The Road Map to
Software Engineering

IEEE Computer Society Publications
The world-renowned IEEE Computer Society publishes, promotes, and distributes a wide variety of authoritative computer science and engineering texts. These books are available from most retail outlets. Visit the CS Store at *http://computer.org/cspress* for a list of products.

IEEE Computer Society / Wiley Partnership
The IEEE Computer Society and Wiley partnership allows the CS Press authored book program to produce a number of exciting new titles in areas of computer science and engineering with a special focus on software engineering. IEEE Computer Society members continue to receive a 15% discount on these titles when purchased through Wiley or at wiley.com/ieeecs.

To submit questions about the program or send proposals, please e-mail dplummer@computer.org or write to Books, IEEE Computer Society, 100662 Los Vaqueros Circle, Los Alamitos, CA 90720-1314. Telephone +1-714-821-8380.
Additional information regarding the Computer Society authored book program can also be accessed from our web site at *http://computer.org/cspress*

The Road Map to Software Engineering

A Standards-Based Guide

James W. Moore

A John Wiley & Sons, Inc., Publication

The Road Map to Software Engineering: A Standards-Based Guide by James W. Moore is recommended by the Software and Systems Engineering Standards Committee of the IEEE Computer Society as a useful guide for software practitioners applying software engineering standards.

All IEEE standards are trademarked. For example, the correct way to reference IEEE 1220 is:

IEEE Std 1220™-1998, *IEEE Standard for Application and Management of the Systems Engineering Process.*

All material quoted from IEEE standards is used by permission.

Published by John Wiley & Sons, Inc., Hoboken, New Jersey.
Published simultaneously in Canada.

For general information on our other products and services or for technical support, please contact our Customer Care Department within the United States at (800) 762-2974, outside the United States at (317) 572-3993 or fax (317) 572-4002.

Wiley also publishes its books in a variety of electronic formats. Some content that appears in print may not be available in electronic formats. For more information about Wiley products, visit our web site at www.wiley.com.

Library of Congress Cataloging-in-Publication Data is available.

ISBN-13 978-0-471-68362-9
ISBN-10 0-471-68362-0

10 9 8 7 6 5 4 3 2 1

To my colleagues who work to transform the software discipline into a recognized engineering profession.

Summary of Contents

Contents

List of Figures

List of Tables

Preface

"Software" is regularly blamed for a large variety of failures—both grand and petty—in our modern world. It is, therefore, ironic that many software developers pay so little attention to placing their profession on a sound engineering basis by using codified approaches that are known to increase the probabilities of success. Fortunately, there are some signs of progress. Two of them provide the basis for this book: the software engineering standards of the IEEE Computer Society and the Society's *Guide to the Software Engineering Body of Knowledge*.

Software Engineering Standards

The first basis for this book is the work of largely anonymous individuals who cooperate in the development of software engineering standards, capturing processes and practices that are effective in improving software development, maintenance, and operation. Considered individually, each of these standards is a technical gem. Taken collectively, though, the corpus of hundreds of standards from dozens of organizations, using a variety of jargon, and having various scopes, can leave the hopeful user with questions rather than answers. Two organizations have stepped up to this challenge. The Software and Systems Engineering Standards Committee (S2ESC) of the IEEE Computer Society (IEEE-CS) has committed to a long-term program to place its 40 or so standards on a consistent basis. As a part of this goal, it cooperates with the international standards committee for software and systems engineering (ISO/IEC JTC 1/SC 7) to "harmonize" their respective collections so that users may choose standards from either collection without fear of contradiction.

The integration of the S2ESC collection and its harmonization with that of SC 7 is a long-term project that may never be finished. There are always new communities joining the scope of the harmonization effort. For example, for roughly a decade, both S2ESC and SC 7 have worked to incorporate and harmonize systems engineering practices into the corpus of software engineering standards. As progress is made in this area, the need to harmonize with standards for enterprise business processes has become apparent and represents a new set of challenges.

Despite the never-ending challenge presented by harmonization, substantial progress has been made in integrating the S2ESC collection. In some sense, this book is a progress report of that integration effort.

Guide to the Software Engineering Body of Knowledge

The second basis for this book is the new 2004 version of the IEEE Computer Society's *Guide to the Software Engineering Body of Knowledge*. A few years ago, one of my colleagues went to a used-book store and returned with a circa 1910 "handbook of electrical engineering." In a single volume of several hundred pages, it summarized the information that an electrical engineer of that era should know and provided reference to additional knowledge. The modern-day *SWEBOK Guide* is the software equivalent of that volume. It provides a basis for the scope and content of software as an engineering discipline. Although software engineers need to know things from other disciplines, the *SWEBOK Guide* describes that portion of their necessary knowledge that characterizes software engineering per se.

Codified Practice

Together, these two sources provide the basis for what I like to call "Codified Software Engineering," a set of knowledge and practices that are applicable most of the time on most projects and which should be applied most of the time. To be sure, there is always a need for continued research, continued experimentation, and continued empirical validation to produce more effective approaches. However, managers of expensive projects who ignore the accepted techniques in favor of alternatives should be aware—and those who are paying the bill should be aware—that experimental engineering carries along its own set of risks. Perhaps the most important contribution of codifying software engineering is to make it clear which aspects of the practice are widely accepted as effective so that innovative alternatives receive the attention and risk management that they deserve.

The Role of This Book

This book provides a single overview of codified software engineering by placing the IEEE software and systems engineering standards—as well as a few standards from other sources—into two important contexts: the context of knowledge provided by the *SWEBOK Guide*, and the context of organizationally adopted processes provided by two important umbrella standards.

The book is intended to appeal to several audiences:

- The most important audience is software engineering practitioners. Because the standards are placed in both the context of topical knowledge areas and the context of commonly recognized processes, it should be easy for practitioners to quickly locate the standards pertinent to questions arising in real projects.

- Closely related to the first audience are professionals interested in their own development as software engineers. The topical organization assists readers in finding "gaps" in their own knowledge and addressing those gaps by consulting the normative literature.
- Another important audience is students of software engineering and their instructors. For this audience, the book is a compendium of "industrial-strength" approaches set in the context of the knowledge that a student should seek to attain.

In considering this book for the latter usage, instructors should note that the *SWEBOK Guide* was one of the principal sources for the joint IEEE/ACM joint curriculum on software engineering.* So the *SWEBOK Guide* itself, as well as this book, should be broadly compatible with courses based on this curriculum.

The book is organized into three parts:

- As is usually the case, the first part of the book is introductory material. Chapter 1 provides an overview of the emerging engineering discipline for software; Chapter 2 provides an overview of software engineering standards-makers, with particular focus on two organizations of particular relevance to this book. The most important chapter—Chapter 3— describes the principles behind the organization of the S2ESC collection. Chapter 4 describes some of the approaches to organizing an integrated collection of software engineering standards.
- The second part of the book organizes software and systems engineering standards by the knowledge areas of the *SWEBOK Guide*.
- The third part of the book organizes software and systems engineering standards by the processes of ISO/IEC 12207, *Software Life Cycle Processes*, and ISO/IEC 15288, *System Life Cycle Processes*—both prepared with the cooperation of S2ESC and both now adopted by IEEE as standards.

Organization by Knowledge Area

One of the many contributions of the *SWEBOK Guide* was the designation of ten *knowledge areas* characterizing the content of software engineering as well as eight *related disciplines* that form the boundary of software engineering. That classification is directly reflected in this part of the book. Chapter 5 gives an overview of the *SWEBOK Guide*. The ten subsequent chapters—Chapters 6 through 15—are each devoted to a single knowledge area. Each one of these chapters begins with a statement of scope and a summary, both excerpted from the *SWEBOK Guide*. The largest part of each chapter is a description of the knowledge area, organized similarly to the treatment in the *SWEBOK Guide*.

_____

* http://sites.computer.org/ccse/

Whenever a software or systems engineering standard would make a contribution to the knowledge area, I note its relevance by inserting a reference that
looks like this example:

Process

IEEE Std 1062, 1998 Edition (R2002)
IEEE Recommended Practice for Software Acquisition
This document recommends a set of useful practices that can be
selected and applied during software acquisition. It is primarily suited
to acquisitions that include development or modification rather than
off-the-shelf purchase.
Allocated to: Software Engineering Management Knowledge Area

The icon on the left—and its label—classify the subject of the standard into
one of seven categories: *document, measure, plan, process, terminology, tool,*
and, in one case, the *world wide web* application area.

The top few lines on the right give the formal designation and title of the
standard. (It should be noted that the designations of IEEE standards are
trademarked, e.g., IEEE Std 1062™.) The next few lines on the right give a
very brief summary of the content of the standard. The final line records a
forced allocation of each standard into a single knowledge area. That's your
cue that a more detailed description of the standard can be found in the
chapter of this book devoted to that knowledge area.

At the end of each chapter is a section providing individual descriptions of
the standards that have been allocated to that knowledge area. The descriptions provide information regarding history and content of the standards, and,
in some cases, plans for revision of the standards.

Chapter 16 describes the eight related disciplines listed by the *SWEBOK
Guide*. This is important because twelve of the standards described by this
book are allocated to the related disciplines rather than to the software engineering knowledge areas. At the end of Chapter 16, you will find descriptions
of those standards.

Two standards don't fall cleanly into any of the knowledge areas or related
disciplines, one because it is too general (a vocabulary standard) and the
second because it is too specific (an application area guide). They are both
described in Chapter 17.

Organization by Process

Recent years have seen great emphasis on software process in the conviction
that improved processes will lead to improved products. Organizations interested in process definition and process improvement inevitably ask how standards can contribute to this endeavor. So Part 3 of this book organizes the
software and systems engineering standards by process. Chapter 18 provides
a history and some important concepts. Chapter 19 organizes the standards
by the software life cycle processes and Chapter 20 organizes them by system
life cycle processes. The icons mentioned above are used to refer to standards
of interest. Their descriptions can be found in the chapters devoted to knowledge areas.

Goals of This Book

Although this book pays great attention to integrated collections of standards, it is not my intention to encourage readers to adopt collections in their entirety. Such a step would cause an individual or an organization to attempt to digest a few thousand pages of highly technical material in a single meal. Instead, the purpose of providing the knowledge and process context is to assist readers in selecting a few standards that suit their needs today, confident that today's selection of standards will not be contradicted by others yet to be adopted.

This book has another important goal. The IEEE Computer Society, in partnership with John Wiley & Sons, has an overall project to provide a series of book devoted to software engineering standards in different areas, e.g., maintenance, verification and validation, testing, quality assurance, etc. We can expect to see those books in future years. In fact, one has already been published—Carma McClure's book on *Software Reuse: A Standards-Based Guide*. In some senses, this book is an entrée to that series—by providing an overview of the entire discipline.

A Few Disclaimers

It's my duty to warn the reader of a few things that may not be completely accurate or precise.* Because I wanted this book to be published at roughly the same time as the 2004 version of the *SWEBOK Guide*, I had to rely on prepublication drafts of the guide. The final published version of the guide may be slightly different from material excerpted in this book.

I think that it makes for turgid prose to always refer to standards in their full, glorious designation, e.g., "IEEE Std 1062™, 1998 Edition (R2002), *IEEE Recommended Practice for Software Acquisition*." The book might double in size if I followed that practice consistently. Therefore, despite the advice of well-meaning editors, I have elided many references. Almost without exception, I omit the trademark designation (™). I typically omit the information regarding the provenance of the standard, e.g., 1998 Edition (R2002). I sometimes shorten the title to its essentials and I often omit the abbreviation "Std." Often, I simply jump to the heart of the matter and refer to the standard by its bare number, 1062. I doubt that readers will be confused by this practice; it certainly improves the readability of the prose.

ISO/IEC 12207 is a special case. When IEEE adopted the standard, it added two parts (volumes), added some appendices to the base volume, and even corrected a few errors. Nevertheless, IEEE/EIA 12207.0 (part 0!) can be regarded as equivalent to ISO/IEC 12207. When I write simply "12207." I mean that either the ISO/IEC or the IEEE/EIA standard apply equally well.

Despite the fact that the software engineering standards development committee of the IEEE Computer Society has evolved in name and scope from SESS to SESC and then S2ESC, I typically use the abbreviation S2ESC unless there is a historical reason to make a distinction.

---

* It's the duty of any engineer—and an exercise for the reader—to learn the difference between the words *accurate* and *precise*.

During the period that I wrote this book, new standards were being developed and existing standards were being revised. I have attempted to "freeze" each standard in time and describe it accordingly so that the treatment is consistent. My strategies for doing this have varied on a case-by-case basis. For example, I have anticipated the 2004 revision of IEEE Std 1012 but have ignored the late-2004 adoption of ISO/IEC 15288 by the IEEE. Nevertheless, it is virtually certain that some inconsistencies have crept into the text.

Finally, I should mention the relationship of this book with my previous one: *Software Engineering Standards: A User's Road Map*, IEEE Computer Society Press, 1997. Both books were intended to fill the same role—to provide an overview of the S2ESC collection of standards at their respective points in time. The books turned out to be very different, though. Lacking a body of knowledge, the previous book paid a lot of attention to the context of software engineering in the hope that the context would provide insight regarding the core. It also paid relatively more attention to the international standards of SC 7. This book is organized on a completely different basis—that of the *SWEBOK Guide*—and is more strongly focused on S2ESC as an integrator of standards, even standards developed by other organizations. Nevertheless, the reader will find some similar material, mostly in the introductory chapters and the chapter on the processes of 12207. I insisted that the words "Road Map" appear in the title of this book as a small warning to buyers that they might already own material similar to some of what they are buying in this book.

My Thanks

Having now written **two** books, I can report that they are the **two** hardest things I have done in my life. (I was disappointed that the second one was not any easier than the first one!) So, I owe thanks to many people—if only for my bad temper during the past several months.

First, I must thank the responsible people at the IEEE Computer Society Press, Angela Burgess and Deb Plummer, for their gentle encouragement during my "slow periods," and the S2ESC book series editor, Roger Fujii. (I also appreciate, but cannot individually acknowledge, the contributions of the anonymous reviewers of this manuscript.)

The development of the *SWEBOK Guide* was a landmark accomplishment in the maturing of software engineering. Alain Abran served with me as an executive editor. Pierre Bourque and Robert Dupuis served as editors. Two dozen or so other individuals—mentioned in the knowledge area chapters—edited particular portions of the *Guide*. Robert Dupuis was primarily responsible for editing the 2004 edition. (Dale Strok and Bob Werner, staffers of the IEEE Computer Society Press, provided editorial services—as volunteers!) Approximately 500 individuals provided review and comment on the guide as it progressed through various stages toward completion. They are named on the SWEBOK web site.*

The IEEE Computer Society has been steadfast in its support of the professionalization of software engineering. A few of the people who have been

---

* http://www.swebok.org

generous to me with their time and attention include Don Bagert, Carl Chang, Kathy Land, Steve McConnell, Fernando Naveda, and Steve Seidman.

During my ten years of service on the Executive Committee of S2ESC, I learned much from my colleagues; Paul Croll, David Schultz, Scott Duncan, Mark Henley, Joe Jarzombek, Dennis Lawrence, Claire Lohr, and John Walz deserve special mention for their contributions to my education.

I have participated in the work of ISO/IEC JTC 1/SC 7 for nearly as many years—most recently as the IEEE Computer Society's liaison representative; I appreciate the support of SC 7's chair, François Coallier, and two successive chairs of its Working Group 7, Stan Magee and Doug Thiele, as well as WG7's current secretary, Bob Johnson. I have learned much from the various national body representatives and other participants in SC 7; unfortunately, they are far too numerous to mention.

An important aspect of software engineering is how organizations define, adopt, assess, and improve their processes. In this area, I have learned much from Terry Rout, David Kitson, Jeanie Kitson, and Perry Deweese.

As the work of SC 7 and S2ESC has extended into systems engineering, there were new things to learn. Ken Crowder, Jerry Lake, Stuart Arnold, Alain Faisandier, and Terry Doran have all been patient with me.

The US Technical Advisory Group to SC 7 has also been a source of knowledge, notably Mike Gayle, its current chair, and Garry Roedler, the US lead to WG7. Finally, Bob Pritchard, the IEEE's administrator of the US TAG to SC 7, insists that I thoroughly understand all the nuances of JTC 1 standardization. (I'm not quite there yet.)

In these standards activities, I met Jack McGarry, Cheryl Jones, and David Card, who taught me most of what I know about software measurement, and Bob Charette, who taught me risk management.

Various staff members at the IEEE Standards Association (IEEE-SA) have been very helpful in providing access to necessary materials, including Executive Director Judy Gorman, Terry DeCourcelle, Mary Lynne Nielsen, Claudio Stanziola, David Ringle, Yvette Ho Sang, and Angela Ortiz. On the JTC 1 side, Witold Suryn (secretary of JTC 1/SC 7) and Keith Brannon (ISO Central Secretariat) have been helpful.

Many of these strands lead back to a single source. Leonard Tripp (now an IEEE Fellow) has served as President of the Computer Society, Chairman of S2ESC, Chairman of the US TAG to SC 7, member of the IEEE-SA Standards Board, Chairman of the CS Professional Practices Committee, founder of the Certified Software Development Professional certification, and "champion" of the SWEBOK project. As far as I know, he was the first to articulate the concept that the integration of software engineering standards into a coherent whole was more important than the individual standards.

I gratefully acknowledge the interest of my employer for the past ten years, The MITRE Corporation, in supporting my participation in many of the standards activities described in this book.* John Slaybaugh, Linda Rosa, Steve

---

* In accordance with the procedures of The MITRE Corporation, I include the following disclaimer: The author's affiliation with The MITRE Corporation is provided for identification purposes only, and is not intended to convey or imply MITRE's concurrence with, or support for, the positions, opinions, or viewpoints expressed by the author.

Huffman, and Lyn van Hoozer have all been notably supportive. MITRE, along with several other organizations, also provided financial support to the Software Engineering Body of Knowledge project and appointed a representative, Chuck Howell, to its Industrial Advisory Board.

Finally and most importantly, I must note that writing a book requires the sacrifice of time that might be spent with the family. I appreciate the support of my wife, Barbara, and my son, David.

Potomac, Maryland   JIM MOORE

Part 1

Background

Chapter *1*

Introduction

On an outside wall of the thirteenth century town hall in Rothenburg-ob-der-Tauber, Germany, hangs an equally old iron *standard* used to measure the length of loaves of bread. Subject to punishment were bakers who made their loaves too short—for cheating their customers—as were those who made their loaves too long—for raising unrealistic expectations. The goal of this chapter is to provide general material about software engineering and software engineering standards and to address the reader's expectations regarding the usefulness of the standards.

1. SOFTWARE ENGINEERING

The Institute of Electrical and Electronics Engineers defines software engineering, in IEEE Std 610.12, as:

> *(1) The application of a systematic, disciplined, quantifiable approach to the development, operation and maintenance of software, that is, the application of engineering to software. (2) The study of approaches as in (1).*

Most of the standards on this subject are practice standards rather than product standards, concerned with norms for the practice of software engineering rather than the interfaces of the products produced.

1.1. Is It Engineering?

One could be excused for denying the premise of this book. With few exceptions, software engineering is not among the engineering professions licensed

---

in the United States and nearly all states have laws forbidding an unlicensed individual from offering services as an "engineer." There an unmistakable signs of change, though [SWEBOK04]:

- Several universities, e.g., the University of New South Wales (Australia), McMaster University (Canada), the Rochester Institute of Technology (US), and the University of Sheffield (UK), offer undergraduate degrees in software engineering.
- In the US, the Engineering Accreditation Commission of the Accreditation Board for Engineering and Technology (ABET) is responsible for the accreditation of undergraduate software engineering programs.
- The Canadian Information Processing Society has published criteria to accredit software engineering undergraduate university programs.
- The Texas Board of Professional Engineers licenses software engineers.
- The Association of Professional Engineers and Geoscientists of British Columbia has begun registering software professional engineers and the Professional Engineers of Ontario has also announced requirements for licensing.
- The Association for Computing Machinery (ACM) and the Computer Society of the Institute of Electrical and Electronics Engineers (IEEE) have jointly developed and adopted a Code of Ethics for software engineering professionals.[1]
- The IEEE Computer Society offers the Certified Software Development Professional certification for software engineering.[2]

Recently, the US Department of Labor recognized "computer software engineer" as a distinct occupation [BLS04]. Most importantly, though, the IEEE Computer Society has published its *Guide to the Software Engineering Body of Knowledge* [SWEBOK04], providing a definitive characterization of the knowledge base underlying a profession. In deference to common usage and these promising developments, this book will use the term "software engineering"; readers may choose to view the term as a statement of a goal or an ideal rather than as a statement of a fact.

Engineering can be viewed as a closed feedback loop as shown in Figure 1. An engineering process consists of related activities performed in response to a statement of *needs* and consuming *resources* to produce a *product*. In order to manage or improve the process, one must exert *control*. Control is a decision-making mechanism that considers *goals* and *constraints* in the formulation of action that is intended to direct or modify the process. The decision to take *action* is based on *measurements*, quantitative evidence regarding the state of the process. Measurements can be made of conditions inside the process, products of the process, and the satisfaction of users of the products [SESC93]. We would expect software engineering standards to contribute to the implementation of such a model with respect to the development, operation, and maintenance of software systems.

---

[1] ACM/CS Software Engineering Code of Ethics and Professional Practice can be found at: http://www.computer.org/certification/ethics.htm.
[2] Information regarding the IEEE CS certification program can be found at http://www. computer.org/certification.

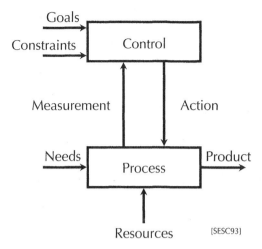

Figure 1. Model of engineering

Indeed, we will find standards related to the process, product, and resources involved in the software discipline. We will find standards describing the treatment of needs in software development, not only as requirements and specifications, but articulating less formal needs from more remote stakeholders. We will find standards describing management plans, measurements, and actions for the purpose of controlling the ongoing processes. Finally, we will find methods to articulate goals and constraints, even informal ones, to guide the managers.

So, even if the software discipline has not yet formalized the empirical underpinnings of an engineering discipline, we will find that, in many ways, it is acting as if it has.

1.2. Relationship to Other Disciplines

Software engineering occupies a position intermediate between, on the one hand, the mathematical and physical disciplines of computer science and technology and, on the other hand, the requirements of the particular application domains, applying the findings of the former to solve problems of the latter (see Figure 2). The techniques for the engineering of software can be viewed, in part, as specializations of those of more general disciplines, such as project management, systems engineering, and quality management. Furthermore, a software project must implement requirements imposed by cross-cutting disciplines like dependability and safety. These contextual disciplines are important to the reader of this book because software engineering standards must often be applied in conjunction with the standards from the other disciplines.

1.3. Body of Knowledge

The engineering style of education deals with rapidly changing technology by teaching well-accepted fundamentals; students are provided little choice regarding their curriculum. As a consequence, there is a set of things that we

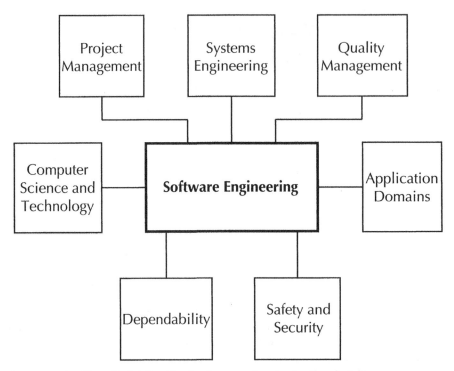

Figure 2. *Relationship of software engineering to other disciplines*

can expect every engineer to know [Parnas95]. The teaching material is based on a common, principle-based body of knowledge, codified by some more-or-less officially designated organization, often enforced by licensing requirements. For software engineering, this need has been filled by the publication of the IEEE Computer Society's *Guide to the Software Engineering Body of Knowledge*, with the purpose of providing "a consensually-validated characterization of the bounds of the software engineering discipline and . . . a topical access to the Body of Knowledge supporting that discipline" [SWEBOK04]. The *SWEBOK Guide* provides a basis for both academic and professional development. The new Software Engineering volume of the joint IEEE-CS/ACM Computing Curriculum[3] is largely based on the knowledge breakdown of the *SWEBOK Guide*—albeit normalized to the needs of undergraduate education. The Computer Society's Certified Software Development Professional (CSDP) certification is gained, in part, through an examination that traces to the *SWEBOK Guide*.

1.4. Fundamental Principles

In other fields, practice standards can be traced to a body of fundamental scientific and engineering principles that constrain the standards. A trivial example is that mechanical engineering standards are constrained by the

---

[3] http://sites.computer.org/ccse/

three-dimensional geometry of physical objects. The codification of software engineering standards is faced by particular challenges in this area. First, the subject of the standards—software—is inherently intangible and unconstrained by the common laws of physics. Second, the discipline is relatively new, compared to other engineering disciplines, and many of its important concepts remain immature. Finally, unlike product interface standards, there are few market forces to cause convergence on selected technologies.

This has caused some problems. Unfettered by any integrating forces of principles or dominant products, some software engineering standards are ad hoc recordings of individual practices claimed to be "best." This is not bad when each standard is considered in isolation, but when the standards are considered as a body, we too often find them to be ***dis***-integrated, capriciously different in detail, overlapping and occasionally contradictory. These characteristics put the erstwhile adopter of the corpus of standards into a difficult situation, because the adopters must themselves develop some mechanism to rationalize, explain, and relate the various standards chosen for implementation.

Part of the solution to the problem is the adoption of a framework of vocabulary, key relationships, and other constraints to which each individual standard must adhere. In fact, IEEE Software and Systems Engineering Standards Committee (S2ESC) and its international counterpart, ISO/IEC JTC 1/SC 7, have taken steps in this direction, efforts that are described elsewhere in this book. Perhaps a more basic requirement is for the identification of a set of fundamental principles that would serve to explain and motivate the provisions of the various standards. There are steps in this direction.

Figure 3 shows a notional depiction of the role of principle standards. The principles of software engineering would be regarded as selected, adapted, and specialized from the principles of engineering in general. The provisions of practice standards would be motivated by the software engineering principles and would be traceable to those principles. So-called "best practices" would be viewed as the detailed implementation of the provisions of the practice standards. Viewed in the other direction, practice standards would be regarded as

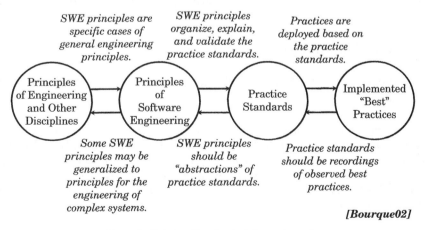

Figure 3. Relationship of principles and practice

descriptions of observed, effective best practices and the principles as abstractions of the practice standards. The principles found to be relevant beyond the scope of software engineering (perhaps those related to complexity, for example) might be considered as general principles of engineering.

In this model, we can view practice standards as existing in a tension between the consolidating and integrating forces exerted by the principles and the expansive and innovative forces exerted by the recognition of new, effective practices.

IEEE S2ESC has participated in efforts to identify fundamental principles for software engineering. A workshop at the 1996 Software Engineering Standards Forum considered candidate principles and developed a set of criteria to be applied to candidates [Jabir98]. Alternating workshops and Delphi exercises produced a candidate set of principles [Bourque02]:

- Apply and use quantitative measurements in decision making
- Build with and for reuse
- Control complexity with multiple perspectives and multiple levels of abstraction
- Define software artifacts rigorously
- Establish a software process that provides flexibility
- Implement a disciplined approach and improve it continuously
- Invest in the understanding of the problem
- Manage quality throughout the life cycle as formally as possible
- Minimize software component interaction
- Produce software in a stepwise fashion
- Set quality objectives for each deliverable product
- Since change is inherent to software, plan for it and manage it
- Since tradeoffs are inherent to software engineering, make them explicit and document them
- To improve design, study previous solutions to similar problems
- Uncertainty is unavoidable in software engineering. Identify and manage it

2. SOFTWARE ENGINEERING STANDARDS

For the purposes of this book, the characterization of standards provided in [SESC93] is helpful:

> A standard can be: (1) an object or measure of comparison that defines or represents the magnitude of a unit; (2) a characterization that establishes allowable tolerances or constraints for categories of items; and (3) a degree or level of required excellence or attainment. Standards are definitional in nature, established either to further understanding and interaction, or to acknowledge observed (or desired norms) of exhibited characteristics or behavior.

Most of the standards described in this book have been developed by Standards Developing Organizations (SDO) operating on the principles of consensus development and voluntary adoption. For the purposes of this book, the organizations are regarded as national (US, with a few exceptions) or international.

2.1. The Nature of Standards[4]

Probably the most important word in the quotation above is the word "acknowledge." Many users have the belief that standards impose mandatory requirements. Of course, they don't because the use of a standard is generally voluntary.[5] In the typical situation, a supplier applies a standard—not because it is required—but because it represents an opportunity to publicly claim conformity, a claim that is "acknowledged" by the marketplace. Suppliers seek this acknowledgment to distinguish themselves from competitors or, at the least, to mark that their products are suitable for a particular use.

Given that suppliers are interested in seeking the acknowledgment of the marketplace, there is an implicit competition among makers of standards to provide the best or most popular opportunity to make these claims. In short, the standards-makers want to maximize the number of users of their standard. One obvious way to do this is to make the conformance requirements easy to achieve or, at least, vague. The approach is shortsighted, though, because such standards gain little respect in the marketplace; hence, claims of conformity are poorly respected and do not provide the competitive advantage desired. In fact, capable suppliers desire the level of difficulty to be set high, to more sharply distinguish themselves from competitors. Left to their own devices, such suppliers would set standards so high as to serve as a barrier to competing products.

Therefore, standards necessarily exist in an uneasy tension between ease and difficulty of conformance. Various makers of standards may trade off the conflicting forces in different ways, leading to different compromises. That's one reason why there may be different standards on the same subject.

More fundamentally, though, consider what a standard does. It divides a class of products into two subclasses—those that conform and those that don't. But, why only two? Is it sensible to have more than two subclasses? In some cases it is, and some standards provide more than one class of conforming product. Furthermore, some standards provide specialized requirements for a specialized subset or niche of products; having many such standards for a particular product class simply provides lots of different subsets, suitable for different purposes.

In short, standards should be viewed simply as a way of naming things. Citing any particular standard, say PDQ-123, is shorthand for a statement that would otherwise be a long explanation of characteristics. PDQ-123 is simply a name for the subclass of products—the subclass that conforms to the provisions of the standard. Having many standards simply means that we have rich space of names and can distinguish among many similar subclasses of products.

---

[4] This section is adapted from an article originally published in [Robillard02].

[5] Nevertheless, in regulatory situations, governments may use their sovereign powers to impose standards that would otherwise be voluntary. Also, dominant customers may be able to coerce the use of selected standards.

With the large opportunity provided by a robust marketplace, you can imagine that there might be many providers of standards. In most of the world, though, there are surprisingly few. Most sources acknowledge three international standards-makers—the International Telecommunications Union, the International Electrotechnical Commission (IEC) for electrical and electronic devices, and the International Organization for Standardization (ISO) for most other things. Joint Technical Committee 1, shared by ISO and IEC, is the committee that makes standards related to information technology. Most nations have a single government-designated standards organization. In addition, there are a few regional standards organizations, mostly serving the European Community. The US breaks the pattern though. Because the US does not designate a single organization, anyone can make standards if they adhere to a few legal requirements. As a result, hundreds of US organizations make standards.

Although every standards organization has different rules, they generally share some similar principles:

- *Consensus:* Product consumers generally expect that relevant standards will be broadly implemented within any particular category of interest. Accordingly, standards-makers strive for broad agreement by applying a principle of consensus in making technical decisions. Although procedures and rules vary, nearly every standards-maker requires some sort of supermajority agreement to approve a technical specification; the number 75% is commonly used.

- *Openness within a community of interest:* The desire for broad agreement suggests that the standards-making process should involve a wide range of interested parties, and many standards-makers have numerical requirements for broad participation. Of course, broad inclusion can slow down the reaching of agreement and can threaten shared interests of some participants. For this reason, the openness principle is the one most often manipulated. Consortia often define the community of interest narrowly by restricting it to those with whom quick agreement can be gained. Standards-makers accredited by ANSI are required to allow anyone with a "material interest" to participate, although participation fees are permitted. International standards-makers define their community of interest as the member nations of the organization—even on technical matters, participation is usually based on national positions.

- *Adherence to process:* Because economic interests often clash in standards-making and because of susceptibility to legal issues (e.g., restraint of trade), standards organizations typically develop a slavish devotion to bureaucratic process. Through strict adherence to process, the standards-maker can demonstrate that all parties have been fairly treated. Consortia often claim that light-weight processes make them faster than formal standards-makers. In fact, though, consortia often develop similarly heavy processes because of the fear of antitrust litigation. Any speed advantage that consortia have can be more correctly attributed to restricting their community of interest to parties among which agreement comes quickly.

- *Separation of technical and management approval:* The emphasis on process means that the development of a standard must be approved in two regards: (1) agreement on technical content and (2) agreement that the process was followed. Accordingly, most standards-makers have some sort of management layer that checks that the process was followed and gives their final approval for publication.

As noted above, a standard provides a product supplier with a voluntary opportunity to make a claim of conformance that is viewed favorably in the marketplace. Failure of any of the principles noted above can diminish the perception of the standard, hence the credibility of the claim. Consortium-based standards, for example, can be unfavorably perceived if the community of interest has been defined to prevent product users from participating with product suppliers in the development of the standard. International standards are sometimes criticized because voting by nation is sometimes viewed as a political process rather than a technical process.

Organizations participate in standardization for a variety of motives. Some products, for example, telephones, serve no useful purpose if they cannot connect to other devices. So their suppliers are eager to develop standards that provide interoperability in a steadily growing range of applications leading to an enlarging market. Some standards stabilize particular dimensions of technology so that investment can be channeled to other technological areas—for example, there is little experimentation in alternative forms of electrical power for supply to the home. Often, organizations participate in standards-making for defensive reasons; they want the standard to look a lot like their existing product so that their customer base—and their own investment—are not left behind by the standard.

Standards that place requirements on processes (a category that includes many software engineering standards) may be a special case. Standards-making in this category is often dominated by users rather than suppliers. In fact, the users are often dominant customers, such as ministries of defense and large aerospace companies. The motivation is to impose process standards as a condition of trade, hence dictating how suppliers will conduct their business, in the belief that better quality products will be the result. Currently, conventional wisdom suggests that organizations will build better products if they are allowed to apply their own processes repeatedly on every project. For this reason, enlightened customers, such as the US Department of Defense, no longer apply such standards as contractual provisions. Nevertheless, the mind-set persists that process standards should be written in a form that coerces behavior rather than offering opportunities for voluntary claims of advantage. Unlike any other standards, documents in this category are often written to be "tailored-down" (as part of a contract negotiation) rather than providing a minimum set of requirements. With no minimum level of performance, any voluntary claim of conformance to a tailored standard is sapped of respect by the suspicion that difficult provisions have been discarded in the tailoring process.

2.2. Scope of Software Engineering Standards

Software engineering standards cover a remarkable variety of topics. Stan Magee and Leonard Tripp organized 29 subjects into the three categories

TABLE 1. Scope of software engineering standardization

Process	Technique or Tool	Applicability
Acquisition	CASE tools	General
Requirements definition	Languages and notations	Defense
Design	Metrics	Financial
Code and test	Privacy	Medical
Integration	Process improvement	Nuclear
Maintenance and operations	Reliability	Process control
Configuration management	Safety	Scientific
Documentation	Security	Shrink-wrap
Project management	Software reuse	Transportation
Quality assurance	Vocabulary	
Verification and validation		

shown in Table 1, for the purpose of organizing their book [Magee97]. This book will use different categories, as explained later.

2.3. Importance of Software Engineering Standards

To consider the importance of software engineering standards, one must consider the uses to which they are put and the benefits that accrue from their application.

2.3.1. Improving the Product Nearly all of the standards discussed in this book are voluntary, that is, an organization makes its own decision, without coercion, to adopt the standard. (This contrasts with regulatory standards, imposed by processes similar to law, and mandated standards, such as military standards, required as a precondition of doing business with a dominant customer.) Organizations often adopt these standards because they improve their products, or improve the perception of their products in a competitive marketplace. Alternatively, the standards may improve the organization's business processes, allowing them to make their products more cost effectively.

Examples of benefits that standards may provide in this regard are the following:

- Some standards are simply statements regarding subjects in which the uniformity provided by agreement is more important than the gains to be made by small, but local, improvements. Standards on terminology, e.g., IEEE Std 610.12, and notations, e.g., the IEEE standards on the IDEF notation, are examples.
- Some standards provide a nomenclature for complex concepts, which, absent standardization, could exhibit detailed differences in characteristics that might ultimately prove crucial. For example, the common term "design review" is used to cover a broad range of alternatives. IEEE Std 1028 provides minimum, essential characteristics for a particular type of review known as an inspection. Agreed nomenclature is helpful in improving communication between concerned parties, particularly those in an acquirer-supplier relationship. For example, is it easier to judge the ade-

quacy of a 20-page explanation of a supplier's verification and validation procedures or a simple claim that they conform to IEEE Std 1012?

- Some standards, in the absence of scientific proof of validity, provide criteria for measurement and evaluation techniques that are, at least, validated by consensus wisdom. For example, IEEE Std 1061 provides a methodology for metrics that can be used as early indicators of later results.

- Some standards record a community consensus of "best practices," that is, techniques broadly regarded as generally effective. For example, IEEE Std 1008 provides requirements and recommendations for the unit testing of code. Some standards, like ISO 9001, provide a "badge" asserting in a supportable fashion that an organization's processes conform to a constellation of best principles and practices [Moore95].

- Some standards provide a framework for communication with customers and suppliers, reducing misunderstanding, and shortening the time (and text) needed to reach agreement. An important example is IEEE/EIA Std 12207, which provides a reference set of software life cycle processes.

- Some standards share techniques that can lead to qualitative improvements in developing software better, faster, or less expensively, for example, IEEE Std 1044 on software anomaly classification.

To be sure, not all observers agree that software engineering standards have been successful. [Pfleeger94] says that the "standards lack objective assessment criteria, involve more process than product, and are not always based on rigorous experimental results." [Fenton96] finds "no evidence that any of the existing standards are effective [in improving] the quality of the resulting software products cost effectively." [Schneidewind96], though, points to success stories such as the organization that has produced nearly error-free code for the space shuttle, in part, through use of software engineering standards. All parties would agree, though, that improvement is desirable.

It should be noted that the criticisms lose their impact when software engineering standards are simply viewed as shorthand names for a collection of practices. For example, the greatest strength of IEEE Std 1028, Software Reviews, is that by adopting the standard, a supplier can economically advise an acquirer of the review practices to be applied. The important point is that the two parties have communicated using a common nomenclature provided by the name and the contents of the standard.

2.3.2. Protecting the Buyer With many products, buyers can make appropriate decisions based on advertising literature, previous experience with the seller, or direct examination. The increasing complexity of technology-based products, however, inevitably causes essential characteristics to remain hidden until after purchase. Standards can play a role when they provide accurate information regarding the suitability of products for specific uses [Brobeck96]. For the most complex of systems, the application of standards by the developer can serve to increase the buyer's confidence in the seller's methods for coping with that complexity. The standards applied by the avionics and nuclear industries are examples.

2.3.3. Protecting the Business   Courts in the United States have used voluntary standards to establish a supplier's "duty of care." Failure to adhere to standards does not necessarily establish negligence but may be considered as evidence when dealing with issues like product safety and liability [Peach94, p. 322]. On the other hand, adherence to the appropriate standards is a strong defense that the supplier was not negligent in its development practices and has taken due care to deliver a product that is safe and fit for its intended use. The introduction of evidence that a product meets a voluntary standard is admissible in 47 of the 50 states [Batik92]. Increasingly, companies are developing liability prevention programs that incorporate voluntary standards as key parts.[6] IEEE Std 1228, *Software Safety Plans*, might be appropriate for such usage.

Florida Power and Light (a winner of the prestigious Deming Award in 1990 [Batik92]), not only applies software engineering standards but sometimes performs causal analysis back to the standards themselves when failures are noted. A major credit reporting firm has applied the entire corpus of IEEE S2ESC standards to its organizational software development processes to further bolster its defenses against potential claims of reckless development, maintenance, and operation of its databases and their accompanying software.

Even in contractual situations where the supplier is dealing with a well-informed buyer, the appropriate application of standards protects both parties by dividing up responsibilities, clarifying terminology, and defining expected practices. An important example of a standard appropriate for this purpose is IEEE/EIA 12207, *Software Life Cycle Processes.*

2.3.4. Increasing Professional Discipline   Even if the practice of software is not yet a proper engineering discipline, it is moving in that direction. A body of practice standards is an essential step because it would serve to define the methods to be expected in the responsible practice of software engineering. An example might the software verification and validation (V & V) standard, IEEE Std 1012.

2.3.5. Introducing Technology   Finally, the Software Engineering Institute notes that standards play a vital role in technology transition. "Standards provide users with common terminology and a framework for communicating about technologies across organizational boundaries. Such communications is particularly critical to acceptance by late adopters." Furthermore, codification of technologies prepares them for adoption [Pollak96]. Examples might include the standards on Computer-Aided Software Engineering (CASE) tool selection and adoption developed by IEEE S2ESC and ISO/IEC JTC 1/SC 7.

---

[6] Of course, the writers of standards assume some liability for their product—the standard. In a famous case, the Sunshine Mine used, for thermal insulation, a foam material incidentally described as "fireproof" in a standard of the American Society for Testing and Materials (ASTM). A fire at the mine was blamed partly on the poorly written standard and ASTM was named as a co-defendant in the lawsuit. Although the lawsuit eventually was dropped, ASTM and other standards organizations have taken steps to protect themselves, and their voluntary participants [Batik92].

2.4. History

Although *software engineering* may not yet be a recognized branch of engineering, the roots of an organized discipline began to emerge in the 1960s and use of the term itself dates back to the now famous 1968 North Atlantic Treaty Organization conference. According to the report, "the phrase 'software engineering' was deliberately chosen as being provocative, in implying the need for software manufacture to be based on the types of theoretical foundations and practical disciplines, that are traditional in the established branches of engineering." [Naur68]

Perhaps because of the federal government's inherent need to conduct its business in an accountable manner, early US software engineering standards were written by its organizations. In 1973, a task force of the National Bureau of Standards concluded that such standards were feasible. Accordingly, three years later, Federal Information Processing Standard Publication (FIPS Pub.) 38, *Guidelines for Documentation of Computer Programs and Automated Systems*, was published. It was organized around the production of 10 documents: functional requirements; data requirements; system/subsystem specifications; program specifications; database specifications; user manual; operations manual; program maintenance manual; test plan; and test analysis report. Meanwhile, in 1974, the US Navy initiated the development of its Mil-Std 1679, *Weapons System Software Development*, one of the first standards treating the usage, control, and management of embedded computer resources [SESC93].

IEEE activity began in 1976 with the creation of the Software Engineering Standards Subcommittee (SESS).[7] Its first standard, IEEE Std 730, *Standard for a Quality Assurance Plan*, was approved for trial use in 1979 and full use two years later. Like FIPS Pub. 38, it was (and remains) oriented toward the documentation requirements, only implicitly placing requirements on the underlying processes.

International standardization activities related to software occurred in various technical committees of the International Organization for Standardization (ISO) and the International Electrotechnical Commission (IEC), depending upon the application area. ISO and IEC agreed in 1987 to form Joint Technical Committee 1 (JTC 1) to deal with the area of information technology (IT). Nevertheless, important work strongly related to IT continues in committees of ISO and IEC.

2.5. Makers of Software Engineering Standards

The need for software engineering standards has been filled by an amount that some would regard as exceeding the requirement. As of 1997, an authoritative source [Magee97] identified 315 standards created and maintained by 55 different international, national, sector, and professional organizations; the number is probably larger now.

---

[7] SESS evolved into the Software Engineering Standards Committee (SESC) and, most recently, the Software and Systems Engineering Standards Committee (S2ESC). Regardless of era, this book will generally refer to S2ESC unless a distinction is important for historical purposes.

The IEEE Software and Systems Engineering Standards Committee (S2ESC) alone maintains about 40 standards comprising a total of more than 2,000 pages. A decade ago, its former chairman, Leonard Tripp, estimated that the typical S2ESC standard takes two to four years to develop and costs (in the labor and travel of volunteers) between $2,000 and $10,000 per page [SESC93].

At the international level, the process is commonly perceived as being even longer and more expensive. One estimate [Spring95] said that ISO standardization typically exceeded seven years in duration. In recent years, though, the average duration has been dropping. ISO management guidelines now require completion of a project within three years.

At the center of software engineering standardization in the United States is the IEEE Computer Society's S2ESC. Its collection has grown from 1 in 1981 to about 40 by the end of 2003. The size and growth of the collection has exposed many stresses and S2ESC has been taking the initiative to address the problems apparent in the world wide corpus of process standards.

The counterpart of S2ESC in the international forum is ISO/IEC JTC 1/SC 7. It inherited an obsolescent set of mainframe-oriented practice standards (on subjects like flowcharts and sequential record processing) when it was formed in 1987 but has turned its attention toward more significant contributions, such as its 1995 standard for software life cycle processes, ISO/IEC 12207, and its 2002 standard for system life cycle processes, ISO/IEC 15288. S2ESC participates in SC 7 through the Computer Society's membership in the US Technical Advisory Group (TAG) that formulates national positions and selects the delegation for meetings of SC 7. The Computer Society also has a category A liaison to SC 7, permitting direct participation except for voting.

These two organizations are not alone in their work. Other relevant standards have been written by US organizations including the American Institute for Aeronautics and Astronautics (AIAA) and the Electronic Industries Alliance (EIA); national organizations like the Canadian Standards Association and Standards Australia; and committees of international organizations, like ISO TC 176 (quality) and IEC TC 56 (dependability). Important contributions have been made by organizations that are not formally accredited to develop standards, including the International Council on Systems Engineering (INCOSE). Even this list is far from complete; [Magee97] lists 55 organizations that have developed relevant standards—and its authors were selective.

Components of the US federal government sometimes write specifications to regulate their own procurement practices. The role of the Department of Defense is well known, particularly with respect to development process standards, but the National Aeronautics and Space Administration (NASA) and the Federal Aviation Agency (FAA) have also written standards.

The most influential government agency in information technology standardization, though, was the Computer Systems Laboratory of the National Institute of Standards and Technology (NIST), "where much of the technology infrastructure that [was] necessary to the United States [was] either created or validated." The Computer Systems Laboratory specialized in information technology. It was formed in 1966, as a result of the Brooks Act, to help resolve the problems of incompatible computer systems in the federal government—

the world's largest purchases of information technology—by making procurement practices more uniform and enlightened. This was accomplished largely through the creation of the famous Federal Information Processing Standards (FIPS) [Cargill97]. In recent years, NIST has been relatively inactive in software engineering standardization, although there are some recent signs of renewed interest.

2.6. Organizational Goals for Using Software Engineering Standards

Not all organizations will have the same goals in the adoption of software engineering standards.[8] Some possibilities are listed here along with the needs that software engineering standards may fill in the achievement of the goals.

Improve and Evaluate Software Competency. An organization may desire processes and measures to calibrate its ability to produce software that is competitive in some or all of the following areas:

- *Quality:* Analyze trends in product and process quality for software organizations.
- *Customer Satisfaction:* Measure the extent to which software satisfies the customers' needs.
- *Cycle Time and Productivity:* Track progress toward goals for software cycle time and productivity improvement.
- *Process Maturity:* Assess progress relative to industry software process benchmarks.
- *Technology:* Assess the application of technology within the organization.

Provide Framework and Terminology for Two-Party Agreements. An organization that specializes in buying or selling software services under contract may desire a uniform framework for defining the relationship and respective responsibilities of the acquirer and the supplier for software and systems containing software, a framework that transcends the scope of any particular contract:

- *Acquisition Process:* Provide the essential actions and criteria to be used by an organization in planning and executing an acquisition for software or software related services.
- *Supply Process:* Provide the essential actions and criteria to be used by an organization in supplying software or software related services to an acquirer.
- *Life Cycle Processes:* Provide the process requirements to be met during the life cycle (definition, development, deployment, operation, etc.) of software or systems containing software.
- *Life Cycle Deliverables:* Provide the requirements for information to be passed between the supplier and the acquirer during the performance of software life cycle processes.

---

[8] The material in this section is adapted from an untitled presentation written by Leonard Tripp for S2ESC.

Evaluate Products of Software Engineering Activities. An organization may need to formulate criteria, processes, and measures to determine the adequacy of a software product to fulfill its mission.

- *External Measurements:* Measurements of completed software products to evaluate the achievement of development goals.
- *Internal Measurements:* Measurement of incomplete software artifacts and development processes to provide early indicators of the achievement of development goals.

Assure High Integrity Levels for Software. An organization may need to develop software for critical applications where safety and dependability are important to protect lives or property.

- *Planning:* A framework to determine that appropriate resources and appropriate controls are provided to ensure treatment of concerns of criticality.
- *Achievement:* Provisions for ensuring that critical requirements for safety and dependability are appropriately treated throughout the providing of the software service
- *Assessment:* Verifiable measurement of the extent to which criticality goals have been achieved.

2.7. Trends

Some trends for the future of software engineering standardization are becoming apparent, particularly in the collections of the major organizations involved in developing these standards. Little progress toward a coherent discipline can be made when each standard is an individual island of practice unrelated to its peers. Recent years, though, have seen a trend toward the recognition of key standards that provide a framework that may be elaborated by other, more detailed ones. Examples include:

- The broadly recognized quality management framework of the ISO 9000 standards.
- The life cycle process framework of the ISO/IEC 12207 standard on software life cycle processes and the newer system life cycle process framework of ISO/IEC 15288.
- Cooperative liaison efforts among standards committees concerned with cross-cutting areas like functional safety, dependability, quality, and software and systems engineering.

ISO and IEC have recognized this trend by designating some of their technical committees as "horizontal"—meaning that they cut across the industry orientation of the other committees. All committees are expected to harmonize their work with that of the horizontal committees.

No one should be surprised at disrespect of software and systems engineering standards if the various collections do not respect and build upon the contributions of other collections. Recent years have seen huge steps toward the harmonization of the important collections. For example:

- S2ESC standards have been used as the basis upon which some SC 7 standards have been drafted. On the other hand, S2ESC has voted to adopt newer SC 7 standards to replace their own standards with a similar scope.
- S2ESC has adopted policies designating various international standards, such as ISO/IEC 9126-1 and the ISO 9000 series as key standards with which its own must harmonize.
- In recent years, S2ESC and SC 7 have entered into a broad agreement to completely harmonize their collections. Competing standards are being merged and each group is filling in "holes" in their collection by adopting standards of the other.

3. USING THIS BOOK

The purpose of this book is to assist users in selecting standards appropriate to their needs. The book emphasizes that a user of software engineering standards should not expect any individual standard to solve all problems, nor should the user treat the entire corpus of standards as a monolith to be adopted in an all-or-nothing fashion. Instead, the book provides a middle course, allowing the selection of coherent subsets of standards, suitable for the achievement of goals specific to an organization.

To achieve this purpose, the book considers the software and systems engineering standards of S2ESC along with a handful of key standards from other sources. The book organizes the standards by showing how each standard can be placed into a coherent context—actually, two of them.

The first context demonstrates how each standard fits into the body of knowledge of software engineering. For this purpose, the book applies the organization provided by the IEEE Computer Society's *Guide to the Software Engineering Body of Knowledge*. Each knowledge area of the *SWEBOK Guide* is summarized and relevant standards are mentioned within the context of the knowledge area. So, for example, users who desire assistance with software requirements management can read the relevant knowledge area description—getting an overview of the subject—and determine how available standards can assist in performing requirements management. In addition, the books performs a forced allocation of each standard to the single knowledge area viewed to be most relevant. At the end of each knowledge area chapter, a section provides detailed descriptions of the standards allocated to the knowledge area.

The second context is a process-oriented context. Many organizations are pursuing process improvement by establishing a set of organizationally adopted processes to be applied by all of their projects, and then improving them on the basis of their experience. The book uses the life cycle processes of IEEE/EIA 12207 and selected other standards to provide an overall process framework. Then other standards are fitted into the various processes to demonstrate how they can be applied in the context of the process.

Whenever a standard is located within the context of a knowledge area or a process, the reference is marked with an icon—something like this:

ISO/IEC 9126-1:2001
Software Engineering—Product Quality—Part 1: Quality Model
This standard provides a model for software product quality covering internal quality, external quality, and quality in use. The model is in the form of a taxonomy of defined characteristics which software may exhibit.
Allocated to: Software Requirements Knowledge Area

Terminology

The reference gives the number, date, and title of the standard along with a brief description of its content. The icon is a third form of categorization—it characterizes the kind of thing that the standard describes: *document*, *measure*, *plan*, *process*, *terminology*, *tool*, or, in one case, the *world wide web*. Finally, the reference states the knowledge area to which this standard has been allocated, hence, which chapter contains a detailed description of the standard.

4. SUMMARY

"Software engineering"—once a provocative euphemism for computer programming—is now rapidly approaching the status of an engineering discipline with strong relationships to other disciplines like systems engineering, quality management, project management, and more. A consensus-based body of knowledge is available, along with an appropriate curriculum and code of ethics. Work continues on the development of a set of fundamental principles.

Standards for software engineering have a variety of uses and roles. Most importantly, though, they provide succinct names for concepts that have many dimensions of variability, hence a tool for buyer and sellers to communicate.

This book is intended to help users find software and systems engineering standards useful in meeting their particular needs. To do this, it organizes the standards in two ways and places them in context. One context is knowledge-oriented and is based on the IEEE Computer Society's *Guide to the Software Engineering Body of Knowledge*. The other is process-oriented and is based on a process framework provided by IEEE/EIA 12207, *Software Life Cycle Processes*, and a few other selected standards. Icons provide a third form of classification—a characterization of the sort of thing, e.g., a process, that the standard describes.

Chapter *2*

Standards-Makers

Most of the standards described in this book have been developed by the Software and Systems Engineering Standards Committee (S2ESC) of the IEEE Computer Society operating under the auspices of the IEEE Standards Association. Nevertheless, a broader overview of standardization is helpful in understanding the role and importance of the standards. This chapter provides an introduction to both international and US standardization from the viewpoint of organization and process. The overview is far from comprehensive. Instead, it selectively pays attention to the organizations most commonly involved in the development of software and systems engineering standards. The first part of the chapter provides a survey of international and US organizations relevant to software and systems engineering. The second part of the chapter concentrates on the two organizations most relevant to this book—S2ESC and its international counterpart, ISO/IEC JTC 1/SC 7.

1. OVERVIEW OF STANDARDS DEVELOPING ORGANIZATIONS

The standards described in this book have been developed by Standards Developing Organizations (SDO) operating on the principles of consensus development and voluntary adoption. For the purposes of classification, the organizations are regarded as national (US, in the case of this book) or international. It must be noted, however, that even this basic distinction oversimplifies the actual situation.[9] Many major standards developers, for example,

---

[9] It turns out that almost every general statement made about standardization is an oversimplification. Nearly every organization and every project involves special circumstances that make it exceptional in some regard. The term *standards organization* may be a not so funny oxymoron.

The Road Map to Software Engineering: A Standards-Based Guide, by James W. Moore
Copyright © 2006 by IEEE Computer Society

the IEEE, include members from many nations, any of whom may contribute to the development of standards. The resulting standards may be adopted by anyone, anywhere on the globe. Nevertheless, for purposes of international standardization, these *trans-national* organizations are regarded as national entities and required to participate via the designated national body. For example, IEEE contributions to international standardization are administered by the American National Standards Institute (ANSI) despite the fact that the standards were developed by members from many nations.

1.1. International Standards Organizations

International standardization is increasingly important because of the growth of global marketplaces. The two organizations most relevant to software engineering are the International Electrotechnical Commission (IEC) and the International Organization for Standardization (ISO). For purposes of standardizing information technology, they have formed a Joint Technical Committee, JTC 1. Nevertheless, several disciplines related to information technology remain within one or the other of the two parent organizations.

As defined by ISO/IEC Guide 2, *Standardization and related activities– General vocabulary*, a standard is a "a document, established by consensus and approved by a recognized body, that provides, for common and repeated use, rules, guidelines or characteristics for activities or their results, aimed at the achievement of the optimum degree of order in a given context." In the case of international standards, consensus is formed among *national bodies*, each presumably representing the interests of producers, users, consumers, and general interest groups within their own country. The processes used by the international organizations include a formal enquiry stage when national bodies are supposed to offer interested parties the opportunity to have their say. Adoption and usage of international standards developed by IEC and ISO is voluntary.[10]

1.1.1. International Electrotechnical Commission (IEC) The International Electrotechnical Commission was formed in 1906 to standardize "the nomenclature and ratings of electrical apparatus and machinery." It currently describes its mission as follows:

> *Through its members, the IEC promotes international cooperation on all questions of electrotechnical standardization and related matters, such as the assessment of conformity to standards, in the fields of electricity, electronics and related technologies.*

The IEC produces a variety of products:

- International Standard (IS): a normative document, developed by consensus and approved by the IEC National Committee members of the responsible committee. It is also possible to develop a Corrigendum or an Amendment to an International Standard.

---

[10] In Europe, though, concurrent standardization by other organizations can have the effect of making the standard equivalent to law.

- Technical Specification (TS): a document that is similar to an IS, but for which full consensus cannot be obtained or on which work continues.
- Technical Report (TR): a document that is descriptive or informative in nature, rather than normative.
- Publicly Available Specification (PAS): a normative document developed outside the IEC but submitted to and approved by the IEC.
- Guide: a non-normative document related to international standardization itself.
- Industry Technical Agreement (ITA): a limited consensus document developed by a light-weight process outside the normal technical organization of the IEC.
- Technology Trend Assessment (TTA): a collaboratively developed document describing new technology that might become the subject of standardization.

IEC documents are published in English and French; some are translated into Russian or Spanish. Published documents are assigned numbers in the range 60,000–79,999 in accordance with an agreement reached in the late 1990s to align numbering with CENELEC.[11]

The members of IEC and its committees are National Committees representing nations. As of mid-2004, 63 nations held some form of membership in IEC. (In the United States, the National Committee is a part of ANSI.) Individual countries adopt IEC standards by using them as the basis for national standards. IEC is managed by a Council that delegates the management of standards activities to a Standardization Management Board. The technical work of the IEC is conducted by Technical Committees (TC) that subdivide the technical scope of the IEC. Three Industry Sector Boards and four advisory committees, including an Advisory Committee on Safety, coordinate activities that may transcend the individual TCs. Technical Committees may form Subcommittees (SC) to deal with designated portions of their scope. National Committees select the TCs and SCs in which they desire to actively participate. Smaller Working Groups (WG) are appointed by TCs or SCs for the purpose of drafting documents. WG members act as individual experts rather than as representatives of their National Committees.

Generally, a project progresses through six formal stages, possibly preceded by a preliminary stage:

0. In the *preliminary* stage, any TC or SC can perform informal work on a new idea.
1. Formal additions to the TC or SC program of work are considered in a *proposal* stage. Typically, a new work item proposal (NP) originates with a National Committee. Its acceptance requires a majority vote of the relevant TC or SC along with a commitment of active support by at least 25% (minimum four) of the National Committees participating in the TC or SC. On approval, it is sometimes called a new work item (NWI).

[11] Older document have been renumbered by adding 60,000 to their original number. For example, IEC 1078 was renumbered as IEC 61078.

2. During the *preparatory* stage, a WG is typically formed and a project editor designated to produce a Working Draft (WD). When suitable for comment, the WD is sent to the IEC Central Office for registration.

3. Now designated as a Committee Draft (CD), the document is circulated, during the *committee* stage, among the members of the appropriate SC or TC for technical comment. When consensus is achieved, the revised document is registered by the IEC Central Office.

4. During the *enquiry* stage, the Committee Draft for Vote (CDV) is circulated for a five-month period to the National Committees participating in the TC or SC. Although formal procedures permit technical comment at this stage, actual practice discourages it. After the incorporation of balloting comments, the revised draft is registered by the Central Office as representing the consensus of the TC or SC.

5. In the *approval* stage, the Central Office circulates the revised document, now called a Final Draft International Standard (FDIS), to all National Committees for a two-month vote on acceptance.

6. The final stage, *publication*, concludes with the actual issuing of the standard by the Central Office.

Documents in progress carry a three-part number indicating the originating TC or SC, a sequence number, and code summarizing the stage of processing. For example, "56/347/CD" would be the 347th document prepared by TC 56, a document at the Committee Draft stage of processing. Project numbers are sometimes more informative than document numbers. They also have a three-part number indicating the responsible TC or SC, the number assigned for the eventual standard, and a sequence of numbers assigning part numbers, amendment numbers, etc. For example, project 49/61178-3-1/A2/f1 would refer, reading right to left, to the first fragment of the second amendment of standard IEC 61178-3-1, as assigned to TC49 [IEC04].

National Committees participate in the TCs and the SCs of IEC by appointing delegations to attend their meetings. In the case of the US, the national delegation is appointed by the US Technical Advisor (TA) designated for the committee. The TA is supported by a Technical Advisory Group (TAG) that also forms national positions on anticipated issues.

Several Technical Committees and Subcommittees of IEC make standards that have some bearing on software and systems engineering. ISO/IEC JTC 1/SC 7 maintains liaison with the following:

- IEC TC 56, Dependability
- IEC TC 62, Electrical Equipment in Medical Practice
- IEC SC 65A, System Aspects of Industrial Process Measurement and Control.

IEC TC 56, Dependability IEC TC 56 is assigned the scope of *dependability*, a term coined in 1989 and intended to be nonquantifiable and broader than the more familiar *reliability*. The scope includes "availability performance and its influencing factors: reliability performance, maintainability performance, and maintenance support performance." Working Group 4, on system aspects of dependability, addresses the relationship between "dependability and integrity from a system perspective" where systems are meant to include hardware, software, and human factors considerations. Originally formed in 1965, the committee's mission was broadened in 1990 to address dependability in a *horizontal* manner cutting across the responsibilities of all other ISO and IEC technical committees [TC56-03].

IEC TC 62, Electrical Equipment in Medical Practice   Established in 1968, IEC TC62 now has the scope "to prepare international standards and technical reports concerning the manufacture, installation and application of electrical equipment used in medical practice and their effects on patients, operators and its environment" [TC62-03].

This TC is notable because it is developing IEC 62304, *Medical device software—Software life cycle processes*, claimed to be a tailoring of the 12207 life cycle process standard that was developed by ISO/IEC JTC 1/SC 7 and adopted by IEEE S2ESC.

IEC SC 65A, System Aspects of Industrial Process Measurement and Control   SC65A is a subcommittee of IEC TC65 on industrial process measurement and control. The SC65A subcommittee has the scope, in part, "to prepare standards dealing with functional safety of electrical/electronic/programmable electronic systems" [TC65-03]. As such, it is responsible for the maintenance of the famous IEC 61508 series of standards on functional safety of electrical, electronic, and programmable electronic safety related systems.

1.1.2. International Organization for Standardization (ISO)   The most well-known international standards developer as well as the world's largest developer of standards, the International Organization for Standardization (ISO),[12] is a nongovernmental federation of national standards bodies, created in 1947 as a successor to the International Federation of the National Standardizing Associations, which had focused primarily on mechanical engineering. Its scope now includes standardization in all fields except electrical and electronic engineering, covered by IEC, and telecommunications, covered by the International Telecommunications Union (ITU). The volume of output is staggering—more than 14,000 standards comprising nearly half a million pages of text.

The members of ISO are national bodies representing countries, 148 of them as of January 2004. ISO standards are developed in a hierarchical organization of Technical Committees (TC), Subcommittees (SC), and Working Groups (WG), the lowest level at which documents are formally drafted. National body membership is distinct for each different ISO TC, SC, and WG; national bodies select the levels and the organizations in which they choose to participate. The standardization operations of ISO are managed by a Technical Management Board that reports to the ISO Council [ISO04].

---

[12] The organization selected "ISO" as its abbreviation precisely because it is not an acronym for the name in any major language and because of its obvious relationship to the Greek word *isos*, meaning "equal."

In overall terms, the ISO standards development process is similar to the IEC process, described earlier, except that the term Final Committee Draft (FCD) is used instead of CDV. Administrative documents are numbered differently from IEC practice; the ISO committee or subcommittee is given, followed by an "N" and a sequential number. For example, the 512th document (from some designated starting point) of ISO TC 176 might be labeled as "ISO/TC176/N512." Documents designated in this manner range in importance from grand policy, through draft standards, to incidental items. To the casual observer, the "N" numbers are notable only because, prior to the assignment of a project number, they may be the only way to identify important items, for example, project proposals.

The US relationship to ISO is managed slightly differently than its relationship to IEC. Rather than having a US National Committee, ANSI itself is the US member body of ISO. The designation of delegates to ISO meetings and the formulation of US positions are controlled by Technical Advisory Groups (TAGs). Each TAG has both a chair and an administrator. In some cases, ANSI delegates the responsibility for TAG administration to a variety of organizations—mostly accredited standards developers.

Several ISO Technical Committees make standards related to software and systems engineering. Notable ones include:

- ISO TC 159, Ergonomics
- ISO TC 176, Quality management and quality assurance

ISO TC 159, Ergonomics   ISO TC 159 is responsible for "standardization in the whole field of ergonomics, including terminology, methodology, usability and human factors data." It defines ergonomics as "the scientific discipline concerned with the interactions among human and other elements of a system." Its SC 4 focuses principally on "human-system interaction." The most famous computing-related product of TC 159 is the 17-part standard ISO 9241, *Ergonomic requirements for office work with visual display terminals* [TC159-01].

ISO TC 176, Quality Management and Quality Assurance   Since their first publication in 1987, the ISO 9000 series has become, arguably, the most successful set of standards ever written in any area that affects information technology. They, and the related ISO 14000 standards for environmental management, are implemented by 610,000 organizations in 160 countries [ISO03]. In many places, the term "ISO" is used to refer to these standards rather than to the organization that created them. The principle underlying the standards is that an organization with a well-defined engineering process is more likely to produce products meeting the needs of its customers than a poorly managed organization. The ISO 9000 series of standards and guidelines specifies an approach to quality management intended to achieve this goal.

The ISO 9000 series of standards are developed and maintained by ISO Technical Committee 176. As of late 2003, 72 nations participated in the development of TC 176 standards. Internally, TC 176 is organized into three subcommittees: SC 1, Concepts and Terminology; SC 2, Quality Systems; and

SC 3, Supporting Technology. Each subcommittee has several working groups, some that appear to have enduring missions and some that seem to be organized for particular tasks [TC176-03].

1.1.3. ISO/IEC JTC 1 Information Technology is a special case. As computing technology evolved, it became clear that the scope for the standardization work of both ISO and IEC overlapped in many areas related to the emerging technologies. In 1987, the two organizations decided to coordinate their efforts by the creation of a new Joint Technical Committee, JTC 1, with responsibility for standardization in the field of information technology. Although JTC 1 also assumed the work programs of IEC TC 47B and TC 83, most of its activity was a continuation of work formerly performed by ISO TC 97, dating back to 1960 [Cargill97].

Membership in JTC 1 and its subcommittees is held by nations—27 participating and 39 observing, as of late 2002—rather than individuals. Participating Members have voting privileges while Observing Members are authorized to attend meetings and to contribute and receive documents. Liaison relationships permit both external and internal (other ISO, IEC, and JTC 1 committees) organizations to participate without voting.

JTC 1 is organized into subcommittees, each dealing with related areas of work, as shown below:

- SC 2, Coded Character Sets
- SC 6, Telecommunications and Information Exchange between Systems
- SC 7, Software and System Engineering
- SC 17, Cards and Personal Identification
- SC 22, Programming Languages, Their Environments and Systems Software Interfaces
- SC 23, Removable Digital Storage Media Utilizing Optical and/or Magnetic Recording Technology for Digital
- SC 24, Computer Graphics and Image Processing
- SC 25, Interconnection of Information Technology Equipment
- SC 27, IT Security Techniques
- SC 28, Office Equipment
- SC 29, Coding of Audio, Picture, and Multimedia and Hypermedia Information
- SC 31, Automatic Identification and Data Capture Techniques
- SC 32, Data Management and Interchange
- SC 34, Document Description and Processing Languages
- SC 35, User Interfaces
- SC 36, Information Technology for Learning, Education, and Training
- SC 37, Biometrics

The subcommittees are further subdivided into Working Groups (WG). JTC 1 uses procedures similar to those of ISO, but in some cases, the technical work is pushed down one level deeper in the hierarchical structure, for example, JTC 1 Subcommittees often perform work analogous to ISO Technical Committees.

JTC 1 produces two main types of products: international standards (IS) and technical reports (TR). Each completed IS is reviewed for currency every five years, resulting in a decision to retain, revise, or withdraw. There are three types of technical reports: a type 1 TR is a document that, although worthwhile, failed to reach consensus as an IS; a type 2 TR is a document on a subject that remains technically immature and on which IS development continues; and a type 3 TR provides material not suitable for a standard but is otherwise of interest, for example, models, frameworks, guidance. Type 1 and 2 technical reports are reviewed after three years with the expectation that they may be revised and designated as standards [JTC1-04].

The JTC 1 development process follows the same six stages previously described for ISO. Each of the key stages has a maximum allowed duration as well as a de facto minimum duration as a consequence of the frequency of meetings and duration of balloting periods. The average duration of the process has been decreasing in recent years and new management guidelines set a limit of 36 months.

US interests in the business of JTC 1 are represented by a Technical Advisory Group (TAG) administered by the International Committee for Information Technology Standards (INCITS) under the procedures prescribed by ANSI, the US member body in JTC 1. The hierarchical structure of JTC 1 is mirrored by a family of TAGs representing US interests at the SC and at the WG levels. The family of US TAGs cooperate under the terms of a Memorandum of Agreement sponsored by the Information Systems Standards Board (ISSB) of ANSI [Gibson95].

1.1.4. Other International Standards-Makers

A third international standards organization, the International Telecommunications Union (ITU), deals exclusively with telecommunications. Unlike ISO and IEC, it is a treaty organization, hence representing governments rather than the private sector.

There are two notable regional organizations in Europe. CEN, the European Committee for Standardization,[13] is the standards organization of the European Union. CENELEC, the European Committee for Electrotechnical Standardization, performs a similar role within its scope. IEC processing of a document is sometimes coordinated with CENELEC. This can lead to powerful results because CENELEC standards have regulatory power within the European Union. Ironically, this consequence may sometimes cause a National Committee to vote affirmatively in IEC but negatively on the same document in CENELEC.

1.2. US Standards Organizations

In the United States, unlike most countries, literally hundreds of trade associations, professional societies, and other groups are permitted to make stan-

---

[13] The N stands for "normalization," the French word for "standardization."

dards. Thousands of individuals and organizations voluntarily contribute their efforts to the development of standards. Most of these standards are developed as part of a voluntary system that is based on principles of due process, openness, and consensus [Baron95]. An important goal of the process is public confidence, not measured by market success, but by being "above reproach" in terms of being fairly developed and supported by consensus [Gibson95].

Some notable characteristics of standards developed by US organizations are listed in [Cargill97]:

- They have been written by a committee of anyone who could attend the meetings.
- They have undergone public scrutiny.
- All technical comments have received responses.
- They are a product of consensus within the committee and within an industry segment or professional community.

Subject to procedures administered by the American National Standards Institute (ANSI), such a standard may be designated as an "American National Standard." Policies of the US government provide that these national standards may be used in federal procurements [Cargill97].

This chapter describes some[14] of the US organizations that make standards relevant to software engineering. A brief history of each organization will be provided along with an overview of its internal structure and procedures.

1.2.1. American National Standards Institute (ANSI)   The most important thing to know about the American National Standards Institute (ANSI) is that it does not make standards. It does provide other important services to the community of US standards developing organizations (SDO). The successor of the American Engineering Standards Committee, formed in 1918, and the American Standards Association,[15] formed in 1928, ANSI is a private, nonprofit, member funded organization that coordinates the development of voluntary US national standards and serves as the US national body to ISO and IEC. ANSI is a federation of more than a thousand companies, about 200 SDOs, a few dozen government agencies, and a handful of educational institutions [ANSI04].

The SDOs that are accredited by ANSI have the opportunity to submit their own standards for ANSI's approval as "Approved American National Standards." It is a requirement to follow an accredited process for the production of standards that is fair, consensus based, and open to participation by all materially interested parties. Approval of a standard by ANSI implies only that the development process was judged to be properly applied; no technical judgment is involved. ANSI does not even check that the standard is within the scope of the submitting organization or that it is consistent with other national standards; it relies on declarations by the submitting organization. Accredited standards developers may write their own procedures or use model

---

[14] [Magee97] describes many more.
[15] Those of a certain age will recall the abbreviation, ASA, as a designation for film speed.

procedures provided by ANSI. In any case, approval of the procedures is a requirement for ANSI accreditation.

ANSI provides a method for public notification that an accredited organization plans to develop a standard in a particular area. Using the Project Initiation Notification System (PINS), the developer places a notice in the ANSI publication, *Standards Action*.

On the completion of a standard, the developer submits it to the ANSI Board of Standards Review (BSR). Notification of this step is published in *Standards Action*, providing interested parties four months to make comment on the submission and appeal[16] if they feel that due process has not been observed. Absent appeal, BSR designates the document as an ANSI standard.

Different SDOs place varying value on the ANSI label. The American Institute of Aeronautics and Astronautics (AIAA) and the Electronic Industries Alliance (EIA), for example, are generally careful to prefix their designation of an approved standard with the label "ANSI". On the other hand, IEEE simply adds a legend to the cover saying that the document is an "Approved American National Standard." Not all standards are submitted to ANSI for processing. The American Society for Testing and Materials (ASTM), a prolific SDO, submits few of its standards. Furthermore, many US standards developers do not even belong to ANSI.

ANSI serves as the US member body for participation in ISO and IEC; all US Technical Advisory Groups (TAG) to these organizations operate under the procedures of ANSI. In some cases, ANSI itself administers the TAG; in other cases, administration is delegated to an SDO.

ANSI is the US distributor of the international standards developed by ISO and IEC, and European regional standards developed by the European Committee for Standardization (CEN) and the European Committee for Electrotechnical Standardization (CENELEC). Furthermore, ANSI receives a portion of the revenues resulting from the sales of American National Standards. This revenue is important for operating their standards activities. According to its 2002 Annual Report, ANSI financed 58 percent of its operation from publication revenue.[17]

Some of the member organizations ([Magee97] lists additional ones) of ANSI responsible for the creation of standards relevant to software engineering are discussed in the following sections.

1.2.2. American Institute of Aeronautics and Astronautics (AIAA)   The American Institute of Aeronautics and Astronautics (AIAA) is the principal professional society serving the aerospace profession and counts 30,000 members worldwide. Its standards are oriented toward the particular requirements of aerospace but are sometimes applied more generally. Standards are created in

---

[16] Formal appeal is rare. It is more common for the submitting organization to revise the submission to deal with any comments.

[17] Other SDOs also finance their standards development and publishing operations through sales of the documents. In some cases, the financial support is crucial. For example, [Cargill97] reports that ASTM receives 80 percent of its revenue in this manner. The issue of payment for standards is always controversial. Obviously, the cost of buying a standard tends to hamper uptake. But, who else should be "taxed" for the legitimate costs of management, publication, and distribution?

Committees on Standards (CoS) under the supervision of a Standards Executive Council (SEC). The AIAA standards program is accredited by ANSI and AIAA participates in international standards activities [AIAA04].

Each of the 25 CoS is assigned a particular scope of standards activity. To draft a standard within that scope, a CoS creates an ad hoc Standards Working Group (SWG) consisting of experts from both inside and outside AIAA. The CoS relevant to this book is Software Systems, responsible for the standardization of application specific characteristics of computer software originating in aerospace [AIAA99].

A draft standard is circulated to the members of the appropriate CoS in a letter ballot. Changes are made in response to negative votes and the members are then permitted to change their vote upon recirculation of the draft. Most documents require a two-thirds vote for approval. If health, safety, or mission critical issues are involved, the threshold for approval is raised to 90 percent along with a requirement to explain why any votes remain negative.

Public review of proposed standards actions coincides with CoS balloting and is invited by notices published in *Aerospace America* and ANSI *Standards Action*. In some cases, the CoS may supplement the public review with a review by selected interested parties or even with public hearings and workshops.

Following successful balloting, and approval by the STC, documents are submitted to ANSI for designation as national standards.

AIAA produces three types of standards documents; the letter prefixing the document's number indicates the type:

- Standards (S): Documents that establish engineering and technical requirements for processes, procedures, practices, and methods. They contain the provisions necessary to verify compliance.
- Recommended Practices (R): Documents that contain authoritative engineering, technical, or design information and data relating to processes, procedures, practices, and methods. They may evolve into standards through application and industry practice.
- Guides (G): Documents that contain technical information in support of Standards and Recommended Practices. Guides provide instructions and data for the application of standards and recommended practices, procedures, and methods. Handbooks are in this category as well as preliminary standards and recommended practices.

AIAA standards groups can also publish Special Project Reports (SP), sometimes as precursors to the other forms of documents, sometimes as proposed government standards or specifications. Special Project Reports are not subjected to the full consensus formation process. Any standard, recommended practice, or guide is reviewed once every five years by the committee that created it to determine if it should be revised, updated, reaffirmed, or canceled.

Two AIAA standards relevant to this book are the following:

- AIAA G-010-1993, *Guide for Reusable Software: Assessment Criteria for Aerospace Applications*
- AIAA R-013-1992, *Recommended Practice for Software Reliability*

The AIAA G-010 standard provides engineering guidance for the use of reusable software components. This standard covers a broad area including domain analysis, component assessment, and reuse libraries. Many of the component assessment guidelines are specific to the programming language Ada 83 (ISO/IEC 8652:1987). The 22-page guide grew out work done in the early 1990s by the DoD's Defense Advanced Projects Research Agency (DARPA), notably the Software Technology for Adaptable, Reliable Systems (STARS) program. It was completed in 1993 by the AIAA's Software Systems Committee. The document provides guidance on "performing domain analysis as the basis for developing criteria for assessing potentially reusable software and establishing a software reuse library." Although the scope is stated as aerospace applications, the guidance seems more broadly applicable. Appendices suggest possible criteria for use in domain analysis, component assessment, and reuse library selection. The component assessment criteria are mostly Ada coding guidelines.

AIAA R-013 is a recommended practice for software reliability, particularly within the context of aerospace systems. The document defines software reliability engineering as "the application of statistical techniques to data collected during system development and operation to specify, predict, estimate, and assess the reliability of software based systems." The document specifies an 11-step generic procedure for estimating software reliability, provides guidance in selecting a model, and recommends three particular models along with providing information on others. Appendices describe approaches to determining the reliability of hardware/software systems and for using reliability models to develop test strategies. Based in part on this document, IBM Federal Systems Division developed a process for onboard space shuttle systems that has achieved a level-5 rating for maturity in the SEI Capability Maturity Model [Schneidewind96]. On the other hand, the document has been criticized for placing undue emphasis on modeling rather than field testing approaches [Knafl95].

1.2.3. Electronic Industries Alliance (EIA)   Founded in 1924, the Electronic Industries Alliance (EIA) is a federation of trade associations representing a broad range of companies involved in electronics manufacturing ranging from companies that produce small electronic parts to multinational corporations that design and manufacture complex systems used by industry, defense, space, and consumers. Although any of EIA's six sector associations can manage its own standards activity, its standards-making process is supervised by a single organization, the Technology Strategy and Standards Department (TS&S). EIA is accredited by ANSI and participates in international standardization activities [EIA04].

EIA standards are typically initiated with a privately developed draft that is submitted to a standards committee. The draft is discussed and eventually approved within the committee by a Committee Letter Ballot. If the document is intended to become an ANSI standard, the draft "Standards Proposal" is then circulated as an industry wide ballot—the so-called "Pink Ballot." Interested parties may purchase a copy of the ballot and cast a vote including comments. Comments are resolved and the draft is improved until a consensus is reached. The result is reviewed by TS&S to ensure that the requirements for due process have been met and then the standard is forwarded to the ANSI Board of Standards Review (BSR) for approval as a national standard. A national standard must be reviewed for currency every five years and may be reaffirmed, revised, or withdrawn. EIA has a mechanism, called an "Interim Standard" (IS),[18] for the trial use of standards that are intended to be quickly revised.

One sector of the EIA, the Government Electronics and Information Technology Association (GEIA), has a deep interest in the federal marketplace and sometimes coordinates its work with the US Department of Defense. When the DoD announced in 1994 its intention to decrease reliance on military standards and correspondingly increase the emphasis on commercial standards, EIA launched several programs to cast the best of the military standards into commercial form. In many cases, this has resulted in the creation of an interim standard (IS), a quick rewrite of the military standard, followed by a longer-term project to create a true commercial standard. Two GEIA standards committees are relevant to this book:

- G 33, Data and Configuration Management Committee
- G 47, Systems Engineering Committee

GEIA standards relevant to this book include the following:

- ANSI/GEIA EIA-632, 2003, *Processes for Engineering a System*
- ANSI/GEIA EIA-649-A, 2004, *National Consensus Standard for Configuration Management*
- GEIA EIA-731, 2002, *Systems Engineering Capability Model*
- GEIA IEEE/EIA 12207 (three parts), 1996, *Software Life Cycle Processes*

EIA-632 is an integrated set of processes that can be used in the engineering or re-engineering of a system. Because it is an outlier in the harmonization currently underway between IEEE S2ESC and ISO/IEC JTC 1/SC 7, the standard is not treated in this book. However, many consider it a legitimate alternative to ISO/IEC 15288 and IEEE Std 1220. The standard is the basis for Version 2a (2004) of the *INCOSE Systems Engineering Handbook*.

EIA-649 addresses configuration management from a system-level viewpoint. It replaced an interim standard, which, in turn, was developed as a replacement for a military standard, Mil-Std 973. The document does not contain normative provisions and is intended for neither conformance nor evaluation. It describes concepts and principles along with terminology that should be observed in the development of system-level practices for CM.

EIA-731 is intended to support the development and improvement of systems engineering capability. It was developed to be a systems-level analog to the famous software capability maturity model developed by the Software Engineering Institute.

[18] EIA's use of "IS" for Interim Standard should not be confused with ISO's use of "IS" to mean International Standard.

GEIA collaborated with the IEEE in the US adoption of ISO/IEC 12207, Software Life Cycle Processes. The result is a three-part standard, IEEE/EIA 12207, which is described throughout this book.

1.2.4. Institute of Electrical and Electronics Engineers (IEEE)   The Institute of Electrical and Electronics Engineers (IEEE) is the world's largest technical professional society with membership numbering more than 360,000 individuals in approximately 175 countries. The organization claims to publish 30 percent of the world's technical literature in electrical engineering, computers, and control technology. The IEEE is organized into 37 Societies, some of which are active in developing standards, including the Computer Society and the Power Engineering Society [IEEE04].

Organizations at three different levels within the IEEE are responsible for the development of standards. First, the IEEE Standards Association (IEEE-SA) is responsible for the encouragement, coordination, and supervision of all IEEE standards activities. Second, a number of "sponsors" have a defined scope of interest in which they may develop standards; most sponsors are within the various Technical Societies. Finally, "working groups" are ad hoc committees that are authorized to draft or revise a standard falling within the scope of a particular sponsor. Because IEEE is a professional society, participants in IEEE standards making generally represent only themselves, not their employers or any other organization, although IEEE has recently made provision for "entity balloting."

IEEE produces three types of standards (with a lowercase "s") documents—Standards (with a capital "S"), Recommended Practices, and Guides. The different types of standards are differentiated by the degree of prescription in their normative requirements. IEEE Standards contain mandatory requirements, generally characterized by the use of the verb "shall." Recommended Practices (RP) present procedures and positions preferred by the IEEE; they are characterized by the use of the verb "should." Guides suggest alternative approaches to good practice but generally refrain from clear cut recommendations; they are characterized by the use of the verb "may." It is important to note, though, that any of the three documents can contain any of the three verb forms. Therefore it is possible to claim conformance with any of the three types of documents, although, in the case of a Guide or even an RP, the claim may not be a strong one. IEEE can produce any of the three types of documents on a "Trial Use" basis. Trial Use standards are approved for a period of two years. At the end of this period, they may be administratively promoted to full use or returned to the sponsor for revision based on comments received during the trial use period.

The numbering of IEEE standards can seem a little complicated. In principle (although there are exceptions), the base number assigned to an IEEE standard has no meaning and the number's relationship to other numbers is not meant to suggest any relationships among the standards. Relationships among standards may be indicated by appending a part number to the base number. For example, standard "123.1" would be related to the "123" standard. It is also possible to add a supplement—an amendment or a corrigenda—to an existing standard with the intention that the supplement eventually will be merged with the base standard. Supplements are indicated by appending a letter to the number. For example, standard "123a" would be regarded as a supplement, a logical part of, the "123" standard.

Standards development projects that have not yet reached final approval are indicated by the presence of a "P" before the number, indicating that the number denotes a "project" rather than a completed standard. One may also find the notation "(R)" following the number of an IEEE standard; this simply denotes a project to revise an existing standard.

The formal IEEE process for developing a standard is delimited by two actions of the IEEE-SA Standards Board: approval of the Project Authorization Request (PAR), resulting in the assignment of a P number to the project; and approval of the final standard for publication, at which point the "P" is removed from the number. The duration of the intervening period is generally limited to four years, although extensions may be granted. During this period the sponsor is responsible for developing a document satisfying the purpose, scope, and other characteristics described in the PAR. Typically, the sponsor accomplishes this goal by creating a Working Group, within which individuals openly and publicly collaborate on a consensus basis to create a draft of a suitable standard. Following the preparation of the draft, a *sponsor ballot* is conducted among a larger group (perhaps the entire membership of the sponsor) to broaden the consensus and improve of the draft. The sponsor ballot may be repeated if necessary as the document is improved to address the concerns of the balloting group. A draft document cannot pass sponsor ballot unless 75 percent of the ballots are returned and the document is approved by 75 percent of those voting. (In practice, higher rates of approval are typically obtained.) Following successful sponsor ballot, the standard is submitted to the IEEE-SA Standards Board for approval and publication.

Approved IEEE standards are usually submitted to ANSI for endorsement as US national standards. Approval is typically routine. IEEE standards are sometimes submitted to international bodies as a basis for their own standardization activities. In turn, IEEE sometimes adopts international standards—sometimes with adaptation to the specific concerns of IEEE.

An approved IEEE standard has a life of five years. At the end of that time it must be reviewed with one of three results: withdrawal, reaffirmation (without change), or revision.[19] Revision is performed by a working group using a process very similar to that for writing a new standard [IEEE04a].

The Software and Systems Engineering Standards Committee (S2ESC) of the IEEE is described later in this chapter. Its collection is described throughout this book.

1.2.5. InterNational Committee for Information Technology Standards (INCITS)

The InterNational Committee for Information Technology Standards (INCITS) calls itself "the primary US focus of standardization in the field of Information and Communications Technology." Its membership is 1,700 organizations from 13 countries. INCITS is probably most famous as the administrator of the J committees responsible for programming language standardization. In all, though, it operates 35 technical committees "encompassing storage, pro-

---

[19] Recently, IEEE-SA added a fourth outcome—stabilization. A stabilized standard remains on the books indefinitely with no requirement for maintenance.

cessing, transfer, display, management, organization, and retrieval of information." INCITS is an ANSI-accredited SDO and is sponsored by the Information Technology Industry Council, a trade association. Those with long memories may recall that INCITS was founded in 1961 as X3, sponsored by the Computer and Business Equipment Association (CBEMA). Its most famous standard is X3.4, the seven-bit ASCII coded character set [INCITS04].

Although INCITS standards, such as the programming language standards, are obviously useful in constructing software systems, INCITS has no systems or software engineering standards. It is relevant to this book because it serves as the US TAG for ISO/IEC JTC 1.

1.2.6. International Council on Systems Engineering (INCOSE) The International Council on Systems Engineering (INCOSE) is an "international professional society for systems engineers whose mission is to foster the definition, understanding, and practice of world class systems engineering in industry, academia, and government." The organization was formed in 1992 and has grown to a membership of more than 5,000 individuals plus more than 40 Corporate Advisory Board members [INCOSE04].

Although it is not an accredited US standards development organization, it does inform its members regarding the development of relevant standards and encourages them to participate. It also has a formal liaison arrangement with ISO/IEC JTC 1/SC 7. INCOSE participation has been prominent in the development and revision of most of the notable systems engineering standards, including ISO/IEC 15288, IEEE Std 1220, and EIA 632.

1.2.7. Project Management Institute (PMI) The Project Management Institute (PMI) was founded in 1969 to promote professionalism in project management. It has since grown to a world-wide membership of 100,000. It provides educational programs, a professional certification program called the Project Management Professional (PMP), and a code of ethics [PMI04].

An enduring interest of PMI has been the collection of a generally accepted body of knowledge that is tangibly represented by their Guide to the Project Management Body of Knowledge [PMI00]. The PMBOK® has been adopted by IEEE as a standard. Since then, PMI has itself become an ANSI-accredited standards developer. As of mid-2004, PMI is developing a revision to the PMBOK® Guide.

2. KEY SOFTWARE AND SYSTEMS ENGINEERING STANDARDS-MAKERS

This section focuses on the standards-making organizations most relevant to this book: at the international level, ISO/IEC JTC 1/SC 7; and at the US level, the IEEE Software and Systems Engineering Standards Committee.

2.1. ISO/IEC JTC 1/SC 7 (Software and Systems Engineering)

ISO/IEC JTC 1/SC 7 is the major source of international standards on software engineering. It was formed in 1987 from three existing technical committees and inherited their programs of work. The terms of reference for SC 7 are defined as the "standardization of processes, supporting tools and supporting technologies for the engineering of software products and systems." SC 7 and its working groups maintain liaison with several ISO and IEC technical committees:

- IEC TC 56, Dependability
- IEC TC 62, Electrical equipment in medical practice
- IEC SC 65A, System aspects of industrial process measurement and control
- ISO TC 159, Ergonomics
- ISO TC 176, Quality management and quality assurance
- ISO TC 184, Industrial automation systems and integration
- ISO TC 210, Quality management and corresponding general aspects for medical devices
- ISO/IEC JTC 1/SC 27, IT security techniques
- ISO/IEC JTC 1/SC 32, Data management and interchange

In addition, SC 7 and its working groups list liaisons—some probably inactive—with a number of external bodies [SC7-04]:

- CEN TC 311, Information systems engineering
- ECMA/TC 33, Portable Common Tool Environment (PCTE)
- EFPUG, European Function Point User's Group
- ESI, European Software Institute
- IEEE Computer Society
- IFPUG, International Function Point User's Group
- INCOSE, International Council on Systems Engineering
- ITU-T, International Telecommunications Union—Telecommunications Standardization Sector
- NATO, North Atlantic Treaty Organization
- OMG, Object Management Group
- PMI, Project Management Institute
- QuEST Forum, a telecommunications industry association

Currently, there are many active Working Groups within SC 7 with scope as listed below:

- WG 2, Documentation of software systems
- WG 4, Tools and Computer-Aided Software/System Engineering (CASE) environments
- WG 6, Software products evaluation and metrics for software products and processes
- WG 7, Life cycle management

- WG 9, System and software assurance
- WG 10, Methods, practices, and application of process assessment
- WG 12, Functional size measurement
- WG 19, Modeling languages, metadata, ODP framework, and ODP components–related standards and projects
- WG 20, Software Engineering Body of Knowledge
- WG 21, Software asset management process
- WG 22, Software and systems engineering consolidated vocabulary.

The subdivision of responsibilities is neither orthogonal nor exhaustive because WGs are formed as their need is perceived rather than in response to an overall strategy.

As of April 2004, SC 7 had completed or was in the process of developing 107 standards [SC7-N3016]. Without exhaustively enumerating the standards, it is possible to list a few of the important categories:

- Vocabulary and the *Guide to the Software Engineering Body of Knowledge* (adopted from the IEEE Computer Society)
- Software and systems life cycle processes
- Process assessment
- Software quality management
- Software product quality models and measurement
- Documentation
- Measurement
- CASE tools
- Electronic data interchange
- Open Distributed Processing

2.2. IEEE Computer Society Software and Systems Engineering Committee

The IEEE Computer Society is the largest association for computer professionals in the world. Founded more than 50 years ago, it is now the largest of the technical societies of IEEE, an organization involved in standards making for nearly a century.

Any Computer Society standards project is assigned to one of ten or so sponsors; a project transcending the scope of any particular sponsor is supervised by the Society's Standards Activities Board, the parent body of the Society's standards sponsor groups. For software and systems engineering standards, the sponsor is the Software and Systems Engineering Standards Committee (S2ESC).[20]

---

[20] Some may recall the name of the group as Software Engineering Standards Committee (SESC). Recently, it formally changed its name and scope to include systems engineering. Involvement in that discipline dates back to the 1994 approval of IEEE Std 1220, *IEEE Standard for the Application and Management of the Systems Engineering Process*, as a trial-use standard.

2.2.1. History S2ESC traces its roots back two decades to the creation of the Software Engineering Standards Subcommittee (SESS) in 1976. Its first standard, IEEE Std 730, *Software Quality Assurance*, was published on a trial use basis three years later. By 1997, the collection had grown to its current size, roughly 40 documents. In addition to the development of standards, S2ESC participates in US or international conferences and workshops regarding software and systems engineering standards. Annually, it sponsors a track at the Software and Systems Technology Conference.

S2ESC cooperates with international standards-making as a member of the US Technical Advisory Group (TAG) to ISO/IEC JTC 1/SC 7. (In addition, IEEE is the organization responsible for administering the TAG.) In 2001, JTC 1 granted the Computer Society the status of a "Category A" liaison to SC 7. This means that the Society acts much as a national body, except that it does not vote. S2ESC and SC 7 are aggressively exploiting the relationship to harmonize and integrate their collections.

Through Memoranda of Agreement or other mechanisms, S2ESC cooperates with other standards-related organizations such as GEIA, PMI, and American Society for Quality Software Division. S2ESC also works closely with the Technical Council on Software Engineering (TCSE) of the IEEE Computer Society, the Software Engineering Institute and the Ukrainian Software Engineering Training Center.

2.2.2. Organization S2ESC cites its scope and mission [S2ESC-FP02] as:

> *Scope: Includes the standardization of processes, products, resources, notations, methods, nomenclatures, techniques, and solutions for the engineering of software and systems dependent on software; as well as the development and promotion of other professional products and services contributing to the maturation of software engineering as a recognized engineering profession.*

> *Mission: To develop and maintain a family of software engineering standards that are relevant, coherent, comprehensive and effective in use. These standards are for use by practitioners, organizations, and educators to improve the effectiveness and efficiency of their software engineering processes, to improve communications between acquirers and suppliers, and to improve the quality of delivered software and systems containing software.... To support and promote a Software Engineering Body of Knowledge, certification mechanisms for software engineering professionals, and other products contributing to a profession of software engineering.*

The management of S2ESC is performed by a chairperson and an executive committee that meets periodically to conduct the business of the S2ESC. In addition, S2ESC has an elected five-member management board. Each member of the management board serves as the point of contact for several of the working groups, planning groups, steering committees, etc.

Like most sponsors, the drafting of standards documents in S2ESC is performed by working groups. In many sponsors, working groups are formed at the recognition of a "good idea" by a number of interested people. Although good ideas remain welcome, S2ESC periodically forms ad hoc planning groups to systematically investigate areas that are strongly related within the discipline as well as areas that cut across other areas of software engineering. Each planning group surveys user needs, the existing base of standards, and technological trends in arriving at recommendations to create new standards, adopt or revise existing ones, or withdraw obsolescent ones. Working groups are often initiated as the result of planning group recommendations. As of May 2004, there were planning groups on three subjects:

- High-Integrity Systems
- Quality Management
- Web Applications

To ensure that each working group remains consistent with its PAR and with planning group recommendations, a series of milestone reviews examine the progress of the working group.

Since 1979, when the S2ESC published its first standard (IEEE Std 730, *IEEE Standard for Software Quality Assurance Plans*), S2ESC standards have provided a high-quality reference for the best practices of software development. Each standard was carefully written to provide the most accurate description of its particular subject.

In the intervening 24 years, the practice of software engineering has grown from an individually practiced craft to a highly organized team operation. There has been growing emphasis on the organizational adoption of processes to be applied repeatedly to every project of the organization. This has presented a new challenge for the S2ESC. Each standard must not only be technically excellent, but must also take its place in an integrated suite of standards that can be adopted in totality or in part by interested organizations and individuals. In order to accomplish this, the S2ESC needed to include an organizing framework, uniform terminology, and clear relationships.

Since 1994, the S2ESC has been following a strategy to achieve the desired level of integration within its collection. Complete integration has not yet been achieved, but substantial progress has been made:

- An organizing framework has been selected.
- The collection has been aligned with key international standards, and efforts are underway to integrate the S2ESC collection with the growing collection of international software and systems engineering standards of ISO/IEC JTC 1/SC 7.
- The collection has been aligned with key standards in related disciplines such as quality management and project management.
- An umbrella standard for software life cycle processes has been adopted.

In the past ten years, important achievements have marked progress toward becoming a true engineering profession. S2ESC has supported each of these initiatives.

- The IEEE Computer Society has published the *Guide to the Software Engineering Body of Knowledge* (SWEBOK).

- The IEEE Computer Society is offering a professional certification, the Certified Software Development Professional (CSDP).
- The IEEE Computer Society and the Association for Computing Machinery (ACM) have collaborated on the adoption of a Software Engineering Code of Ethics.

2.2.3. Integration of Collection with ISO/IEC JTC 1/SC 7

The IEEE Computer Society and S2ESC have always enjoyed a close, if informal, working relationship with SC 7. S2ESC has adopted and adapted SC 7 standards to fill holes in its collection and to provide common strategic direction, notably the adoption of ISO/IEC 12207 so that both organizations could share fundamental software life cycle processes. As the SC 7 collection grew, though, important differences started to appear between the two collections. These differences presented a dilemma for users who might desire to "pick and choose" among the offerings of the two organizations. Furthermore, the strategy of "adopt and adapt" resulted in the two organizations having standards that were substantively identical, but annoyingly different in the details. Clearly, a more tightly managed relationship had become necessary.

In 2000, JTC 1 granted the IEEE Computer Society a Category A liaison relationship with SC 7, a relationship that was implemented by S2ESC in the following year. During 2002, the two organizations worked together to develop a coordination procedure and a "Vision of Outcomes" to guide the direction of coordination. That vision and its 2004 update [SC7-N3069] have directed the harmonization efforts since that time.

The liaison relationship is based on four principles:

- The collections of SC 7 and S2ESC should be consistent and complementary—harmonized. Users should able to select and apply standards from both collections without contradiction.
- Both organizations should respect the consensus achieved by the other organization and avoid creating multiple variants of the documents.
- Whenever possible, coordination of a standard should commence by one organization adopting a standard of the other organization, so that coordination begins with a shared baseline.
- Maintenance / revision of adopted documents should be accomplished through a coordinated process so both organizations have the same standard.

Computer Society representatives now directly participate in a variety of SC 7 projects with the goal of harmonization. When appropriate, S2ESC provides leadership by providing IEEE standards for adoption by SC 7. Alternatively, S2ESC sometimes adopts SC 7 standards. In addition to four SC 7 standards previously adopted, S2ESC is in the process of adopting two additional fundamental standards—ISO/IEC 15288, *System Life Cycle Processes*, and ISO/IEC 90003, the application of ISO 9001 to software. S2ESC is planning to adopt these standards without change, except for the addition of informative material describing their relationship to other IEEE standards.

In a few cases, the two organizations have different standards covering the same scope; in these cases, work is underway to merge the two documents. A summary of major harmonization projects appears below:

- *Key concepts:* SC 7 is adopting the IEEE Computer Society's *Guide to the Software Engineering Body of Knowledge* as ISO/IEC Technical Report 19759.

- *Vocabulary:* S2ESC has contributed IEEE Std 610.12-1990, *IEEE Standard Glossary of Software Engineering Terminology*, to a new SC 7 project that will attempt to develop a unified terminology for the standards of the two organizations.

- *Software Life Cycle Processes:* S2ESC adopted ISO/IEC 12207 in 1996[21]; so both organizations already share a process framework. S2ESC policy suggests the use of ISO/IEC 15939, *Software Measurement Process*. S2ESC developed a risk management process, IEEE Std 1540, and "fast-tracked" it to SC 7; with minor changes, the result is currently being adopted by both organizations under the number 16085. SC 7 has agreed to withdraw its Technical Report on configuration management and will instead refer to IEEE Std 828. The two organizations have approved a plan to merge IEEE Std 1058 and ISO/IEC TR 16326 to provide a single standard on software project management. Furthermore, the merger of IEEE Std 1219 and ISO/IEC 14764, *Software Maintenance*, is nearing completion.

- *System Life Cycle Processes:* IEEE is participating in the ongoing SC 7 project to harmonize the life cycle process requirements for systems (ISO/IEC 15288) and software (ISO/IEC 12207). S2ESC is revising IEEE Std 1220, *Application and Management of the Systems Engineering Process*, for "fast-track" to SC 7. Finally, IEEE has contributed IEEE/EIA 12207.1, *Software Life Cycle Data*, to the project to develop an SC 7 standard for system and software life cycle data.

- *Measurement:* As mentioned previously, S2ESC uses ISO/IEC 15939 as its process for software measurement. In addition, its policies recommend the taxonomy of quality factors provided by ISO/IEC 9126-1, *Software Product Quality Model*.

- *Internet Best Practices:* SC 7 has requested IEEE to "fast-track" IEEE Std 2001, *Recommended Practice for the Internet—Web Site Engineering, Web Site Management, and Web Site Life Cycle*.

- *Certification:* IEEE Computer Society is leading an SC 7 study group to develop approaches for "portability" of software engineering certifications across national boundaries.

In addition, IEEE is contributing to the maintenance of standards that it has adopted by providing comments to their SC 7 revision projects. Other cooperative projects are under study.

---

[21] S2ESC has not adopted the amendments recently developed by SC 7. The group has decided to wait for "the other shoe to drop" when SC 7 harmonizes its software and systems life cycle processes.

3. SUMMARY

International standardization operates in a hierarchical organized structure of committees defined by technical scope. US standardization is less strictly organized, with hundreds of organizations operating more or less independently in overlapping scopes to produce standards. Given the untidiness of the real world, it may not be surprising that both systems deal with nearly identical problems of coordination.

For software and systems engineering, the most important standards-makers are the Software and Systems Engineering Standards Committee of the IEEE Computer Society and its international counterpart, ISO/IEC JTC 1/SC 7. They are currently cooperating to harmonize their respective collection.

Chapter 3

Principles of the S2ESC Collection

Because of the broad scope of S2ESC, and because of its desire to better integrate its collection of standards for software engineering, S2ESC has adopted a number of plans and policies to guide the evolution of its collection.

Beginning early in the decade of the 1990s, the S2ESC initiated a set of long-range planning activities with the ultimate intention of reorganizing itself and its collection to better achieve its mission. These strategic planning efforts laid the groundwork for a continuing process to better integrate the S2ESC collection so that users may select standards without fear of inconsistencies among them. Looking into the 21st century, S2ESC has captured and updated the results of the planning efforts in a set of policies and plans[22] for the management of the collection. These plans and policies can be grouped into five themes that are described in the remainder of this chapter:

- Strategic relationships with other standards collections
- Clear relationship between system and software
- Emphasis on organizationally adopted processes
- Uniform process framework based on IEEE/EIA 12207 and related standards
- Architectural coherence

1. STRATEGIC RELATIONSHIPS WITH OTHER STANDARDS COLLECTION

As the integrated suite of software engineering standards becomes more comprehensive, it is inevitable that it intersects with other disciplines and with

[22] See http://standards.computer.org/sesc/s2esc_pols/polndex.htm.

The Road Map to Software Engineering: A Standards-Based Guide, by James W. Moore
Copyright © 2006 by IEEE Computer Society

standards developed by other organizations. We must address the question of whether, for example, to re-invent project management in a software project management standard or to adopt an existing, broader standard on general project management and describe its relationship to managing a software project. S2ESC has chosen to designate strategic relationships with organizations writing standards in the various areas that form the context of software engineering. This section describes the relationships selected by S2ESC to organize its collection.

Principle: S2ESC standards should be consistent with recognized terminology and concepts of computer science and software engineering. Consistency should be maintained with IEEE Std 610.12, *Glossary of Software Engineering Terminology*, and with the IEEE Computer Society's *Guide to the Software Engineering Body of Knowledge*.

IEEE Std 610 is a multi-volume computer dictionary dealing with many disciplines including computer science and computer engineering. The portion of the vocabulary relevant to software engineering is gathered in part (volume) 12 of that standard, formally designated as IEEE Std 610.12. The *SWEBOK Guide* [SWEBOK04] is a consensually validated document that characterizes the content of software engineering, provides a topical organization of the discipline, and points to key references forming the field's body of knowledge. It can be regarded as the summary of the software engineering that any experienced practitioner should know.

S2ESC policy designates other disciplines or collections as having a strategic relationship with the S2ESC collection. For most of the disciplines, a specific source for standards is designated as the target for coordination.

- Quality management
- Project management
- Dependability
- Safety

In addition, S2ESC policy provides that its collection should be coordinated with the collection of the relevant international standards committee, ISO/IEC JTC 1/SC 7, with the goals of minimizing inconsistency. Finally, the collection aims to be consistent with the various maturity models popular in the software engineering community.

In implementing coordination with each other, standards-developers sometimes cross-adopt each others' documents or develop "bridge" documents describing the detailed relationship between the two collections. In such cases, the relevant document might be found in either or both collection. It should be noted that ISO/IEC JTC 1/SC 7 is pursuing similar goals for coordination. In some cases, the relevant bridge document can be found in the SC 7 collection.

> **Principle**: S2ESC has the ideal of consistency with the software and system engineering standards of ISO/IEC JTC 1/SC 7. S2ESC standards should be consistent with the vocabulary and process architecture of IEEE/EIA 12207.

Ideally, all S2ESC standards would be consistent with the standards of SC 7. That ideal is complicated because of the different adoption processes used by the two organizations. In cases where uniformity is very important, S2ESC has adopted SC 7 standards as part of its own collection.[23] IEEE/EIA 12207 is an example. The joint IEEE/EIA committee adopted ISO/IEC 12207 and supplemented it with additional material. The process architecture provided by IEEE/EIA 12207 is described later in this chapter.

> **Principle**: S2ESC standards should be consistent with the ISO quality management standards. Vocabulary is provided by ISO 8402:1994, *Quality Management and Quality Assurance—Vocabulary*. Quality management requirements are provided by ISO 9001:1994, *Quality Systems—Model for Quality Assurance in Design, Development, Production, Installation, and Servicing*. The relationship to software engineering is provided by ISO 9000-3:1997, *Guidelines for the Application of 9001 to . . . Computer Software*.

With the great emphasis on ISO 9000 certification around the world, it would be folly if software engineering standards prescribed processes inconsistent with ISO 9001. This principle is intended to achieve the desired relationship. Of course, the principle is slightly out of date because ISO TC 176 replaced its quality management standards during 2000. The current obstacle to updating the principle is the status of the bridge document, ISO 9000-3. ISO TC 176 transferred responsibility for the document to ISO/IEC JTC 1/SC 7, which produced a revision, called ISO/IEC 90003. Currently S2ESC is adopting the standard and will supplement it with an informative annex describing the relationship to IEEE standards. When that is completed (ca 2005), it is reasonable to expect S2ESC to update its consistency policy.

> **Principle**: S2ESC has the goal of consistency with the project management standards of the Project Management Institute (PMI), notably IEEE Std 1490.

Project management is a general discipline that can be specialized and applied to the management of software projects. S2ESC does not seek to write standards in the general area. Instead, S2ESC standards should describe the application of the general principles to software projects. The general principles of project management can be found in the PMI's *Guide to the Project Man-*

---

[23] Recent implementation of the Category A liaison relationship of the IEEE Computer Society in ISO/IEC JTC 1/SC 7 will make it substantially easier to coordinate the collections.

agement Body of Knowledge which has been adopted by S2ESC as IEEE Std 1490-2003. This goal is not completely realized because IEEE Std 1058, *Software Project Management Plans*, is not fully reconciled with IEEE Std 1490, and because PMI is about to release a revised version of the *PMBOK® Guide*.

Principle: S2ESC has the goal of consistency with the dependability standards of IEC TC 56. S2ESC standards on reliability, availability and maintainability should be consistent with the vocabulary and concepts of ISO/IEC 15026, *System and Software Integrity Levels*.

IEC TC 56 has the responsibility for standards related to system *dependability*, defined as a nonquantitative concept combining reliability, availability, maintainability, and maintenance support. Ideally, the S2ESC treatment of these subjects would be consistent with the standards of TC 56. S2ESC has taken a first step by designating ISO/IEC 15026 (developed by SC 7 in coordination with TC 56) as a "bridge" document. As SC 7 work continues in this area, additional documents may be designated. This goal is not fully realized; several S2ESC standards address reliability as a distinct topic. Furthermore, SC 7 is revising 15026 to become a more comprehensive document.

Principle: S2ESC has the goal of consistency with the functional safety standards of IEC SC 65A. Currently, consistency should be maintained with IEEE Std 1228:1994, *Software Safety Plans*.

This ideal is largely unimplemented. In 1998, following roughly 15 years of work, IEC SC 65A released its seven-part standard on functional safety for programmable, electromechanical systems. Its relationship to software engineering is still being explored. In the meantime, IEEE Std 1228, *Software Safety Plans*, is the best available bridge because of its coordination with standards from the nuclear power industry.

2. CLEAR RELATIONSHIP BETWEEN SYSTEM AND SOFTWARE

The extension of S2ESC standards to increasingly complex systems has served to emphasize the importance of the relationships between systems and software engineering. Some S2ESC efforts, such as IEEE Std 1362, *Guide for Concept of Operations Document*, and IEEE Std 1233, *Guide for Developing System Requirements Specifications*, directly address well-understood aspects of the interface between the two disciplines. Some of the relationships, though, are the subject of disagreement. For example, S2ESC planning efforts have shown that responsible professionals disagree on whether the concept of "software safety" makes any sense—some claiming that only system-level analysis is meaningful and others claiming that a body of software techniques should be articulated and systematically applied in conjunction with the system analysis. In the face of such fundamental disagreements, progress is made slowly and formal relationships must be carefully formulated.

Recent work in both S2ESC and ISO/IEC JTC 1/SC 7 is yielding agreement on some substantial issues in this area. One fundamental basis for agreement is provided by a simple convention:

Principle: According to IEEE/EIA 12207, *Software Life Cycle Processes*, software is always part of a system.

If nothing else, software always requires a processor for its execution and it often requires a human interface. Therefore, software development is **always** coupled with some form of systems engineering and software requirements are **always** derived from the requirements for the system.

The 12207 standard describes the minimum systems engineering activities needed to provide the context for a software project. Both the acquisition and supply processes of 12207 contain provisions for developing system requirements. The development process includes activities to analyze and evaluate the system requirements, if not already done, and to create a system architectural design that allocates the requirements to identified hardware, software and manual items. The development process also includes activities to perform system integration testing and system qualification testing based, in part, on the system requirements. The verification and validation processes also reference the system requirements.

Work by ISO/IEC JTC 1/SC 7 will provide additional details but is expected to retain the principle that software is always part of a system. The recently completed ISO/IEC 15288, *System Life Cycle Processes*, includes an implementation process that is employed to develop and deliver an element of a system. An element could be any of hardware, software, or training. Although the text references ISO/IEC 12207 for the creation of software elements, it is clear that the fit between the two documents is not yet perfect. The responsible working group is conducting a collective harmonization project to improve the fit between 12207, 15288, and a short list of other key documents. Meanwhile, to prepare for the international harmonization, S2ESC is adopting ISO/IEC 15288 to provide a reference set of system life cycle processes.

3. EMPHASIS ON ORGANIZATIONALLY ADOPTED PROCESSES

It has become clear that capable organizations do not invent new software processes for each new project. Instead, they have a sound base of organizationally adopted processes that are adapted and applied to the specific requirements of each new project. Therefore, the focus for the application of best practices, including software engineering standards, must be at the organizational level rather than at the project level. Furthermore, processes and practices are most effectively applied when supported by appropriate tooling and procedures. This requires investment—investment most economically applied across an organization's entire set of projects rather than borne by individual ones. To meet this need, S2ESC standards are intended to be suitable for organization level adoption. IEEE/EIA 12207 leads the way by providing a comprehensive set of processes that that encompass the entire software life cycle. In particular, when adopting the ISO/IEC standard, the IEEE added specific conformance provisions targeted to organizational adoption.

Key Terminology: According to ISO Guide 2, *General Vocabulary*, "conformance" is the fulfillment by a product, process or service of the requirements specified in a standard. The word "compliance" should not be used for this purpose.

The words "conformance" and "compliance" are often confused and used interchangeably. Conformance implies voluntary usage and compliance implies coerced usage. The point is raised here because one of the key standards, 12207, uses the word "compliance" in situations where "conformance" would be the appropriate word. The reason is that the writers of the standard originally intended it to be applied only in two-party situations where the standard would be "stapled to" the contract and the supplier would "comply" with the requirements of the contract. The 12207 standard was generalized to a wider variety of situations, but the word was never changed. This book generally uses the word "conformance" and its cognates for the concept of satisfying the requirements of a standard, even when discussing 12207.

Principle: S2ESC standards should be written in a manner that makes them suitable for adoption at the organizational level. Individual projects would adapt the processes provided by the performing organization taking advantage of tooling and procedures supplied by the organization.

The most obvious ramification of this principle is a recognition that some S2ESC standards might have to provide two distinct forms of flexibility—a degree of flexibility permitted to the organization adopting the process and a degree of flexibility permitted to the project adapting the organizational process. Flexibility provided to the project often takes the form of "parameterizing" the provisions of the standard with information taken from the specific project. For example, IEEE/EIA 12207, subclause 5.5.6.5 requires the archiving of data from a retired software product in accordance with the provisions of the contract for the job. Flexibility provided to the organization is discussed below.

Principle: S2ESC standards should be written in a manner permitting unilateral claims of conformance. Vague phrasing should be avoided. All requirements of the standard should be testable in an objective fashion. Standards should not be written in a manner that encourages "tailoring," in the sense of permitting arbitrary changes or deletions of the requirements of the standard.

Traditionally, many software engineering standards have been implicitly intended for usage in a two-party situation, i.e., an agreement between an acquirer and a supplier. Suggested guidance rather than firm requirements may make sense in such a situation because the two parties have the opportunity to determine the precise application in their specific situation. It also makes sense for the standard to include many provisions that may not apply in the general case; the two parties are reminded of them and have the opportunity to modify or remove them.

There are problems with this approach though. Tailoring demands a level of expertise that is often unavailable. In such cases, uninformed and risk-averse personnel often provide a tailoring that is too conservative, retaining inappropriate and costly provisions. More importantly, though, tailoring prevents the repeated execution of a single process, thus denying the benefits that an organization would gain from the increasing maturity of a repeated process.

The alternative is for supplier organizations to develop their own life cycle processes and to compete, in part, based upon the desirability and suitability of those processes. For this purpose, an organization desires credible evidence that its processes are sound and wants to cite that evidence in its proposals. Of course, adherence to applicable standards is one strong form of evidence. However, standards suitable for two-party tailoring may be unsuitable for the purpose of unilateral claims of conformance. A claim of conformance to a tailored standard raises the question of the extent of the tailoring. An unscrupulous claimant may have gutted essential provisions of the standard but still gets to make the same claim of conformity as a responsible claimant who implements all of the provisions of the standard.

For this reason, tailorable standards are not well suited for unilateral claims of conformance. It may be appropriate to provide some flexibility in the provisions of standards, but the choices made by the claimant should be clear in the statement of conformity. IEEE/EIA 12207 provides a good example. In the original ISO/IEC 12207 standard the only tool for achieving flexibility was tailoring, defined as deleting inapplicable provisions. When the joint IEEE/EIA committee adopted the standard, they added an annex providing additional mechanisms for making more precise claims. IEEE/EIA 12207 permits an absolute claim of conformance, which asserts conformance to all requirements without any tailoring whatsoever. To permit reasonable flexibility, though, IEEE/EIA 12207 permits conformance to be claimed on a process by process basis. For example, an organization in the business of software development, but not operation or maintenance, might make a claim of "absolute conformance to the development process"—a very precise claim. If ISO/IEC 12207 were used as the basis, the organization could only make a claim of conformance to a tailored version of 12207—a vague claim that includes both responsible and irresponsible tailorings of the standard.

4. UNIFORM PROCESS FRAMEWORK BASED ON 12207

Fundamental to the coherence of the S2ESC collection is agreement on the terminology for the processes that contribute to the life cycle of software and systems development. S2ESC has decided to adopt the process framework provided by IEEE/EIA 12207 and to apply that framework in all new and revised standards. The framework provides unifying principles for both software engineering processes and the data generated by those processes.

4.1. Process Framework

> **Principle**: S2ESC standards are based upon an enumerated and categorized list of reference processes, each implementing a specified list of objectives.

This principle results from the simple observation that some users wish to apply more than one S2ESC standard at a time. For this to be feasible, the standards must be based upon a commensurable set of processes. The principle satisfies this need by listing the S2ESC processes and defining their scope by means of a list of objectives. The list is not static but grows in a controlled fashion. Currently the processes on the list are those provided by IEEE/EIA 12207 along with a handful of additional ones provided by complementary standards. The process objectives were added as an annex of IEEE/EIA 12207 when the standard was adopted.

The current list of reference processes and the source of their objectives is provided in Table 2.

The left column of the table lists a process category for each process. The 12207 standard provides all but one of the categories and the 1517 standard provides the other. They are:

- *Primary:* Each primary process serves a principal participant in a software project. The primary *business* processes define the activities of the acquirer and supplier. The primary *technical* processes define the technical activities of the project—development, operation, or maintenance.

- *Supporting:* "A supporting process supports another process as an integral part with a distinct purpose and contributes to the success and quality of the software project. A supporting process is employed and executed, as needed, by another process" [IEEE/EIA 12207.0, 4.1.1.2].

- *Organizational:* The organizational processes are inherent to an organization that participates in a software project. When undertaking a project, an organization creates an instance of each corresponding organizational process for application to the project.

- *Cross-Project:* This category may be unique to software reuse. It includes a domain engineering process that inherently spans more than a single project by producing components for use in multiple projects.

ISO/IEC JTC 1/SC 7 has amended ISO/IEC 12207 to enlarge the list of reference processes and describe them in terms of purpose and outcomes. SC 7 plans additional work to harmonize the processes of 12207 with those of ISO/IEC 15288. S2ESC has decided to defer adopting the ISO amendment to 12207, preferring to wait until the harmonization efforts are substantially completed. However, it has decided to adopt the current ISO/IEC 15288 to provide an interim set of references processes for the system life cycle.

TABLE 2. Reference processes of S2ESC

Process Category	Process Name	Objectives defined by
Primary—Business	Acquisition	IEEE/EIA 12207.0, G.1 and IEEE Std 1517, C.1
	Supply	IEEE/EIA 12207.0, G.14 and IEEE Std 1517, C.8
Primary—Technical	Development	IEEE/EIA 12207.0, G.4 and IEEE Std 1517, C.3
	Operation	IEEE/EIA 12207.0, G.11 and IEEE Std 1517, C.6
	Maintenance	IEEE/EIA 12207.0, G.9 and IEEE Std 1517, C.5
Supporting	Documentation	IEEE/EIA 12207.0, G.5
	Configuration Management	IEEE/EIA 12207.0, G.3
	Quality Assurance	IEEE/EIA 12207.0, G.13
	Verification	IEEE/EIA 12207.0, G.17
	Validation	IEEE/EIA 12207.0, G.16
	Joint Review	IEEE/EIA 12207.0, G.8
	Audit	IEEE/EIA 12207.0, G.2
	Problem Resolution	IEEE/EIA 12207.0, G.12
	Measurement	ISO/IEC 15939, 4.1
	Asset Management	IEEE Std 1517, C.2
Organizational	Management	IEEE/EIA 12207.0, G.10
	Infrastructure	IEEE/EIA 12207.0, G.7
	Improvement	IEEE/EIA 12207.0, G.6
	Training	IEEE/EIA 12207.0, G.15
	Risk Management	IEEE Std 1540, 5.0 (without sub-clauses)
	Reuse Program Administration	IEEE Std 1517, C.7
Cross-Project	Domain Engineering	IEEE Std 1517, C.4

As the S2ESC collection evolves, its standards will be revised to utilize the reference processes and avoid defining processes which subdivide, combine, overlap, or cut across the specified ones.

Key Terminology: A *process* is not a *procedure*. A procedure is a time-sequenced series of steps intended for execution by individuals who do not need to know the objective. A process, however, provides a set of continuing responsibilities to parties who pursue those responsibilities in full understanding of the objective to be achieved. The activities specified by a process are selected because they are strongly coupled and because they are executable by a single party.

One reason for the success of ISO/IEC 12207 is the level of description used for process requirements. Several earlier standards attempted to describe similar processes but failed because they were "overly prescriptive." That term means that the standards required actions that, in full detail, were inappropriate in some situations. For example, requirements on the sequence of execution bound some of the standards to a waterfall life-cycle—not the appropriate choice for all situations. ISO/IEC 12207 managed to avoid entire categories of inappropriate requirements with a few simple rules.

ISO/IEC 12207 (and the IEEE/EIA adoption) describes each process as a collection of activities regarded as a continuing responsibility to obtain or maintain an objective. For example, the software architectural design activity of the development process calls for the allocation of requirements to the items of the system and demands that traceability is maintained. There is no distinct activity for updating the system architecture if the system requirements change. The necessity for tracking changes is implicit in the convention that the software architectural design is a continuing responsibility of the developer, not a step to be completed at some particular point in time.

One might wonder how the activities of each process were determined. The writers of the 12207 standard followed two rules: activities within a process should be strongly coupled and each process should be executable by a single party. Strong coupling is a principle borrowed from software design. It means that the activities within a given process should have a stronger relationship to each other than to activities outside the process. The rule that each process should be executable by a single party ensures that responsibility for the performance of the process can be precisely located. No process of 12207 imposes joint responsibility. Even the Joint Review process assigns distinct responsibilities to the two parties—the reviewed party and the reviewing party—who are executing it concurrently.

In general, S2ESC standards do not describe procedures because successful procedures are highly dependent on context. It is simply very difficult for a standard to provide a sensible procedure without imposing all sorts of superfluous requirements or lapsing into imprecise vagueness. The definition of procedures is best left to organizations that adopt S2ESC standards; they should provide tools and procedures to their various projects.

Principle: Evaluation is integral to a process.

The concept here is simple. Every process should contain requirements for the evaluation of the products that it produces. Stated another way, those with the responsibility to perform a process should not depend upon some other party to evaluate the products that they produce. (Of course, some users will seek the assurance provided by external evaluation, but any external evaluation is performed in addition to the evaluation inherent in the process.) Several of the S2ESC standards model their processes on a Plan-Do-Check-Act cycle; each process contains activities to make a plan, execute the plan, check for the satisfactory execution of the plan, and perform any appropriate actions for correction or improvement.

Process A

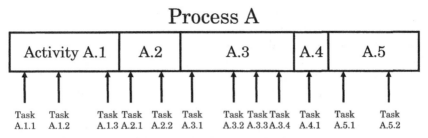

Figure 4. *Relationship of process, activity, and task in IEEE/EIA 12207*

Key Terminology: Processes are subdivided into *activities*. Activities contain a number of discrete tasks that provide requirements, recommendations, or permissions.

When users attempt to apply more than one process standard at a time, it is a great inconvenience if the various standards use different terminology to describe the structure of the processes. So S2ESC has adopted the convention that its processes should be described as stated above. The breakdown from the process into activities is a subdivision, i.e., the scope of all of the activities combined is that of the process. Activities do not overlap; instead they completely divide the scope of the process.

Tasks, on the other hand, are discrete provisions for the performance of an activity. Each task might be a requirement (typically marked by the verb "shall"), a recommendation ("should"), or a permission ("may"). Figure 4 may be helpful in seeing the distinction between process, activity, and task.

In the figure, the scope of Process A is indicated by the width of the box. The scope is subdivided into five activities. The scopes of the various activities do not overlap and precisely cover the scope of the process. The tasks, however, don't cover any scope. They represent individual provisions within the scope of the activity. Said another way, adding or deleting an activity of a process would change its scope; adding or deleting a task would not.

4.2. Data Framework

Executing the processes of 12207 requires the production of data. S2ESC has adopted the data framework of IEEE/EIA 12207.1 as a unifying principle for its collection.

Principle: The 12207 standard requires the recording of data but does not require the data to be gathered into documents of any particular content or format. The data requirements of 12207 can be satisfied with an electronic database.

The 12207 standard was written with the intention that organizations could apply or define their own documentation sets or standards to satisfy the requirements of the standard. The organization would simply explain how its documents correlate to the data requirements of 12207. The Documentation process of 12207 was provided for this purpose.

When the joint IEEE/EIA committee adopted ISO/IEC 12207, they decided to provide an aid to mapping data requirements to documents. This aid is IEEE/EIA 12207.1. The heart of IEEE/EIA 12207.1 is its Table 1, the *information item* matrix. Each of the 84 rows of this matrix corresponds to one or more provisions of 12207 calling for the recording of data. Each row gives a name to the information item, cross-references it to the corresponding clauses of IEEE/EIA 12207.0, categorizes it by *kind*, references content requirements, and cites standards that might be helpful.

Key Terminology: IEEE/EIA 12207.1 categorizes all information items into seven kinds:

Description: "Describe a planned or actual function, design, performance or process."

Plan: "Define when, how, and by whom specific activities are to be performed, including options and alternatives, as required."

Procedure: "Define in detail when and how to perform certain jobs, including needed tools."

Record: "Describe the materials an organization retains."

Report: "Describe the results of activities such as investigations, assessments, and tests."

Request: "Record information needed to solicit a response."

Specification: "Specify a required function, performance, or process." [IEEE/EIA 12207.1, 5]

For approximately half of the information items listed in the matrix, the content is described only by the kind of data. Table 3 summarizes the generic content requirements for each of the seven kinds of data.

Approximately half of the information items listed in IEEE/EIA 12207.1 have more extensive content requirements, provided by Clause 6 of the standard. In no case, though, are these content requirements as extensive as the Data Item Descriptions (DIDs) familiar to the users of military standards for software development. There are few surprises in the data framework, but some users would prefer more detailed content requirements. In many cases, 12207.1 cites other standards—including those from other organizations—that might provide the desired detail.

One surprise may be the distinction made between a *specification* and a *description*. Only one specification is listed in the table of information items— the systems requirements specifications. All documents that derive their content from the system specification—system architecture, software requirements, software architecture, software design, database design, software interface design—are categorized as descriptions.

TABLE 3. Generic content requirements for the seven kinds of data specified by IEEE/EIA 12207.1

Contents	Description	Plan	Procedure	Record	Report	Request	Specification
Date of issue and status	•	•	•		•		•
Date of initiation						•	
Date recorded				•			
Date/time frame				•			
Scope	•	•	•	•	•	•	•
Subject				•		•	
Issuing organization	•	•	•	•	•		•
Approval authority		•	•				•
Originator						•	
Contributors					•		
References	•	•	•	•	•		•
Macro (higher level) references		•	•				
Micro (lower level) references		•	•				
Message					•		
Context	•				•		
Introduction					•		
Notation for description	•						
Body	•			•	•		•
Conclusions and recommendations					•		
Summary	•				•		
Glossary	•	•	•	•	•		•
Bibliography					•		
Change history	•	•	•		•		•
Change procedures		•					
Planned activities and tasks		•					
Schedules		•					
Estimates		•					
Cost		•					
Resources and their allocation		•					
Responsibilities and authority		•					
Interfaces among parties involved		•					
Quality control measures		•					
Risks		•					
Environment and infrastructure		•					

TABLE 3. Continued

Contents	Description	Plan	Procedure	Record	Report	Request	Specification
Training		•					
Relationship to other procedures			•				
Inputs and outputs			•				
Ordered description of the steps to be taken			•				
Identification of requested item, service, or response						•	
Detailed description, including suspense date						•	
Justifications						•	
Delivery instructions							•
Assurance requirements							•
Conditions, constraints, and characteristics							•

This distinction is not yet implemented across the entire S2ESC collection. IEEE Std 830-1998 is still titled *IEEE Recommended Practice for Software Requirements Specifications*; it assumes that all of the requirements of a software-intensive system are incorporated into the single document. Currently, Appendix B of IEEE Std 830 notes the discrepancy with 12207.1. It can be anticipated that a future revision of 830 will make it completely compatible with 12207.

The current inconsistency is a matter of terminology and has little operational impact. Because 12207.1 specifies data rather than documents, it permits incorporating multiple data items into a single document. In a software-intensive system, it would be completely reasonable to combine the system requirements specification and the software requirements description in a single document, as is done in the current 830 standard.

5. ARCHITECTURAL COHERENCE

If users of standards are expected to pick and apply a single standard as a point solution, then there would be no need for the standards to have any defined relationships among themselves. It is more likely, though, that various users will need to select several standards according to their needs and apply them in unison. An overall organization of the collection assists users in easily finding the standards appropriate to their needs. A degree of uniformity among the standards assists users in applying them together. For this purpose, S2ESC has developed an architecture for its collection.

5.1. Consistency

The S2ESC architecture begins with principles of consistency:

> **Principle**: IEEE software engineering standards should be internally consistent and consistent across the collection of standards.
>
> **Principle**: It is more important to optimize the technical quality of the overall collection of S2ESC than that of any individual standard.

The first principle states that it is not enough for individual standards to effect a consistent treatment of their individual subject matter, but that all S2ESC standards, taken as a group, should effect a consistent treatment of the subject of software engineering. The second principle makes a tradeoff; it suggests that overall consistency of the collection is a more important goal than the excellence in any individual standard. For example, suppose that S2ESC is offered a brilliant treatment of some particular subject that is premised on a structure of processes completely different than that of the 12207 standard. The principle suggests that a more mundane, but consistent treatment is to be preferred because it contributes to the excellence of the collection as a whole.

Of course, an insistence upon consistency begs an extended definition of that term. S2ESC has adopted the following:

- The S2ESC collection should be free from internal contradiction, in the sense that no two standards impose contradictory requirements for conformance.
- There should be operational consistency among the standards, in the sense that related standards can be used together on a project.
- The individual standards, and the collection as a whole, should satisfy a designated set of S2ESC consistency policies.

Some might object that a strict requirement for consistency across the entire collection might stifle innovation or the treatment of innovative subjects. S2ESC has recognized that possibility and is considering designation of a "foundation" subset of its collection. The foundation collection would be completely subject to the consistency policies. However, designated standards would be placed outside the foundation and relieved of the requirement of consistency. Standards might be placed outside the foundation if they deal with new technologies or niche applications, if they deal with subjects that fall outside the S2ESC architecture, or if they are temporary or transitional in nature.

5.2. Product Quality Model

> **Key Terminology**: S2ESC standards use the taxonomy of software product quality characteristics provided by ISO/IEC 9126-1.

When one specifies a product, one usually starts by specifying the functional characteristics required of the product. Of course, these are different in each product and there is little that a software engineering standard can say on the subject. There is another class of characteristics, though, sometimes called "nonfunctional" or "quality" characteristics. S2ESC calls them *product quality* characteristics in order to clearly distinguish them from the quality characteristics of processes. Users of software engineering standards are often interested in these characteristics. In fact, the pursuit of these characteristics is often what motivates an engineering approach to software development. Because S2ESC standards often address product quality characteristics, a uniform taxonomy is helpful so that different standards use the same terminology to address the same subject. Fortunately, ISO/IEC JTC 1/SC 7 has developed a standard that provides this taxonomy in the form of a product quality model, ISO 9126-1, *Software Engineering—Product Quality—Part 1: Quality Model*. The model provides six characteristics with each characteristic broken down into several subcharacteristics:

- *Functionality:* The ability of the product to provide functions meeting stated and implied needs. Subcharacteristics include suitability, accuracy, interoperability, security, and compliance.
- *Reliability:* The ability of the product to maintain its specified level of performance. Subcharacteristics include maturity, fault tolerance, recoverability, and compliance.
- *Usability:* The ability of the product to be understood, learned, used, attractive. Subcharacteristics include understandability, learnability, operability, attractiveness, and compliance.
- *Efficiency:* The ability of the product to provide appropriate performance relative to the resources consumed. Subcharacteristics include time behavior, resource utilization, and compliance.
- *Maintainability:* The ability of the product to be modified. Subcharacteristics include analyzability, changeability, stability, testability, and compliance.
- *Portability:* The ability of the product to be transferred from one environment to another. Subcharacteristics include adaptability, installability, co-existence, replaceability, and compliance.

Readers may note that "compliance" is a subcharacteristic of all six of the characteristics. It refers to the adherence to regulations, conventions, standards, or other norms related to the characteristic.

Despite the importance of the product quality model, it exposes a problem in attempting to coordinate one's collection with international standards. In general, the hundreds of international standards-making committees have great difficulty in achieving consistency among their collections. One of the inconsistencies is illustrated here. IEC TC 56 defines "dependability" as including subcharacteristics of "reliability" and "maintainability"; here in the SC 7 model those two subcharacteristics appear as top-level characteristics without mention of dependability. Although annoying, the inconsistency causes no contradiction in actual usage.

5.3. Process Abstraction Model

One difficulty with some process standards is that they describe processes at different levels of abstraction, making it difficult to determine how a process described in one standard might relate to a process described in another. It is useful to designate a (small) number of process abstraction levels and confine standards to those levels. S2ESC has done this.

Principle: S2ESC uses the Basili model [Basili92] to describe process abstraction levels. Each S2ESC standards describes processes at the *reference* or the *conceptual* level of the Basili model. The *implementation* level is better left to organizations adopting S2ESC standards.

The Basili framework, with terminology modified to match IEEE/EIA 12207, provides for three levels of abstraction in representing processes:

- The *reference* level, representing agents that carry out the processes. Decisions represented at this level are the selection of a coherent and cohesive set of activities that may be sensibly performed by a single agent. Such a set of activities is a process.
- The *conceptual* level, representing the flow of control and data among the agents. Decisions at this level include the logical relationships among the agents both for control and for the communication of data.
- The *implementation* level, representing the implementation, both technical and organizational, of the agents and their interfaces. Decisions at this level include mapping the agents to the management organization of the particular project or enterprise and the selection of policies, procedures, and tools to enable the agents to perform their tasks.

These levels are not to be regarded as successive functional decompositions. In fact, any one of them can be independently refined into greater details. The distinction between the former two levels permits discussion of the objectives of the processes independently of their detailed relationships. The distinction between the latter two levels permits discussion of processes independently of the structure of the organization that will implement them.

Both the international and the US versions of 12207 are examples of reference-level process descriptions. IEEE Std 1074, *Developing Life Cycle Processes*, is a tool that can be applied by a process architect to create conceptual-level process descriptions implementing the requirements of the 12207 standard. Projects can develop policies and procedures that provide the implementation-level descriptions of the processes complying with the standards.

This model for process abstraction has not yet been uniformly implemented across the S2ESC collection. Many of software process standards of IEEE S2ESC straddle the reference and conceptual level of abstraction. The authors of these standards—written when process description tools were not in general usage—generally resorted to the artifice of specifying a plan, the contents of which implicitly impose process requirements. Flows of data were generally unspecified except for the flows to and from the plan's manager.

6. SUMMARY

To better integrate its collection of standards and to form clearer relationships with other collections, S2ESC has adopted a number of policies that are applied to its collection as a whole. This chapter has described the policies by grouping them into five themes:

- Strategic relationships with other standards collections
- Clear relationship between system and software
- Emphasis on organizationally adopted processes
- Uniform process framework based on IEEE/EIA 12207 and related standards
- Architectural coherence

Chapter *4*

Organizing a Standards Collection

The sheer number of standards in a large collection is a barrier to their application. A user needs some sort of organizing principle so that he or she can find the way to the particular standard that is needed. S2ESC has organized its collection in various ways at different times. This chapter will review some of them.

1. ORGANIZING BY TOPIC

In 1997, the IEEE Standards Association published a 2,400-page volume [IEEESA97] containing most of the standards of the then-SESC. The standards were organized by eight topics:

- Documentation
- Life Cycle Processes
- Measurement (including reliability)
- Plans
- Project Management
- Reuse
- Terminology
- Tools

The classification was forced—a standard was placed in a single category, even if it were relevant to several. If this organization were applied to today's collection, the result would be something like that shown below. This organization would omit one current standard, IEEE Std 2001, *Recommended Practice for the Internet—Web Site Engineering, Web Site Management, and Web Site Life Cycle.*

1.1. Standards for Documentation

The following S2ESC standards prescribe or recommend the format and/or content of documentation of software or software-related products:

- IEEE Std 829, *Software Test Documentation*
- IEEE Std 830, *Recommended Practice for Software Requirements Specifications*
- IEEE Std 1016, *Recommended Practice for Software Design Descriptions*
- IEEE Std 1063, *Software User Documentation*
- IEEE Std 1233, *Guide for Developing System Requirements Specifications*
- IEEE Std 1362, *Guide for Information Technology—System Definition—Concept of Operations (ConOps) Document*
- IEEE Std 1465, *Adoption of International Standard ISO/IEC 12119: 1994(E), Information Technology—Software packages—Quality requirements and testing*
- IEEE Std 1471, *Recommended Practice for Architectural Description of Software Intensive Systems*
- IEEE/EIA 12207.1, *Industry Implementation of International Standard ISO/IEC 12207:1995, Standard for Information Technology—Software Life Cycle Processes—Life cycle data*

1.2. Standards for Life Cycle Processes

The following S2ESC standards prescribe or recommend requirements for processes or activities of the software life cycle:

- IEEE Std 1008, *Software Unit Testing*
- IEEE Std 1028, *Software Reviews*
- IEEE Std 1062, *Recommended Practice for Software Acquisition*
- IEEE Std 1074, *Developing Software Life Cycle Processes*
- IEEE Std 1219, *Software Maintenance*
- IEEE Std 1220, *Application and Management of the Systems Engineering Process*
- IEEE/EIA 12207.0, *Industry Implementation of International Standard ISO/IEC 12207:1995, Standard for Information Technology—Software life cycle processes*
- IEEE/EIA 12207.2, *Industry Implementation of International Standard ISO/IEC 12207:1995, Standard for Information Technology—Software life cycle processes—Implementation considerations*

1.3. Standards for Measurement

The following S2ESC standards prescribe or recommend measures for various aspects of software size, productivity, and quality:

- IEEE Std 982.1, *Dictionary of Measures to Produce Reliable Software*
- IEEE Std 1045, *Software Productivity Metrics*
- IEEE Std 1061, *Software Quality Metrics Methodology*
- IEEE Std 14143.1, *Adoption of ISO/IEC 14143-1:1998, Information Technology—Software Measurement—Functional Size Measurement—Part 1: Definition of Concepts*

1.4. Standards for Plans

Today, the boundary between disciplined and undisciplined software development is marked by the existence of defined processes. Prior to that, the boundary was defined by the existence of various types of plans. These S2ESC standards prescribe or recommend the content of various plans related to software:

- IEEE Std 730, *Software Quality Assurance Plans*
- IEEE Std 828, *Software Configuration Management Plans*
- IEEE Std 1012, *Software Verification and Validation*
- IEEE Std 1228, *Software Safety Plans*

1.5. Standards for Project Management

Modern approaches to disciplined software development emphasize management planning and control. The following S2ESC standards support various aspects of project management:

- IEEE Std 1044, *Classification for Software Anomalies*
- IEEE Std 1058, *Software Project Management Plans*
- IEEE Std 1490, *Guide: Adoption of PMI Standard, A Guide to the Project Management Body of Knowledge*
- IEEE Std 1540, *Software Life Cycle Processes—Risk Management*

1.6. Standards for Reuse

S2ESC has one standard relevant to the processes of software reuse:

- IEEE Std 1517-1999, *Information Technology—Software Life Cycle Processes—Reuse Processes*

1.7. Standards for Terminology

S2ESC has one terminology standard, albeit an aging one:

- IEEE Std 610.12, *Glossary of Software Engineering Terminology*

1.8. Standards for Tools

S2ESC has several standards related to tools. Notation standards are also lumped into this category because notations are typically supported by tools.

- IEEE Std 1175.1, *Guide for CASE Tool Interconnections—Classification and Description*
- IEEE Std 1320.1, *Functional Modeling Language—Syntax and Semantics for IDEF0*
- IEEE Std 1320.2, *Conceptual Modeling Language—Syntax and Semantics for IDEF1X97 (IDEFobject)*
- IEEE Std 1420.1, *Information Technology—Software Reuse—Data Model for Reuse Library Interoperability: Basic Interoperability Data Model (BIDM)*
- IEEE Std 1420.1a, *Supplement to IEEE Standard for Information Technology—Software Reuse—Data Model for Reuse Library Interoperability: Asset Certification Framework*
- IEEE Std 1420.1b, *Trial-Use Supplement to IEEE Standard for Information Technology—Software Reuse—Data Model for Reuse Library Interoperability: Intellectual property Rights Framework*
- IEEE Std 1462, *Adoption of International Standard ISO/IEC 14102:1995, Information Technology—Guideline for the evaluation and selection of CASE tools*

2. ORGANIZING BY OBJECT

In 1999, the IEEE Standards Association published a four-volume edition [IEEESA99] containing most of the standards of the then-SESC. This edition used two principles to group the standards: *levels of prescription* and *objects of software engineering*.

2.1. Levels of Prescription

By their nature, all standards provide some level of prescription; they include requirements that must be satisfied if one is to claim conformance or recommendations regarding best practice. Nevertheless, the level of prescription varies widely both in form and level of detail. Characterizing the levels of prescription is a useful tool for categorizing standards:

- *Terminology* standards provide definitions and unifying concepts for a collection of standards. In many cases, they do not include any explicit requirements, only the implicit demand of applying a uniform terminology.
- *Collection guides* do not provide requirements—only information. A collection guide surveys a group of related standards and provides advice to users on how suitable standards may be selected for their use. This book is the collection guide for the S2ESC standards.

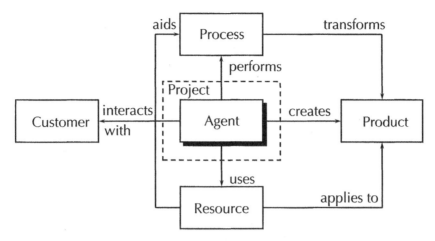

Figure 5. *Objects of software engineering*

- *Principle standards* provide high-level requirements that might be satisfied in a wide variety of ways. They emphasize goals rather than specific means for achieving the goals.
- *Element standards* are the most familiar form. They contain requirements more detailed than those of principle standards and prescribe a particular approach to achieving the goals prescribed in a principle standard.
- *Application guides* emphasize recommendations and guidance. They provide advice on how element standards may be implemented in particular situations.
- *Technique standards* are the most detailed and prescriptive. They generally describe notations or procedures rather than processes. They provide very specific requirements presumably for those cases where small deviations might have large consequences.

2.2. Objects of Software Engineering

S2ESC standards can be viewed as addressing four interacting objects of software engineering—customer, process, resource and product—and their relationship with the software project as depicted in Figure 5.

In this view, software engineering is performed by a project. The project interacts with *customers* and uses *resources* to perform *processes* resulting in the creation of *products*. Each S2ESC standard can be viewed as addressing one or more of the four objects that form the context of the project. Using this approach, the current collection could be classified as shown in Table 4.

3. ORGANIZING BY KNOWLEDGE AREA

Since the publication of the 1999 edition of the then-SESC standards, an exciting development has occurred. The IEEE Computer Society's Software

TABLE 4. S2ESC standards organized by level of prescription and object

	Customer	Process	Product	Resource
Terminology	610.12, Vocabulary			
Collection Guide	For the 1999 S2ESC collection, James W. Moore, *Software Engineering Standards: A User's Road Map* [Moore97]. For the current collection, this book.			
Principle Standards	12207.0, Software Life Cycle Processes			
Element Standards	1062 Software Acquisition 1220 Systems Engineering Process 1228 SW Safety Plans 1233 System Requirements Specification 1362 Concept of Operations	730 SW Quality Assurance Plans 828 SW Configuration Management Plans 1008 SW Unit Testing 1012 SW V&V 1028 SW Reviews 1045 SW Productivity Metrics 1058 SW Project Management Plans 1074 Developing SWLC Processes 1219 SW Maintenance 1490 Project Management BOK 1517 Reuse Processes 1540 Risk Management Process	982.1 Measures for Reliable SW 1061 SW Quality Metrics Methodology 1063 SW User Documentation 1465 SW Package Quality Requirements	829 SW Test Documentation 830 SW Requirements Specification 1016 SW Design Descriptions 1175 CASE Tool Interconnection 1320.1 and .2 IDEF 1420.1, 1a, 1b Reuse Library Interoperation 1462 Evaluation and Selection of CASE Tools 1471 Architecture Description 2001 Internet Best Practices 14143.1 Functional Size Measurement
Application Guides	12207.1 and 12207.2, Guides to Software Life Cycle Processes			
Technique Standards	1044, Classification of Anomalies			

Engineering Body of Knowledge project has produced a consensus description of the scope of software engineering and the knowledge that is generally accepted within that scope. The *Guide to the Software Engineering Body of Knowledge* [SWEBOK04], sometimes simply called the *SWEBOK Guide*, subdivides the relevant knowledge into ten knowledge areas. This book organizes the S2ESC standards in the same fashion.[24]

In this book, the S2ESC standards are grouped by the ten knowledge areas of the *SWEBOK Guide* and its additional chapter for related disciplines:

- Software Requirements
- Software Design
- Software Construction
- Software Testing
- Software Maintenance
- Software Configuration Management
- Software Engineering Management
- Software Engineering Process
- Software Engineering Tools and Methods
- Software Quality
- Related Disciplines

The reader will find a chapter for each of the SWEBOK knowledge areas. Within each chapter, the knowledge area is summarized and the standards relevant to that knowledge area are described in context. Because the S2ESC collection has a scope broader than the SWEBOK, it contains some standards that do not fall within the ten Knowledge Areas. However, the *SWEBOK Guide* does have a chapter on "Related Disciplines." So does this book, and standards related to project management, quality management, and systems engineering are described in that chapter.

Finally, the S2ESC collection includes a general terminology standard, IEEE Std 610.12 and one standard specific to an application area, IEEE Std 2001, *Internet Best Practices*. Those standards are described in an additional chapter—Chapter 17, Other IEEE Software Engineering Standards.

4. ORGANIZING BY PROCESS

Another way to organize the standards is by using a process reference model. S2ESC has provided a process reference model based on the processes of IEEE/EIA 12207.0 and a few complementary standards. A major part of this book takes a process-oriented view of the collection.

The current **systems** engineering standards of S2ESC are a problem because they fit uneasily into a framework of software life cycle processes and

---

[24] The most recent published edition [IEEESA03] of the S2ESC collection also follows this organization.

S2ESC has not yet adopted a policy providing a process framework for the systems life cycle. As of mid-2004, S2ESC was moving to adopt ISO/IEC 15288, *System Life Cycle Processes*, as an IEEE standard. Anticipating that move, this book classifies the systems engineering standards using the technical processes of ISO/IEC 15288.

5. SUMMARY

Because of the relatively large number of software and systems engineering standards, it is difficult for readers to easily identify standards of interest unless some organizing principles are provided. This chapter first described two historical methods of organizing the S2ESC collection—by topic and by object—and then described the two organizations that are used in this book—by knowledge area and by process.

Part 2

A Knowledge-Oriented View

Chapter 5

Overview of the Software Engineering Body of Knowledge

The *Guide to the Software Engineering Body of Knowledge* was developed by the IEEE Computer Society to underlay its professional development activities for software engineers by characterizing the things that a practicing software engineer should know. The *SWEBOK Guide* can be used to organize the software and systems engineering standards of the IEEE Computer Society's Software and Systems Engineering Standards Committee (S2ESC).

1. PURPOSE OF THE *SWEBOK GUIDE*

The purpose of the *Guide to the Software Engineering Body of Knowledge* is to "provide a consensually-validated characterization of the bounds of the software engineering discipline and to provide a topical access to the Body of Knowledge supporting the discipline" [SWEBOK04].

The various phrases of this statement provide important insight into the nature of the *SWEBOK Guide*:

- *Software engineering discipline:* The *Guide* takes an engineering viewpoint to software, rather than a scientific viewpoint. It emphasizes the construction of useful artifacts and it emphasizes a disciplined approach to solving a problem rather than the particular technologies that are needed to effect a solution. Although the *Guide* is not *normative*—it does not provide direction or recommendations—it does draw from the normative literature as a source of generally accepted practice.

The Road Map to Software Engineering: A Standards-Based Guide, by James W. Moore
Copyright © 2006 by IEEE Computer Society

- *Body of knowledge:* The existence of a recognized and accepted body of knowledge is a prerequisite for recognition as a legitimate engineering discipline and a profession. The *SWEBOK Guide* is not that body of knowledge; rather it is an organized set of references to the literature containing that knowledge. In general, the references are made to recent literature so that the treatment is current and the material is accessible. As technologies are replaced and practice evolves, the body of knowledge will change.

- *Topical access:* The *SWEBOK Guide* provides a topical access to the literature by subdividing it into ten broad knowledge areas. Each knowledge area description provides additional taxonomical breakdown into topics and subtopics, explaining just enough for the reader to find the items of interest. The reader is then directed to the literature for an authoritative treatment of the item. In many cases, the reader is directed to a standard.

- *Characterization of the bounds:* Information selected for treatment in the *Guide* is intended to describe the boundaries of the software engineering discipline—not the limits of what software engineers should know. A practicing software engineer should have knowledge of many other disciplines, but it is not the task of the *SWEBOK Guide* to describe that knowledge. Instead, the *Guide* describes the knowledge that characterizes software engineering and also includes a list of related disciplines from which practicing engineers should draw.

- *Consensually validated:* The test for inclusion of material in the *Guide* is "general acceptance," i.e. "the . . . knowledge applies to most projects most of the time, and widespread consensus validates its value and effectiveness" [PMI00]. Expressed in terms of the US style of education, the *Guide* is oriented toward the knowledge that should be mastered by a graduate with four years of experience. Knowledge that is advanced or in the nature of research was excluded as well as knowledge that is more specialized than general application. Consensual validation was achieved in a direct method, by using three public review cycles that elicited roughly 10,000 comments from more than 500 reviewers in 42 countries.

2. STRUCTURE OF THE KNOWLEDGE-BASED ORGANIZATION

The *Guide* is divided into ten knowledge areas plus a chapter on related disciplines. A brief description of the scope of each chapter is provided below:

- *Software requirements:* the elicitation, analysis, specification, and validation of software requirements—those properties that must be exhibited to solve a real-world problem

- *Software design:* the process and the result of software architectural design—describing the system's top-level structure and organization and identifying its components—and software detailed design—describing each component sufficiently to allow for its construction

- *Software construction:* the detailed creation of working, meaningful software through a combination of coding, validation, unit testing, integration testing, and debugging
- *Software testing:* the dynamic verification of the behavior of a program on a finite set of test cases, suitably selected from the usually infinite executions domain, against the expected behavior
- *Software maintenance:* the totality of activities—both pre- and post-delivery—to provide cost-effective support to the software system throughout its life cycle
- *Software configuration management:* the discipline of identifying and controlling the configuration of a system and its software components to maintain integrity and traceability
- *Software engineering management:* the application of management activities—including measurement—to ensure that the development and maintenance of software is systematic, disciplined, and quantified
- *Software engineering process:* the definition, implementation, measurement, management, change, and improvement of software engineering processes
- *Software engineering tools and methods:* software development tools and environments and methods to develop software
- *Software quality:* software quality considerations—the degree to which a set of inherent characteristics fulfills requirements—that transcend the individual life cycle processes of the software

The related disciplines are listed below. The three that will be treated by this book are briefly described:

- *Computer engineering*
- *Computer science*
- *Management*
- *Mathematics*
- *Project management:* the application of knowledge, skills, tools, and techniques to project activities to meet project requirements.
- *Quality management:* coordinated activities to direct and control an organization with regard to quality
- *Software ergonomics*
- *Systems engineering:* an interdisciplinary approach and means to enable the realization of successful systems.

Taken together, the ten SWEBOK knowledge areas plus three of the related disciplines cover the scope of nearly all of the S2ESC standards. Two standards, though, do not fit neatly into the taxonomy. IEEE Std 610.12, *Glossary of Software Engineering Terminology*, is too general to be fitted into any one knowledge area; IEEE Std 2001, *Recommended Practice for the Internet*, is an application of the standards to a particular application domain. These two standards are described in Chapter 17, prosaically named, "Other IEEE Software Engineering Standards."

Each of the S2ESC standards, along with a handful of standards from other sources, has been assigned to one of the chapters, because it falls within the knowledge area or the related discipline. Each chapter describes the scope of the knowledge area or related discipline and provides a brief overview using material excerpted from the *SWEBOK Guide*. The body of the chapter is a more extended treatment of the material that cites the appropriate standards within appropriate context. Each of the standards assigned to the chapter receives a more detailed treatment at the end of the chapter.

Inevitably, many of the standards are applicable to more than one knowledge area. The standards are mentioned in each relevant knowledge area and a reference directs the reader to the chapter containing the detailed description.

3. SUMMARY

The ten knowledge area of the *SWEBOK Guide* plus three related disciplines—project management, quality management, and systems engineering—span the scope of the S2ESC standards collection. In the following chapters, the S2ESC standards—as well as a handful of standards from other sources—are presented in the context of the knowledge areas and the related disciplines.

Chapter **6**

Knowledge Area: Software Requirements

In developing a sound approach to software engineering, the requirements area is often one of the first ones chosen for improvement. That's because one cannot possibly hope to engineer a satisfactory product without knowing what it is supposed to do. Despite that obvious homily, many software projects still fail due to failure to manage requirements.

This chapter surveys the concepts, processes, and activities related to software requirements as well as the standards supporting them. The chapter is organized according to the subject's treatment in the *Guide to the Software Engineering Body of Knowledge* [SWEBOK04], and much of the text is paraphrased from that source. (The knowledge area editors for the chapter in the *SWEBOK Guide* were Peter Sawyer and Gerald Kotonya.) The relevant IEEE software engineering standards, as well as a few from other sources, are described in the context of the knowledge described by the SWEBOK. At the end of the chapter, the standards allocated to this knowledge area are described in greater detail. Cross-references to other chapters provide access to descriptions of the other applicable standards.

1. KNOWLEDGE AREA SCOPE

The scope of the Software Requirements Knowledge Area is defined by [SWEBOK04] as being

> ... concerned with the elicitation, analysis, specification, and validation of software requirements. ... Software requirements express the needs and constraints placed on a software product that contribute to the solution of some real-world problem.

The Road Map to Software Engineering: A Standards-Based Guide, by James W. Moore
Copyright © 2006 by IEEE Computer Society

2. KNOWLEDGE AREA SUMMARY

The *SWEBOK Guide* divides the Software Requirements Knowledge Area into seven subareas—an organization followed by this chapter. The Introduction of the *SWEBOK Guide* summarizes this knowledge area as follows:

A requirement is defined as a property that must be exhibited in order to solve some real-world problem.

*The first knowledge subarea is **Software Requirements Fundamentals**. It includes definitions of software requirements themselves, but also of the major types of requirements: product vs. process, functional vs. nonfunctional, emergent properties. The subarea also describes the importance of quantifiable requirements and distinguishes between systems and software requirements.*

*The second knowledge subarea is the **Requirements Process**, which introduces the process itself, orienting the remaining five subareas and showing how requirements engineering dovetails with the other software engineering processes. It describes process models, process actors, process support and management, and process quality and improvement.*

*The third subarea is **Requirements Elicitation**, which is concerned with where software requirements come from and how the software engineer can collect them. It includes requirement sources and elicitation techniques.*

*The fourth subarea, **Requirements Analysis**, is concerned with the process of analyzing requirements to*

- *Detect and resolve conflicts between requirements*
- *Discover the bounds of the software and how it must interact with its environment*
- *Elaborate system requirements to software requirements*

Requirements analysis includes requirements classification, conceptual modeling, architectural design and requirements allocation, and requirements negotiation.

*The fifth subarea is **Requirements Specification**. Requirements specification typically refers to the production of a document, or its electronic equivalent, that can be systematically reviewed, evaluated, and approved. For complex systems, particularly those involving substantial non-software components, as many as three different types of documents are produced: system definition, system requirements specification, and software requirements specification. The subarea describes all three documents and the underlying activities.*

*The sixth subarea is **Requirements Validation**, the aim of which is to pick up any problems before resources are committed to addressing the requirements. Requirements validation is concerned with the process of examining the requirements documents to ensure that they are defining the right system (that is, the system that the user expects). It is subdivided into descriptions of the conduct of requirements reviews, prototyping, and model validation and acceptance tests.*

*The seventh and last subarea is **Practical Considerations**. It describes topics which need to be understood in practice. The first topic is the iterative nature of the requirements process. The next three topics are fundamentally about change management and the maintenance of requirements in a state which accurately mirrors the software to be built, or that has already been built. It includes change*

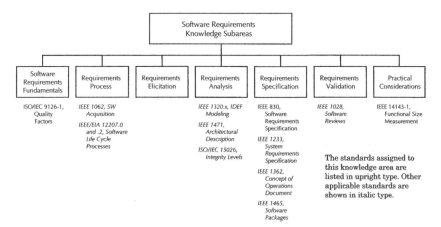

Figure 6. *Software Requirements knowledge area and its standards*

management, requirements attributes, and requirements tracing. The final topic is requirements measurement.

The knowledge area breakdown is illustrated in Figure 6, which also shows the standards relevant to this knowledge area.

3. KNOWLEDGE AREA DESCRIPTION

3.1. Software Requirements Fundamentals

The critical role of requirements in providing well-engineered systems has led to the practice of referring to the area as "requirements engineering" despite the fact that this is not a recognized engineering discipline. The point of the term is to emphasize the need for discipline and rigor in dealing with requirements. In most instances, the need for a software product is expressed as a real-world problem to be solved, a problem that is often independent of any particular technology. Requirements express the needs and constraints placed on a product to solve the real-world problem. Because software is part of a larger system (if only the processor on which it executes) both system requirements and software requirements must be expressed. In fundamental terms, though, the two are managed similarly. In software-intensive systems, the two are often combined.

A primary objective of requirements engineering is to allocate requirements to particular components of a system, including the software components. Strictly speaking, the initial activity of requirements elicitation applies only to the development of system requirements. Because of the pervasive role of software in many systems, though, it is often appropriate for software requirements specialists to be involved in requirements elicitation.

When system and software requirements are expressed distinctly, the software requirements documents establish a key interface between the system and software engineering activities. A specification of a properly allocated set of requirements constitutes an agreement on the role of the software component in the system. From this viewpoint, the software requirements activity is a mediation between the systems and software engineers.

A *requirement* is a property that must be expressed by the completed system in order to contribute to the solution of the problem. Requirements are often categorized as *product* and *process* requirements. Product requirements refer to the completed product and process requirements place constraints on the development of the product—often to achieve desired life cycle characteristics such as maintainability. Product requirements are often classified as *functional* and *nonfunctional*. The functional requirements describe some discrete functionality to be expressed by the completed system. Nonfunctional requirements are often called "ilities" because they typically describe emergent properties of the system, such as compatibility, reliability, and performance. Because of the difficulty of quantifying nonfunctional requirements, customers often specify process requirements on the premise that a good process will lead to a product expressing the desired characteristics.

It is helpful to have a taxonomy of nonfunctional properties of software. There are many different lists of properties, often called "quality factors." One taxonomy can be regarded as authoritative because it has been developed and refined through three versions of international standardization:

Terminology

ISO/IEC 9126–1:2001
Software Engineering—Product Quality—Part 1: Quality Model
This standard provides a model for software product quality covering internal quality, external quality, and quality in use. The model is in the form of a taxonomy of defined characteristics which software may exhibit.
Allocated to: Software Requirements Knowledge Area

System requirements are sometimes called "user requirements" but, in reality, they typically come from a variety of stakeholders including users, customers (the ones who pay the bill), regulators, other developers who may reuse portions of the product in their own product, market analysts, and product planners. In addition, some requirements are implicit in the intended use of the system, e.g., interoperability requirements. It is helpful to maintain a business case for the system that clearly explains its intended benefits and the risks to achieving those benefits. For some systems, formal hazard analysis is a vital method for specifying critical requirements such as safety, security, and privacy. In some cases, these critical requirements may have to be verified via simulation rather than live testing.

A good statement of requirements must be clear, unambiguous, quantified (where possible), complete, consistent, and testable. To facilitate handling large bodies of requirements, each requirement should be uniquely identifiable and prioritized. Often, a requirements baseline is placed under formal configuration management.

Completeness is difficult to attain because it is often economically infeasible to contact all stakeholders. Furthermore, stakeholders typically hold implicit assumptions regarding the system that may never be expressed without careful elicitation. For this reason, the requirements analyst must have the "big picture" of the system and may often use conceptual aids to focus discussion with stakeholders. Examples include graphics, prototypes, simulations, sample outputs, and scenarios.

Rarely is it true that all stakeholders have a consistent view of the desired product. In fact, their desires may often be contradictory. The analysis of requirements may involve restatement of desires to improve consistency or a tradeoff among desired properties. In many cases, desired properties that fall outside the business case must be discarded as too expensive or technically infeasible. Dealing with these issues requires a full understanding of the constraints placed upon the project, including budget, schedule, resources, and regulation.

Verifiability is an important property of the requirements because it contributes to the cost of developing the acceptance tests for the system. Because testing can be costly, requirements must sometimes be specified in a different manner to reduce the cost of testing. Sometimes alternative verification methods may be used in place of testing.

When a complete and coherent set of requirements is attained, they must then be allocated to the components of the system. In complex systems, this allocation involves the description of an architectural design for the system—a design that, at the least, designates the major items comprising the system and their relationships to each other. System requirements are allocated to the items. Typically, the system requirements and the architectural design are formally approved and treated as a baseline for future work.

It is rarely the case that the allocated system requirements are suitable for immediate implementation. In the case of the system's software items, software requirements analysis must be performed to produce a set of software requirements that are *derived* from the system requirements allocated to the software item.

In practice, system requirements are rarely completely understood before implementation commences. Although there are various reasons for the phenomenon, they can generally be summarized by saying that the cost of lost opportunity in delaying is judged to exceed the anticipated cost of rework induced by premature implementation. Some life cycle models provide a formalized iteration or revisiting of the requirements activity. Regardless of whether it is planned or not, it is a fact of life that requirements change during system development. Requirements management therefore spans the entire life cycle.

Good requirements engineering demands that the result of the activity be expressed in some tangible form, typically documents. For complex systems, it is useful to provide a document that describes the system from the user's point of view. In particular, when the new system replaces an existing one, it is necessary to describe how the user can accomplish the same functions (the required ones, at least) on the new system. This document is sometimes called a User Requirements Document or a Concept of Operations Document (often abbreviated as ConOps). It should be written in a form that is readable by users and other stakeholders.

Of course, there must be a reviewed and approved statement of the system requirements. This is usually called a System Requirements Specification. It often forms part of the agreement between acquirer and supplier. Hence, it must be capable of analysis and approval by both sides, even though it is usually written more formally than the ConOps.

For each software item, there should be a recording of the software requirements derived from the system requirements allocated to each software item. Although this is sometimes called a Software Requirements Specification, IEEE/EIA 12207.1 prefers to call it a Software Requirements Description. The term "description" is used in preference to "specification" to express the fact that the requirements are not primary but are instead derived.

The use of natural language is unavoidable in these documents because of its richness and accessibility. Nevertheless, it is wise to restrict natural language to a highly stylized form. For example, all requirements should be expressed using the verb "shall," to distinguish them from merely desirable items marked by the verb "should."

The principal readers of the Software Requirements Description are software engineers; therefore, its form of expression may be more formal and rigorous than any of the others. In some cases, it may be appropriate to supplement the natural language statement of requirements with a more formal notation. A de facto standard for this purpose is the Unified Modeling Language™ (UML), but alternatives exist, including the IEEE standards for IDEF modeling, described later in this chapter.

The requirements documents should be verified, validated, reviewed, approved, baselined, and placed under configuration management. Verification means that the requirements should be checked for the key characteristics described above— clear, unambiguous, quantified (where appropriate), complete, consistent, and testable. Validation means that the requirements should be checked to ensure that they indeed describe the needs for the system. Stakeholders should review the documents and appropriate ones should formally approve them. Baselining means that the acquirer and supplier agree that the documents provide the basis for further development. Configuration management ensures that the inevitable changes to the requirements baseline will be properly authorized.

An important verification activity is requirements tracing. The documentation of the requirements (or a database of requirements) must make clear the source of all derived requirements. Requirements should be traceable from user needs to system requirements and then to software requirements. Ultimately, the requirements should be traceable to design items, to code, to tests and to acceptance tests. Without this sort of traceability, analyzing the impact of requested changes is merely a guessing game.

The inevitability of changes in requirements implies that requirements must be managed throughout the development of the system. The impact of changes must be analyzed. When approved, changes must propagate forward and backward in the chain of documents and engineering artifacts so that the changes are consistently described and implemented. Modern requirements management tools assist in these activities.

3.2. Requirements Process

The key standard describing the activity of requirements engineering is IEEE/EIA 12207.0:

Process

IEEE/EIA 12207.0-1996
Industry Implementation of International Standard ISO/IEC12207:1995,
Standard for Information Technology-Software Life Cycle Processes
This standard provides a framework of processes used across the entire
life cycle of software.
Allocated to: Software Engineering Process Knowledge Area

Processes and activities for requirements engineering are described in these clauses of 12207.0:

- The acquirer's description of the concept or need for a system is described in clause 5.1.1.
- The acquirer's definition and analysis of system requirements is described in clause 5.1.1.
- The acquirer's analysis of software requirements is described in clause 5.1.1.
- The developer's analysis, specification, and evaluation of system requirements is described in clause 5.3.2, directly followed by system architectural design.
- The developer's analysis, specification, and evaluation of software requirements is described in clause 5.3.4, directly followed by software architectural design.
- The verification of requirements is treated in clause 6.4.2.3.
- Validation that the requirements and the product meet the intended use is described in clause 6.5.2.

Note that either the acquirer or the developer can take the responsibility for analysis of requirements. When the acquirer performs the activity, the standard says that the acquirer should execute the same process as the developer.

Acquiring software induces special needs for requirements management because changes in requirements may require contractual modification and induce extra cost. These characteristics are treated in an IEEE recommended practice:

Process

IEEE Std 1062, 1998 Edition (R2002)
IEEE Recommended Practice for Software Acquisition
This document recommends a set of useful practices that can be selected
and applied during software acquisition. It is primarily suited to acquisitions
that include development or modification rather than off-the-shelf purchase.
Allocated to: Software Engineering Management Knowledge Area

The ordering of the activities in the standard may cause one to think that a waterfall life cycle model is required. This is not the case; the standard disclaims any temporal relationships among the activities. They can be easily mapped into any of the other popular life cycle models: spiral, evolutionary delivery, or incremental development. Of course, the spiral model places additional demands on risk management and all of the alternatives place greater demands on configuration management of the requirements.

3.3. Requirements Elicitation

Requirements elicitation is the initial activity of identifying stakeholders and establishing relationships with the development team to begin discovering requirements. Successful elicitation requires attention to various items:

- *Goals:* This refers to the overall goals of the project. Although they are obviously central to the success of the project, they are often vaguely formulated and need to be converted to clear, verifiable requirements. The perception of project success or failure may depend on these expectations!
- *Domain Knowledge:* The users of the system operate in a domain that may be unfamiliar to the requirements engineer. Learning their business and their jargon can help the engineer discover tacit assumptions as well as formulate tradeoffs.
- *System Stakeholders:* Often systems prove unsatisfactory because they have satisfied one group of interested parties at the expense of another. The requirements engineer must find all of the stakeholders and ensure that their viewpoints are represented.
- *Operational Environment:* The system's requirements are deeply affected by the context in which it operates. Interoperability requirements are an obvious example.
- *Organizational Environment:* Any system implements business processes and must fit into a corporate structure, while satisfying various cultural needs. The requirements engineer must be careful to address these "political" factors when determining requirements.

Of course, the requirements engineer must eventually call on the stakeholders to express their perceived needs. This is difficult because some interested parties may be uncooperative or inarticulate. Inevitably, important key assumptions will remain unstated. Requirements elicitation must be an active activity and may be aided by some techniques including interviews, scenarios, prototypes, facilitated meetings, and direct observation.

3.4. Requirements Analysis

Requirements analysis has the goal of determining the bounds of a system and how it interacts with its context; detecting and resolving conflicts among the requirements; and elaborating system requirements to become software requirements. It includes activities of requirements classification, conceptual modeling, architectural design and requirements allocation, and requirements negotiation. Some additional activities are appropriate when the system must exhibit critical properties, like safety or security.

3.4.1. Requirements Classification   Requirements can be classified in a number of ways, including:

- Functional or nonfunctional
- Primary (i.e., directly from a stakeholder), or derived from other requirements. (Some classifications distinguish emergent properties arising from the interaction of the system's components.)
- Product or process
- Priority, e.g., mandatory, highly desirable, desirable, optional
- Scope, i.e., allocation to components
- Volatility or stability. (This can assist in planning for future evolution of the system.)

3.4.2. Conceptual Modeling The purpose of conceptual modeling is to aid in understanding of the problem rather than prototyping a solution. Factors affecting the choice of the modeling method include the nature of the problem, the expertise of the modeler, the customer's process requirements, and the availability of suitable tools.

One popular modeling method is IDEF,[25] described in the two IEEE standards listed below:

Tool

IEEE Std 1320.1–1998 (R2004)
IEEE Standard for Functional Modeling Language—
Syntax and Semantics for IDEF0
This standard defines the IDEF0 modeling language used to represent decisions, actions, and activities of an organization or system. IDEF0 may be used to define requirements in terms of functions to be performed by a desired system.
Allocated to: Software Engineering Tools and Methods Knowledge Area

Tool

IEEE Std 1320.2–1998 (R2004)
IEEE Standard for Conceptual Modeling Language—
Syntax and Semantics for IDEF1X 97 (IDEF object)
This standard defines two conceptual modeling languages, collectively called IDEF1X97 (IDEFObject). The language support the implementation of relational databases, object databases, and object models.
Allocated to: Software Engineering Tools and Methods Knowledge Area

3.4.3. Architectural Design and Requirements Allocation Architectural design is a point of overlap between requirements engineering and system design. The goal is to identify subsystems or components that interact to produce a system with the required characteristics. The allocation of functionality to the components is crucial in bridging the gap between the overall desired behavior and behavior that can be implemented in a practical fashion. Architectural design is related to conceptual modeling but not identical; conceptual model-

---

[25] IDEF is often decoded as "Integrated Definition," but was originally a compound acronym for "ICAM Definition" where ICAM stood for "Integrated Computer Aided Manufacturing."

ing operates in the problem state and architectural design is the first step into the solution space. The correspondence of objects and functions in the two representations may not be direct.

IEEE/EIA 12207.0 places minimal requirements on the design and evaluation of architecture, primarily requiring the allocation of requirements.

	System	**Software**
Design	*From IEEE/EIA 12207.0, Clause 5.3, Development Process:* 5.3.3 System architectural design. This activity consists of the following tasks, which the developer shall perform or support as required by the contract: 5.3.3.1 A top-level architecture of the system shall be established. The architecture shall identify items of hardware, software, and manual operations. It shall be ensured that all the system requirements are allocated among the items. Hardware configuration items, software configuration items, and manual operations shall be subsequently identified from these items. The system architecture and the system requirements allocated to the items shall be documented.	*From IEEE/EIA 12207.0, Clause 5.3, Development Process:* 5.3.5 Software architectural design. For each software item (or software configuration item, if identified), this activity consists of the following tasks: 5.3.5.1 The developer shall transform the requirements for the software item into an architecture that describes its top-level structure and identifies the software components. It shall be ensured that all the requirements for the software item are allocated to its software components and further refined to facilitate detailed design. The architecture of the software item shall be documented. 5.3.5.2 The developer shall develop and document a top-level design for the interfaces external to the software item and between the software components of the software item. 5.3.5.3 The developer shall develop and document a top-level design for the database. 5.3.5.4 The developer should develop and document preliminary versions of user documentation. 5.3.5.5 The developer shall define and document preliminary test requirements and the schedule for Software Integration.

Evaluation	*From IEEE/EIA 12207.0, Clause 5.3, Development Process:* 5.3.3.2 The system architecture and the requirements for the items shall be evaluated considering the criteria listed below. The results of the evaluations shall be documented. a) Traceability to the system requirements; b) Consistency with the system requirements; c) Appropriateness of design standards and methods used; d) Feasibility of the software items fulfilling their allocated requirements; e) Feasibility of operation and maintenance.	*From IEEE/EIA 12207.0, Clause 5.3, Development Process:* 5.3.5.6 The developer shall evaluate the architecture of the software item and the interface and database designs considering the criteria listed below. The results of the evaluations shall be documented. a) Traceability to the requirements of the software item; b) External consistency with the requirements of the software item; c) Internal consistency between the software components; d) Appropriateness of design methods and standards used; e) Feasibility of detailed design; f) Feasibility of operation and maintenance.
Review		*From IEEE/EIA 12207.0, Clause 5.3, Development Process:* 5.3.5.7 The developer shall conduct joint review(s) in accordance with 6.6.

The existence of nonfunctional requirements typically requires an architecture that is far richer than a hierarchical decomposition, because the architecture must be usable to explain how the interaction of the functional components will achieve the desired nonfunctional characteristics. IEEE has a recommended practice for architectural descriptions that provides for multiple viewpoints in describing the architecture of a system:

IEEE Std 1471–2000
IEEE Recommended Practice for
Architectural Description of Software Intensive Systems
This document recommends a conceptual framework and content for the architectural description of software-intensive systems.
Allocated to: Related Disciplines Chapter, Systems Engineering

Document

3.4.4. Requirements Negotiation A more common term might be "conflict resolution." When various requirements conflict or when resources do not permit all requirements to be treated, then choices must be made among them. Consultation is often required to find a suitable tradeoff. In some cases, it may be advisable to maintain a contractual record of such decisions.

3.4.5. Requirements in High-Integrity Systems Some systems have particularly high requirements for reliability, dependability, safety, security, privacy, or other critical properties. In developing these systems, we refer to an "integrity" requirement. Software components of the system will have an integrity requirement negotiated with systems engineers. ISO/IEC 15026, *System and Software Integrity Levels*, is relevant.

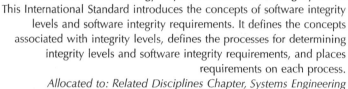

ISO/IEC 15026:1998
Information Technology—System and Software Integrity Levels
This International Standard introduces the concepts of software integrity levels and software integrity requirements. It defines the concepts associated with integrity levels, defines the processes for determining integrity levels and software integrity requirements, and places requirements on each process.
Allocated to: Related Disciplines Chapter, Systems Engineering

Tool

3.5. Requirements Specification

To most engineers, "specification" refers to the assignment of a numerical value to a design goal. Physical devices typically have a small number of such specifications and are often characterized and purchased on the basis of their "spec sheet." Software systems, on the other hand, have a large number of requirements and focus is placed on the problem of maintaining consistency among the requirements and with the user's needs. Therefore, in software jargon, "requirements specification" usually refers to the production of a document or other artifact that can be systematically reviewed, evaluated, and approved. For a complex system, as many as three different types of documents are created—system definition, system requirements, and software requirements. For projects to develop a simple software product, one document may suffice.

3.5.1. The System Definition Document System requirements are sometimes expressed in one document or two. A separate Concept of Operations document is useful in describing the planned system from the users' viewpoint. Separating the two documents may allow the System Requirements Specification to be written in a more formal manner—a manner that might make it inaccessible to end-users. The Concept of Operations document often contrasts the new system with the one that it replaces so that the value of the project is defined. To achieve communication with end-users, the document often includes scenarios illustrating how common tasks will be accomplished with the new system.

IEEE has a suitable guide for the content and format of the Concept of Operations Document.

IEEE Std 1362–1998
IEEE Guide for Information Technology—System Definition—
Concept of Operations (ConOps) Document
This document provides guidance on the format and content of a Concept of Operations (ConOps) document, describing characteristics of a proposed system from the users' viewpoint.
Allocated to: Related Disciplines Chapter, Systems Engineering

Document

3.5.2. System Requirements Specification All software, when executed, is part of a system—even if the remainder of the system consists only of the processor on which the software is executed. A corollary of this fact is that, from a conceptual point of view, software requirements are distinct from system requirements and are derived from the system requirements. IEEE/EIA 12207.1 applies that distinction in stating that the documentation of software requirements is a *description*, because the requirements are all derived from the system requirements *specification*. Of course, this is a legalistic distinction. In many software-intensive systems, it is customary to state system and software requirements in the same document. In any case, documenting the requirements in some form is a fundamental precondition for success.

The System Requirements Specification states the high-level system requirements from the perspective of the problem domain. Because its readership includes customers, planners, and marketing representatives, it is essential for the document to confine itself to the domain viewpoint. It should include the context of the system, environment, constraints, and assumptions. Of course, it must specify the requirements—both functional and nonfunctional. It may include various models.

The requirements statement plays several important roles throughout the development of the system:

- It is the basis for agreement between the acquirer and the developer.
- It forces a rigorous assessment of the requirements prior to commencing implementation.
- It provides a basis for estimating product cost, schedule and risks.
- It is the starting point in developing plans for verification and validation.
- It provides an informed basis for transferring a product to a new host or a new user community.
- It provides a basis for future enhancement of the product.

IEEE/EIA 12207.0 places specific provisions on the system requirements specification:

> *From IEEE/EIA 12207.0, Clause 5.3, Development Process:*
>
> 5.3.2.1 . . . The system requirements specification shall describe: functions and capabilities of the system; business, organizational and user requirements; safety, security, human-factors engineering (ergonomics), interface, operations, and maintenance requirements; design constraints and qualification requirements.

IEEE has a suitable guide for the activity and the result of system requirements specification:

Document

IEEE Std 1233, 1998 Edition (R2002)
IEEE Guide for Developing System Requirements Specifications
This document provides guidance on the development of a System Requirements Specification, covering the identification, organization, presentation, and modification of requirements. It also provides guidance on the characteristics and qualities of requirements.
Allocated to: Related Disciplines Chapter, Systems Engineering

3.5.3. The Software Requirements Specification In complex systems, the statement of system requirements is an inadequate basis for commencing software design. Instead, system requirements must be allocated to software items. The derived software requirements are analyzed and allocated to finer structures to provide a basis for implementation.

IEEE/EIA 12207.0 places specific provisions on the software requirements description of each software item in the system. It uses the term "quality characteristics" to mean "nonfunctional requirements":

From IEEE/EIA 12207.0, Clause 5.3, Development Process:

5.3.4.1 ... The developer shall establish and document software requirements, including the quality characteristics specifications, described below. Guidance for specifying quality characteristics may be found in ISO/IEC 9126.

a) Functional and capability specifications, including performance, physical characteristics, and environmental conditions under which the software item is to perform;

b) Interfaces external to the software item;

c) Qualification requirements;

d) Safety specifications, including those related to methods of operation and maintenance, environmental influences, and personnel injury;

e) Security specifications, including those related to compromise of sensitive information;

f) Human-factors engineering (ergonomics), including those related to manual operations, human-equipment interactions, constraints on personnel, and areas needing concentrated human attention, that are sensitive to human errors and training;

g) Data definition and database requirements;

h) Installation and acceptance requirements of the delivered software product at the operation and maintenance site(s);

i) User documentation;

j) User operation and execution requirements;

k) User maintenance requirements.

IEEE has a well-regarded recommended practice for the content of a Software Requirements Description:

Document

IEEE Std 830–1998
IEEE Recommended Practice for Software Requirements
Specifications
This document recommends the content and characteristics of a
Software Requirements Specification. Sample outlines are provided.
Allocated to: Software Requirements Knowledge Area

Software packages intended for off-the-shelf purchase may have special needs for requirements management. Those needs are treated by an ISO/IEC standard that has been adopted by the IEEE.

Tool

IEEE Std 1465–1998 (R2004)
IEEE Standard: Adoption of International Standard
ISO/IEC 12119:1994(E), Information Technology—
Software Packages—Quality Requirements and Testing
This standard describes quality requirements specifically suitable for software packages and guidance on testing the package against those requirements.
Allocated to: Software Quality Knowledge Area

Evaluation can be performed on the quality of requirements documents. Quality indicators include size, readability, specification depth, text structure, as well as counts of the word "shall," weak phrases, and options. The quality of the requirements document is correlated with project success and product quality.

The evaluation of requirements should be a normal part of requirements engineering. IEEE/EIA 12207.0 says that system and software requirements must be evaluated for the following characteristics:

From IEEE/EIA 12207.0, Clause 5.3, Development Process:	*From IEEE/EIA 12207.0, Clause 5.3, Development Process:*
5.3.2.2 The system requirements shall be evaluated considering the criteria listed below. The results of evaluations shall be documented. a) Traceability to acquisition needs; b) Consistency with acquisition needs; c) Testability; d) Feasibility of system architectural design; e) Feasibility of operation and maintenance.	5.3.4.2 The developer shall evaluate the software requirements considering the criteria listed below. The results of the evaluations shall be documented. a) Traceability to system requirements and system design; b) External consistency with system requirements; c) Internal consistency; d) Testability; e) Feasibility of software design; f) Feasibility of operation and maintenance.

Typically, acquirers demand additional assurance of the soundness of the requirements. Additional verification activities can provide the needed assurance. IEEE/EIA 12207.0 provides a suitable verification activity to address the quality of the specification:

From IEEE/EIA 12207.0, Clause 6.4, Verification Process:

6.4.2.3 Requirements verification. The requirements shall be verified considering the criteria listed below:

   a) The system requirements are consistent, feasible, and testable.
   b) The system requirements have been appropriately allocated to hardware items, software items, and manual operations according to design criteria.
   c) The software requirements are consistent, feasible, testable, and accurately reflect system requirements.
   d) The software requirements related to safety, security, and criticality are correct as shown by suitably rigorous methods.

3.6. Requirements Validation

It is normal for the validation of requirements to be included in project plans. "Validating requirements" means to gain assurance that the requirements documents correctly define the system that the user expects to receive.

   IEEE/EIA 12207.0 treats validation as an activity extending the full duration of the life cycle.

From IEEE/EIA 12207.0, Clause 6.5, Validation Process:

6.5.2 Validation. This activity shall consist of the following tasks:

6.5.2.1 Prepare selected test requirements, test cases, and test specifications for analyzing test results.

6.5.2.2 Ensure that these test requirements, test cases, and test specifications reflect the particular requirements for the specific intended use.

6.5.2.3 Conduct the tests in subclauses 6.5.2.1 and 6.5.2.2, including:

   a) Testing with stress, boundary, and singular inputs;
   b) Testing the software product for its ability to isolate and minimize the effect of errors; that is, graceful degradation upon failure, request for operator assistance upon stress, boundary, and singular conditions;
   c) Testing that representative users can successfully achieve their intended tasks using the software product.

6.5.2.4. Validate that the software product satisfies its intended use.

6.5.2.5 Test the software product as appropriate in selected areas of the target environment.

   As you can see, there is little here to address the early validation of requirements beyond the evaluation tasks built into the development process. Four mechanisms are typically used for validation—reviews, prototyping, model validation, and acceptance tests.

3.6.1. Requirements Reviews In this method, teams of reviewers are assigned to look for errors, mistaken assumptions, lack of clarity, and deviations from standard practices. Often, the review is conducted as a formal meeting where the reviewers follow a systematic protocol to look for the problems. Often, customer representatives are included in the review team. Reviews are typically conducted before any baseline of requirements is approved.

IEEE has a standard suitable for use in conducting requirements reviews:

Process

IEEE Std 1028–1997 (R2002)
IEEE Standard for Software Reviews
This standard defines five types of software reviews and procedures for their execution. Review types include management reviews, technical reviews, inspections, walk-throughs, and audits.
Allocated to: Software Quality Knowledge Area

IEEE/EIA 12207.0 requires a joint review of the specified software requirements and the creation of a baseline (clause 5.3.4.3). It also requires a joint review of the software architectural design (clause 5.3.5.7).

3.6.2. Prototyping Prototyping is used to validate the engineer's interpretation of the system requirements as well as eliciting new ones. The advantage is that dynamic behavior of the planned system can be demonstrated. A disadvantage is that cosmetic issues may distract the user from considering fundamental aspects of the function.

3.6.3. Model Validation If models are used to express requirements, then the models themselves must be validated. Methods depend on the nature of the models but static analysis and formal reasoning are sometimes applicable.

3.6.4. Acceptance Tests Of course, actual acceptance testing is not performed until the system is completed. The planning of the acceptance testing, though, can assist in validating the requirements, notably in assuring that the requirements are testable.

IEEE/EIA 12207.0 requires that both system requirements and software requirements be evaluated for testability (clauses 5.3.2.2 and 5.3.4.2). In addition, preliminary test requirements for software items are developed as a part of the software architectural design (clause 5.3.5.5).

3.7. Practical Considerations

Requirements management spans the entire life cycle of the system. Its fundamental concern is to manage the inevitable changes in software requirements as the system progresses through development and operation. Although it has aspects of configuration management, there are additional needs that must be respected when requirements are first formulated. For example, it is helpful if requirements have been carefully classified and if rationales have been maintained. Most fundamentally, there is a need for unique identification of requirements so that they can be unambiguously cited when necessary.

Another fundamental need is requirements traceability. Unless the requirements can be traced forward and backward, there can be no ability to analyze the impact of proposed changes. Of course, it is necessary to establish formal procedures for agreeing to changes in requirements, particularly when the requirements are part of a baseline agreed to by the customer.

The concept of impact analysis suggests that it is desirable to have a concept of the "size" of a set of requirements. Having a measurement of the size of the requirements is useful in the same way as knowing the square footage of a planned house. It doesn't completely predict the cost of the building but it helps to provide an estimate. Furthermore, the size of the requirements is often a useful denominator for other measurements, e.g., number of problem reports per requirements-size. Traditionally, the size of the requirements base is estimated using "function-point counting." An international standards committee has generalized the concept of function point counting to be "functional size measurement" and has written a standard describing its essential characteristics; their standard was adopted by the IEEE with a few minor changes.

Measure

IEEE Std 14143.1–2000
IEEE Adoption of ISO/IEC 14143–1:1998, Information Technology—
Software Measurement—Functional Size Measurement—
Part 1: Definition of Concepts
This standard describes the fundamental concepts of a class of measures collectively known as functional size.
Allocated to: Software Requirements Knowledge Area

Despite the creation of the generalized standard, most functional size measurement is performed using a de facto standard method maintained by the International Function Point Users Group (IFPUG). However, alternatives exist; the major ones—including IFPUGs—have been adopted as ISO/IEC standards.

4. STANDARDS IN THE SOFTWARE REQUIREMENTS KNOWLEDGE AREA

4.1. IEEE Std 830–1998, IEEE Recommended Practice for Software Requirements Specifications

This S2ESC standard is a Recommended Practice originally approved in 1984 and revised in 1993 and again in 1998 to improve consistency with IEEE/EIA 12207. It is written in the form of guidance, providing many recommendations of good practice but no requirements.

The document is based on the premise that the software requirements specification is intended to be a complete and unambiguous specification of the characteristics required of the completed software product. Three audiences are addressed:

a) Software acquirers, to accurately describe what they wish to obtain;

b) Software suppliers, to understand exactly what the customer wants;

c) Individual practitioners, to accomplish the following goals:

    1) Develop a standard software requirements specification (SRS) outline for their own organizations;

TABLE 5. Outline of software requirements specification suggested by IEEE Std 830

Table of Contents
1. Introduction
    1.1 Purpose
    1.2 Scope
    1.3 Definitions, acronyms, and abbreviations
    1.4 References
    1.5 Overview
2. Overall description
    2.1 Product perspective
    2.2 Product functions
    2.3 User characteristics
    2.4 Constraints
    2.5 Assumptions and dependencies
3. Specific requirements
Appendixes
Index

2) Define the format and content of their specific software requirements specifications;

3) Develop additional local supporting items such as an SRS quality checklist, or an SRS writer's handbook.

Issues to be addressed by the requirements specification include functionality, external interfaces, performance, nonfunctional requirements, and design constraints.

The document recommends that a requirements specification should be correct, unambiguous, complete, consistent, ranked for importance and/or stability, verifiable, modifiable, and traceable.

The recommended practice addresses some special issues related to a requirements specification including joint preparation, evolution, prototyping, embedded design requirements, and embedded project requirements.

It suggests an outline for an SRS (shown in Table 5) and provides substantial additional detail for use in various situations.

The document is not completely reconciled with the provisions of IEEE/EIA 12207.1. An annex suggests minor additions to the provisions that would provide complete compatibility.

4.2. ISO/IEC 9126–1:2001, Software Engineering—Product Quality—Part 1: Quality Model

Many sources provide lists of software "ilities" or quality factors. This standard provides an authoritative source, refined by consensus and three versions of revision and application. IEEE S2ESC has adopted a policy to use these definitions in its own standards. The standard first defines three views of software quality:

- *Internal Quality:* quality that can be measured during development or maintenance of the product.

- *External Quality:* quality that can be measured when the product is executed.
- *Quality in Use:* quality as seen by the user while the product is applied in the intended fashion.

The standard provides two taxonomies of characteristics and subcharacteristics applicable to the three views. The taxonomy of characteristics applicable to the external and internal views is:

- *Functionality:* Suitability, Accuracy, Interoperability, Security, Functionality compliance
- *Reliability:* Maturity, Fault tolerance, Recoverability, Reliability compliance
- *Usability:* Understandability, Learnability, Operability, Attractiveness, Usability compliance
- *Efficiency:* Time behavior, Resource utilization, Efficiency compliance
- *Maintainability:* Analyzability, Changeability, Stability, Testability, Maintainability compliance
- *Portability:* Adaptability, Installability, Co-existence, Replaceability, Portability compliance

(At first glance, the subcharacteristics for "compliance" may be puzzling. They refer to conformance to designated regulations and standards for the characteristic.)

The taxonomy of characteristics relevant to the view of quality in use is:

- Effectiveness
- Productivity
- Safety
- Satisfaction

The standard introduces the concept of evaluating quality from each of several viewpoints: those of the user, the developer, and the manager. Measures related to the characteristics are suggested in other parts of the multi-part standard. Processes for evaluating the quality factors are described in another multi-part standard, ISO/IEC 14598. The responsible committee, ISO/IEC JTC 1/SC 7/WG 6, is planning to repackage the set of related standards as a single series beginning with the number 25000.

4.3. IEEE Std 14143.1–2000, Implementation Note for IEEE Adoption of ISO/IEC 14143-1:1998 Information Technology—Software Measurement—Functional Size Measurement—Part 1: Definition of Concepts

ISO/IEC 14143–1 was developed by ISO/IEC JTC 1/SC 7 to define the concept of "functional size measurements" (FSM) of software. This is typically known as "function point counting." Functional size measurement is intended to measure the size of software in a manner independent of its implementation, by examining the functions required by the user. Most existing methods trace their parentage to a method, known as function point analysis, proposed by Alan Albrecht of IBM [Albrecht81]. Since his paper, various alternatives have been proposed, either—depending on one's point of view—lessening the value of the technique as inconsistencies accumulate or increasing the value as applied to specific problems. An important principle of FSM methods is that they are independent of nonfunctional requirements (including performance requirements). This does not diminish the importance of such requirements in the project planning, estimating, and measurement processes. However, the *functional size* itself is independent of such requirements. The nonfunctional requirements are typically introduced later as adjustments applied during the analysis of the results and the use of the results for estimation.

The ISO/IEC standard defines the fundamental concepts of FSM and the principles of applying FSM with the intention of promoting consistent interpretations. It does not endorse any specific method for measurement. An important de facto standard for function point counting is maintained by the International Function Point Users' Group (IFPUG).[26]

IEEE adopted the standard in 2000 with minor modifications intended to improve compatibility of terminology with the other IEEE software engineering standards.

5. SUMMARY

This chapter has provided an overview of the Software Requirements knowledge area of the IEEE Computer Society's *Guide to the Software Engineering Body of Knowledge*. Several IEEE and ISO/IEC standards have been offered as relevant to the knowledge area.

The presentation has been divided into seven subsections:

- *Fundamentals*: ISO/IEC 9126–1 is a useful taxonomy for nonfunctional requirements.
- *Requirements Process*: IEEE/EIA 12207.0 provides useful provisions for the Software Requirements Engineering process, particularly when supplemented with the process provisions of IEEE Std 1233 and 830 on system and software requirements specification, respectively. IEEE Std 1062 includes provisions relevant to requirements engineering when one is acquiring software.
- *Requirements Elicitation*: No standards specific to this subject are listed.
- *Requirements Analysis*: IEEE Std 1471 places requirements on architectural description. IEEE standards 1320.1 and 1320.2 describe two forms of the IDEF conceptual modeling language. ISO/IEC 15026 deals with the concept of integrity levels applied to systems with critical properties, such as safety.

---

[26] Three important functional size measurement methods have been adopted as ISO/IEC standards: ISO/IEC 19761, *COSMIC*; ISO/IEC 20926, *IFPUG 4.1 (Unadjusted)*; and ISO/IEC 20968, *Mk II*. ISO/IEC 20926 is identical to the popular IFPUG method except that it excludes the post-counting adjustment factors.

- *Requirements Specification*: IEEE standards 1362, 1233, and 830 provide suggested formats for the Concept of Operations document, the System Requirements Specification, and the Software Requirements Specification. The standards also include provisions on conducting the requirements specification activity. IEEE Std 1465 deals with requirements engineering when one is developing "off-the-shelf" software packages.
- *Requirements Validation*: IEEE Std 1028 may be helpful in the conduct of validation reviews.
- *Requirements Management*: IEEE Std 14143–1 provides the concept of a "functional size" of a body of requirements.

Chapter *7*

Knowledge Area: Software Design

Treatment of "design" may be an important issue in the acceptance of the software discipline as an engineering profession. Vincenti [Vincenti90] says that engineering describes the practices of organizing the design, construction, and operation of any artifice that transforms the physical world around us to meet some recognized need. Of the three, he states that design is basic because it conditions the knowledge required for the creation of the artifice. He differentiates *normal design*—the application of known solutions in new or more stringent conditions—from *radical design* where new solutions must be created. Finally, he states that the bulk of day-to-day engineering is involved with normal design. Except in some niches, this is not true for software engineering today; the technologies for saving, recalling, and reapplying known designs are relatively new. In much of the field, it remains the norm to reinvent a design.

This chapter surveys the concepts, processes, and activities related to software design as well as the standards supporting them. The chapter is organized according to the subject's treatment in the *Guide to the Software Engineering Body of Knowledge* [SWEBOK04], and much of the text is paraphrased from that source. (The knowledge area editor for the chapter in the *SWEBOK Guide* was Guy Tremblay.) The relevant IEEE software engineering standards, as well as a few from other sources, are mentioned in the context of the knowledge described by the SWEBOK. At the end of the chapter, the standards allocated to this knowledge area are described in greater detail. Cross-references to other chapters provide access to descriptions of the other relevant standards.

1. KNOWLEDGE AREA SCOPE

The scope of the Software Design Knowledge Area is explained by [SWEBOK04]:

The Road Map to Software Engineering: A Standards-Based Guide, by James W. Moore
Copyright © 2006 by IEEE Computer Society

Design is defined . . . as both "the process of defining the architecture, components, interfaces, and other characteristics of a system or component" and "the result of [that] process." Viewed as a process, software design is the software engineering life cycle activity in which software requirements are analyzed in order to produce a description of the software's internal structure that will serve as the basis for its construction. More precisely, a software design (the result) must describe the software architecture—that is, how software is decomposed and organized into components—and the interfaces between those components. It must also describe the components at a level of detail that enable their construction.

In a standard listing of software life cycle processes such as IEEE/EIA 12207 Software Life Cycle Processes . . . , software design consists of two activities that fit between software requirements analysis and software construction:

- *Software architectural design (sometimes called top-level design): describing software's top-level structure and organization and identifying the various components*
- *Software detailed design: describing each component sufficiently to allow for its construction.*

. . . the current KA description does not discuss every topic the name of which contains the word "design." In Tom DeMarco's terminology . . . , the KA discussed in this chapter deals mainly with D-design (decomposition design, mapping software into component pieces). However, because of its importance in the growing field of software architecture, we will also address FP-design (family pattern design, whose goal is to establish exploitable commonalities in a family of software). By contrast, the Software Design KA does not address I-design (invention design, usually performed during the software requirements process with the objective of conceptualizing and specifying software to satisfy discovered needs and requirements), since this topic should be considered part of requirements analysis and specification.

2. KNOWLEDGE AREA SUMMARY

The *SWEBOK Guide* divides the Software Design Knowledge Area into six subareas—an organization followed by this chapter. The Introduction of the *SWEBOK Guide* summarizes this knowledge area as follows:

According to the IEEE definition [IEEE 610.12-90], design is both "the process of defining the architecture, components, interfaces, and other characteristics of a system or component" and "the result of [that] process." The KA is divided into six subareas.

*The first subarea presents **Software Design Fundamentals**, which form an underlying basis to the understanding of the role and scope of software design. These are general software concepts, the context of software design, the software design process, and the enabling techniques for software design.*

*The second subarea groups together the **Key Issues in Software Design**. They include concurrency, control and handling of events, distribution of components, error and exception handling and fault tolerance, interaction and presentation, and data persistence.*

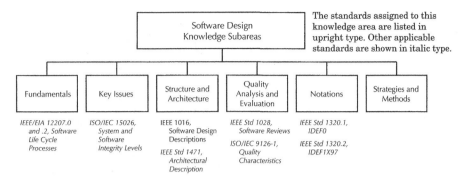

Figure 7. *Software Design knowledge area and its standards*

*The third subarea is **Software Structure and Architecture**, the topics of which are architectural structures and viewpoints, architectural styles, design patterns, and, finally, families of programs and frameworks.*

*The fourth subarea describes **Software Design Quality Analysis and Evaluation**. While there is an entire KA devoted to software quality, this subarea presents the topics specifically related to software design. These aspects are quality attributes, quality analysis, and evaluation techniques and measures.*

*The fifth subarea is **Software Design Notations**, which are divided into structural and behavioral descriptions.*

*The last subarea describes **Software Design Strategies and Methods**. First, general strategies are described, followed by function-oriented design methods, object-oriented design methods, data-structure-centered design, component-based design, and others.*

The knowledge area breakdown is illustrated in Figure 7, which also shows the standards relevant to this knowledge area.

3. KNOWLEDGE AREA DESCRIPTION

3.1. Software Design Fundamentals

3.1.1. General Design Concepts Software is not the only field that involves design; design is a form of general problem solving that is applied in all engineering fields for the creation of artifacts to solve problems. [Budgen94] suggests that software design is an example of a wicked problem—problems that do not have immediately testable solutions and that lead to an indefinitely long series of additional problems that may be more complex. In navigating such a maze, it is important to formulate goals and constraints, represent key features of the problem, consider alternatives, and evaluate potential solutions.

3.1.2. Context of Software Design Although design is a key activity in the development of a software solution, it is necessary to understand how design relates to other important activities. The standards referenced in the next section are helpful in this regard.

3.1.3. Software Design Process   Software design is often treated as a two-step activity: architectural design provides a decomposition into software components; and detailed design describes the behavior of the components. Both of the design activities and the processes forming the context of software design are described in the following standard:

Process

IEEE/EIA 12207.0-1996
Industry Implementation of International Standard
ISO/IEC 12207:1995, Standard for Information Technology–
Software Life Cycle Processes
This standard provides a framework of processes used across the entire
life cycle of software.
Allocated to: Software Engineering Process Knowledge Area

Processes and activities for design are described in these clauses of 12207.0:

- System architectural design is described in clause 5.3.3, directly followed by software requirements analysis.
- Software architectural design is described in clause 5.3.5.
- Software detailed design is described in clause 5.3.6, directly followed by software coding and testing.
- Verification of design is treated in clause 6.4.2.4.

The ordering of the activities in the standard may cause one to think that a waterfall life cycle model is required. This is not the case; the standard disclaims any temporal relationships among the activities. They can be easily mapped into any of the other popular life cycle models: spiral, evolutionary delivery, or incremental development.

3.1.4. Enabling Techniques   It is possible to identify certain principles that underlay nearly all of the software design methodologies. These enabling techniques include:

- *Abstraction:* selective suppression of detail so that things that are different in detail can be treated as if they are alike for some purposes.
- *Coupling and cohesion:* the strength of relationships within modules (cohesion) versus the strength of relationships among modules (coupling).
- *Decomposition and modularization:* solving a design problem by subdividing the system or software into parts that satisfy selected criteria.
- *Encapsulation and information hiding:* packaging the parts of the software so that selected details are inaccessible to other parts.
- *Separation of interface and implementation:* specifying an interface for usage of the software part that is relatively independent of the manner in which the part is implemented.
- *Sufficiency, completeness, and primitiveness:* typically applied criteria for successful specification of an abstraction.

3.2. Key Issues of Software Design

Aside from the application functionality of a software system, there are a number of key issues that cross-cut the system and affect its success in systemic ways.

- *Concurrency:* in systems with multiple threads of execution, how to schedule and synchronize the execution for efficiency and correctness.
- *Control and Handling of Events:* how to organize the software system to properly react to temporal and external events.
- *Distribution of Components:* in systems that span multiple processors, how to decompose the system into software parts that can communicate effectively.
- *Error and Exception Handling:* how to cope with hardware and software faults and exceptional conditions.
- *Interaction and Presentation:* how to organize the system to effectively and efficiently react to its users. (This issue is distinct from the design of the user interface.)
- *Data Persistence:* how to handle long-lived data.

An important issue in some designs is the contribution of software components to the dependability of a high-integrity system, particularly concurrent systems where errors or exceptions may propagate among related components. An international standard introduces the concept of an integrity level and explains how system designers and software designers interact in the design of high-integrity systems:

Tool

ISO/IEC 15026:1998
Information Technology—System and Software Integrity Levels
This International Standard introduces the concepts of software integrity levels and software integrity requirements. It defines the concepts associated with integrity levels, defines the processes for determining integrity levels and software integrity requirements, and places requirements on each process.
Allocated to: Related Disciplines Chapter, Systems Engineering

3.3. Software Structure and Architecture

ISO/IEC 12207 and many other sources treat architecture as the decomposition of the system or software into constituent parts and the allocation of functional requirements to those parts. During the 1990s, there was growing interest in architecture as the approach to capturing design information that could be reused in multiple contexts. So far, there is little agreement on the details of the various approaches but some principles are emerging from the continuing discussion.

3.3.1. Architectural Structures and Viewpoints Many authors agree that no single representation of a design is appropriate to deal with all of the issues that affect design. Therefore, there is growing agreement that architectures should be described with multiple views, each illuminating an aspect of the design showing specific properties. Common examples include the logical view (showing function), the process view (showing concurrency), the physical view (showing distribution), and the development view (showing decomposition). Of course, other views have been suggested. The key idea is that a software design is a multi-faceted artifact produced by the design process and generally composed of relatively independent and orthogonal views.

Architectural design, including the role of IEEE Std 1471 in multi-view architectural description, was discussed in Chapter 6, Knowledge Area: Software Requirements.

Document

IEEE Std 1471-2000
IEEE Recommended Practice for
Architectural Description of Software Intensive Systems
This document recommends a conceptual framework and content for the
architectural description of software-intensive systems.
Allocated to: Related Disciplines Chapter, Systems Engineering

In the 12207 standard, the software architectural design results in the identification of software components and their allocated software requirements. The identified components are now the subject of detailed design:

From IEEE/EIA 12207.0, Clause 5.3, Development Process:

5.3.6 Software detailed design. For each software item (or software configuration item, if identified), this activity consists of the following tasks:

5.3.6.1 The developer shall develop a detailed design for each software component of the software item. The software components shall be refined into lower levels containing software units that can be coded, compiled, and tested. It shall be ensured that all the software requirements are allocated from the software components to software units. The detailed design shall be documented.

5.3.6.2 The developer shall develop and document a detailed design for the interfaces external to the software item, between the software components, and between the software units. The detailed design of the interfaces shall permit coding without the need for further information.

5.3.6.3 The developer shall develop and document a detailed design for the database.

5.3.6.4 The developer shall update user documentation as necessary.

5.3.6.5 The developer shall define and document test requirements and schedule for testing software units. The test requirements should include stressing the software unit at the limits of its requirements.

5.3.6.6 The developer shall update the test requirements and the schedule for Software Integration.

The output of the design activity is a description of the software design. IEEE has a Recommended Practice for this description.

Document

IEEE Std 1016-1998
IEEE Recommended Practice for Software Design Descriptions
This document recommends content and organization of a Software
Design Description.
Allocated to: Software Design Knowledge Area

3.3.2. Architectural Styles An architectural style, sometimes called a macro-architectural pattern, is a set of constraints that identify a family of architectures. A number of styles have been identified by various authors. Some of the better known ones include pipe and filter, layered, client-server, model-view-controller, and blackboard.

3.3.3. Design Patterns Design patterns are a method of describing common solutions to a problem within a given context. (They may represent an important mechanism for moving software development from radical design to normal design, in Vincenti's parlance.) Architectural styles may be seen as describing high-level organization of systems while design patterns treat more local problems. Oddly enough, there aren't any **standards** describing design patterns, although the so-called Gang of Four book [Gamma95] probably counts as a de facto standard.

3.3.4. Families of Programs and Frameworks One approach to large scale reuse is to develop families of programs, called *software product lines*, that capture common functionality and are customized to particular applications. In object-oriented programming, this notion is realized as a *framework*, a partially completed subsystem that is extended and specialized through instantiation of plug-ins.

3.4. Software Design Quality Analysis and Evaluation

Evaluation of the "quality" of a software design is generally intended to mean evaluation of the expected quality of the system that will result from the implementation of the design. Therefore, design quality analysis and evaluation is inherently indirect and predictive in nature.

3.4.1. Quality Attributes Consideration of a number of attributes of quality, sometimes called "ilities," is important in obtaining a good design. One useful distinction is to separate qualities observable at run-time (e.g., performance, reliability, usability), from those not observable in execution (e.g., portability, reusability, testability), and those intrinsic to the architecture or design (e.g., traceability, consistency, completeness). The design process should interact with the requirements process to ensure that the requirements related to these quality factors are verifiable in an appropriate manner. Many different lists of quality factors have been proposed. One notable source for a taxonomy of attributes is an international standard:

Terminology

ISO/IEC 9126-1:2001
Software Engineering—Product Quality—Part 1: Quality Model
This standard provides a model for software product quality covering internal quality, external quality, and quality in use. The model is in the form of a taxonomy of defined characteristics which software may exhibit.
Allocated to: Software Requirements Knowledge Area

3.4.2. Quality Analysis and Evaluation Tools There are three categories of approaches for software quality analysis and verification: static analysis, simulating and prototyping, and software design reviews. The 12207 standard provides for integral evaluation by the developer of the results of the software detailed design:

From IEEE/EIA 12207.0, Clause 5.3, Development Process:

5.3.6.7 The developer shall evaluate the software detailed design and test requirements considering the criteria listed below. The results of the evaluations shall be documented.

  a) Traceability to the requirements of the software item;
  b) External consistency with architectural design;
  c) Internal consistency between software components and software units;
  d) Appropriateness of design methods and standards used;
  e) Feasibility of testing;
  f) Feasibility of operation and maintenance.

5.3.6.8 The developer shall conduct joint review(s) in accordance with 6.6.

As you can see, the result of the design activity is approved in a review. IEEE provides a standard for the conduct of reviews:

Process

IEEE Std 1028-1997 (R2002)
IEEE Standard for Software Reviews
This standard defines five types of software reviews and procedures for their execution. Review types include management reviews, technical reviews, inspections, walk-throughs, and audits.
Allocated to: Software Quality Knowledge Area

In some situations, there may be a need for additional assurance that the detailed design is sound. IEEE/EIA 12207.0 provides a suitable verification activity to address the soundness of the design:

From IEEE/EIA 12207.0, Clause 6.4, Verification Process:

6.4.2.4 Design verification. The design shall be verified considering the criteria listed below:

  a) The design is correct and consistent with and traceable to requirements.
  b) The design implements proper sequence of events, inputs, outputs, interfaces, logic flow, allocation of timing and sizing budgets, and error definition, isolation, and recovery.
  c) Selected design can be derived from requirements.
  d) The design implements safety, security, and other critical requirements correctly as shown by suitably rigorous methods.

3.4.3. Measures Measures can be used to estimate aspects of the size, structure, or quality of a software design. Many of them depend on the approach used for producing the design, so they are often classified as being suitable for function-oriented design (e.g., based on structure charts) or object-oriented design (e.g., based on class diagrams).

3.5. Software Design Notations

There are a large number of notations and special-purpose languages that are useful in describing software designs. They can be classified in various ways including structure versus behavior, or architectural design versus detailed design. Some apply only in the context of certain design methods. The two lists below are categorized by structure versus behavior, or equivalently, static versus dynamic:

Structural (static) view:

- Architecture Description Languages (ADL): textual, often formal, languages used to describe an architecture in terms of components and connectors
- Class and object diagrams: diagrams used to show a set of classes (and objects) and their relationships
- Component diagrams: used to show a set of components and their relationships
- CRC Cards: used to denote the name of components (class), their responsibilities and the names of their collaborating components
- Deployment diagrams: used to show a set of (physical) nodes and their relationships and, thus, to model the physical aspects of a system
- Entity-Relationship Diagrams (ERD): used to define conceptual models of data stored in information systems
- Interface Description Languages (IDL): programming-like languages used to define the interface (name and types of exported operations) of software components
- Jackson structure diagrams: used to describe the structure of data in terms of sequence, selection and iteration
- Structure charts: used to describe the calling structure of programs

Behavioral (dynamic) view:

- Activity diagrams: used to show the flow of control from activity to activity
- Collaboration diagrams: used to show the interactions that occur among a group of objects, where the emphasis is on the objects, their links, and the messages they exchange on these links
- Data flow diagrams: used to show the flow of data among a set of processes
- Decision tables and diagrams: used to represent complex combination of conditions and actions

- Flowcharts and structured flowcharts: used to represent the flow of control and the associated actions to be performed
- Formal specification languages: textual languages that use basic notions from mathematics (e.g., logic, set, sequence) to rigorously and abstractly define the interface and behavior of software components, often in terms of pre/post-conditions
- Pseudo-code and Program Design Languages (PDL): structured, programming-like languages used to describe, generally at the detailed design stage, the behavior of a procedure or method
- Sequence diagrams: used to show the interactions among a group of objects, with the emphasis on the time-ordering of messages
- State transition and state-chart diagrams: used to show the flow of control from state to state in a state machine

Two design notations are described by IEEE standards:

Tool

IEEE Std 1320.1-1998 (R2004)
IEEE Standard for
Functional Modeling Language—Syntax and Semantics for IDEF0
This standard defines the IDEF0 modeling language used to represent decisions, actions, and activities of an organization or system. IDEF0 may be used to define requirements in terms of functions to be performed by a desired system.
Allocated to: Software Engineering Tools and Methods Knowledge Area

Tool

IEEE Std 1320.2-1998 (R2004)
IEEE Standard for Conceptual Modeling Language—
Syntax and Semantics for IDEF1X 97 (IDEF object)
This standard defines two conceptual modeling languages, collectively called IDEF1X97 (IDEFObject). The language support the implementation of relational databases, object databases, and object models.
Allocated to: Software Engineering Tools and Methods Knowledge Area

IDEF0 is an example of the "activity diagram" form of behavioral notation. IDEF1X97 is a hybrid of various forms of structural notation, perhaps primarily "class and object diagram." Of course, the most common design notation is a de facto standard—Unified Modeling Language (UML™).[27] It is also a hybrid of various forms of notation listed previously.

3.6. Software Design Strategies and Methods

Designers apply both *strategies* and *methods* in producing designs. The Design Knowledge Area of the *SWEBOK Guide* differentiates the two: strategies provide an overall approach; and methods generally provide specific notations,

---

[27] A form of UML is about to be standardized as ISO/IEC 19501-1, *Information technology—Unified Modeling Language (UML)—Part 1: Specification*. However, the standardized language may lack recent revisions described in textbooks.

procedures, and heuristics. Of course, both are useful as a means of capturing and transferring knowledge as well as providing uniformity in team design efforts.

General strategies include divide-and-conquer and stepwise refinement, top-down or bottom-up, data abstraction and information hiding, design heuristics, patterns, and iterative and incremental approaches.

Function-oriented (structured design) rests upon the successive decomposition of functions into smaller subfunctions and their assignment to hierarchically organized components.

Object-oriented design has evolved from the early object-based approaches where nouns in functional descriptions were equated with objects and verbs were equated with methods. Modern approaches depend heavily on the use of inheritance and polymorphism.

Data-structured design is generally practiced as a specific method, for example Jackson Structured Design or Warnier-Orr. In general, the control structure of the program is derived from an examination of the input and output data structures.

Of course, there are other approaches including some based on applying formal or highly rigorous methods.

4. STANDARDS IN THE SOFTWARE DESIGN KNOWLEDGE AREA

4.1. IEEE Std 1016-1998, IEEE Recommended Practice for Software Design Descriptions

The 1998 version of this Recommended Practice is a complete rewrite of a document first approved in 1987. The 16-page document is intended to specify content and organization of Software Design Descriptions (SDD). It is not limited by the size or complexity of the software or system but is intended for application only to systems designed via functional decomposition—a shortcoming that may be remedied by a current revision effort. Because it is a Recommend Practice rather than a Standard, it generally provides advice regarding good practices rather than verifiable requirements. The primary audience for its recommendations is software designers. However, those in closely related parts of the software life cycle—requirements analysts, implementers, and testers—must also be able to use the SDD, not to mention quality assurance and configuration management personnel.

IEEE Std 1016 defines the SDD as "a representation of a software system that is used as a medium for communicating software design information." The SDD represents the software system as decomposed into a number of *design entities*—elements that are structurally and functionally distinct from other elements and that are separately named and referenced. Each entity is described by a number of named characteristics or properties called *attributes*. The standard recommends a minimum set of ten attributes:

- Identification, the unique name of the design entity
- Type, for example, subprogram, module, procedure, data store
- Purpose of the entity including functional and performance requirements

TABLE 6. Four design views from IEEE Std 1016

Design view	Scope	Entity attributes	Example representations
Decomposition description	Partition of the system into design entities	Identification, type, purpose, function, subordinates	Hierarchical decomposition diagram, natural language
Dependency description	Description of the relationships among entities and system resources	Identification, type, purpose, dependencies, resources	Structure charts, data flow diagrams, transaction diagrams
Interface description	List of everything a designer, programmer or tester needs to know to use the design entities that make up the system	Identification, function, interfaces	Interface files, parameter tables
Detail description	Description of the internal design details of an entity	Identification, processing, data	Flowcharts, N-S charts, PDL

- Function, notably the relationship between inputs and outputs or the type of information that is stored
- Subordinates, used to trace decomposed requirements and identify structural relationships
- Dependencies, including timing conditions, ordering requirements, data sharing, etc.
- Interface, the rules or methods for interacting with other entities
- Resources used by the entity including storage, time, shared data, and external devices
- Processing, notably algorithms to be used by the entity and contingencies for unusual conditions
- Data internal to the entity including representation, semantics, formats, ranges, and validation criteria

A table in the standard (reproduced verbatim as Table 6) recommends four design views for organizing the presentation of the design entities and their attributes:

IEEE Std 1016 provides an example table of contents but levies no requirement on the format of the description. An annex lists additional material that should be included with the SDD for conformance to the data recommendations of ISO/IEC 12207.1.

5. SUMMARY

This chapter has provided an overview of the Software Design knowledge area of the IEEE Computer Society's *Guide to the Software Engineering Body of*

Knowledge. Nine IEEE and ISO/IEC standards have been offered as relevant to the knowledge area.

The presentation has been divided into six subsections corresponding to the knowledge break-down provided in the *SWEBOK Guide*.

- *Fundamentals*: IEEE/EIA 12207.0 provides useful provisions for the Software Design process.

- *Key Issues*: Cross-cutting design issues were briefly described. ISO/IEC 15026 is useful for dealing with high-integrity systems.

- *Structure and Architecture*: IEEE Std 1471 places requirements on architectural description. IEEE Std 1016 describes the desired output of the detailed design activity.

- *Quality Analysis and Evaluation*: ISO/IEC 9126-1 provides a taxonomy of quality characteristics. IEEE Std 1028 describes reviews useful for design evaluation.

- *Notations*: IEEE standards 1320.1 and 1320.2 describe two forms of the IDEF conceptual modeling language.

- *Strategies and Methods*: A brief overview of alternative approaches is provided.

Chapter **8**

Knowledge Area: Software Construction

Although many of the SWEBOK knowledge areas serve to distinguish the discipline of software engineering from the craft of computer programming, the construction knowledge area marks the connection between the two.

"Software construction is a fundamental act of software engineering: the construction of working, meaningful software through a combination of coding, validation, and testing (unit testing) by a programmer. Far from being a simple mechanistic 'translation' of good design into working software, software construction burrows deeply into difficult issues of software engineering. It requires the establishment of a meaningful dialog between a person and a computer—a 'communication of intent' that must reach from the slow and fallible human to a fast and unforgivingly literal computer. Such a dialog requires that the computer perform activities for which it is poorly suited, such as understanding implicit meanings and recognizing the presence of nonsensical or incomplete statements. On the human side, software construction requires that developers be logical, precise, and thorough so that their intentions can be accurately captured and understood by the computer. The relationship works only because each side possesses certain capabilities that the other lacks. In the symbiosis that is software construction, the computer provides astonishing reliability, retention, and (once the need has been explained) speed of performance. Meanwhile, the human being provides creativity and insight into how to solve new, difficult problems, plus the ability to express those solutions with sufficient precision to be meaningful to the computer" [Bollinger01].

This chapter surveys the concepts, processes, and activities related to software construction as well as the standards supporting them. The chapter is organized according to the subject's treatment in the *Guide to the Software*

Engineering Body of Knowledge [SWEBOK04], and much of the text is paraphrased from that source. (The knowledge area editor for the chapter in the *SWEBOK Guide* was Steve McConnell.[28]) The relevant IEEE software engineering standards, as well as a few from other sources, are mentioned in the context of the knowledge described by the SWEBOK. At the end of the chapter, the standard allocated to this knowledge area is described in greater detail. Cross-references to other chapters provide access to descriptions of the other relevant standards.

1. KNOWLEDGE AREA SCOPE

The scope of the Software Construction Knowledge Area is explained by [SWEBOK04]:

> *The term software construction refers to the detailed creation of working, meaningful software through a combination of coding, verification, unit testing, integration testing, and debugging.*

> *The Software Construction Knowledge Area is linked to all the other KAs, most strongly to Software Design and Software Testing. This is because the software construction process itself involves significant software design and test activity. It also uses the output of design and provides one of the inputs to testing, both design and testing being the activities, not the KAs in this case. Detailed boundaries between design, construction, and testing (if any) will vary depending upon the software life cycle processes that are used in a project. . . .*

> *Among the Related Disciplines of Software Engineering, the Software Construction KA is most akin to computer science in its use of knowledge of algorithms and of detailed coding practices, both of which are often considered to belong to the computer science domain. . . .*

2. KNOWLEDGE AREA SUMMARY

The *SWEBOK Guide* divides the Software Construction Knowledge Area into three subareas—an organization followed by this chapter. The Introduction of the *SWEBOK Guide* summarizes this knowledge area as follows:

> *Software construction refers to the detailed creation of working, meaningful software through a combination of coding, verification, unit testing, integration testing, and debugging. The KA includes three subareas.*

> *The first subarea is **Software Construction Fundamentals**. The first three topics are basic principles of construction: minimizing complexity, anticipating change, and constructing for verification. The last topic discusses standards for construction.*

> *The second subarea describes **Managing Construction**. The topics are construction models, construction planning, and construction measurement.*

---

[28] Earlier versions of this SWEBOK chapter were edited by Terry Bollinger, Philippe Gabrini, and Louis Martin.

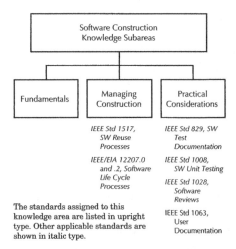

Figure 8. *Software Construction knowledge area and its standards*

*The third subarea covers **Practical Considerations**. The topics are construction design, construction languages, coding, construction testing, reuse, construction quality, and integration.*

The knowledge area breakdown is illustrated in Figure 8, which also shows the standards relevant to this knowledge area.

3. KNOWLEDGE AREA DESCRIPTION

3.1. Basic Concepts of Construction

There are four basic principles of software construction:

- Minimizing Complexity
- Anticipating Change
- Constructing for Validation
- Applying Standards

Minimizing complexity is related to the limited human ability to retain complex information in working memory. This limitation affects the ability to solve complex problems, such as debugging software. The principle suggests that code should be simple and readable.

The principle of *anticipating change* is appropriate because most useful software systems change over time—even before their initial construction is complete. In many cases, some dimensions of change can be predicted and code can be constructed in anticipation of those changes. Even if the direction of change is completely unknown, there are general-purpose techniques that ease the problems in changing code.

Constructing for validation suggests that code should be constructed in a manner that facilitates the finding of errors, whether by testing or by other validation techniques.

The use of these principles is assisted by the selection of appropriate standards, including standards for programming languages and external application program interfaces (APIs). A large project will find it easier to achieve these principles if all programmers follow a uniform style. In this case, the applicable standards do not necessarily describe a "best practice" but instead require all programmers to make a consistent selection from a possibly arbitrary set of choices. Such standards are typically developed by the applying organization rather than by an external standards body.

3.2. Managing Construction

3.2.1. Construction Methods Many different approaches to software development are suggested by the literature. Some, such as extreme programming and the other "agile methods," provide a central role for the construction activity, often intermingling design, coding, testing, and even requirements specification. More traditional construction approaches distinguish coding from other activities and enforce some sort of controlled "handoff" among the activities. In such cases, construction consists primarily of coding and unit testing.

For most approaches, particularly the more traditional ones, the following standard provides suitable processes:

Process

IEEE/EIA 12207.0-1996
Industry Implementation of International Standard ISO/IEC
12207:1995, Standard for Information Technology–
Software Life Cycle Processes
This standard provides a framework of processes used across the entire life cycle of software.
Allocated to: Software Engineering Process Knowledge Area

Processes and activities for construction are described in these clauses of 12207.0:

- Following the design activities, software coding and testing is described in clause 5.3.7.
- Software integration is described in clause 5.3.8.
- Software qualification testing is described in clause 5.3.9 and is followed by system integration.
- Verification of code is treated in clause 6.4.2.5.

The ordering of the activities in the standard may cause one to think that a waterfall life cycle model is required. This is not the case; the standard disclaims any temporal relationships among the activities. They can be easily mapped into any of the other popular life cycle models: spiral, evolutionary delivery, or incremental development.

The requirements of the IEEE/EIA 12207 are straightforward. In the software coding and testing activity, the developer must develop and document each software unit and database provided by the design, as well as the procedures and data for testing them. The standard provides for requirements-based testing of the units and databases, and is silent on other forms of testing. It requires that the result of testing be documented. In addition, the developer must update user documentation and the test requirements and schedule for software integration. The results are evaluated for traceability to requirements and design, consistency of requirements and design, test coverage, appropriateness of coding methods and standards, and feasibility of proceeding.

The software integration activity is based on an integration plan that describes test requirements, procedures, data, responsibilities and schedule for integrating the software units and components to produce a software item. The resulting unit is tested to ensure that it meets the requirements allocated to the unit. User documentation is updated and the developer prepares for qualification testing. The results of software integration are evaluated for traceability to requirements and design, consistency of requirements, test coverage, appropriateness of test methods and standards, conformance to expected results, and feasibility of proceeding. The results of software integration are formally reviewed.

Software qualification testing is based on qualification test cases and procedures developed by the software integration activity. User documentation is updated again. The results are evaluated for test coverage, conformance to expected results, and feasibility of proceeding. The activity is closed with a formal audit and preparation of the deliverable software product for installation, acceptance, or system integration.

If additional verification is desired, the code verification activity may be executed. This activity applies the following criteria to the code: traceable to design and requirements, testable, correct, and compliant with requirements and coding standards. Consideration of correctness includes consideration of

- proper event sequence
- consistent interfaces
- correct data and control flow
- completeness
- appropriate allocation timing and sizing budgets
- error definition, isolation, and recovery

In addition, it is verified that code implementing safety-related or other critical requirements has demonstrated to be correct via "suitably rigorous methods." Portions of the code may be selected for a demonstration that the implementation is derivable from design or requirements.

For organizations performing systematic software reuse, an additional standard is appropriate:

Process

IEEE Std 1517-1999 (R2004)
IEEE Standard for Information Technology—
Software Life Cycle Processes—Reuse Processes
This standard provides life cycle processes for systematic software reuse
suitable for use with IEEE/EIA 12207.
Allocated to: Software Engineering Process Knowledge Area

Aside from adding requirements to the existing activities of IEEE/EIA 12207, IEEE Std 1517 also provides three additional processes supporting systematic reuse—reuse program management, asset management, and domain engineering.

3.2.2. Construction Planning   The choice of construction approach strongly affects the nature of the planning that is appropriate for construction. These decisions are typically reflected in the chosen life cycle and the development plan.

From IEEE/EIA 12207.0, Clause 5.3, Development Process:

5.3.1.1   If not stipulated in the contract, the developer shall define or select a software life cycle model appropriate to the scope, magnitude, and complexity of the project. The activities and tasks of the Development Process shall be selected and mapped onto the life cycle model. . . .

5.3.1.3   The developer shall select, tailor, and use those standards, methods, tools, and computer programming languages (if not stipulated in the contract) that are documented, appropriate, and established by the organization for performing the activities of the Development Process and supporting processes (clause 6).

3.2.3. Construction Measurement   Of course, the construction activity produces numerous artifacts, providing ample opportunities for measurement. Measurement can be applied to support project progress evaluation, process improvement, and quality assurance. A particular use of measurement is to provide early estimates of various desired qualities factors. One hopes to measure artifacts available during construction to predict the achievement of desired qualities in the completed product. The ISO/IEC 9126 series of standards supports this approach; its various parts provide a taxonomy of quality factors and various measurements useful at different points of product development. The various uses of measurement are described in other chapters of this book.

3.3. Practical Considerations

Construction is the activity in which software engineering must come to grips with the messy nature of the real world. Perhaps it is not surprising that construction is driven by practical considerations and remains more craft-like than most aspects of software engineering.

3.3.1. Construction Design   It is inevitable that coders engage in design activity. In some cases, the design activity stops at some predetermined level of detail, allowing for the coders to make the remaining decisions. In other cases, coders find themselves coping with unanticipated circumstances, just as a carpenter might make up for a detailed flaw in a building's plan. The principles of design, whether applied within a design activity or a construction activity, are the same and are treated in Chapter 7, Knowledge Area: Software Design.

3.3.2. Construction Languages Construction languages receive a lot of attention, perhaps more than they deserve. One can consider languages to be of four types: configuration languages (e.g., some program generators) to customize an installation or usage of an item; toolkit languages (e.g., human-computer interface generators) to build components from parts; programming languages for general purpose construction; and domain-specific languages (e.g., lex, yacc, TCL) used for specific purposes. Many of the common programming languages are defined by standards or de facto specifications.

3.3.3. Coding Various techniques important to the quality of software are applied during the coding process. Examples include buffer overrun checking, proper use of control structures, discipline in use of serially reusable resources and mutual exclusion, and conventions for naming variables and laying out code. Generally, these techniques are not specified by external standards but are often the subject of internal standards or guidelines published by the developing organization itself.

3.3.4. Construction Testing Construction typically includes two types of testing—unit testing and integration testing. The purpose of unit testing is to ensure that the coded units correctly perform some level of function before more systematic testing begins. Both forms of testing are typically based on requirements.

IEEE has a standard specifically dedicated to software unit testing:

Process

IEEE Std 1008-1987(R2003)
IEEE Standard for Software Unit Testing
This standard describes a sound approach to software unit testing and the concepts and assumptions on which it is based.
Allocated to: Software Testing Knowledge Area

An integrated approach to testing and its documentation is described by an IEEE standard:

Document

IEEE Std 829-1998
IEEE Standard for Software Test Documentation
This standard describes the form and content of a basic set of documentation for planning, executing, and reporting software testing.
Allocated to: Software Testing Knowledge Area

3.3.5. Construction Quality Many of the engineering techniques to improve quality are applicable during software construction. However, they are generally specialized to focus on the code and test artifacts produced by construction. Of course, testing and debugging are two prominent techniques. Most software engineers also recommend the use of technical reviews to examine the artifacts. IEEE provides an applicable standard:

Process

IEEE Std 1028-1997 (R2002)
IEEE Standard for Software Reviews
This standard defines five types of software reviews and procedures for their execution. Review types include management reviews, technical reviews, inspections, walk-throughs, and audits.
Allocated to: Software Quality Knowledge Area

3.3.6. Integration An important activity of construction is the integration of the separately developed artifacts into a software item ready for delivery or incorporation into a larger system. The strategy for integrating components will affect the need to develop test drivers and test scaffolding.

IEEE/EIA 12207 treats user documentation as a result of integration. User documents are first drafted during the software architectural design activity and successively updated by software detailed design, software coding and testing, software integration, and software qualification testing. An IEEE standard may be helpful in the development of user documentation:

Document

IEEE Std 1063-2001
IEEE Standard for Software User Documentation
This standard provides minimum requirements for the structure, content, and format of user documentation—both printed and electronic.
Allocated to: Software Construction Knowledge Area

3.3.7. Construction Tools Software construction can be performed in a mostly manual fashion (aside from the necessary language processor) or can be performed in a highly automated fashion. Examples of tools include compilers, specialized editors, test generators, coverage analyzers, and debuggers. The primary obstacle to the use of tools is not their availability, but the need to integrate them into a comprehensive and interoperable environment.

4. STANDARDS IN THE SOFTWARE CONSTRUCTION KNOWLEDGE AREA

4.1. IEEE Std 1063-2001, IEEE Standard for Software User Documentation

This 19-page standard strives to set a good example for documentation by including a bibliography and an index. It was originally developed in 1987 but was completely revised to its current form in 2001. It provides minimum requirements for user documentation—whether printed or electronic—of systems containing software. The standard places requirements on both the content and the format of the documentation. The following components of user documentation are described:

- Identification data
- Table of contents (in documents longer than eight pages)
- List of illustrations (optional)
- Introduction
- Information for use of documentation
- Concept of operations
- Procedures (in instructional documents)
- Information on commands (in reference documents)
- Error messages and problem resolution
- Glossary (if documentation contains unfamiliar terms)
- Related information sources (optional)

- Navigational features
- Index (in documents longer than 40 pages)
- Search capability (in electronic documents)

5. SUMMARY

This chapter has provided an overview of the Software Construction knowledge area of the IEEE Computer Society's *Guide to the Software Engineering Body of Knowledge*. Seven IEEE and ISO/IEC standards have been offered as relevant to the knowledge area.

The presentation has been divided into three subsections corresponding to the knowledge breakdown provided in the *SWEBOK Guide*.

- *Fundamentals*: Key concepts are described.
- *Managing Construction*: IEEE/EIA 12207.0 and IEEE Std 1571 provide useful processes for construction.
- *Practical Considerations*: IEEE standards 829 and 1008 support testing, while IEEE Std 1028 describes technical reviews. IEEE Std 1063 provides requirements for software user documentation.

Chapter 9

Knowledge Area: Software Testing

Testing is the second oldest of the activities related to software engineering—its necessity discovered only a few hours later than the first activity, construction. The pioneers of computing quickly discovered that the implacably literal nature of computing made it far more difficult than imagined to program computers correctly. In the "code and fix" era of computing—before the appreciation of engineering approaches to software—testing was the primary tool for achieving correctness in software. A large variety of testing techniques have arisen during the 60 or so years of the computing age.

This chapter surveys the concepts, processes, and activities related to software testing as well as the standards supporting them. The chapter is organized according to the subjects treatment in the *Guide to the Software Engineering Body of Knowledge* [SWEBOK04], and much of the text is paraphrased from that source. (The knowledge area editors for the chapter in the *SWEBOK Guide* were Antonia Bertolino and Eda Marchetti.) Several relevant IEEE software engineering standards are mentioned in the context of the knowledge described by the *SWEBOK Guide*. At the end of the chapter, the standards allocated to this knowledge area are described in greater detail. Cross-references to other chapters provide access to descriptions of the other relevant standards.

1. KNOWLEDGE AREA SCOPE

The scope of the Software Testing Knowledge Area is defined by [SWEBOK04] as follows:

> *Testing is an activity performed for evaluating product quality, and for improving it, by identifying defects and problems.*

The Road Map to Software Engineering: A Standards-Based Guide, by James W. Moore
Copyright © 2006 by IEEE Computer Society

Software testing consists of the dynamic verification of the behavior of a program on a finite set of test cases, suitably selected from the usually infinite executions domain, against the expected behavior.

. . . Software testing is now seen as an activity which should encompass the whole development and maintenance process and is itself an important part of the actual product construction. Indeed, planning for testing should start with the early stages of the requirement process, and test plans and procedures must be systematically and continuously developed, and possibly refined, as development proceeds.

. . . Testing must be seen . . . primarily as a means for checking not only whether [fault] prevention has been effective, but also for identifying faults in those cases where, for some reason, it has not been effective. It is perhaps obvious but worth recognizing that, even after successful completion of an extensive testing campaign, the software could still contain faults. . . .

In the Software Quality KA (See topic 3.3 Software Quality Management Techniques), software quality management techniques are notably categorized into static techniques (no code execution) and dynamic techniques (code execution). . . . This KA focuses on dynamic techniques.

Software testing is also related to software construction. . . . Unit and integration testing are intimately related to software construction, if not part of it.

2. KNOWLEDGE AREA SUMMARY

The *SWEBOK Guide* divides the Software Testing Knowledge Area into five subareas—an organization followed by this chapter. The Introduction of the *SWEBOK Guide* summarizes this knowledge area as follows:

Software Testing consists of the dynamic verification of the behavior of a program on a finite set of test cases, suitably selected from the usually infinite executions domain, against the expected behavior. It includes five subareas.

*It begins with a description of **Software Testing Fundamentals**. First, the testing-related terminology is presented, then key issues of testing are described, and finally the relationship of testing to other activities is covered.*

*The second subarea is **Test Levels**. These are divided between the targets of the tests and the objectives of the tests.*

*The third subarea is **Test Techniques**. The first category includes the tests based on the tester's intuition and experience. A second group comprises specification-based techniques, followed by code-based techniques, fault-based techniques, usage-based techniques, and techniques relative to the nature of the application. A discussion of how to select and combine the appropriate techniques is also presented.*

*The fourth subarea covers **Test-Related Measures**. The measures are grouped into those related to the evaluation of the program under test and the evaluation of the tests performed.*

*The last subarea describes the **Test Process** and includes practical considerations and the test activities.*

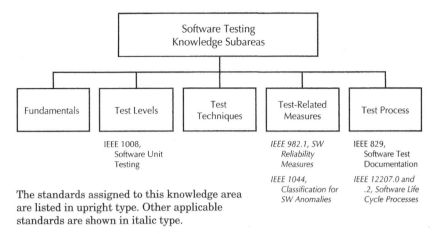

Figure 9. Software Testing knowledge area and its standards

The knowledge area breakdown is illustrated in Figure 9, which also shows the standards relevant to this knowledge area.

3. KNOWLEDGE AREA DESCRIPTION

In its traditional role, testing is the activity of executing code for the purpose of finding and correcting defects. As any practitioner knows, though, no substantial software product is defect-free and the absence of defects does not ensure a quality product. Therefore, modern practitioners view testing as one of a set of techniques that are applied to improve the quality of a software product. Roughly speaking, those techniques can be categorized as static or dynamic depending on whether or not they involve actual execution of the code. Dynamic techniques are treated here while static techniques are treated in the chapter on Software Quality.

The role of testing in the software life cycle has also expanded. Testing is no longer reviewed as the activity that follows coding. Instead, test planning is now undertaken in the early stages of a project, and the test plans are revised as the project progresses. Tests are executed throughout the life cycle to assess quality of the product. Test planning itself is a verification activity that can contribute to product quality through early identification of problems in the statement of requirements.

3.1. Basic Concepts and Definitions

The *SWEBOK Guide* characterizes testing as follows: "Software testing consists of the **dynamic** verification of the behavior of a program on a **finite** set of test cases, suitably **selected** from the usually infinite executions domain, against the specified **expected** behavior." The bolded terms provide insight into the nature and limitations of testing.

- The word "dynamic" implies that testing is, by definition, performed by executing the program. Of course, this means that any single test case is restricted to dealing with a single set of input conditions. Without further analysis, any one test case can only verify the correctness of the program for a single input from an indefinitely large domain.

- The word "finite" suggests that the set of test cases is probably small in comparison to the size of the domain of inputs. Therefore, testing inherently involves a trade-off between the desired quality and the resources needed for testing.

- The word "selected" is notable because different test techniques select their test cases in different ways. Appropriate selection of techniques and the corresponding test cases is a complex problem.

- The word "expected" is important because testing is useless if one cannot compare the results of program execution with a known correct answer. For large test sets, the problem of knowing the correct answer—the so-called *oracle* problem—is similarly large.

In performing software testing, it is essential to distinguish between the cause for a malfunction and the results of the malfunction; the cause is called a *fault* or *defect* and the observed results are the *failure*. Testing reveals failures, but it is the faults that must be removed. Sometimes, though, the fault cannot be unambiguously identified because a variety of code modifications might each suffice to remedy the problem. Therefore, some authors refer to *failure-causing inputs*—the set of inputs that reveal the failure.

For most large software projects, testing is performed not once but at several stages in the development, on different ensembles of the system components. Therefore, the *target of the test* varies during system development. Testing is conducted with a more-or-less specifically defined purpose in mind—the *test objective*. "Breaking the program" to identify defects is one popular objective, but there are others, including reliability measurement, usability evaluation, and acceptance from a supplier. Clear matching of appropriate test objectives with test targets is a purpose of test planning; typically, different objectives are sensible for different targets. Together, the test target and test objective determine how the *test set* is identified. Two types of *test criteria* are generally applied: *test selection*—which test cases contribute to the objective—and *test adequacy*—how much testing is enough.

Test techniques are selected to accomplish the test objective, but they should not be confused. The technique is an aid to accomplishing the objective. For example, achieving a specified level of branch coverage is not the objective, merely a means to improve the chances of finding faults. To avoid misunderstanding, one should distinguish *test measures*, which evaluate the characteristics of the test set, from product measures, e.g, reliability.

In a complex software product development, testing approaches need to be formulated as a controlled and repeatable *test process*. Because these processes are labor intensive, they are typically supported by *test tools*.

The preceding overview motivates the organization of the remainder of this section:

- Test levels (targets and objectives)
- Test techniques
- Test-related measures
- Managing the test process

3.2. Test Levels

3.2.1. Test Targets Typically, in the development of a large software system, three different levels of testing are distinguished: *unit*, *integration*, and *system*. Different life cycle models will iterate and interleave these forms of testing in different ways.

Unit testing verifies that individual software units function as expected in isolation. Unit testers typically have visibility of the code and the support of debugging tools. Unit testing is usually performed during the coding activity, typically after a clean compile, often by the same programmers who performed the coding. It varies in formality. Sometimes the results of unit testing are not systematically captured.

IEEE has a standard specifically dedicated to software unit testing:

Process

IEEE Std 1008–1987(R2003)
IEEE Standard for Software Unit Testing
This standard describes a sound approach to software unit testing-and the concepts and assumptions on which it is based,
Allocated to: Software Testing Knowledge Area

Integration testing consists of verifying the interaction between components that have already been unit tested. Except for very small and simple systems, it is not sensible to put all of the components together at once for a so-called "big bang" test. Instead, components are typically accreted in a fashion that might be driven by hierarchy or by following functional threads. Hierarchical techniques are sometimes classified as *top-down*, requiring *stubs* for missing low-level components, or *bottom-up*, requiring *drivers* for missing high-level components. Sometimes, integration is performed in a staged fashion; sometimes it is performed continuously as the system evolves.

System testing requires the addition of nonsoftware components to verify interfaces and overall properties of the system as a whole. Even in a system that is nearly pure software, system testing is appropriate to evaluate nonfunctional characteristics such as performance, reliability, usability, etc.

3.2.2. Test Objectives Any testing should be conducted with a specific objective in mind. After all, without an objective, how does one know when to stop? Different objectives are appropriate for evaluating different characteristics or at different points in the life cycle:

- *Acceptance or qualification testing*, marking the acquirer's acceptance of the system from the developer
- *Installation testing*, verifying that the system operates in its intended environment

- *Alpha/beta testing*, evaluating the system when operated in possibly unanticipated ways by the intended users
- *Conformance testing* or *functional testing*, verifying that the behavior of the system conforms to its specifications
- *Reliability evaluation*, measuring the observed reliability of the system in operation
- *Regression testing*, verifying that modifications have not caused unintended changes
- *Performance testing*, evaluating factors such as capacity and response time
- *Back-to-back testing*, verifying that two ostensibly equivalent systems provide the same results
- *Recovery testing*, verifying capability to recover from serious failures
- *Configuration testing*, verifying that different configurations of the same system provide the same results
- *Usability testing*, evaluating the ease of using the system
- *Test-driven development*, using test case development as a surrogate for requirements specification

Some testing is intended to evaluate nonfunctional properties that emerge from the operation of the system. These include reliability, performance, usability, behavior when stressed to design limits, and recovery from unusual conditions.

3.3. Test Techniques

In many cases, the goal of testing is to "break" the program for the purpose of revealing defects. The tester achieves economy and efficiency by testing the system with test cases drawn from different classes of executions deemed to be equivalent. The principle is to perform a systematic analysis of program behaviors by using a representative cross-section of test cases.

This section summarizes various testing techniques available to testers. Because there are many different techniques that are not homogeneously classified, it is difficult to provide a single overall organization. An alternative organization is to classify the techniques as *black-box*, where the tester has no knowledge of the design of the component, or *white-box*, where the tester applies design knowledge to generate and select test cases.

3.3.1. Experience-Based The most common form of testing generates ad hoc test cases based on the tester's intuition and experience. It is particularly useful for the exploration of special situations not easily generated by more formalized techniques. Two clear difficulties with the approach are variability from individual to individual and the lack of effectiveness measures. An advantage is the adaptive nature of the testing—the tester can pursue situations that provide unexpected results or side-effects.

3.3.2. Specification-Based In this category of techniques, the specifications for the test target are analyzed to produce the test cases. Specific techniques include:

- *Equivalence partitioning*: The domain of input values is divided into subsets that are deemed to be equivalent for the property being tested. A representative set of tests (perhaps only one from each subset) are selected for execution.
- *Boundary-value analysis*: Test cases are chosen from the boundaries of the input domain on the rationale that extreme values may generate erroneous behavior. A variety, called *robustness testing*, uses values outside the domain.
- *Decision table*: Decision tables specify a relationship between classes of inputs and outputs. Test cases are derived from each instance of the relationship.
- *Finite-state-machine-based*: If the program is modeled as a finite-state machine, test cases can be generated to exercise selected states and transitions among them.
- *Formal specifications*: If the program is formally specified, one can automatically generate test cases as well as a test oracle.
- *Random testing*: This technique is based on a statistical formulation of the intended usage of the input domain. It is sometimes used as a forecaster of reliability in the field.

3.3.3. Code-Based   In this category of techniques, tests are generated from an examination of the code to be tested. Two techniques are:

- *Control flow testing*: These techniques attempt to achieve some stated degree of coverage of a program's paths of control, or combinations, thereof. Exhaustive techniques are computationally infeasible, so compromise criteria are typically used.
- *Data flow testing*: These techniques attempt to achieve some stated degree of coverage of the data in the program. A test case traverses a definition and usage of a variable.

3.3.4. Fault-Based   In this category, test cases are generated with the purpose of revealing specified types of faults. Two techniques are:

- *Error guessing*: These techniques involve the generation of test cases specifically contrived to create a failure. Often such tests are based on historical information of faults discovered in earlier projects.
- *Mutation testing*: A mutant is derived from the original code by introducing a small change. Originally mutation testing was developed to evaluate test cases—one kept the cases that were effective in distinguishing the mutant from the original. However, one can also generate additional test cases designed to "kill" the "surviving" mutants on the rationale that they will also detect other errors. This technique is sometimes used to generate regression tests.

3.3.5. Usage-Based   In this category, test cases are generated to evaluate reliability objectives based on usage profiles. Two techniques are:

- *Operational profile*: This technique generates test cases to reflect statistical properties expected in actual usage of the system. In this manner, it is intended that the operational reliability of the system can be estimated.
- *Software Reliability-Engineered Testing (SRET)*: This is an overall methodology for system testing guided by reliability objectives, expected field usage, and the criticality of designated operations.

3.3.6. Based on Nature of Application
A variety of specialized techniques are applicable to software systems that are constructed, integrated, or operated in a particular fashion. They include:

- Object-oriented testing
- Component-based testing
- Web-based testing
- Graphical user interface (GUI) testing
- Concurrent program testing
- Protocol conformance testing
- Testing of distributed systems
- Testing of real-time systems
- Testing of safety-critical systems

3.3.7. Selecting and Combining Techniques
Specification-based testing and code-based testing are often termed as *functional testing* versus *structural testing*. These should not be viewed as competing approaches but as complementary. They should be selected as appropriate for test objectives and test targets. The selection of particular test cases can be *deterministic* or *random*.

3.4. Test-Related Measures

Measurement is necessary for meaningful quality analysis. Various quality factors must be traded against each other—if only for the allocation of project resources. The general topic of quality measurement is treated in Chapter 15, Knowledge Area: Software Quality. Measurement is also necessary to achieve effective yet economical planning and execution of tests. Test measures are used for two purposes: to evaluate the program being tested; and to evaluate the thoroughness of the test set itself.

3.4.1. Evaluation of the Program Being Tested
The first category of measurements count or predict faults or failures in the program being tested. There are several categories including:

- *Planning aids*: These measures describe program size, complexity, and structure so that testing may be appropriately allocated to the components of the software product.
- *Types, classification, and statistics of faults*: Fault classification is important in characterizing the faults discovered. Historical information of this sort can predict future faults and assist in the allocation of testing effort.

- *Fault density*: This is an overall measure of the product under test. The fault density is the ratio of the number of faults to the size of the component. It is typically evaluated for each class of faults.
- *Life test, reliability evaluation*: These measures attempt to forecast properties of the system in actual usage. They are helpful in determining when to stop testing.
- *Reliability growth models*: These are models that predict the growth in reliability of the system as faults are fixed. They are helpful in forecasting test budgets.

IEEE has a standard specifically dedicated to measures for reliability. These measures may be useful in evaluating the program being tested:

Measure

IEEE Std 982.1-1988
IEEE Standard Dictionary of Measures to Produce Reliable Software
This Standard provides a set of measures for evaluating the reliability of a software product and for obtaining early forecasts of the reliability of a product under development.
Allocated to: Software Quality Knowledge Area

IEEE has a standard specifically dedicated to fault classification. It may be helpful in planning and collecting fault and failure data for measurement purposes:

Tool

IEEE Std 1044-1993 (R2002)
IEEE Standard Classification for Software Anomalies
This standard provides a uniform approach to the classification of anomalies found in software and its documentation. It includes helpful lists of anomaly classifications and related data.
Allocated to: Software Quality Knowledge Area

3.4.2. Evaluation of the Tests The second category of measures looks at the test cases themselves to estimate their effectiveness in finding faults. There are several categories including:

- *Coverage measures*: When tests are generated from specifications or code, one can derive ratios that are measures of thoroughness. It is typical to demand that all of the requirements be tested. Often one is required to test a certain percentage of the branches or the blocks of code within a program.
- *Fault seeding*: It is possible to seed a program with faults and then evaluate the test set based on the percentage of seeded faults that are discovered.
- *Mutation score*: When using mutation testing (described above), one can evaluate the test set based on the percentage of mutants detected in the total number generated.

There are analytic studies concerning the effectiveness of various testing techniques. Publicly accessible "open source" projects provide a fertile source for these studies.

3.5. Managing the Test Process

Testing activities represent an obvious trade-off between cost and quality. For testing to be both efficient and effective, it must be a well-managed execution of a defined process.

3.5.1. Management Concerns   There are important issues in managing the test process. Perhaps the most important is a positive attitude toward testers as a contributor to the success of the system. In too many organizations, testers are considered as inferior to coders and as hungry consumers of project budgets. Some enlightened organizations form partnerships between coders and testers to work together in ensuring software quality. Some particular issues are noted below:

- *Egoless programming*: Maintaining a collaborative attitude is important in a process that has the objective of revealing failure. An attitude of joint ownership rather than individual ownership of code may be helpful.
- *Test guides*: Collaborative sharing of the goals of testing may be an effective supplement (or even replacement) for detailed test planning.
- *Test process management*: Like other development and maintenance activities, testing should be planned and controlled.
- *Test documentation and work products*: Documentation of test plans and results is useful for demonstrating achievement of goals as well as performing forensic analysis.
- *Internal versus independent test team*: Considerations of cost and criticality may lead to a decision that a test team should be independent rather than a part of the code construction team, at least during some parts of the life cycle.
- *Estimation and measurement*: Because testing can consume an important portion of the development budget, it is important to estimate the effort and monitor its effectiveness.
- *Termination*: The decision to terminate testing depends on evaluations of both the quality of the test set and the quality of the artifact being tested. Obviously, quantitative goals are to be preferred. Hence measurement is appropriate.
- *Test reuse and test patterns*: This may be simply organized facilities for regression testing or it might involve reusing overall test regimes in similar systems.

3.5.2. Test Activities   Testing should not be an ad hoc activity. Like other development activities, it should have a defined process and should produce a defined set of products. The output of testing is not only a high-quality system, but historical information useful in developing the next system or modifying the current one. In formalizing the test process, it will be necessary to determine the relationship of the test team to the implementers. Different choices may be appropriate for different test objectives and at different stages of the project. The importance of test measurement has already been discussed. It follows that estimation of test resources will be based on measured experience in similar projects. It is important to evaluate both the system being tested and the effectiveness of the testing process. The decision to terminate testing will be based on both sets of results considered in conjunction with the risks of stopping and the costs of continuing. The best of organizations will develop a repository of test materials—including plans, scripts, and test cases—to be used in future projects.

Effective testing involves several activities:

- *Planning*: Key aspects of test planning include provision and coordination of necessary personnel, management of test facilities and equipment, and contingencies for undesired outcomes. Multiple versions or configurations will introduce additional complications.
- *Test case generation*: For most testing (possibly excluding unit testing), test cases and the expected results should be documented and placed under configuration management.
- *Test environment development*: Perhaps more than coders, testers need a highly automated environment suitable for the controlled repetition of test scripts. The test environment should be compatible with the development environment to ensure that important results can be transmitted between testers and implementers.
- *Execution*: Beyond the level of unit testing, testing should be performed in accordance with documented procedures and scripts. In many cases, execution is overseen by quality assurance personnel or customer representatives for the purpose of building confidence in the thoroughness of the process.
- *Test results evaluation*: Of course, the expected result of a test should be known in advance, but not all unexpected results are bad results. In some cases, further analysis is required. Sometimes, there will be a formal review or other process to analyze test results.
- *Problem reporting*: Test results and problem reports should be logged as an input to change management. All unanticipated anomalies should be logged for later analysis.
- *Defect tracking*: Failures should be related to faults. A comprehensive reporting system can support causal analysis efforts leading to improvements in the development process.

The key standard describing the activities of software testing is IEEE/EIA 12207.0:

Process

IEEE/EIA 12207.0-1996
Industry Implementation of International Standard ISO/IEC
12207:1995, Standard for Information Technology-
Software Life Cycle Processes
This standard provides a framework of processes used across the entire
life cycle of software.
Allocated to: Software Engineering Process Knowledge Area

The 12207 standard includes testing in several activities of the development process:

- Software coding and testing
- Software integration
- Software qualification testing
- System integration
- System qualification testing
- Software installation
- Software acceptance support

However, test planning begins earlier. Three activities—software architectural design, software detailed design, and software coding and testing—document and update test requirements and schedule for the software integration activity. Furthermore, the latter two activities evaluate their products for feasibility of testing. The testing activities of the 12207 standard are described in Chapter 19, Software Life Cycle Processes.

A systematic approach to testing involves a flow of products:

- Test plan
- Test design specifications
- Test case specifications
- Test procedure specifications
- Test execution
- Test reports

This integrated approach to testing is described by an IEEE standard:

Document

IEEE Std 829-1998
IEEE Standard for Software Test Documentation
This standard describes the form and content of a basic set of documentation for planning, executing, and reporting software testing.
Allocated to: Software Testing Knowledge Area

4. STANDARDS IN THE SOFTWARE TESTING KNOWLEDGE AREA

4.1. IEEE Std 829–1998, IEEE Standard for Software Test Documentation

The S2ESC standard for software test documentation, IEEE Std 829, was first approved in 1983 and revised in 1998 for improved compatibility with IEEE/EIA 12207.1. It specifies the form and content of a set of basic document that may be used to carry out a software testing program. It does not specify a minimum acceptable set of such documents, instead assuming that the project plans will designate the appropriate set. The standard prescribes one document for test planning, three for test specification, and four for test reporting. Annexes provide examples of application. The relationships among the various documents are depicted in Figure 10.

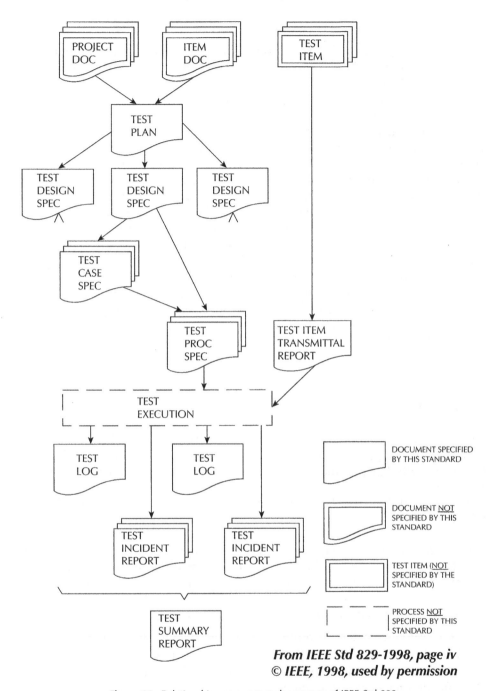

Figure 10. Relationships among test documents of IEEE Std 829

4.2. IEEE Std 1008–1987, IEEE Standard for Software Unit Testing

The primary objective of IEEE Std 1008 is to provide a standard approach to the software unit testing. Completed by S2ESC in 1987 and repeatedly reaffirmed, this 24-page standard is intended to be applied as a basis for comparison of test practices, a source of ideas to modify those practices, and a replacement for less effective practices.

The document provides an integrated approach to systematic unit testing based on requirements, design, and implementation information to determine the completeness of testing. The required testing process is a hierarchy of phases, activities, and tasks. Performance of each activity is required; each of the activity's required tasks must be performed or the results of their prior performance must be available for reverification. The 1008 standard is consistent with IEEE Std 829 on software test documentation and requires the use of the test design specification and the test summary report specified in 829.

The specified unit testing process is applicable to either new or modified code. The standard does not address software debugging, other aspects of comprehensive software verification, or related processes like configuration management and quality assurance.

Appendixes of the standard include usage guidelines, concepts and assumptions, and references for additional information.

5. SUMMARY

This chapter has provided an overview of the Software Testing knowledge area of the IEEE Computer Society's *Guide to the Software Engineering Body of Knowledge*. Six IEEE standards have been offered as relevant to the knowledge area.

The presentation has been divided into five subsections provided by the *SWEBOK Guide*:

- *Fundamentals*: Testing reveals failures, but it is the underlying faults that must be removed. Testing must address different test targets with appropriate test objectives. Test techniques are chosen to address the test objectives.
- *Test Levels*: IEEE Std 1008 describes software testing at the unit level.
- *Test Techniques*: Test techniques were classified a variety of ways.
- *Test-Related Measures*: IEEE 982.1 provides a dictionary of measures useful in evaluating software reliability. IEEE Std 1044 provides a classification for software anomalies.
- *Managing the Test Process*: IEEE/EIA 12207.0 provides useful provisions for the Software Testing, particularly when supplemented with the documentation provisions of IEEE Std 829.

Chapter *10*

Knowledge Area: Software Maintenance

Maintenance takes its place with development and operation as one of the three fundamental processes in the life of a software product. It's probably safe to say that no substantial software product ever escapes maintenance during its life. The only question is whether or not the maintenance is planned and conducted in a disciplined manner.

This chapter surveys the concepts, processes and activities related to software maintenance as well as the standards supporting them. The chapter is organized according to the subject's treatment in the *Guide to the Software Engineering Body of Knowledge* [SWEBOK04], and much of the text is paraphrased from that source. (The knowledge area editors for the chapter in the *SWEBOK Guide* were Thomas M. Pigoski and Alain April.) The relevant IEEE software engineering standards, as well as a few from other sources, are mentioned in the context of the knowledge described by the *SWEBOK Guide*. At the end of the chapter, the standards allocated to this knowledge area are described in greater detail. Cross-references to other chapters provide access to descriptions of the other relevant standards.

1. KNOWLEDGE AREA SCOPE

The scope of the Software Maintenance Knowledge Area is defined by [SWEBOK04] as being

> ... *software maintenance is defined as the totality of activities required to provide cost-effective support to software. Activities are performed during the pre-delivery stage, as well as during the post-delivery stage. Pre-delivery activities include*

The Road Map to Software Engineering: A Standards-Based Guide, by James W. Moore
Copyright © 2006 by IEEE Computer Society

planning for post-delivery operations, for maintainability, and for logistics deter-mination for transition activities. Post-delivery activities include software modi-fication, training, and operating or interfacing to a help desk.

2. KNOWLEDGE AREA SUMMARY

The *SWEBOK Guide* divides the Software Maintenance Knowledge Area into four subareas—an organization followed by this chapter. The Introduction of the *SWEBOK Guide* summarizes this knowledge area as follows:

Once in operation, anomalies are uncovered, operating environments change, and new user requirements surface. The maintenance phase of the life cycle commences upon delivery, but maintenance activities occur much earlier. The Software Maintenance KA is divided into four subareas.

*The first one presents **Software Maintenance Fundamentals**: definitions and terminology, the nature of maintenance, the need for maintenance, the majority of maintenance costs, the evolution of software, and the categories of maintenance.*

*The second subarea groups together the **Key Issues in Software Maintenance**. These are the technical issues, the management issues, maintenance cost estima-tion, and software maintenance measurement.*

*The third subarea describes the **Maintenance Process**. The topics here are the maintenance processes and maintenance activities.*

***Techniques for Maintenance** constitute the fourth subarea. These include program comprehension, re-engineering, and reverse engineering.*

The knowledge area breakdown is illustrated in Figure 11, which also shows the standards relevant to this knowledge area.

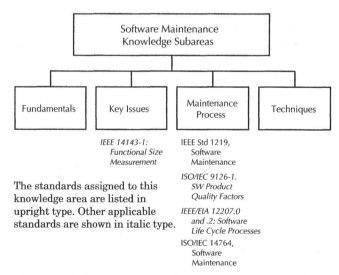

Figure 11. *Software Maintenance knowledge area and its standards*

3. KNOWLEDGE AREA DESCRIPTION

3.1. Fundamentals

Software maintenance is an integral part of the software life cycle but historically it has not received the same attention as development. Recently, though, the subject is attracting more attention as organizations focus on the total life cycle cost of their information technology. Because maintenance is expensive, it is an important contributor to that cost. Recent events, such as the Year 2000 rollover and the increased interest in open source products, also increase the attention paid to maintenance.

Perceived needs for change begin immediately when a software product commences operation. In many cases, functionality has been deferred from software development or defects have already been noted. Sources for change requirements include anomalies discovered in operation, evolution in the requirements of the users, and changes to the operating environment of the software. The software maintenance process reacts to these demands by logging and tracking change requests, analyzing the impact of proposed changes, modifying the software product, testing it, releasing a new version, and training its users. Hence, software maintenance activities not only span the full life cycle of the software product, but also impute a life cycle to the change activity itself.

The IEEE standard for software maintenance, IEEE Std 1219, defines its subject as: "Modification of a software product after delivery to correct faults, to improve performance or other attributes, or to adapt the product to a modified environment." IEEE/EIA 12207.0 includes maintenance as one of the primary life cycle processes and defines maintenance as "modification to code and associated documentation due to a problem or a need for improvement. The objective is to modify the existing software product while preserving its integrity."

Of course, the reason for maintenance is to ensure that the system continues to meet the requirements of its users. Maintenance activity must be performed for any of the following reasons:

- Correct faults
- Correct requirements and design flaws
- Improve the design
- Implement enhancements
- Interface with other systems
- Adapt software products to changes in their context, e.g., hardware and telecommunications
- Migrate legacy systems
- Retire outdated systems

In performing maintenance activity, one must simultaneously preserve the operation of the existing system while maintaining control over the desired changes. Functions must be improved or added while preventing system performance from degrading.

Although maintenance is often perceived as fixing bugs, in fact, studies show that over 80 percent of the maintenance activity over the entire life cycle of a software product is noncorrective in nature. A tendency to group improvement actions with corrective actions leads to a misleadingly high perception of the cost of correction.

Maintenance may be better regarded as the activity dealing with the software product's evolution over its life cycle. In this view, maintenance is similar to development although it retains some unique characteristics, such as a greater emphasis on problem reporting and configuration management. An emphasis on evolution rather than correctness led Manny Lehman to formulate the so-called Laws of Software Evolution, based on the premise that large systems are never complete and continue to evolve. The evolution inherently leads to greater complexity unless one undertakes specific actions to counteract the trend. In this view, software development is simply the first step in its evolution and software maintenance is the same as development with the additional constraint of the existing system.

The traditional categorization of maintenance—*corrective*, *perfective*, and *adaptive*—led to the definition in IEEE Std 1219 quoted above. To this list, some authors would add a category of *preventive maintenance*. ISO/IEC 14764 incorporates all four categories as follows:

- *Corrective maintenance*: Reactive modification of a software product performed after delivery to correct discovered problems.
- *Adaptive maintenance*: Modification of a software product performed after delivery to keep a computer program usable in a changed or changing environment.
- *Perfective maintenance*: Modification of a software product after delivery to improve performance or maintainability.
- *Preventive maintenance*: Modification of a software product after delivery to detect and correct latent faults in the software product before they become effective faults.

Preventive maintenance is typically employed on systems required to implement some critical property such as safety or security.

3.2. Key Issues in Software Maintenance

Maintenance presents some difficult challenges. Aside from the obvious problem of finding and fixing bugs in large codes developed by others, there are problems of competing with developers for resources, planning for future releases while maintaining old releases, and reacting to demands for emergency maintenance.

3.2.1. Technical Issues

- *Limited understanding*: Perhaps 40–60 percent of maintenance effort is devoted to understanding the code that is to be changed. Effective documentation and configuration management can help with the problem.
- *Testing*: Full regression testing is almost always economically infeasible for large systems. Special techniques must be applied to select appropriate test sets.
- *Impact analysis*: Maintainers must analyze not only the impact of change on the software, but upon the users and organizations relying on the software to do their jobs.
- *Maintainability*: Maintainability is one of the quality characteristics defined by ISO/IEC 9126-1. Inadequate attention during development can induce devastating costs during maintenance. The problem can be alleviated by selecting coding standards, documentation standards, and test tools during development.

3.2.2. Management Issues

- *Alignment with organizational objectives*: Return on investment is not clear for maintenance activities. Therefore it can be difficult to compete against developers for resources.
- *Staffing*: Maintainers are often perceived as less competent than developers so only the less competent are willing to accept maintenance roles—or maybe only the less competent are offered such roles.
- *Process*: Unique activities of maintenance, e.g., service level agreements for maintenance, present issues not present in development. If management is focused on development, these issues may be treated inadequately.
- *Organizational aspects of maintenance*: In one way or another, maintenance is often outsourced—sometimes to another company, sometimes to another organization within the same company.

3.2.3. Cost Estimation   The factors causing excessive maintenance costs are generally known. Unfortunately, though, it is usually too late to correct these causes after maintenance begins; they are set by decisions made during development. Regardless of cost levels, estimating the cost of a maintenance action is essential. Experience-based estimation is sometimes satisfactory, especially if historical data is available. Parametric maintenance cost models are available but necessarily depend on an estimate of the "functional size" of the change. One helpful standard is:

Measure

IEEE Std 14143.1-2000
IEEE Adoption of ISO/IEC 14143-1:1998, Information Technologh—
Software Measurement—Functional Size Measurement—
Part 1: Definition of Concepts
This standard describes the fundamental concepts of a class of measures collectively known as functional size.
Allocated to: Software Requirements Knowledge Area

3.2.4. Measurement   Trading quality against cost is particularly difficult—and particularly important—when performing maintenance. For these reasons, it is appropriate to continue (and enhance) any measurement program initiated during software development. In some cases, it may be necessary to initiate a set of maintenance measures. The Practical Software Measurement [McGarry01] method recommends using an issue-driven approach.

3.3. Maintenance Process

Maintenance processes are treated systematically by a number of modern standards and the maturity of those processes is treated by various capability models.

3.3.1. Maintenance Process Models   Maintenance is one of the three primary technical processes of IEEE/EIA 12207.0:

Process

IEEE/EIA 12207.0-1996
Industry Implementation of International Standard ISO/IEC
12207:1995, Standard for Information Technology—
Software Life Cycle Processes
This standard provides a framework of processes used across the entire life cycle of software.
Allocated to: Software Engineering Process Knowledge Area

The maintenance process is described in clause 5.5 of the 12207 standard. Six activities are provided:

- Process implementation: develop plans, establish procedures for tracking problem reports and requests, and provide for configuration management.
- Problem and modification analysis: perform impact analysis for requested changes, verify the problem, consider alternative solutions, and obtain approval.
- Modification implementation: determine which software units and documents must be changed (as well as the affected versions) and use the 12207 development process to implement the changes, supplemented by regression testing and other mechanisms to ensure that other functionality is unaffected.
- Maintenance review/acceptance: conduct a review and gain acceptance.
- Migration: develop migration plans (addressing requirements, tooling, conversion, and verification, as well as support for the old environment), notify users, conduct parallel operation as appropriate, and archive and maintain accessibility to old documentation and products and data.
- Software retirement: develop retirement plans (addressing cessation of support, residual support, archiving, and transition to new products), notify users, conduct parallel operation, provide training to users, and

archive and maintain accessibility to old documentation and products and data.

IEEE has a standard specifically dedicated to Software Maintenance:

Process

IEEE Std 1219-1998
IEEE Standard for Software Maintenance
This standard describes a process for software maintenance and its management.
Allocated to: Software Maintenance Knowledge Area

The IEEE standard provides much additional guidance—notably planning for maintenance—but aggregates its activities differently than those of the 12207 standard. For that reason, some users prefer to use an ISO/IEC standard for maintenance:

Process

ISO/IEC 14764:1999
Information Technology—Software Maintenance
This standard provides guidance on implementing the maintenance process provided in ISO/IEC 12207.
Allocated to: Software Maintenance Knowledge Area

The ISO/IEC 14764 standard has the advantage that it maps directly to 12207. In fact, it contains no requirements beyond those of 12207, merely guidance. The IEEE and ISO/IEC JTC 1/SC 7 have initiated a project to merge the two documents so that both organizations will share a single maintenance process standard that is fully compatible with 12207.

3.3.2. Maintenance Activities The actual implementation of change is performed using the development process of 12207, strengthening the viewpoint of maintenance as a special case of software evolution. However, maintenance does induce some special considerations.

Unique Activities Some of the unique activity involved in maintenance is related to the initiation of a change. Maintainers must pay particular attention to analyzing the impact of a proposed change. The activity is similar to the impact analysis of requirements management but necessarily involves an end-to-end look at all artifacts of the software product. In addition, it must address the impact on the system's users who may have to accomplish their work in a different manner. Maintainers must also perform a risk analysis, considering the possibility that change may adversely affect portions of the system that are operating acceptably.

The special relationship of maintainers to users is described in part by the Operation process of 12207:

From IEEE/EIA 12207.0, Clause 5.4, Operation Process:

5.4.1 Process implementation. This activity consists of the following tasks:

5.4.1.2 The operator shall establish procedures for receiving, recording, resolving, tracking problems, and providing feedback. Whenever problems are encountered, they shall be recorded and entered into the Problem Resolution Process (6.8).

5.4.1.3 The operator shall establish procedures for testing the software product in its operation environment, for entering problem reports and modification requests to the Maintenance Process (5.5), and for releasing the software product for operational use.

. . .

5.4.4 User support. This activity consists of the following tasks:

5.4.4.2 The operator shall forward user requests, as necessary, to the Maintenance Process (clause 5.5) for resolution. These requests shall be addressed and the actions that are planned and taken shall be reported to the originators of the requests. All resolutions shall be monitored to conclusion.

5.4.4.3 If a reported problem has a temporary work-around before a permanent solution can be released, the originator of the problem report shall be given the option to use it. Permanent corrections, releases that include previously omitted functions or features, and system improvements shall be applied to the operational software product using the Maintenance Process (5.5).

Supporting Activities   All of the supporting and management processes of the IEEE/EIA 12207 standard are applicable to maintenance. Some, however, need additional emphasis.

PROBLEM RESOLUTION   As noted above, the operation process employs the problem resolution process to receive and track problem reports from the users of the system. In many cases, problem reports and other user requests are forwarded to the maintenance process, thus initiating a maintenance action.

MAINTENANCE PLANNING   Planning for maintenance is essential because the maintenance portion of the life cycle lasts far longer than development. This planning should begin during the development process. The development process requires that all items needed for maintenance must be deliverable products of the development (clause 5.3.1.5), and that maintenance requirements are part of the system requirements analysis (clause 5.3.2.1) and the software requirements analysis (5.3.4.1).

In addition, "feasibility of operation and maintenance" is an evaluation requirement of system requirements (clause 5.3.2.2), system architecture (clause 5.3.3.2), software requirements (5.3.4.2), software architecture (5.3.5.6), software detailed design (5.3.6.7), software code and unit test results (5.3.7.5), software integration plan, tests and test results (5.3.8.5), software qualification tests and test results (5.3.9.3), integrated system (5.3.10.3), and system qualification test results (5.3.11.2). In addition, 12207 requires particular attention to safety specifications related to maintenance (clause 5.3.4.1).

ISO/IEC 9126-1 provides four subcharacteristics for maintainability that may be measured:

- *Analyzability*: Measures of the maintainer's effort or resources expended in trying to diagnose deficiencies or causes of failure, or in identifying parts to be modified.
- *Changeability*: Measures of the maintainer's effort associated with implementing a specified modification.
- *Stability*: Measures of the unexpected behavior of software, including that encountered during testing.
- *Testability*: Measures of the maintainer's and users' effort in trying to test the modified software. Measurement of the maintainability of software can be performed using available commercial tools.

Terminology

ISO/IEC 9126-1:2001
Software Engineering—Product Quality—Part 1: Quality Model
This standard provides a model for software product quality covering internal quality, external quality, and quality in use. The model is in the form of a taxonomy of defined characteristics that software may exhibit.
Allocated to: Software Requirements Knowledge Area

Other parts of the ISO/IEC 9126 series suggest specific measurements related to the subcharacteristics of maintainability.

CONFIGURATION MANAGEMENT Good configuration management is essential to maintenance. The CM system must provide all relevant artifacts applicable to a maintenance issue to assist in impact analysis, particularly considering that some software products are fielded in multiple versions. Because maintenance is an error-prone activity, it is appropriate to track the extent of change that has occurred in components of the system. This supports making the decision to redevelop a component rather than to change it.

QUALITY ASSURANCE, VERIFICATION, AND VALIDATION Just as for development, these processes are used to assure the correct implementation of new functionality. In the case of maintenance, though, they bear the additional burden of ensuring that functions that were supposed to be unchanged are, in fact, not changed.

3.4. Techniques for Maintenance

Software maintenance requires the use of some techniques that are unique to the maintenance process, or, at least, specialized for that purpose.

- *Program Comprehension*: Because of the vital necessity for economically comprehending the code to be changed, assistive tools are particularly helpful.
- *Re-engineering*: Most sources agree that there is a time when software components should be redeveloped rather than modified. Few sources agree on the criteria for making that decision. "Refactoring"—transforming the organization of code without changing its function—is a technique discussed widely in current literature.
- *Reverse Engineering*: This refers to a systematic approach to studying the code to recreate lost or missing documentation or to recover design. Tooling is becoming available for this purpose.

4. STANDARDS IN THE SOFTWARE MAINTENANCE KNOWLEDGE AREA

4.1. IEEE Std 1219–1998, IEEE Standard for Software Maintenance

S2ESC has a standard suitable for use in implementing the maintenance process, the 47-page IEEE Std 1219, approved in 1992, and revised in 1998 for better fit with IEEE/EIA 12207.1. The standard describes an iterative process for managing and executing the maintenance activity for software regardless of size, complexity, criticality, or application. It has its own *process model* of *phases* that differ slightly from the activities prescribed by the maintenance process of 12207. For each phase, inputs, outputs, and controls are specified. Measures for each phase are also provided. Finally, the standard suggests other S2ESC standards that may be applied in detailing its phase requirements.

Although the current 1219 standard is not completely reconciled with the 12207 standard, it should be a useful tool in implementing a maintenance process conforming to the requirements of 12207. The most troublesome misfit of the two is in a basic premise. The 12207 maintenance process would execute the development process in order to create a software change and then return to the maintenance process for the remaining work, for example, assuring that the untouched code still works. In the 1219 standard, required development activities are simply subsumed into the maintenance process. This difference is more legalistic than substantive and simply introduces a degree of awkwardness in the explanation of how organizational processes relate to the two standards.

The standard includes a suggested outline of a Maintenance Plan, shown in Table 7.

Annex D suggests minor changes and additions to the outline that would provide conformance with IEEE/EIA 12207.1.

4.2. ISO/IEC 14764:1999, Information Technology—Software Maintenance

In 1999, ISO/IEC JTC 1/SC 7 completed its own standard on software maintenance. The document is notable because it contains no requirements beyond those already levied by ISO/IEC 12207. It provides only guidance—albeit

TABLE 7. Outline of Maintenance Plan suggested by IEEE Std 1219

1. Introduction
2. References
3. Definitions
4. Software Maintenance Overview
   4.1 Organization
   4.2 Scheduling Priorities
   4.3 Resource Summary
   4.4 Responsibilities
   4.5 Tools, Techniques, and Methods
5. Software Maintenance Process
   5.1 Problem/Modification Identification/Classification and Prioritization
   5.2 Analysis
   5.3 Design
   5.4 Implementation
   5.5 System Testing
   5.6 Acceptance Testing
   5.7 Delivery
6. Software Maintenance Reporting Requirements
7. Software Maintenance Administrative Requirements
   7.1 Anomaly Resolution and Reporting
   7.2 Deviation Policy
   7.3 Control Procedures
   7.4 Standards, Practices, and Conventions
   7.5 Performance Tracking
   7.6 Quality Control of Plan
8. Software Maintenance Documentation Requirements

extensive guidance—in implementing those requirements. The guidance is particularly helpful in the predelivery aspects of maintenance, i.e., planning for maintainability while the product is still under development.

Knowledgeable reviewers find it difficult to choose between the IEEE standard and the ISO/IEC standard because both have their strengths. Accordingly, in 2003 IEEE and ISO/IEC JTC 1/SC 7 agreed to cooperate on a revision of ISO/IEC 14764 that would incorporate the best of both documents.

5. SUMMARY

This chapter has provided an overview of the Software Maintenance knowledge area of the IEEE Computer Society's *Guide to the Software Engineering Body of Knowledge*. Six IEEE and ISO/IEC standards have been offered as relevant to the knowledge area.

The presentation has been divided into four subsections provided by the *SWEBOK Guide*:

- *Basic Concepts*: Maintenance activity can be classified as adaptive, corrective, perfective or preventive. In many cases, it is useful to view development and maintenance as a unified process of evolution.

- *Key Issues*: IEEE Std 14143-1 provides the concept of a "Functional Size" of a proposed change to a set of requirements.
- *Maintenance Process*: IEEE/EIA 12207.0 provides useful provisions for the Software Maintenance process, particularly when supplemented with the process provisions of IEEE Std 1219 or ISO/IEC 14764. ISO/IEC 9126-1 defines characteristics of maintainability useful in planning for maintenance.
- *Techniques:* Some techniques, such as re-engineering, are unique or specialized for the maintenance process.

Chapter 11

Knowledge Area: Software Configuration Management

Software Configuration Management may be the most widely accepted aspect of software engineering. Businesses using code-and-fix methods typically "discover" the need for configuration management before they appreciate the need for other disciplines. Unfortunately, this discovery is typically made after a serious loss is experienced. Software configuration management is part of a more general CM discipline, but has enough special characteristics to merit distinct treatment.

This chapter surveys the concepts, processes, and activities related to software configuration management as well as the standards supporting them. The chapter is organized according to the subject's treatment in the *Guide to the Software Engineering Body of Knowledge* [SWEBOK04], and much of the text is paraphrased from that source. (The knowledge area editors for the chapter in the *SWEBOK Guide* were John A. Scott and David Nisse.) The relevant IEEE software engineering standards, as well as a few from other sources, are mentioned in the context of the knowledge described by the *SWEBOK Guide*. At the end of the chapter, the standard allocated to this knowledge area is described in greater detail. Cross-references provide access to descriptions of other relevant standard.

1. KNOWLEDGE AREA SCOPE

The scope of the Software Configuration Management Knowledge Area is defined by [SWEBOK04] as follows:

> *[Software] Configuration Management . . . is the discipline of identifying the configuration of a system at distinct points in time for the purpose of systematically*

The Road Map to Software Engineering: A Standards-Based Guide, by James W. Moore
Copyright © 2006 by IEEE Computer Society

controlling changes to the [software] configuration, and maintaining the integrity and traceability of the configuration throughout the system life cycle.

2. KNOWLEDGE AREA SUMMARY

The *SWEBOK Guide* divides the Software Configuration Management Knowledge Area into six subareas—an organization followed by this chapter. The Introduction of the *SWEBOK Guide* summarizes this knowledge area as follows:

> *Software Configuration Management (SCM) is the discipline of identifying the configuration of software at distinct points in time for the purpose of systematically controlling changes to the configuration and of maintaining the integrity and traceability of the configuration throughout the system life cycle. This KA includes six subareas.*
>
> *The first subarea is **Management of the SCM** Process. It covers the topics of the organizational context for SCM, constraints and guidance for SCM, planning for SCM, the SCM plan itself, and surveillance of SCM.*
>
> *The second subarea is **Software Configuration Identification**, which identifies items to be controlled, establishes identification schemes for the items and their versions, and establishes the tools and techniques to be used in acquiring and managing controlled items. The first topics in this subarea are identification of the items to be controlled and the software library.*
>
> *The third subarea is **Software Configuration Control**, which is the management of changes during the software life cycle. The topics are: first, requesting, evaluating, and approving software changes; second, implementing software changes; and third, deviations and waivers.*
>
> *The fourth subarea is **Software Configuration Status Accounting**. Its topics are software configuration status information and software configuration status reporting.*
>
> *The fifth subarea is **Software Configuration Auditing**. It consists of software functional configuration auditing, software physical configuration auditing, and in-process audits of a software baseline.*
>
> *The last subarea is **Software Release Management and Delivery**, covering software building and software release management.*

The knowledge area breakdown is illustrated in Figure 12, which also shows the standards relevant to this knowledge area.

3. KNOWLEDGE AREA DESCRIPTION

According to IEEE Std 610.12, a system is a "collection of components organized to accomplish a specific function or set of functions" and its configuration is "the functional and physical characteristics of hardware or software as set forth in technical documentation or achieved in a product." Normally, the functional and physical characteristics are referenced in a shorthand fashion by

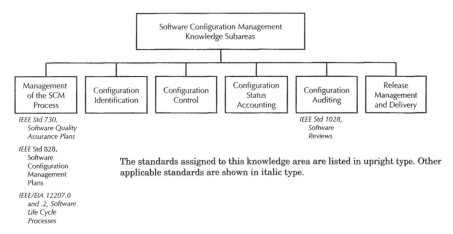

Figure 12. *Software Configuration Management knowledge area and its standards*

citing a version. It is important that versions claimed as identical are actually identical. So configuration management is the discipline of identifying the configuration of a system at distinct points in time for the purpose of systematically controlling changes to the configuration and maintaining the integrity and traceability of the configuration throughout the system life cycle.

Configuration management is a system-level discipline and there are norms for providing configuration management at the system level, for example, EIA-649:1998, *National Consensus Standard for Configuration Management*. Configuration management is also considered critical to quality management; ISO TC 176 (the maintainers of the famous ISO 9000 series of quality management standards) cite configuration management as one way to achieve the "product identification and traceability" requirements of ISO 9001:2000 and provide configuration management guidance in ISO 10007:2003, *Quality management systems—Guidelines for configuration management*.

The system level principles of CM apply to software. Since software presents some difficult challenges, though, the treatment of the subject is often specialized for application to software. This chapter follows that principle. The six subareas of this chapter correspond directly with the six activities specified as a part of the configuration management process by IEEE/EIA 12207.0. This treatment is typical except that many sources do not separately treat the final activity, software release management and delivery.

Process

IEEE/EIA 12207.0-1996
Industry Implementation of International Standard ISO/IEC
12207:1995, Standard for Information Technology–
Software Life Cycle Processes
This standard provides a framework of processes used across the entire life cycle of software.
Allocated to: Software Engineering Process Knowledge Area

The configuration management process is described in clause 6.2 of the 12207 standard. Six activities are provided:

- Process implementation, including planning
- Configuration identification
- Configuration control
- Configuration status accounting
- Configuration evaluation
- Release management and delivery

3.1. Management of the Software Configuration Management Process

According to the treatment provided by IEEE/EIA 12207.0, configuration management is a supporting process. Unlike some supporting processes, though, its usage is not optional. Clauses 5.3.1.2 and 5.5.1.3 require the developer and the maintainer, respectively, to place their work under configuration management. Clause 5.1.5.3 requires the acquirer to take the responsibility for configuration management following acceptance of the product. Other supporting processes of the 12207 standard also depend upon CM. Clauses 6.1.1.1 and 6.1.3.2 of the documentation process place document products under configuration management and the verification process checks that the CM of the documents followed the specified procedures (6.4.2.7). The joint review process (6.6.3.1) checks that changes to products are under CM. Finally, the infrastructure process suggests applying CM to important portions of the infrastructure (7.2.3). We will see later, though, that the artifacts of the development process do not have to be under CM for their entire life.

3.1.1. Organizational Context for Software Configuration Management Although software configuration management is typically assigned to a specific organization or individual, it necessarily interacts with various processes and organizations. Obviously, if software is part of a larger system, there are system-level CM activities with which software CM must be consistent. Quality assurance activities often depend upon configuration records maintained by the CM process.

Perhaps the closest relationship, though, is with the development process because it is the development process that identifies configuration items. The system architectural design activity of 12207 establishes a top-level architecture by the identification of *items* of hardware, software and manual operation. Clause 5.3.3.1 goes on to state that *configuration items* are **subsequently** identified from those items [emphasis added]. Clause 5.3.10.1 states that the system is integrated by aggregating the configuration items. So, we know that items are identified relatively early but that formal configuration management of the items can be delayed until system integration. This distinction is made for a purpose; Annex E.14 explains that the configuration management of configuration items is intended to be more rigorous than for items that have not been so designated. So, when is an item chosen for the transition from informal control to rigorous CM? The timing of this transition is determined by the development planning for the particular project. Of course, these choices depend, in part, upon the life cycle model selected for the development project.

We will return to this subject when *baselines* are described later in this chapter.[29]

3.1.2. Constraints and Guidance for Software Configuration Management

Some projects are not completely free to select configuration management practices. In many cases, policies and procedures are imposed from the corporate level to ensure uniformity. In two-party situations, the acquirer may impose specific requirements. Occasionally, regulatory bodies impose constraints. Formal and de facto standards provide a source for "best practices."

3.1.3. Planning for Software Configuration Management

Planning for configuration management is inherent in the responsibilities of the developer. Clause 5.3.1.2 of IEEE/EIA 12207.0 requires that the outputs of development be placed under configuration management and Clause 6.2.1 requires that a configuration management plan be developed—either standalone or as part of a system CM plan:

> 6.2.1.1 ... The plan shall describe: the configuration management activities; procedures and schedule for performing these activities; the organization(s) responsible for performing these activities; and their relationship with other organizations, such as software development or maintenance. The plan shall be documented and implemented.

The IEEE provides a standard useful in the development of a software CM plan:

Plan

IEEE Std 828-1998
IEEE Standard for Software Configuration Management Plans
This standard specifies the content of a Software Configuration Management plan along with requirements for specific activities.
Allocated to: Software Configuration Management Knowledge Area

Typically, the plan is reviewed by the quality assurance process and is among the plans that QA periodically monitors for process compliance. Many users of the standard apply it in conjunction with the IEEE quality assurance standard.

Plan

IEEE Std 730-2002
IEEE Standard for Software Quality Assurance Plans
This standard specifies the format and content of Software Quality Assurance plans.
Allocated to: Software Quality Knowledge Area

---

[29] For ease of expression, this paragraph contains many temporal references, e.g., "earlier," "timing," etc. Of course, the 12207 standard disclaims levying any temporal requirements. The temporal references are intended to refer to spans of activities in the development process regardless of how they are mapped to a life cycle model.

IEEE Std 730 also provides a summary set of requirements for configuration management. In some cases, they would suffice and the use of 828 would not be necessary.

Organization and Responsibilities   To prevent confusion, the configuration management plan should identify the organizations that will perform or be involved with configuration management. Clause 4.2.1 of IEEE Std 828 requires the identification of organizational units, their functional roles, and the relationships among them. Organizational unit is interpreted broadly, including, for example, customers and vendors. The plan also identifies the activities that are allocated to the organizational units. Review boards are given special treatment; the plan must describe their purpose, objectives, membership, life span, scope of authority and procedures. External constraints on the plan are identified.

The plan must identify and describe the functions and tasks to perform CM. IEEE Std 828 states that these activities are typically grouped into four functions:

- Configuration identification
- Configuration control
- Status accounting
- Configuration audits and reviews

Of course, this organization closely matches the *SWEBOK Guide's* breakdown of the SCM knowledge area, the activities of the IEEE/EIA 12207.0 CM process, and the subsections of this chapter.

Resources and Schedules   IEEE Std 828 requires the identification of "software tools, techniques, equipment, personnel and training necessary for the implementation of the specified SCM activities." Schedule issues are addressed by specifying sequencing and coordination of the SCM activities and relating them to the overall project schedule as either absolute dates or dates relative to other activities.

Tool Selection and Implementation   It is common to accomplish SCM functions using special-purpose tools. In some cases, the tools are integrated with the development team's environment; in other cases, they are dedicated to the SCM organization. Tool support is available for:

- The configuration library
- Software change request and approval procedures
- Code and change management
- Reporting status and collecting measurements
- Auditing
- Managing and tracking documentation
- Performing software builds
- Managing and tracking software releases

It is an all-too-common mistake to believe that configuration management tools can obviate the CM process itself. The tools themselves can be used in many ways, some sound and some unsound.

Vendor/Subcontractor Control When portions of the software are purchased from vendors or developed through subcontracts, a number of additional issues are raised. The most important question is when the software should enter configuration management. If a subcontractor performs CM during its development, one must consider how their CM process is to be monitored.

Interface Control In large systems, configuration management is often given the responsibility to manage the interfaces between the various hardware and software items of the system. Typically, interface changes require configuration management actions, sometimes authorized by a Configuration Control Board.

3.1.4 Software Configuration Management Plan
The results of SCM planning are documented in a plan. IEEE Std 828 includes a table (shown here as Table 8) listing six classes of information to be included in the plan:
The plan must be regarded as a "living document" and should include the procedures to be used for its own modification.

3.1.5 Surveillance of Software Configuration Management
Of course, to be useful, the configuration management plan must be executed. Use of tooling provides some aid to uniform implementation of the plan and has the desirable side effect of generating measurements that may be useful in project planning and process improvement. Because of the consequences of loss of configuration control, the execution of the SCM plan is usually monitored in some way, possibly by the quality assurance process. Like a financial accounting system, periodic audits are useful in confirming that the integrity of the plan has been maintained.

TABLE 8. Six classes of SCM planning information in IEEE Std 828

Class of information	Description
Introduction	Describes the Plan's purpose, scope of application, key terms, and references
SCM management	(Who?) Identifies the responsibilities and authorities for accomplishing the planned activities.
SCM activities	(What?) Identifies all activities to be performed in applying to the project.
SCM schedules	(When?) Identifies the required coordination of SCM activities with other activities in the project.
SCM resources	(How?) Identifies tools and physical and human resources required for execution of the Plan
SCM plan maintenance	Identifies how the plan will be kept current while in effect

3.2. Software Configuration Identification

Software configuration identification is the activity forming the foundation for the remaining SCM activities because it identifies the items to be controlled. The 12207 standard places a minimum set of requirements on this activity:

> 6.2.2.1 A scheme shall be established for the identification of software items and their versions to be controlled for the project. For each software configuration item and its versions, the following shall be identified: the documentation that establishes the baseline; the version references; and other identification details.

We've already learned that software configuration items are the same software items identified by the system architectural design activity, but after the point when they enter configuration management. Now, we are ready to look at the mechanism by which they come under the control of SCM; it is the *baseline*. Each software item identified by the system architectural design eventually becomes a software configuration item by being included in an approved baseline. Subsequent baselines might approve revised versions of the software configuration item.

A baseline is defined in the 12207 standard as a formally approved version of a configuration item. In a two-party situation, the formal approval is provided jointly by the acquirer and the supplier. The development process of the ISO/IEC standard includes three thresholds when baselines are established:

- Clause 5.3.4.3 states that a baseline of the software requirements is established following a joint review at the completion of the software requirements analysis activity.
- Clause 5.3.9.5 states that a baseline of the software design and code is established following an audit at the completion of software qualification testing.
- Clause 5.3.11.4 states that a baseline of the software design and code is established following an audit at the completion of system qualification testing.

All three of these thresholds are deleted by the errata sheet of the IEEE/EIA version of the standard. Instead, the developer is required, as a part of implementation of the development process, to "establish baselines for each configuration item, at appropriate times, as determined by the acquirer and the supplier" (Clause 5.3.1.2(e)). The *SWEBOK Guide* differentiates among the following types of baselines:

- The *functional baseline* for the reviewed system requirements
- The *allocated baseline* for the reviewed software requirements allocation and interface specification
- The *developmental baseline* for the evolving software configuration at selected times
- The *product baseline* for the completed software product provided for system integration

It is important to note that baselines are formally approved; in a two-party situation, they are typically approved by both supplier and acquirer. Often, the approval is made as the result of some sort of formal review or other acceptance activity. It is implicit in this concept that items that have been baselined are regarded as less changeable than items that have not. Often, additional administrative procedures—possibly executed by a Change Control Board—are imposed to approve a change to a baselined item.

The lean nature of the requirements of 12207 is apparent in the clause quoted previously. The requirement treats only the code of the software items and their associated design and requirements allocation.[30] Furthermore, identification is performed only at the item level, not at the more detailed component or unit level. IEEE Std 828 is more inclusive:

> 4.3.1 ... Configuration identification activities shall identify, name, and describe the documented physical and functional characteristics of the code, specifications, design, and data elements to be controlled for the project. The documents are acquired for configuration control. Controlled items may be intermediate and final outputs (such as executable code, source code, user documentation, program listings, databases, test cases, test plans, specifications, and management plans) and elements of the support environment (such as compilers, operating systems, programming tools, and test beds).
>
> The Plan shall identify the project configuration items (CI) and their structures at each project control point. The Plan shall state how each CI and its versions are to be uniquely named and describe the activities performed to define, track, store, and retrieve CIs.

The standard goes on to provide detailed requirements for identifying, naming, and acquiring configuration items. Even the items required by IEEE Std 828 may not be sufficient. The *SWEBOK Guide* provides a more complete list of potential items including plans, specifications, design documentation, testing materials, software tools, source and executable code, code libraries, data and data dictionaries, and documentation for installation, maintenance, operations, and software use. One must strike a balance between providing adequate visibility to project management and selecting a reasonable number of items to control.

Simple identification of the configuration items may not be adequate to meet other project goals. It may be necessary to maintain information regarding the structure and relationships of the configuration items to support traceability, impact analysis, product evolution, and version control. Version control can be particularly difficult—even a research topic—in situations where a single product must operate in a variety of environments or support differing selections of functionality. The *SWEBOK Guide* suggests the following terminology:

- A *version* of a software item is an identified state of an evolving item.
- A *revision* is a new version that replaces the old version.
- A *variant* is a new version that does not replace the old version.

---

[30] However, clause 6.1.1.1 suggests that documents should also be placed under SCM.

Identified software configuration items are typically retained in a software library. Typically, libraries provide mechanisms for differentiating final products from work in progress and for regressing to previous versions when appropriate. One common mechanism is to provide a working library for items being coded, a support library for items being tested, and a master library for finished products. Tools for operating libraries typically provide some level of security mechanism as an administrative protection from changes that have not been approved. Many library tools can also provide measurements of progress.

3.3. Software Configuration Control

Software configuration control has the purpose of managing changes during the software life cycle. It provides the means to suggest changes, approve them, and support their implementation. The activity may also provide the means for granting and tracking waivers of selected project requirements. It is the presence of this activity that characterizes the distinction between software version control and software configuration management. The 12207 standard places the following requirement on the activity:

> 6.2.3.1 The following shall be performed: identification and recording of change requests; analysis and evaluation of the changes; approval or disapproval of the request; and implementation, verification, and release of the modified software item. An audit trail shall exist, whereby each modification, the reason for the modification, and authorization of the modification can be traced. Control and audit of all accesses to the controlled software items that handle safety or security critical functions shall be performed.

IEEE Std 828 seems to be completely consistent:

> 4.3.2 . . . Configuration control activities request, evaluate, approve or disapprove, and implement changes to baselined CIs. Changes encompass both error correction and enhancement. The degree of formality necessary for the change process depends on the project baseline affected and on the impact of the change within the configuration structure.
>
> For each project software library identified according to 4.3.1.3, the Plan shall describe the change controls imposed on the baselined CIs. The Plan shall define the following sequence of specific steps:
>
> a) Identification and documentation of the need for a change;
> b) Analysis and evaluation of a change request;
> c) Approval or disapproval of a request;
> d) Verification, implementation, and release of a change.
>
> The Plan shall identify the records to be used for tracking and documenting this sequence of steps for each change. Any differences in handling changes based on the origin of the request shall be explicitly documented.

The standard goes on to provide additional details for requirements on procedures for requesting, evaluating, approving, and implementing changes. All of the procedures are to be described in the Software Configuration Management Plan.

A change request typically identifies the configuration item to be changed, describes the desired change, and characterizes the need and urgency of the change. Changes may be requested by anyone, but one important source are corrections resulting from problem reports. Regardless, the nature of the change (e.g., defect or enhancement) is typically noted in the change request, providing the opportunity to separate the two types in change activity measurements. Once the request is received, it is analyzed to assess the impact on other parts of the system. The result is evaluated by a designated management authority to determine if the change should be accepted, modified, deferred, or rejected. In many cases, the authority rests with a Change Control Board that represents appropriate stakeholders. Large projects may have multiple levels of change authority (even multiple levels of CCBs) depending on criteria such as criticality (e.g., safety) of the items to be changed, budget and schedule impact, or point in the life cycle. The activities of a CCB are often audited by a quality assurance process to ensure that procedures are being correctly implemented.

Implementation of the change request process is assisted by supporting tools to track change requests and their disposition. It is often helpful to link change tracking to problem reporting so that the two categories of items can be reconciled.

It is likely that a number of approved changes would be implemented at the same time. For this reason, it is appropriate to track which changes are associated with particular software versions and baselines so that their implementation can be verified. Tooling is typically used to support this tracking, often associated with library check-in/out support and version control. Such a library might be under the exclusive control of SCM or might be provided to the entire development team (with appropriate controls) as part of an integrated development environment.

One particular form of change request is permission to deviate from plans or requirements that cannot be practically implemented at a given point in the life cycle. The configuration control activity provides an appropriate focus for considering and tracking such requests.

The relatively heavy weight of change control for configuration managed items is the biggest argument for delaying the inclusion of items in a baseline until relatively late in their development. IEEE/EIA 12207.0 treats the application of CM to an item as a black-and-white difference. Most applications of the standard will probably want to take a more graded approach whereby additional controls are gradually placed on the items as they become more mature. Such an approach would conform to the standard as long as the most restrictive controls conform to the requirements of the 12207 CM process and are applied to all software items at some point prior to system integration.

3.4. Software Configuration Status Accounting

Software configuration status accounting is the reporting and recording of information needed for the management of the software configuration. The 12207 standard places this requirement on the activity:

6.2.4.1 Management records and status reports that show the status and history of controlled software items including baseline shall be prepared. Status reports should include the number of changes for a project, latest software item versions, release identifiers, the number of releases, and comparisons of releases.

IEEE Std 828 places corresponding requirements on the Software Configuration Management Plan:

4.3.3 Configuration status accounting activities record and report the status of project CIs.

The Plan shall include information on the following:

   a) What data elements are to be tracked and reported for baselines and changes;

   b) What types of status accounting reports are to be generated and their frequency;

   c) How information is to be collected, stored, processed, and reported;

   d) How access to the status data is to be controlled.

If an automated system is used for any status accounting activity, its function shall be described or referenced.

The following minimum data elements shall be tracked and reported for each CI: its initial approved version, the status of requested changes, and the implementation status of approved changes. The level of detail and specific data required may vary according to the information needs of the project and the customer.

Obviously, there are two parts to this activity: recording the data and reporting the data. The recording is often supported by a database management system that captures configuration item identification, change requests and their status, and the incorporation of changes within software versions. The reporting capability should address ad hoc requests for information as well as routine reporting. When designing the reporting, one should consider the possibility that the reports may be usable as quality assurance records and for providing development measurements.

3.5 Software Configuration Auditing

According to IEEE Std 1028, an audit provides "an independent evaluation of conformance of software products and processes to applicable regulations, standards, guidelines, plans, and procedures." The *SWEBOK Guide* states that an the software configuration management auditing activity determines the extent to which an item satisfies the required functional and physical characteristics." The 12207 standard calls this activity "software configuration **eval-**

uation" because it uses the term "audit" to describe a distinct process that might be employed, among other things, to implement the evaluation:

6.2.5.1 The following shall be determined and ensured: the functional completeness of the software items against their requirements and the physical completeness of the software items (whether their design and code reflect an up-to-date technical description).

IEEE Std 828 places requirements on the planning for the configuration audits:

4.3.4 Configuration audits determine to what extent the actual CI reflects the required physical and functional characteristics. Configuration reviews are management tools for establishing a baseline.

The Plan shall identify the configuration audits and reviews to be held for the project. At a minimum, a configuration audit shall be performed on a CI prior to its release.

For each planned configuration audit or review, the Plan shall define the following:

    a) Its objective;

    b) The CIs under audit or review;

    c) The schedule of audit or review tasks;

    d) The procedures for conducting the audit or review;

    e) The participants by job title;

    f) Documentation required to be available for review or to support the audit or review;

    g) The procedure for recording any deficiencies and reporting corrective actions;

    h) The approval criteria and the specific action(s) to occur upon approval.

Note that IEEE Std 828 requires a configuration audit prior to a configuration item's release, defined as "the formal notification and distribution of an approved version." Although the 12207 standard lacks this requirement (and has a slightly different definition of "release"), the same intent is found in clauses 5.3.9.4 (software qualification testing) and 5.3.11.3 (system qualification testing).

The *SWEBOK Guide* suggests that informal configuration audits might be conducted at various points in the life cycle, but that two types of formal audits are often required in software being developed under contract: the Functional Configuration Audit (FCA) and the Physical Configuration Audit (PCA). The FCA checks that the item is consistent with its specifications and often relies on the results of testing, verification and validation activity. The PCA, in a software context, determines that the design and reference documentation is consistent with the software product as it was actually built.

IEEE has a standard suitable for the conduct of audits:

Process

IEEE Std 1028-1997 (R2002)
IEEE Standard for Software Reviews
This standard defines five types of software reviews and procedures for their execution. Review types include management reviews, technical reviews, inspections, walk-throughs, and audits.
Allocated to: Software Quality Knowledge Area

3.6. Software Release Management and Delivery

The *SWEBOK Guide* notes that in much CM literature, the topic of release management is not treated separately. However, the editor of the knowledge area decided to follow the lead of the 12207 standard is this regard:

> 6.2.6.1 The release and delivery of software products and documentation shall be formally controlled. Master copies of code and documentation shall be maintained for the life of the software product. The code and documentation that contain safety or security critical functions shall be handled, stored, packaged, and delivered in accordance with the policies of the organizations involved.

Frankly, it is not exactly clear what is meant by "release" in this context. The 12207 standard defines "release" as "a particular version of a configuration item that is made available for a specific purpose (for example, test release)." Of course, 12207 does not require that items be under configuration management before entering test. It's probably best to interpret this provision as principally applying to the release of the software that is to be delivered to the customer, while understanding that it could also be applied early in the life cycle of projects that are highly controlled. The *SWEBOK Guide* suggests that release procedures can be applied to any distribution of a software configuration item outside the development activity. It identifies version control as the key problem and a properly controlled software library as the solution to the problem.

To build the software for release, one must combine the correct revisions and variants of the software items, using appropriate configuration data, and build instructions into an executable program for delivery. In most practical situations, it is necessary for SCM to be able to rebuild previous releases for recovery, problem identification, and maintenance. This means that tools, build instructions, and configuration data must also be under the configuration management as well as the code. Tooling is available to support this aspect of software configuration management. The process and products of system build can be the subject of quality assurance (see 12207 clause 6.3.2.3) and the reports resulting from the software build may be legitimate quality assurance records.

In a two-party situation, the timing and selection of releases are probably determined by contract or other agreement between the acquirer and the supplier. In one-party situations, the timing and content of releases can be more problematic. Issues include the extent of new functionality, the severity of problems in the prior release, and the dependability of functions in the old release versus their anticipated dependability in the new one.

Packaging the release involves more than simply selecting the appropriate variants of the software items; appropriate documentation must also be provided. In contractual situations, this is sometimes provided in a Version Description document describing new capabilities, known problems, and platform requirements. Releases of commercial product software may have to address this problem by providing and maintaining variants of user documentation that must also be placed under CM and related to the implementing code.

In some cases, the release management activity must keep track of the customers or users of the various releases so that problem reports can be treated appropriately.

4. STANDARDS IN THE SOFTWARE CONFIGURATION MANAGEMENT KNOWLEDGE AREA

4.1. IEEE Std 828–1998, IEEE Standard for Software Configuration Management Plans

The S2ESC standard for software CM plans, IEEE Std 828, was originally written in 1983 and revised in 1990. The 1998 revision is a complete rewrite that, among other changes, reconciles the 17-page standard with the data requirements of IEEE/EIA 12207.1. At one time, there was a companion guide, IEEE Std 1042, that was withdrawn because of the practical difficulties in synchronizing the consensus process for two distinct documents covering the same ground.

The concerns of the document are described in its introduction: "Software configuration management (SCM) is a formal engineering discipline that, as part of the overall system configuration management, provides the methods and tools to identify and control the software throughout its development and use. SCM activities include the identification and establishment of baselines; the review, approval, and control of changes; the tracking and reporting of such changes; the audits and reviews of the evolving software product; and the control of interface documentation and project supplier SCM."

The standard is based on the premise that configuration management, at some level of formality, occurs in all software projects. Proper planning of the activity and effective communication of the plan increases its effectiveness. Hence, the standard prescribes the minimum required contents of an SCM plan. Developing the required plan will implicitly induce process requirements on the conduct of the project. Those requirements are intended to be consistent with those of IEEE Std 730 on software quality assurance plans.

5. SUMMARY

This chapter has provided an overview of the Software Configuration Management knowledge area of the IEEE Computer Society's *Guide to the Software Engineering Body of Knowledge*. Four IEEE standards have been offered as relevant to the knowledge area.

The presentation has been divided into six subsections corresponding to the *SWEBOK Guide* and the activities of IEEE/EIA 12207:

- *Management of the SCM Process*: IEEE/EIA 12207 places requirements on the activities of the software configuration management process. IEEE Std 828 contains provisions useful in planning for SCM, particularly when used in conjunction with IEEE Std 730.

- *Software Configuration Identification*: Items are placed under CM control at various points in their life cycle and are managed via the designation of baselines.

- *Software Configuration Control*: Configuration changes are managed during the life cycle.

- *Software Configuration Status Accounting*: Reports are provided to support management.

- *Software Configuration Auditing*: IEEE Std 1028 contains provisions useful for conducting audits.

- *Software Release Management and Delivery*: Software "releases" for various purposes are built and recorded.

Chapter *12*

Knowledge Area: Software Engineering Management

Management involves the activities and tasks undertaken by people for the purpose of planning and controlling the activities of others in order to achieve objectives that could not be achieved by individual action. *Project management* is a system of management procedures, practices, technologies, skill, and experience applied to managing an engineering project [Thayer95].

The most important tenet in the study of management is a principle called the *universality of management* [Fayol49, Koontz72] stating that:

- Management performs the same functions of planning, organizing, staffing, directing, and controlling regardless of the nature of the activity being managed.
- Management functions are characteristic duties of managers, but the specific practices, techniques, and methods are particular to the nature of the activity being managed.

This concept permits us to apply general management principles to the particular needs of software project management [Thayer84].

This chapter surveys the concepts, processes, and activities related to software engineering management as well as the standards supporting them. The chapter is organized according to the subject's treatment in the *Guide to the Software Engineering Body of Knowledge* [SWEBOK04], and much of the text is paraphrased from that source. (The knowledge area editors for the chapter in the *SWEBOK Guide* were Dennis Frailey, Stephen G. MacDonell, and Andrew R. Gray.) The relevant IEEE software engineering standards, as well as a few from other sources, are mentioned in the context of the knowledge described by the SWEBOK. In all, 14 relevant standards will be mentioned. At the end of the chapter, the standards allocated to this knowledge area are described in greater detail. Cross-references to other chapters provide access to descriptions of the other relevant standards.

1. KNOWLEDGE AREA SCOPE

The scope of the Software Engineering Management Knowledge Area is defined by [SWEBOK04] as follows:

> *Software Engineering Management can be defined as the application of management activities—planning, coordinating, measuring, monitoring, controlling, and reporting—to ensure that the development and maintenance of software is systematic, disciplined, and quantified . . .*

> *The Software Engineering Management KA therefore addresses the manage-ment and measurement of software engineering. While measurement is an important aspect of all KAs, it is here that the topic of measurement programs is presented. . . .*

> *With respect to software engineering, management activities occur at three levels: organizational and infrastructure management, project management, and measurement program planning and control. The last two are covered in detail in this KA description . . .*

2. KNOWLEDGE AREA SUMMARY

The *SWEBOK Guide* divides the Software Engineering Management Knowledge Area into six subareas—an organization followed by this chapter. The Introduction of the *SWEBOK Guide* summarizes this knowledge area as follows:

> *The Software Engineering Management KA addresses the management and measurement of software engineering. While measurement is an important aspect of all KAs, it is here that the topic of measurement programs is presented. There are six subareas for software engineering management. The first five cover software project management and the sixth describes software measurement programs.*

> *The first subarea is **Initiation and Scope Definition**, which comprises determination and negotiation of requirements, feasibility analysis, and process for the review and revision of requirements.*

> *The second subarea is **Software Project Planning** and includes process planning, determining deliverables, effort, schedule and cost estimation, resource allocation, risk management, quality management, and plan management.*

> *The third subarea is **Software Project Enactment**. The topics here are implementation of plans, supplier contract management, implementation of measurement process, monitor process, control process, and reporting.*

> *The fourth subarea is **Review and Evaluation**, which includes the topics of determining satisfaction of requirements and reviewing and evaluating performance.*

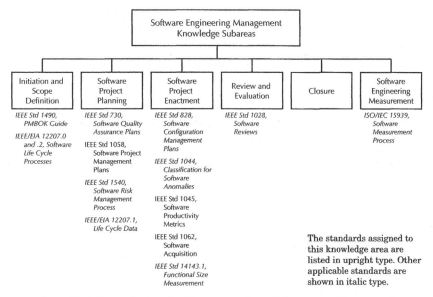

Figure 13. *Software Engineering Management knowledge area and its standards*

The fifth subarea describes **Closure**: *determining closure and closure activities.*

Finally, the sixth subarea describes **Software Engineering Measurement,** *more specifically, measurement programs. Product and process measures are described in the Software Engineering Process KA. Many of the other KAs also describe measures specific to their KA. The topics of this subarea include establishing and sustaining measurement commitment, planning the measurement process, performing the measurement process, and evaluating measurement.*

The knowledge area breakdown is illustrated in Figure 13, which also shows the standards relevant to this knowledge area.

3. KNOWLEDGE AREA DESCRIPTION

Although organizational and infrastructural management are not within the scope of this knowledge area, some aspects of software engineering place unusual stresses upon those levels of management. Because the uniform use of processes across the organization provides savings in tooling and increases in effectiveness, software engineering induces unusual needs for corporate standards and policies, and the accompanying investment in tools. Furthermore, corporations must initiate organization-level feedback mechanisms to capture historical data as the basis for future cost estimation and to improve the organizational processes. Personnel management is stressed by software engineering because of the need to hire, retain, and retrain highly competent people in a context of short technology half-lives. Software reuse can be pursued to reduce costs and increase productivity but is substantially more difficult to institutionalize software reuse than the corresponding programs for hardware devices.

Despite those organizational effects, this chapter treats *software project management*, a specific instance of *project management*. Project management itself is the subject of a professional discipline, described in the Project Management Institute's Guide to the Project Management Body of Knowledge. This document is discussed in the chapter on Related Disciplines.

IEEE Std 1490-2003
IEEE Guide: Adoption of PMI Standard, A Guide to the
Project Management Body of Knowledge (PMBOK® Guide)
This document is the IEEE adoption of the Project Management Body of Knowledge defined by the Project Management Institute. It identifies and describes generally accepted knowledge regarding project management.
Allocated to: Related Disciplines Chapter, Quality Management

Terminology

While it is undeniable that software project management is an example of the more general project management discipline, there are some characteristics of software projects that justify distinct treatment:

- The inherent complexity of software, particularly the impact of changing requirements, is often poorly appreciated by the customer.
- Software is often built iteratively, with multiple deliveries.
- A peculiar match of creativity and discipline is required to develop useful software.
- The degree of novelty is often high
- The technology changes rapidly.

Measurement (or the need for measurement) pervades the discipline of software engineering. The subject is treated in this chapter because it addresses the most important issue in managing software—the perception (with substantial truth) that software projects are always late and over-budget, delivering incomplete functionality of questionable quality. Management without measurement would lack rigor and could not address this perception.

The organization of this chapter is process oriented. The first five topics correspond roughly to the activities of the management process in IEEE/EIA 12207.0 and the final topic corresponds to the measurement process provided by ISO/IEC 15939.

IEEE/EIA 12207.0-1996
Industry Implementation of International Standard ISO/IEC
12207:1995, Standard for Information Technology–
Software Life Cycle Processes
This standard provides a framework of processes used across the entire life cycle of software.
Allocated to: Software Engineering Process Knowledge Area

Process

3.1. Initiation and Scope Definition

According to IEEE/EIA 12207.0, the management process is classified as an organizational process. This means that the organization, rather than the project, ensures that the management process exists and is functional. An instance of the management process is created for each new project. When the project management process is created, the manager first establishes feasibility by ensuring that appropriate resources (personnel, materials, technology, and environment) are adequate and that the schedule for completion is achievable. Of course, this is a preliminary treatment; the provision of resources and the creation of a schedule do not always coincide with the formal beginning of a project. A project manager should take this requirement as a continuing responsibility for the duration of the project.

Early in the project, it is important to determine and negotiate the requirements for the project. Note that the project requirements may include items beyond the technical requirements of the product or service to be provided. For instance, the organization or the acquirer may levy requirements for processes, methodologies, reporting, and infrastructure. Considering the viewpoints of the various stakeholders, the manager must characterize the scope, objectives, and constraints of the project and negotiate that characterization with the other involved parties. This creates a shared understanding of the bounds of the project.

The determination of the feasibility of the project involves consideration of technical, operational, financial factors—not to mention socio-political considerations. Various kinds of resources will be required and needs for all of them must be estimated, even if only inaccurate estimates are possible at this early time.

Changes in requirements are inevitable. Changes do not necessarily mean that the acquirer doesn't know what is desired; in fact, the users' legitimate needs will evolve during the duration of the project. Therefore, it is essential to reach agreement on the mechanism for reviewing and revising requirements at appropriate points during the project.

3.2. Software Project Planning

The management process of IEEE/EIA 12207.0 provides a terse description of project planning:

7.1.2.1 The manager shall prepare the plans for execution of the process. The plans associated with the execution of the process shall contain descriptions of the associated activities and tasks and identification of the software products that will be provided. These plans shall include, but are not limited to, the following:

  a) Schedules for the timely completion of tasks;
  b) Estimation of effort;
  c) Adequate resources needed to execute the tasks;
  d) Allocation of tasks;
  e) Assignment of responsibilities;
  f) Quantification of risks associated with the tasks or the process itself;
  g) Quality control measures to be employed throughout the process;
  h) Costs associated with the process execution;
  i) Provision of environment and infrastructure.

A more extended treatment of software project management plans can be found in an IEEE standard:

Plan

IEEE Std 1058-1998
IEEE Standard for Software Project Management Plans
This standard describes the format and contents of a software project management plan.
Allocated to: Software Engineering Management Knowledge Area

For guidance in software project management, some users prefer ISO/IEC Technical Report 16326, *Guide for the Application of ISO/IEC 12207 to Project Management*. As its title suggests, the document is closely aligned to the 12207 standard. In fact, the only normative provisions of 16326 are quoted from 12207. Everything else is guidance, derived from the *PMBOK® Guide* and ISO 10006, *Guidelines for Quality Management in Projects*, part of the ISO 9000 family of standards. ISO/IEC JTC 1/SC 7 and the IEEE have made the decision to collaborate in merging IEEE Std 1058 into the next revision of ISO/IEC TR 16326.

3.2.1. Process Planning In its best form, planning the software project will be based on selecting appropriate organizationally adopted processes and adapting them for the current project. The manager chooses a life cycle model appropriate to the needs of the acquirer and the characteristics of the project and fits the processes into the model. Typically, the project is described as a hierarchical decomposition of tasks, each having assigned results (perhaps deliverables), characterized quality goals, allocated resources, and assigned schedule. Enlightened organizations will evaluate the risks to the project plan and establish a mechanism for re-evaluating the risks. Quality management mechanisms will be established. As before, it is important to understand that project planning is an iterative activity and a continuing responsibility.

3.2.2. Deliverables The deliverables of the project may include more than a completed software product. There may be additional needs for support, user training, and operation. Documentation forms an important category. Different acquirers have different needs according to their plans for life cycle sustainment of the system. The documentation process of IEEE/EIA 12207 is suitable for this purpose. Its first activity is the development of a documentation plan:

6.1.1.1 A plan, identifying the documents to be produced during the life cycle of the software product, shall be developed, documented, and implemented. For each identified document, the following shall be addressed:

a) Title or Name;

b) Purpose;

c) Intended audience;

d) Procedures and responsibilities for inputs, development, review, modification, approval, production, storage, distribution, maintenance, and configuration management;

e) Schedule for intermediate and final versions.

An IEEE standard can provide help in preparing this plan:

Document

IEEE/EIA 12207.1-1996
Industry Implementation of International Standard ISO/IEC
12207:1995, Standard for Information Technology—
Software Life Cycle Processes—Life Cycle Data
This document provides guidance on recording data resulting from the
life cycle processes of IEEE/EIA 12207.0.
Allocated to: Software Engineering Process Knowledge Area

The heart of this standard is an 84-row cross-reference table that characterizes every information item produced by the processes described in IEEE/EIA 12207.0. The information items can be combined into documents suitable to the needs of the project while informing the manager of the process source of the data. The standard also provides guidance for the minimum required content of the information items.

3.2.3. Effort, Schedule, and Cost Estimation Based on the breakdown of tasks, the expected effort of each task is estimated. Capable organizations will have historical data available to assist in preparing these estimates. Of course, interdependencies among tasks must be resolved. If schedule duration becomes an issue, it may be necessary to perform analyses to reduce the critical path length. Introducing parallel activities can induce risk and increase the cost and effort needed for rework. Even at the beginning of the project, this activity is inherently iterative and involves negotiation among many involved parties.

3.2.4. Resource Estimation With a roughly costed hierarchy of tasks, one can allocate resources (personnel, materials, technology, and environment) to the tasks. In some cases, critical resources (e.g., expertise) may be in short supply and the task hierarchy may have to be restructured or restructured to meet the constraints. Team size and structure may also become an issue in determining the extent to which activities may be conducted concurrently.

3.2.5. Risk Management No project ever goes right. There is always a need to resolve problems that occur during the course of the project. A manager is handicapped in reacting to problems if they come as surprises. The discipline of risk management is applied to identify and mitigate risks before they become problems. Two kinds of risks are relevant—risks to the conduct of the project and risks to the operation of the completed product. Both should be anticipated and managed.

IEEE provides a standard risk management process:

Process

IEEE Std 1540-2001
IEEE Standard for Software Life Cycle Processes—
Risk Management
This standard provides a life cycle process for software risk management
suitable for use with IEEE/EIA 12207.
Allocated to: Software Engineering Process Knowledge Area

The process described in IEEE Std 1540[31] is designed to "plug into" the process framework of IEEE/EIA 12207.0. It provides six activities:

- Plan and implement risk management
- Manage the project risk profile
- Perform risk analysis
- Perform risk monitoring
- Perform risk treatment
- Evaluate the risk management process

The treatment of risk—addressing problems that haven't happened yet—always competes for resources with the ongoing management of the project—including problems that have already happened. Some organizations prefer to use dedicated staff for risk analysis and monitoring while giving line management the responsibility for risk treatment. In this way, decisions regarding the application of resources rest with the line managers while top management is apprised of the overall risk profile of the project.

In high-risk projects, it may be appropriate at its outset to negotiate policies and criteria for abandonment of the project.

3.2.6. Quality Management Because of tight schedules and competition for resources, managers are unlikely to get something if they don't ask for it—quality is no different in that regard. The desired quality of products must be characterized in measurable terms. Often processes (rather than direct measurement) are used to evaluate the achievement of quality. An IEEE standard is helpful:

Plan

IEEE Std 730-2002
IEEE Standard for Software Quality Assurance Plans
This standard specifies the format and content of Software Quality
Assurance plans.
Allocated to: Software Quality Knowledge Area

IEEE Std 730 provides an overview of quality assurance planning. It takes a broad look at the problem and explains how quality considerations are involved in all aspects of managing the project.

3.2.7. Plan Management It is obvious that the project must be managed during its execution, but perhaps not so obvious that the plan itself must be managed. Despite the fact that nearly continuous change destabilizes any plan, the plan itself must not be allowed to float and become meaningless. The project must adopt a discipline for monitoring, reviewing and revising plans that they are stable in application while responsive to change.

---

[31] IEEE Std 1540 was recently adopted by JTC 1 via the fast-track process as ISO/IEC 16085. JTC 1/SC 7 and S2ESC are jointly revising the standard for approval by both organizations. The resulting standard will be numbered as ISO/IEC 16085 and IEEE Std 16085, respectively.

3.3. Software Project Enactment

The management process of IEEE/EIA 12207.0 requires the manager to control the execution of the project by monitoring and reporting progress, and investigating, analyzing, and resolving problems that arise. This can be a substantial burden in an organization that does not use a process-based approach to project execution. On the other hand, enacting project processes—especially ones based on organizationally mature processes—supplements the manager's attention with a number of additional control mechanisms. This section considers some of the issues that arise in controlling a project.

3.3.1. Supplier Contract Management   To a harried manager, subcontracting a portion of the project must seem like an easy way to conserve and focus management time and attention. Of course, subcontracting introduces its own problems. IEEE offers a recommended practice for software acquisition:

Process

IEEE Std 1062, 1998 Edition (R2002)
IEEE Recommended Practice for Software Acquisition
This document recommends a set of useful practices that can be selected and applied during software acquisition. It is primarily suited toacquisitions that include development or modification rather than off-the-shelf purchase.
Allocated to: Software Engineering Management Knowledge Area

Although the standard includes within its scope the purchase of completed software, it specializes in the acquisition of software development. It characterizes acquisition in nine steps:

- Planning organizational strategy
- Implementing the organization's process
- Determining the software requirements
- Identifying potential suppliers
- Preparing contract documents
- Evaluating proposals and selecting the suppliers
- Managing supplier performance
- Accepting the software
- Using the software

3.3.2. Process Monitoring   Management has a continuing responsibility to monitor the execution of the project to determine its progress toward its goals in terms of deliverables and completed project requirements. The manager should monitor the expenditure of effort and other resources, accumulated costs, expended schedule, and changes to the project's risk profile. Measurement data is crucial to performing clear analysis. An IEEE standard describes productivity measurement:

Measure

IEEE Std 1045-1992 (R2002)
IEEE Standard for Software Productivity Metrics
This standard provides a consistent terminology for software productivity measures and defines a consistent way to measure the elements that go into computing software productivity.
Allocated to: Software Engineering Management Knowledge Area

The standard is remarkable, not for its scope, but for its precision. It defines an "input primitive"—staff hours—and three "output primitives"—source statements of code, function points, and document pages—and a number of relationships between them. The concept is simple, but successful implementation of productivity measurement requires dealing with a morass of details in defining the primitives. The standard serves as a guide in navigating those details.

One of the "output primitives" mentioned in IEEE Std 1045 is function points. Function point counting is a popular measurement primitive because it is relatively independent of implementation and can be calculated as soon as requirements are defined. Function points belong to a class of measures called "functional size" that are defined in this IEEE standard:

Measure

IEEE Std 14143.1-2000
IEEE Adoption of ISO/IEC 14143-1:1998, Information Technology—
Software Measurement—Functional Size Measurement—
Part 1: Definition of Concepts
This standard describes the fundamental concepts of a class of measures collectively known as functional size.
Allocated to: Software Requirements Knowledge Area

3.3.3. Process Control   A manager must control the project's processes by taking corrective action when anomalies arise. However, the appropriate correction is not always clear from the observed anomaly. Defect analysis or root-cause analysis is often required in order to determine the process failure that is leading to the defects. Software anomalies typically arise in such numbers and are so elusive in their cause that individual defect analysis is not appropriate. Instead, defects must be grouped into categories for analysis. Software anomaly classification is treated by this IEEE standard:

Tool

IEEE Std 1044-1993 (R2002)
IEEE Standard Classification for Software Anomalies
This standard provides a uniform approach to the classification of anomalies found in software and its documentation. It includes helpful lists of anomaly classifications and related data.
Allocated to: Software Quality Knowledge Area

The standard describes the processing of anomalies from their initial discovery to their final disposition, as well as suggestions for categories into which anomalies may be classified. A minimum set of classification data is prescribed.

Perhaps the best known process for controlling software projects is configuration management (CM). Software professionals may consider configuration management to be a subject specific to software, but software CM is actually a subset of a far broader discipline. From the viewpoint of project management, it is cited as a "technique" of the "overall change control process" in the PMBOK® Guide, and can be used not only to control the software product but also to control the overall management process. CM also has an important relationship to systems engineering processes; particularly for software projects that are a part of the development of an encompassing system, it may be desirable to view software CM as an instance of systems level CM. Finally, CM can be regarded as an aspect of quality management; ISO 10007 provides guidance from this viewpoint.

Because CM is well rooted in a broader discipline, software CM was probably the first software discipline to achieve widespread agreement. Nearly all sources describe it similarly. IEEE provides an excellent standard on the subject:

Plan

IEEE Std 828-1998
IEEE Standard for Software Configuration Management Plans
This standard specifies the content of a Software Configuration Management plan along with requirements for specific activities.
Allocated to: Software Configuration Management Knowledge Area

3.4. Review and Evaluation

The management process of IEEE/EIA 12207.0 requires that software products and plans should be evaluated and the evaluated results assessed for achievement of objectives and completion of plans.

Evaluations of the progress toward achieving product objectives are often considered at major project milestones are reached. The scheduling of these milestone reviews is typically considered an important part of project planning. The form and scope of the reviews, though, vary depending on the project life cycle model and other characteristics of the product and project. An IEEE standard deals with project reviews:

Process

IEEE Std 1028-1997 (R2002)
IEEE Standard for Software Reviews
This standard defines five types of software reviews and procedures for their execution. Review types include management reviews, technical reviews, inspections, walk-throughs, and audits.
Allocated to: Software Quality Knowledge Area

IEEE Std 1028 specifies the characteristics of five different types of reviews and audits—management review, technical review, inspection, walk-through, and audit. It does not specify reasons for conducting a review or provide requirements for using the results; instead it focuses on the conduct of the review itself. For each review type, it specifies responsibilities, inputs, entry criteria, procedures, exit criteria, and outputs.

Of course, project managers must also review the performance of personnel. Although important, this subject is not treated by IEEE standards.

3.5. Closure

Project closure may seem an existential issue—when it's over, it's over! Software projects are sufficiently complex, though, that intuition regarding completion cannot be trusted. The management process of IEEE/EIA 12207.0 states that "the manager shall determine whether the process is complete taking into account the criteria as specified in the contract or as part of organization's procedure" and "check the results and records of the software products, activities, and tasks employed for completeness." It goes on to say that the results should be appropriately archived.

In a two-party situation, legal considerations may advise formal agreement from the acquirer that the project is completed. Often, a suitable acceptance procedure is defined at the outset of the project. Mature software organizations will want to perform a post-mortem analysis of the project to draw lessons to be utilized for organizational improvement.

3.6. Software Engineering Measurement

The need for measurement pervades the practice of software engineering. Unfortunately, organizations implementing comprehensive measurement programs are still somewhat unusual. During the past decade, there has been a growth in interest in providing practical measurement programs, e.g., the Defense Department's Practical Software Measurement program [McGarry01]. Just as organizations have learned to focus on process definition and assessment, we can hope that they will begin implementing quantitative approaches to software project management.

The *SWEBOK Guide* provides the following definition "Measurement refers to the assignment of values and labels to aspects of software engineering (products, processes, and resources . . .) and the models that are derived from them whether these models are developed using statistical, expert knowledge, or other techniques."

Various measurement standards have been described throughout this book as they relate to the subject of the measurements. A unifying standard is this international standard on the process of software measurement:

ISO/IEC 15939:2002
Software Engineering—Software Measurement Process
This standard provides a life cycle process for software measurement suitable for use with IEEE/EIA 12207.
Allocated to: Software Engineering Process Knowledge Area

Process

In addition to describing a process for measurement, the standard also provides a framework of concepts and vocabulary that have been harmonized with the ISO vocabulary of metrology [ISO93]. Nevertheless, readers will often encounter terminology differences; for example, the term "metrics" is often used (even in standards) in place of the correct term—"measures."

ISO/IEC 15939 was written to describe a process that can be "plugged into" the framework of processes described in the 12207 standard. The standard describes four activities as part of the measurement process:

- *Establish and Sustain Measurement Commitment:* This involves determining organizational objectives (e.g., "be first to the marketplace"), defining the scope of measurement (e.g., project, site, enterprise), obtaining staff commitment, and allocating resources for the measurement program.
- *Plan the Measurement Process:* One must characterize the organizational unit in terms of processes, application domains, technology, and organizational interfaces. Based on the scope and organizational objectives, one identifies information needs and select measures addressing the information needs. Finally, data collection, analysis, and reporting procedures are defined as well as criteria for evaluating the collected information. The procedures must be deployed, provided with resources, and supported by tools and technology.
- *Perform the Measurement Process:* It is important that measurement is not viewed as an additional burden levied upon already overworked staff. Data collection must be integrated with existing processes. Of course, additional resources must be allocated for the analysis, aggregation, and communication of data.
- *Evaluate Measurement:* An important result of measurement is organizational improvement. Management should evaluate the information products and the measurement process against their intent and determine appropriate improvements.

4. STANDARDS IN THE SOFTWARE ENGINEERING MANAGEMENT KNOWLEDGE AREA

4.1. IEEE Std 1045-1992, IEEE Standard for Software Productivity Metrics

The S2ESC standard for software productivity metrics, 1045, was completed in 1992 and reaffirmed in 2003. The purpose of the 32-page standard is to assist the user in collecting consistent productivity data to be used for management and process improvement. It provides "a foundation to accurately measure software productivity . . . through a set of precisely defined units of measure."

The standard defines a framework for measuring and reporting the data by defining measurement primitives that are input to the software project and output from the software project, and relationships between them. The basic "input primitive" is staff-hours. The basic "output primitives" are source statements, function points, and document pages. Productivity can be evaluated by various mathematical operations on these primitives. There's nothing surprising about any of this; the strength of this standard is the degree of precision used in defining the primitives and their relationships. An additional clause provides a discussion of the factors that affect productivity.

The terminology used in this standard is not the same as the framework of terms provided by ISO/IEC 15939. However, users should have little difficulty in applying the standards together.

4.2. IEEE Std 1058-1998, IEEE Standard for Software Project Management Plans

The 1998 version of this standard merged two predecessor documents, 1058.1 and 1058a, into a single document. This 20-page document is the key standard in the IEEE S2ESC collection for project management requirements focusing specifically on software. It specifies the format and content of a software project management plan (SPMP) but does not prescribe techniques for developing the plan or managing the project. The standard is addressed to software project managers and personnel who prepare and update plans and control adherence to those plans. It is intended to be applicable to all forms of software projects, not merely those concerned with new product development. Projects of all sizes can make use of this standard although smaller ones may require less formality.

A user may claim "content compliance" with the standard if all of the required information is included. "Format compliance" may be claimed if the plan is arranged in the recommended structure. A plan that is in "format compliance" with the standard would be organized as shown in Table 9.

The 1998 revision of the standard made it thoroughly consistent with the process requirements of IEEE/EIA 12207.0 and the data requirements of IEEE/EIA 12207.1. Project management experts advise me that it is not thoroughly reconciled with IEEE Std 1490, the adoption of the Project Management Institute's Project Management Body of Knowledge. The inconsistencies with that document, though, are unlikely to cause substantial difficulties in applying the standard.

IEEE S2ESC and ISO/IEC JTC 1/SC 7 have recently agreed to cooperate on a joint revision that merges IEEE Std 1058 and ISO/IEC Technical Report 16326 resulting in a single standard for software project management. The resulting standard is likely to be numbered as 16326 by both organizations.

4.3. IEEE Std 1062, 1998 Edition, IEEE Recommended Practice for Software Acquisition

This is the key IEEE standard for the software acquisition process. It was approved in 1993 as a "recommended practice," meaning that its provisions are generally recommendations rather than requirements. The 1998 edition, which was reaffirmed in 2002, incorporated an annex explaining the document's relationship with the data provisions of IEEE/EIA 12207.1. The 43-page document provides a set of practices that are useful in the management and execution of software acquisition. Software is treated in three categories— off-the-shelf, modified, and fully developed—but the document claims to be better suited to the latter two categories. The practice encompasses nine steps covering a broad scope ranging from planning the overall strategy through follow-up on the use of the acquired software. A number of checklists are provided in an annex. The document recommends the preparation of an acquisition plan in the format shown in Table 10. (You can see the nine steps of acquisition in clause 5 of the plan's outline.)

The document may be applied in a variety of contexts: to implement the acquisition requirements of an ISO 9001 quality management system; to detail the management process of a project that will acquire software products; to

TABLE 9. Outline of software management plan suggested by IEEE Std 1058

1. Overview
   1.1 Project summary
       1.1.1 Purpose, scope, and objectives
       1.1.2 Assumptions and constraints
       1.1.3 Project deliverables
       1.1.4 Schedule and budget summary
   1.2 Evolution of the SPMP
2. References
3. Definitions
4. Project organization
   4.1 External interfaces
   4.2 Internal structure
   4.3 Roles and responsibilities
5. Managerial process plans
   5.1 Project start-up plan
       5.1.1 Estimation plan
       5.1.2 Staffing plan
       5.1.3 Resource acquisition plan
       5.1.4 Project staff training plan
   5.2 Work plan
       5.2.1 Work activities
       5.2.2 Schedule allocation
       5.2.3 Resource allocation
       5.2.4 Budget allocation
   5.3 Control plan
       5.3.1 Requirements control plan
       5.3.2 Schedule control plan
       5.3.3 Budget control plan
       5.3.4 Quality control plan
       5.3.5 Reporting plan
       5.3.6 Metrics collection plan
   5.4 Risk management plan
   5.5 Project closeout plan
6. Technical process plans
   6.1 Process model
   6.2 Methods, tools, and techniques
   6.3 Infrastructure plan
   6.4 Product acceptance plan
7. Supporting process plans
   7.1 Configuration management plan
   7.2 Verification and validation plan
   7.3 Documentation plan
   7.4 Quality assurance plan
   7.5 Reviews and audits plan
   7.6 Problem resolution plan
   7.7 Subcontractor management plans
   7.8 Process improvement plan
8. Additional plans
9. Plan annexes
10. Plan index

TABLE 10. Outline of software acquisition plan suggested by IEEE Std 1062

1. Introduction
2. References
3. Definitions
4. Software acquisition overview
   4.1 Organization
   4.2 Schedule
   4.3 Resource summary
   4.4 Responsibilities
   4.5 Tools, techniques, and methods
5. Software acquisition process
   5.1 Planning organizational strategy
   5.2 Implementing the organization's process
   5.3 Determining the software requirements
   5.4 Identifying potential suppliers
   5.5 Preparing contract documents
   5.6 Evaluating proposals and selecting the suppliers
   5.7 Managing supplier performance
   5.8 Accepting the software
   5.9 Using the software
6. Software acquisition reporting requirements
7. Software acquisition management requirements
   7.1 Anomaly resolution and reporting
   7.2 Deviation policy
   7.3 Control procedures
   7.4 Standards, practices, and conventions
   7.5 Performance tracking
   7.6 Quality control of plan
8. Software acquisition documentation requirements

implement the acquisition side of the acquirer/supplier relationship described by the 12207 standard; or to implement the activities required by 12207 for the management of subcontractors.

The body of the document references several other IEEE S2ESC standards to provide detailed implementation of the steps involved in software acquisition. It also references ISO/IEC 9126 as a framework of quality characteristics that might be required in acquired software.

5. SUMMARY

This chapter has provided an overview of the Software Engineering Management knowledge area of the IEEE Computer Society's *Guide to the Software Engineering Body of Knowledge*. Fourteen IEEE and ISO/IEC standards have been offered as relevant to the knowledge area. The presentation has been divided into six subsections provided by the *SWEBOK Guide*:

- *Initiation and Scope Definition:* Software project management is part of a more general project management disciplines described in IEEE Std

1490. An overall description of software project management is provided by the management process of IEEE/EIA 12207.0.

- *Software Project Planning:* A detailed treatment of software project planning can be found in IEEE Std 1058. The documentation process of 12207 and the guidance of IEEE/EIA 12207.1 assist in planning documentation of a project. IEEE Std 1540 complements 12207 with a risk management process. A detailed treatment of quality assurance is contained in IEEE Std 730.

- *Software Project Enactment:* IEEE Std 1062 guides the manager in acquiring software components or development. IEEE Std 1045 provides rigorous definitions for productivity measurement and IEEE Std 14143.1 defines the class of "functional size" measures. IEEE Std 1044 deals with defect classification and IEEE Std 828 adds detail to the configuration management process.

- *Review and Evaluation:* IEEE Std 1028 defines five types of management reviews.

- *Closure:* The management process of 12207 treats project closure.

- *Software Engineering Measurement:* ISO/IEC 15939 complements the 12207 standard with a process for systematic measurement.

Chapter *13*

Knowledge Area: Software Engineering Process

Of all the subjects in the discipline of software engineering, process is the one receiving the most attention today. It is commonly believed that the implementation of a sound software development process is strongly correlated with the production of high-quality software products. Of course, this attitude is not unique to software development—the ISO 9000 standards apply the same premise to the management of all organizations.

This chapter surveys the concepts, processes, and activities related to software engineering process as well as the standards supporting them. The chapter is organized according to the subject's treatment in the *Guide to the Software Engineering Body of Knowledge* [SWEBOK04], and much of the text is paraphrased from that source. (The knowledge area editor for the chapter in the *SWEBOK Guide* was Khaled El Emam.) The relevant IEEE software engineering standards, as well as a few from other sources, are mentioned in the context of the knowledge described by the SWEBOK. In all, 16 relevant standards will be mentioned. At the end of the chapter, the standards allocated to this knowledge area are described in greater detail. Cross-references to other chapters provide access to descriptions of the other relevant standards.

1. KNOWLEDGE AREA SCOPE

The scope of the Software Engineering Process Knowledge Area is defined by [SWEBOK04] as being

> *The Software Engineering Process KA can be examined on two levels. The first level encompasses the technical and managerial activities ... that are performed*

The Road Map to Software Engineering: A Standards-Based Guide, by James W. Moore
Copyright © 2006 by IEEE Computer Society

during software acquisition, development, maintenance, and retirement. The second is the meta-level, which is concerned with the definition, implementation, assessment, measurement, management, change, and improvement of the software life cycle processes themselves. The first level is covered by the other KAs in the Guide. This KA is concerned with the second.

The term "software engineering process" can be interpreted in different ways, and this may cause confusion.

- *One meaning, where the word "the" is used, as in "the software engineering process," could imply that there is only one right way of performing software engineering tasks. This meaning is avoided in the Guide, because no such process exists. Standards such as IEEE 12207 speak of software engineering processes, meaning that there are many processes involved, such as Development Process or Configuration Management Process.*
- *A second meaning refers to the general discussion of processes related to software engineering. This is the meaning intended in the title of this KA, and the one most often intended in the KA description.*
- *Finally, a third meaning could signify the actual set of activities performed within an organization, which could be viewed as one process, especially from within the organization. This meaning is used in the KA in a very few instances.*

This KA applies to any part of the management of software life cycle processes where procedural or technological change is being introduced for process or product improvement.

This KA does not explicitly address human resources management . . . and systems engineering. . . .

It should be noted that systems engineering processes are out of the scope of the *SWEBOK Guide* but are treated in this book. The subject is briefly mentioned in this chapter and treated more completely in Chapter 16, Related Disciplines, as well as Chapter 20, System Life Cycle Processes.

2. KNOWLEDGE AREA SUMMARY

The *SWEBOK Guide* divides the Software Engineering Process Knowledge Area into four subareas—an organization followed by this chapter. The Introduction of the *SWEBOK Guide* summarizes this knowledge area as follows:

The Software Engineering Process KA is concerned with the definition, implementation, assessment, measurement, management, change, and improvement of the software engineering process itself. It is divided into four subareas.

*The first subarea presents **Process Implementation and Change**. The topics here are process infrastructure, the software process management cycle, models for process implementation and change, and practical considerations.*

*The second subarea deals with **Process Definition**. It includes the topics of software life cycle models, software life cycle processes, notations for process definitions, process adaptation, and automation.*

*The third subarea is **Process Assessment**. The topics here include process assessment models and process assessment methods.*

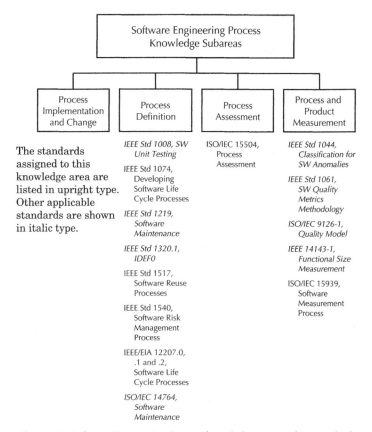

Figure 14. *Software Engineering Process knowledge area and its standards*

*The fourth subarea describes **Process and Product Measurements**. The software engineering process covers general product measurement, as well as process measurement in general. Measurements specific to KAs are described in the relevant KA. The topics are process measurement, software product measurement, quality of measurement results, software information models, and process measurement techniques.*

The knowledge area breakdown is illustrated in Figure 14, which also shows the standards relevant to this knowledge area.

3. KNOWLEDGE AREA DESCRIPTION

The objective of software engineering process is to introduce new or better individual, project or organizational processes to actual practice. The subject is relevant to organizations of all sizes. Improvement can be performed at any scale, including small organizations, small teams, and individuals.

3.1. Process Implementation and Change

This topic addresses the situation when processes are deployed within a project or organization, or changed. In both cases, practices must be changed. In tougher situations, corporate culture may be affected.

3.1.1. Process Infrastructure Meaningful process engineering requires an infrastructure appropriate to the size of the organization or team. As in any form of business investment, management commitment must be obtained, resources must be identified and responsibilities must be assigned to the appropriate parts of the organization. It is not appropriate to leave this job to the developers—their primary function is to produce software systems. Instead, one must establish a process team that communicates with the process users, but that has distinct resources and roles. Two types of infrastructure are popularly used—a Software Engineering Process Group and an Experience Factory. An SEPG is typically a team that cuts across the various needed parts of the organization. An Experience Factory is an improvement organization that is parallel to the project organization.

IEEE/EIA 12207 contains some provisions concerning the general infrastructure needed by a project, including its process infrastructure. It does this by defining an infrastructure process and assigning responsibilities to that process:

From IEEE/EIA 12207.0, Clause 7.2, Infrastructure Process:

7.2.1 Process implementation. This activity consists of the following tasks:

7.2.1.1 The infrastructure should be defined and documented to meet the requirements of the process employing this process, considering the applicable procedures, standards, tools, and techniques.

7.2.1.2 The establishment of the infrastructure should be planned and documented.

7.2.2 Establishment of the infrastructure. This activity consists of the following tasks:

7.2.2.1 The configuration of the infrastructure should be planned and documented. Functionality, performance, safety, security, availability, space requirements, equipment, costs, and time constraints should be considered.

7.2.2.2 The infrastructure shall be installed in time for execution of the relevant process.

7.2.3 Maintenance of the infrastructure. This activity consists of the following task:

7.2.3.1 The infrastructure shall be maintained, monitored, and modified as necessary to ensure that it continues to satisfy the requirements of the process employing this process. As part of maintaining the infrastructure, the extent to which the infrastructure is under configuration management shall be defined.

The "process implementation" of clause 7.2.1 actually refers to the implementation of the Infrastructure Process itself. As you can see, the provisions are very general.

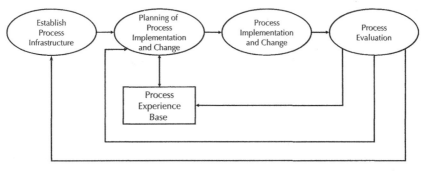

Adapted from [SWEBOK01]

Figure 15. *Model of the software process engineering cycle*

3.1.2. Plan-Do-Check-Act Cycle It should be obvious that a good process is not the end-goal of any business—its real objectives are the products and services that it sells to others. The emphasis on process, particularly in the software industry, rests on the premise that good products result from the execution of good processes. As a corollary then, process improvement should result in product quality improvement. Since software quality is so difficult to measure, process improvement—even in the absence of validation—is often pursued as a business goal in itself.

Figure 15 depicts process engineering in the form of the commonly-known "Plan-Do-Check-Act" (PDCA) cycle.[32] The rectangle is a repository of data gathered from experience. The ovals are activities. The activities are sequenced in a never-ending cycle permitting continuous feedback and improvement of software engineering processes.

The activity to "Establish Process Infrastructure" includes gaining management commitment, identifying resources, and designating responsibilities. This might be a one-time activity in a perfect world, but in the real world, it is a continuous activity competing with other organizational initiatives for resources and attention. The core activities of process engineering are the two shown in the middle of the figure. The objective of the "Planning" activity is to understand the goals of the business and its needs for process, identify its strengths and weaknesses, and make a plan for change. The objective of the "Implementation" activity is execute the plan, including tool deployment, procedural changes, and staff training. The objective of "Process Evaluation" is to determine if the expected benefits actually occurred and to adjust plans accordingly. The "Process Experience Base" is a repository of lessons learned and other experience from past improvement activities; it can be applied to make future plans more realistic.

3.1.3. Models for Process Implementation and Change Two well-known paradigms for process improvement are the Quality Improvement Paradigm (QIP)

---

[32] The figure is adapted from one provided in [SWEBOK01]. It has the same content, but has been rearranged to be comparable to similar figures in IEEE Std 1540 and ISO/IEC 15939.

[SEL96], and the IDEAL (Initiating, Diagnosing, Establishing, Acting & Learning) model of the SEI [Briand99].

3.1.4. Practical Considerations Process implementation is an example of organizational change and is fraught with all the same difficulties. Typically, successful organizations treat process implementation as a project in its own right, with appropriate management and review procedures. In many cases, substantial technology transfer is also required. The evaluation of process implementation can be either qualitative or quantitative. The evaluation can focus on the process itself or on the outcomes of the process implementation, for example, product characteristics or financial results.

IEEE/EIA 12207.0 provides organizational level processes that are relevant to process implementation and change. The Improvement Process places requirements on establishing, assessing, measuring, controlling, and improving processes:

From IEEE/EIA 12207.0, Clause 7.3, Improvement Process:

7.3.1 Process establishment. This activity consists of the following task:

7.3.1.1 The organization shall establish a suite of organizational processes for all software life cycle processes as they apply to its business activities. The processes and their application to specific cases shall be documented in organization's publications. As appropriate, a process control mechanism should be established to develop, monitor, control, and improve the process(es).

7.3.2 Process assessment. This activity consists of the following tasks:

7.3.2.1 A process assessment procedure should be developed, documented, and applied. Assessment records should be kept and maintained.

7.3.2.2 The organization shall plan and carry out review of the processes at appropriate intervals to assure their continuing suitability and effectiveness in the light of assessment results.

7.3.3 Process improvement. This activity consists of the following tasks:

7.3.3.1 The organization shall effect such improvements to its processes as it determines to be necessary as a result of process assessment and review. Process documentation should be updated to reflect improvement in the organizational processes.

7.3.3.2 Historical, technical, and evaluation data should be collected and analyzed to gain an understanding of the strengths and weaknesses of the employed processes. These analyses should be used as feedback to improve these processes, to recommend changes in the direction of the projects (or subsequent projects), and to determine technology advancement needs.

7.3.3.3 Quality cost data should be collected, maintained, and used to improve the organization's processes as a management activity. These data shall serve the purpose of establishing the cost of both the prevention and resolution of problems and non-conformity in software products and services.

Another relevant process, Training, addresses a wide range of training needs, including management and software engineering, for personnel in the organization. Both the Improvement and Training processes can be considered to apply at the organizational level for deploying organizationally adopted processes. However, either can also be applied at the project level. The Supply process of 12207 has provisions intended to ensure the availability of appropriate processes and trained personnel on each project:

From IEEE/EIA 12207.0, Clause 5.2, Supply Process:

5.2.4 Planning. This activity consists of the following tasks: . . .

5.2.4.2 If not stipulated in the contract, the supplier shall define or select a software life cycle model appropriate to the scope, magnitude, and complexity of the project. The processes, activities, and tasks of this International Standard shall be selected and mapped onto the life cycle model. . . .

5.2.4.5 The supplier shall develop and document project management plan(s) based upon the planning requirements and options selected in 5.2.4.4. Items to be considered in the plan include but are not limited to the following: . . .

b) Engineering environment (for development, operation, or maintenance, as applicable), including test environment, library, equipment, facilities, standards, procedures, and tools; . . .

o) Training of personnel (see 7.4).

Each of the other processes of 12207 begins with a Process Implementation activity to ensure that appropriate organizational or project-specific processes are applied to the job.

3.2. Process Definition

Software engineering processes are defined for a number of reasons ranging from human communication to automated support of execution. The form of definition—policy, standard, procedure, etc.—depends greatly on its intended usage.

It's a common fallacy that a single set of processes can be defined that will be useful in all enterprises. (The US Department of Defense made that mistake in applying military standards like MIL-STD-2167 to all of its acquisitions; now the DoD allows contractors to define their own processes.) In defining its processes, an enterprise must consider a number of factors:

- Organizational imperatives—for example, ISO 9000 conformance.
- Organizational competencies—for example, systems engineering or project management.
- Industry sector characteristics—for example, requirements for dependability or safety.

- Demands of dominant customers—for example, military standards for defense acquisitions.
- Organizational size, strategic plans, customs, and cultures.

Every organization has a different set of factors affecting its process requirements. That's why no single "best" set of processes can be defined that is suitable to all enterprises.

The real payoff comes from the implementation of procedures, templates, tools, training and other infrastructural support at the enterprise level. It is these resources that enable repeatable execution of processes, portability of staff and the resulting organizational improvement. Finally, of course, enterprise policies must be established to motivate usage of the enterprise processes, to systematically monitor execution for desirable changes, and to complete the cycle of organizational improvement.

Processes can be described at different levels of abstraction. One useful way of classifying the levels of abstraction was provided by Victor Basili. In performing his work on the "component factory," Basili needed to provide appropriate process descriptions. He and his colleagues [Basili92, Heineman94] found that three different forms of description seem useful:

- The *Reference* view describes a process as a coherent, cohesive set of activities that can sensibly be performed by a single agent.
- The *Conceptual* view describes flow of control and data among the agents.
- The *Implementation* view maps the agents to the organization chart and selects policies, procedures, and tools to implement the processes.

The following sections describe standards that contribute to the reference and conceptual views. The implementation view is not specified by standards; instead it is provided by the adopting organization through its provision of corporate policies, procedures and tools.

3.2.1. Life Cycle Models

A life cycle model provides a high-level characterization of the temporal relationships among processes during the life cycle of a software product or service. At the reference level of description, processes may be independent of the life cycle model. At the conceptual and implementation levels, though, the processes depend upon the life cycle model. Commonly used models include waterfall, incremental delivery, evolutionary development, prototype-based, reuse-based, and automated synthesis. Both the Supply and Acquisition processes of IEEE/EIA 12207.0 require early selection of a life cycle model for any software project. Guidance for selecting among the first three mentioned models is provided in Annex I of IEEE/EIA 12207.2.

3.2.2. Software Life Cycle Processes

Life cycle processes per se have no temporal ordering. The temporal relationships among the processes are provided by the life cycle model. In defining life cycle processes, organizations may draw upon a variety of sources. A rich source is provided by available standards. It must be noted, though, that the standards do not describe the processes themselves. Instead, the standards describe characteristics that the processes should have and the organizations define processes that meet the requirements of the standards. There are two good reasons for implementing processes that conform to standards: (1) the standards are a summary of good practice in this area; and (2) a claim of conformance to a standard can be used as a shorthand description in describing organizational processes to customer and suppliers. Suitable standards are available at both the reference and conceptual levels of the Basili framework.

Reference-Level Process Standards   The most important reference-level standard for software engineering processes is IEEE/EIA 12207.0 (or its near-identical twin ISO/IEC 12207). The 12207 standard describes seventeen processes useful during the life cycle of a software product or service. The processes are described at the reference level of the Basili framework:

Process

IEEE/EIA 12207.0-1996
Industry Implementation of International Standard ISO/IEC 12207:1995, Standard for Information Technology— Software Life Cycle Processes
This standard provides a framework of processes used across the entire life cycle of software.
Allocated to: Software Engineering Process Knowledge Area

Another standard, IEEE/EIA 12207.2 takes the normative text of 12207.0 and supplements it with guidance that has been found to be useful in the acquisition of complex software-intensive systems.

Document

IEEE/EIA 12207.2-1997
Industry Implementation of International Standard ISO/IEC 12207:1995, Standard for Information Technology— Software Life Cycle Processes—Implementation Considerations
This document provides guidance for the implementation of the life cycle processes of IEEE/EIA 12207.0.
Allocated to: Software Engineering Process Knowledge Area

SC 7 also has a guide to the implementation of their version of the 12207 standard—ISO/IEC Technical Report 15271. Seeing the value of the process descriptions in 12207, SC 7 has recently written a similar standard for system life cycle processes, ISO/IEC 15288. Although that standard is beyond the scope of the *SWEBOK Guide*, it is mentioned here because it provides a system context for the processes of the 12207 standard. More detail on ISO/IEC 15288 can be found in Chapter 16, Related Disciplines, as well as Chapter 20, System Life Cycle Processes.

The 12207 standard was intended to describe a minimum set of processes applicable to the life cycle of all software products and services. Some circumstances demand additional processes, though. Two IEEE standards provide additional processes that "plug-into" the process framework already provided by 12207. IEEE Std 1540 provides a process for software risk management and IEEE Std 1517 provides a set of additional processes suitable for implementing systematic software reuse. In addition, ISO/IEC 15939, mentioned later in this chapter, provides a plug-in for a measurement process.

IEEE Std 1540-2001
IEEE Standard for Software Life Cycle Processes—
Risk Management
This standard provides a life cycle process for software risk management
suitable for use with IEEE/EIA 12207.
Allocated to: Software Engineering Process Knowledge Area

IEEE Std 1517-1999 (R2004)
IEEE Standard for Information Technology—
Software Life Cycle Processes—Reuse Processes
This standard provides life cycle processes for systematic software reuse
suitable for use with IEEE/EIA 12207.
Allocated to: Software Engineering Process Knowledge Area

Because the 12207 standard attempts to provide a **minimum** set of process requirements that are applicable to all systems, there are some circumstances where more detailed process requirements or guidance are desirable. Three standards are useful in this regard:

IEEE Std 1008-1987 (R2003)
IEEE Standard for Software Unit Testing
This standard describes a sound approach to software unit testing, and
the concepts and assumptions on which it is based.
Allocated to: Software Testing Knowledge Area

ISO/IEC 14764:1999
Information Technology—Software Maintenance
This standard provides guidance on implementing the maintenance
process provided in ISO/IEC 12207.
Allocated to: Software Maintenance Knowledge Area

IEEE Std 1219-1998, *Software Maintenance*, is an alternative to ISO/IEC 14764 but is not strictly built upon the requirements of the maintenance process provided by the 12207 standard.

IEEE Std 1219-1998
IEEE Standard for Software Maintenance
This standard describes a process for software maintenance and
its management.
Allocated to: Software Maintenance Knowledge Area

Conceptual Level Process Standards The transition from the reference level of process definition to the conceptual level requires the definition of interfaces to the reference level processes and characterization of the flows of control and data that provide the communication between the processes. An important aid in making this transition from the reference processes of 12207 is provided by IEEE/EIA 12207.1. This guide lists all of the data that is produced by the processes of IEEE/EIA 12207.1 and provides some characterization of that data:

Document

IEEE/EIA 12207.1-1996
Industry Implementation of International Standard ISO/IEC
12207:1995, Standard for Information Technology—
Software Life Cycle Processes—Life Cycle Data
This document provides guidance on recording data resulting from the
life cycle processes of IEEE/EIA 12207.0.
Allocated to: Software Engineering Process Knowledge Area

However, the key IEEE standard at the conceptual level is IEEE Std 1074. This standard provides a set of process building blocks that can be applied to define processes based on the requirements of 12207 or other life cycle process standards:

Process

IEEE Std 1074-1997
IEEE Standard for Developing Software Life Cycle Processes
This standard describes an approach for the definition of software life
cycle processes.
Allocated to: Software Engineering Process Knowledge Area

Unfortunately, the clarity of 1074 is diminished by some language that would make one think that it is a reference-level standard and itself provides the minimum requirements for software development processes, rather than deferring to other standards. A revision is underway to solve that problem.

3.2.3. Notations for Process Definitions Various notations, ranging from natural language to highly formal language, can be used to describe processes. The *SWEBOK Guide* mentions dataflow diagrams, Statecharts, Entry-Task-Validation-Exit (ETVX) modeling, Actor-Dependency Modeling, Structured Analyis and Design Technique (SADT), Petri Nets, rule-based, and Systems Dynamics. Three notations are well supported by standards. IEEE/EIA 12207 uses a disciplined decomposition approach to describe processes in terms of a hierarchy—process/task/activity. The hierarchy is described in Chapter 3, Principles of the S2ESC Collection. ISO/IEC 15504, mentioned previously in this chapter, describes processes by a statement of their purpose and a set of outcomes that may be assessed. (This approach has been taken up in SC 7's amendment to ISO/IEC 12207.) Finally, IDEF0 may be used to describe processes in progressive levels of detail:

Tool

IEEE Std 1320.1-1998 (R2004)
IEEE Standard for
Functional Modeling Language—Syntax and Semantics for IDEF0
This standard defines the IDEF0 modeling language used to represent
decisions, actions, and activities of an organization or system. IDEF0
may be used to define requirements in terms of functions to be
performed by a desired system.
Allocated to: Software Engineering Tools and Methods Knowledge Area

3.2.4. Process Adaptation   The definition of organizational processes follows a life cycle similar to that of software development. Requirements must be elicited, analyzed, specified, and validated; and then managed for the life of the organization. Investment must be applied to the development of procedures, guides, and tooling to implement the processes. Furthermore, the processes must be actively maintained in the face of changing needs and circumstances.

It is important to note that no predefined set of processes is suitable for all organizations. They should always be adapted to the needs and drivers of the organization. Most process standards, e.g., 12207, contain recommendations for adaptation.[33]

3.2.5. Automation   Processes may be implemented with a degree of automation—either to guide humans in the execution of the process or to directly enact the process. The tools are often provided as part of a process-centered development environment. In some cases, they are driven by the notations mentioned above.

3.3. Process Assessment

Process assessment is generally performed using a benchmarking paradigm. This is often implemented by measuring the *maturity* or *capability* of an organization's processes, comparing it against a norm, and deciding where improvement will be most effective. The norm for comparison is generally called a *process assessment model* and the means for measurement is generally called a process *assessment method*. The model captures some recognized version of good practices. The method provides a mechanism for determining if an organization implements those practices.

The most commonly used model in the United States is the Software Capability Maturity Model® (SW-CMM®) [Paulk93]. The US Department of Defense has generalized the model to include systems engineering processes; the result is called the Capability Maturity Model Integration® (CMMI®) [CMMI00].

There are two architectures for capability models, known as *continuous* and *staged*. The continuous model provides distinct evaluations of individual areas while the staged models provide overall assessment of organizational capability keyed to a roadmap for improvement.

A process assessment model is used in conjunction with a process assessment method to place focus on selected goals. For example, the SW-CMM model was applied by both the CMM-Based Appraisal for Internal Process Improvement (CBA-IPI) and Software Capability Evaluation (SCE) methods to address process improvement and supplier capability, respectively.

An emerging international standard on this subject is ISO/IEC 15504. The original Technical Report can be regarded as a trial use standard while the final version is under development:

---

[33] Some refer to adaptation as "tailoring." Unfortunately, this word, in the minds of many, refers to the discredited practice in Defense standards of permitting acquirers to change any provision of the standard, thus defeating supplier efforts to implement repeatable organizational processes. Unfortunately, some standards still permit free tailoring.

Process

ISO/IEC TR 15504 (nine parts)
Information Technology—Software Process Assessment
This technical report would provide requirements on methods for
performing process assessment as a basis for process improvement or
capability determination.
Allocated to: Software Engineering Process Knowledge Area

By definition, a Type 2 Technical Report, like TR 15504, is a work in progress—a preliminary product is published while work continues on a final standard. SC 7 has followed this strategy with its process assessment standard. The new version of 15504 will be published in five parts when completed.

Process

ISO/IEC (Draft) 15504 (five parts)
Information Technology—Process Assessment
This draft standard would provide requirements on methods for
performing process assessment as a basis for process improvement or
capability determination.
Allocated to: Software Engineering Process Knowledge Area

The version under development has been broadened to deal with the assessment of any business process—not just software. It provides a two-dimensional model of capability and processes. The process dimension is supplied by reference to an externally supplied process reference model that defines process based on a statement of purpose and a set of outcomes. (SC 7's amendment to ISO/IEC 12207 was motivated, in part, by the need for a process reference model suitable for use by 15504.) The capability dimension is provided by the new 15504 and consists of six process capability levels and associated attributes. An assessment is a set of process attribute ratings for each assessed process.

Other notable examples of assessment models are Trillium [April95] and Bootstrap [Haase94].

3.4. Process and Product Measurement

It seems fundamentally obvious that one must be able to measure process and product characteristics before one can hope to improve them. Nevertheless, effective means for measurement are relatively recent additions to software engineering as practiced. One barrier has been a confusing diversity of terminology for measurement and the measurement process. For example, the term "metric" has often been used to describe the combination of a measurement with a judgment regarding acceptability—a very simplistic model. New standards are providing richer models and better processes.

Most modern references suggest a goal-oriented approach to performing measurement. One starts with information needs and decides how to measure them rather than starting with measurements and figuring out how to use them. An international standard describes this approach.

Process

ISO/IEC 15939:2002
Software Engineering—Software Measurement Process
This standard provides a life cycle process for software measurement
suitable for use with IEEE/EIA 12207.
Allocated to: Software Engineering Process Knowledge Area

The standard provides a framework for describing measurement and a process for selecting, collecting, analyzing and interpreting measurements. The process is designed to be a "plug-in" to the 12207 standard.

3.4.1. Process Measurement   The idea behind measuring processes is to identify strengths and weaknesses for the purpose of evaluation, e.g., return on investment, and improvement. However, process measures are also useful in managing the project. Typically, a big assumption underlies most process measurement approaches—the assumption that the process has a close relationship to desired project outcomes despite the context in which the process is executed. Of course, in the real world, the relationship may not be as close or as obvious as desired. The introduction of additional inspections, for example, may reduce the cost of testing, but may delay entry into testing. Project resources have to be adjusted accordingly.

One important factor in the context of the process is the fidelity with which it is executed. Modern approaches to evaluating processes try to separate the process outcomes from the organization's capability to execute the processes. The recent Amendment to ISO/IEC 12207 provides a statement of purpose and outcomes for a large number of software life cycle processes. The revision of ISO/IEC 15504 to a standard provides a model for evaluating the capability of organizations implementing any set of processes defined by their purpose and outcomes.

3.4.2. Software Product Measurement   Three important categories of product measurement include product size, product structure, and product quality. There are available standards for size and quality.

Product size is often measured in terms of source lines of code. However, it is possible to measure the size of the requirements set by counting function points. IEEE Std 14143-1 provides the principles of functional size measurement:

Measure

IEEE Std 14143.1-2000
**IEEE Adoption of ISO/IEC 14143-1:1998, Information Technology—
Software Measurement—Functional Size Measurement—
Part 1: Definition of Concepts**
This standard describes the fundamental concepts of a class of
measures collectively known as functional size.
Allocated to: Software Requirements Knowledge Area

To measure the quality of software, one first needs a lexicon of characteristics to be measured and a method for measuring them. Two standards are helpful:

Terminology

ISO/IEC 9126-1:2001
Software Engineering—Product Quality—Part 1: Quality Model
This standard provides a model for software product quality covering internal quality, external quality, and quality in use. The model is in the form of a taxonomy of defined characteristics which software may exhibit.
Allocated to: Software Requirements Knowledge Area

The standard provides three models of quality—internal (while under development), external (as a completed artifact), and in-use (as meeting the users needs)—and a taxonomy of characteristics and subcharacteristics for each model. The terms and their classification are useful in selecting characteristics for measurement.

The second necessity is a methodology for measuring the characteristics. The developers of ISO/IEC 9126-1 are working on an extensive program of measurement standards. For now though, this IEEE standard is a compact description of a useful approach:

Measure

IEEE Std 1061-1998 (R2004)
IEEE Standard for a Software Quality Metrics Methodology
This standard describes a methodology–spanning the entire life cycle–for establishing quality requirements and identifying, implementing, and validating the corresponding measures.
Allocated to: Software Quality Knowledge Area

3.4.3. Quality of Measurement Results Two important issues in any form of measurement are *reliability* (Are there errors in the measured values?) and *validity* (Are we actually measuring the right thing?). For software processes, a critical aspect is *predictive validity*—does an improvement in the measured value during development actually predict an improved result in the product? The theory of measurement provides a scientific approach to the question. Useful practical information can be found in IEEE Std 1061, mentioned above.

3.4.4. Software Information Models The measurement process of ISO/IEC 15939 includes a series of activities similar to that shown in Figure 15, notably including the aggregation of a base of experience. Some organizations apply this historical data to develop models that will have predictive power for future projects. Of course, validation of such models involves substantial effort beyond merely collecting the data. Validation can be complicated when changes are made in the organizational process as a result of improvement efforts.

3.4.5. Process Measurement Techniques In order to perform process improvement, it is helpful to gather, analyze and interpret data regarding the performance of the processes. Furthermore, process measurement can be helpful in managing the project. It is possible to measure outcomes of processes or the processes themselves. Card [Card91] describes two general paradigms:

- *Analytic paradigm*: relying on quantitative evidence to make improvement decisions
- *Benchmarking paradigm*: identifying a successful organization to emulate

The second paradigm requires the assumption that imitating the practices of another successful organization will lead to success. Of course, one can apply both paradigms. The process assessment methods described previously are examples of the benchmarking paradigm.

When quantitative evaluation is impossible, there is a role for qualitative techniques—notably in identifying and analyzing process problems. Analysis might be applied as a diagnostic technique before changing a process or as an evaluation technique after a process change. A few common techniques are listed below:

- *Experimental Studies*: Setting up simulations, experiments, or dual projects to evaluate the likely result of a change in process.
- *Process Definition Review*: This is a technical review intended to spot deficiencies or potential improvements in a process definition. It is often performed as a comparison against a benchmark, such as the 12207 standard.
- *Root Cause Analysis*: This approach centers on defects that have been observed in the execution of a deployed process. One starts from the failure to achieve a process outcome and traces back a chain of causality to find the portion of the process that permitted the defect to occur. In performing causal analysis, one must use or develop defect categories in order to group data meaningfully. Orthogonal Defect Classification is a method for determining categories.
- *Statistical Process Control*: One can place software processes under statistical process control. The usual techniques, including control charts, can be used to analyze process instabilities.
- *Personal Software Process*: The Personal Software Process [Humphrey95] is a method for individuals to meaningfully collect and apply process measurement.

The IEEE has a standard that may be useful in practicing defect classification:

Tool

IEEE Std 1044-1993 (R2002)
IEEE Standard Classification for Software Anomalies
This standard provides a uniform approach to the classification of anomalies found in software and its documentation. It includes helpful lists of anomaly classifications and related data.
Allocated to: Software Quality Knowledge Area

4. STANDARDS IN THE SOFTWARE ENGINEERING PROCESS KNOWLEDGE AREA

4.1. IEEE Std 1074-1997, IEEE Standard for Developing Software Life Cycle Processes

S2ESC originally developed IEEE Std 1074 in 1991, performed minor revisions in 1995, and revised it in 1997 to better harmonize with IEEE/EIA 12207. The 88-page document is a standard for generating processes for software development and maintenance. It does not itself provide life cycle processes nor does it provide a life cycle model. The user, a process architect, must define the intended life cycle of the software, select a life cycle model, and then apply the standard to define processes suiting those needs.

As explained above, the 1074 standard is best understood at the contextual level of the Basili model. The resource that it provides to the architect is a set of 17 predefined and interrelated activity groups, composed from 65 activities, along with specified inputs and outputs, and entry and exit criteria. The architect composes the activity groups to create appropriate processes. (Requirements for those processes may be provided by other standards, notably 12207.) Finally, the processes may be augmented with organizational process assets, such as policies, standards, procedures, etc., to create implementable processes. (This last step may be regarded as leading into the implementation level of the Basili model.)

The 17 Activity Groups and 65 Activities of the 1074 standard are shown in Table 11.

Unfortunately, IEEE Std 1074-1997 contains language that suggests that it provides the minimum requirements for processes rather than deferring to other standards, such as 12207, for this purpose. A revision project is currently underway to address the problem.

4.2. IEEE Std 1517-1999, IEEE Standard for Information Technology—Software Life Cycle Processes—Reuse Processes

Although IEEE/EIA 12207.0 mentions software reuse, it does not provide the processes necessary to implement systematic software reuse on an organizational basis. IEEE Std 1517 was approved in 1999 to address that need. Along with adding activities and tasks to the existing processes of 12207, the 43-page standard also specifies new processes specifically oriented to software reuse. In particular, it adds the following new processes:

Category of Process	Processes
Organizational	Reuse Program Administration
Supporting	Asset Management
Cross-Project	Domain Engineering

Of course, the organizational and supporting categories of processes already exist in 12207. The cross-project category was invented in 1517 to deal with processes that span selected projects.

Like 12207, the standard structures processes as a hierarchy of processes composed of activities containing tasks. It describes the responsibilities inherent in the processes at the reference level of the Basili model but does not describe steps to be performed, temporal relationships, and data and control flows. The scope of the standard includes developing components from reusable components but not the integration of software packages provided in forms other than source code.

The document contains several useful annexes, including one describing categories of tools useful in supporting software reuse.

TABLE 11. Activities described by IEEE Std 1074

Section within IEEE Std 1074	Activity Groups	Activities
Project Management	Project Initiation	Create SW Life Cycle Process (SLCP) Perform Estimations Allocate Project Resources Define Metrics
	Project Planning	Plan Evaluations Plan Configuration Management Plan System Transition Plan Installation Plan Documentation Plan Training Plan Project Management Plan Integration
	Project Monitoring and Control	Manage Risks Manage the Project Identify SLCP Improvement Needs Retain Records Collect and Analyze Metric Data
Pre-Development	Concept Exploration	Identify Ideas or Needs Formulate Potential Approaches Conduct Feasibility Studies Refine and Finalize the Idea or Need
	System Allocation	Analyze Functions Develop System Architecture Decompose System Requirements
	Software Importation	Identify Imported Software Requirements Evaluate Software Import Sources Define Software Import Method Import Software
Development	Requirements	Define and Develop Software Requirements Define Interface Requirements Prioritize and Integrate Software Requirements
	Design	Perform Architectural Design Design Data Base Design Interfaces Perform Detailed Design
	Implementation	Create Executable Code Create Operating Documentation Perform Integration
Post-Development	Installation	Distribute Software Install Software Accept Software in Operational Environment
	Operation and Support	Operate the System Provide Technical Assistance and Consulting Maintain Support Request Log
	Maintenance	Identify Software Improvement Needs Implement Problem Reporting Method Reapply Software Life Cycle
	Retirement	Notify User Conduct Parallel Operations Retire System

TABLE 11. Continued

Section within IEEE Std 1074	Activity Groups	Activities
Integral	Evaluation	Conduct Reviews Create Traceability Matrix Conduct Audits Develop Test Procedures Create Test Data Execute Tests Report Evaluation Results
	Software Configuration Management	Develop Configuration Identification Perform Configuration Control Perform Status Accounting
	Documentation Development	Implement Documentation Produce and Distribute Documentation
	Training	Develop Training Materials Validate the Training Program Implement the Training Program

4.3. IEEE Std 1540-2001, IEEE Standard for Software Life Cycle Processes—Risk Management

IEEE/EIA 12207.0 mentions risk management in several places, but does not require a systematic treatment of risk. IEEE Std 1540 was developed that fill that need. The 24-page standard was published in 2001 to provide a risk management process that plugs cleanly into the process framework provided by 12207. The standard depicts the process as shown in Figure 16.

The figure illustrates the fundamental relationship of the risk management processes to the other processes of 12207. Risk Management monitors, analyzes, and may even make recommendations, but action requests are forwarded to the other processes for implementation. This permits risk treatment to be properly prioritized, resourced, and managed by the appropriate parties.

The 1540 standard suggests the content of three documents: risk management plan, risk action request, and risk treatment plan. The suggested content of the risk management plan is shown Table 12. The suggested content of a Risk Treatment Plan is shown in Table 13.

Currently, the IEEE standard is undergoing minor revision jointly with ISO/IEC JTC 1/SC 7. The primary intent is to harmonize the vocabulary of the standard with the vocabulary of ISO Guide 73 on risk management. It is also possible that the scope of the standard will be extended to include system-level risk management. The resulting standard will be shared by both JTC 1 and IEEE; it will be designated as ISO/IEC 16085 and IEEE Std 16085.

4.4. IEEE/EIA 12207, Software Life Cycle Processes

The 12207 standard occupies an important role in software process standardization for reasons in addition to its content. It is the first software process standard in recent history that has been widely viewed as a framework with

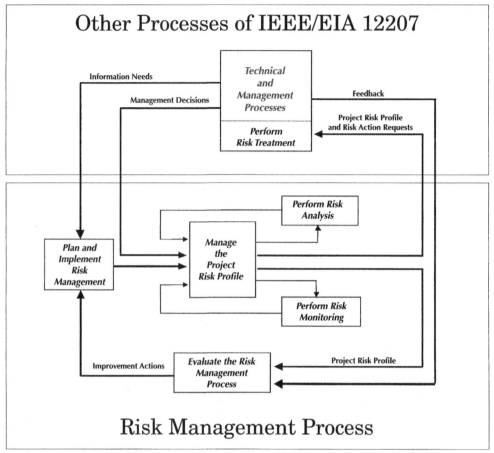

From IEEE Std 1540-2001, page 6, ©IEEE, 2001, used by permission

Figure 16. *Risk management process of IEEE Std 1540 and its relationship to other processes*

which other standards should be unified.[34] IEEE S2ESC has adopted a policy that its other standards will be harmonized with 12207.

ISO/IEC 12207.0 was originally approved by ISO/IEC JTC 1 in 1995 following development by an international working group of JTC 1/SC 7. Shortly thereafter, a joint committee of IEEE and the Electronics Industry Alliance (EIA) considered the document for adoption in the US. They chose to leave the body of the document untouched, aside from a one-page errata sheet, and to replace the annexes. The 75-page result was approved in 1996. They also wrote two additional parts, described later in this chapter.

---

[34] IEEE Std 730 on Software Quality Assurance may have briefly occupied a similar role when there were few other software engineering process standards and when the ISO 9000 series had yet to be developed.

TABLE 12. Outline of risk management plan content suggested by IEEE Std 1540

1. Overview
    1.1 Date of Issue and Status
    1.2 Issuing Organization
    1.3 Approval Authority
    1.4 Updates
2. Scope
        [Define the boundaries and limitations of risk on the project]
3. Reference Documents
4. Glossary
5. Risk Management Overview
        [Describe the specifics of risk management for this project or organization's situation.]
6. Risk Management Policies
        [Describe the guidelines by which risk management will be conducted.]
7. Risk Management Process Overview
8. Risk Management Responsibilities
        [Define the parties responsible for performing risk management.]
9. Risk Management Organization
        [Describe the function or organization assigned responsibility for risk management within
        the organizational unit.]
10. Risk Management Orientation and Training
11. Risk Management Costs and Schedules
12. Risk Management Process Description
        [If there is an organizational risk management process that is being used for this project or
        situation, refer to it. If adaptation of the process is appropriate, describe the adaptations
        made. Describe the procedures that implement the risk management process. If no
        organizational process exists, describe the risk management process and procedures to be
        used for the project or situation.]
    12.1 Risk Management Context
    12.2 Risk Analysis
    12.3 Risk Monitoring
    12.4 Risk Treatment
        [Describe how risks are to be treated. If a standard management process exists for handling
        deviations or problems, refer to this process. If risks require a separate risk treatment
        activity due to specific circumstance, describe this activity.]
13. Risk Management Process Evaluation
        [Describe how this project or organization will gather and use measurement information
        to help improve the risk management process for the project and/or for the
        organization.]
    13.1 Capturing Risk Information
    13.2 Assessing the Risk Management Process
    13.3 Generating Lessons Learned
14. Risk Communication
        [Describe how risk management information will be coordinated and communicated
        among stakeholders, such as what risks need reporting to which management level.]
    14.1 Process Documentation and Reporting
    14.2 Coordinating Risk Management with Stakeholders
    14.3 Coordinating Risk Management with Interested Parties
15. Risk Management Plan Change Procedures and History

TABLE 13. Outline of risk treatment plan suggested by IEEE Std 1540

1. Overview
  1.1 Date of Issue and Status
  1.2 Issuing Authority
  1.3 Approval Authority
  1.4 Updates
2. Scope
3. Reference Documents
4. Glossary
5. Planned Risk Treatment Activities and Tasks
  [Describe the specifics of the risk treatment selected for a risk or combination of risks found to be unacceptable. Describe any difficulties that may be found in implementing the treatment.]
6. Treatment Schedule
7. Treatment Resources and their Allocation
8. Responsibilities and Authority
  [Describe who is responsible for ensuring that the treatment is being implemented and their authority.]
9. Treatment Control Measures
  [Define the measures that will be used to evaluate the effectiveness of the risk treatment.]
10. Treatment Cost
11. Interfaces among Parties Involved
  [Describe any coordination among stakeholders or with the project's master plan that must occur for the treatment to be properly implemented.]
12. Environment/Infrastructure
  [Describe any environmental or infrastructure requirements or impacts, e.g., safety or security impacts that the treatment may have.]
13. Risk Treatment Plan Change Procedures and History

4.4.1. IEEE/EIA 12207.0-1996, Industry Implementation of International Standard ISO/IEC 12207:1995, Standard for Information Technology—Software Life Cycle Processes

The[35] 12207 standard specifies three classes of processes: *primary*, *organizational*,[36] and *supporting*. (There is also a special *tailoring* process, constrained in the IEEE/EIA version of the standard, that is applied to adapt the requirements of the other processes to deal with project-specific circumstances.) The primary processes identify five major roles played by an organization in the life cycle of software: *acquisition*, *supply*, *development*, *maintenance*, and *operation*. In the model chosen by the standard, an acquirer and a supplier enter into an agreement for the completion of a particular product or service. The supplier then executes one of the other three primary processes to perform the development, maintenance, or operations appropriate to the performance of the agreement. It is important to understand that—like the reference level of the Basili model—the agents performing the processes are roles to be assumed rather than permanent organizational entities. For example, a developer choosing to purchase a component of the soft-

[35] Much of the material in this section is based on Annex E of IEEE/EIA 12207.0. The principal drafter of the annex was Raghu Singh, the project editor of ISO/IEC 12207.
[36] It would have been more convenient if the writers of 12207 had used the word "enterprise" instead of "organizational." Used as the name of a specific class of processes, the term is easily confused with the concept of implementing project-level processes uniformly across an organization.

ware system would additionally execute the acquirer role. Or, a maintainer electing to rewrite a portion of the system could execute the developer role to do that job or could execute the acquirer role to arrange for some other organization to perform the development.

Any of the primary processes can invoke one or more of the supporting processes to accomplish appropriate objectives. (The supporting processes can be regarded as process subroutines.) The eight supporting processes are: *documentation, configuration management, quality assurance, verification, validation, joint review, audit*, and *problem resolution*.

Finally, four processes are regarded as inherent to an organization at the enterprise level: *management, infrastructure, improvement*, and *training*. Initiating any of the primary processes has the effect of instantiating the management process and the other appropriate organizational processes.

The life cycle processes of 12207 are deliberately broad and are intended to cover the entire life of software from conception through retirement—not just the development effort. Each of the processes of 12207 is hierarchically decomposed into a set of *activities* and then *tasks*—although, in some cases, the tasks are better regarded as simply individual requirements on the activities.

Evaluation is built into each of the processes rather than segregated. There are processes for verification, validation, and quality assurance, but these are all in addition to the fundamental requirements for evaluation incorporated in each process. The integral nature of evaluation is a consequence of a more general principle of total quality management—each of the primary processes incorporates its own "plan-do-check-act" cycle inherited from its instantiation of the organizational management process. For this reason, 12207 may be a better choice than IEEE Std 730 for implementing software processes intended to comply with the requirements of ISO 9001.

Although 12207 does not prescribe systems engineering life cycle processes, it does prescribe the minimum systems engineering context necessary for the successful execution of the software processes. The systems engineering context is specified as a set of activities intended to be executed by systems engineering processes or delegated to the 12207 developer. These activities include system requirements, system architecture, system integration, and system qualification testing.

The standard is intended to be independent of development technologies and methodologies and useful for any form of life cycle model, for example, waterfall, incremental, spiral, etc. In fact, one of the specified responsibilities of the supplier's role is to select a life cycle model[37] and map the requirements of the standard to that model. Furthermore, the developer is specifically tasked to detail the development portion of the model. Using the Basili model, we can understand those responsibilities as moving from the reference to the conceptual level of process implementation.

The 12207 standard is written in language appropriate for a contractual agreement between the acquirer and the supplier. It is a premise that even

---

[37] It is intentional that the supplier must describe the entire life cycle rather than merely the process being contracted. The motivation is to force contractors to take a broader view of the life cycle impact of their decisions.

within a single organization, some form of agreement must be reached between the party desiring the software and the party supplying the software. The formal contract-oriented provisions can be omitted for work performed within a single enterprise.

Although 12207 requires that certain information be documented, it does not prescribe any recording medium, format, or detailed content requirements. The documentation process is intended to plan and implement such requirements.

In 2002, ISO/IEC JTC 1/SC 7 completed an amendment to the international version of the standard. The amendment provides statements of purpose and outcomes for the processes of 12207 as well as many others. The amendment is to be regarded as a first step toward a harmonization of the 12207 process definition standard and the 15504 process assessment standard. The amendment will also play a future role in the harmonization of the 12207 software life cycle process standard with the 15288 system life cycle process standard. The amendment is an important future step toward improved integration of the standards but has little immediate impact on users of the standards. IEEE has not adopted the amendment and will probably wait for more concrete harmonization to occur.

4.4.2. IEEE/EIA 12207.1-1996, IEEE/EIA Guide for Information Technology—Software Life Cycle Processes—Life Cycle Data   The IEEE/EIA project to adapt 12207 has added two additional parts to the standard. The basic standard, described above, is 12207.0, i.e., part 0. IEEE/EIA 12207.1, i.e., part 1, is a 30-page guidance document providing recommendations expanding on the data objectives that were added as an annex of part 0. For those desiring guidance on how specific documents or electronic data should be associated with specific processes, part 1 provides recommendations on the content of various possible documents. In all, IEEE/EIA 12207 offers four different levels of detail regarding data recording:

- The two-page Annex H of 12207.0 lists general objectives for the recording of life cycle data, including purpose, operations, characteristics, types, and presentation form.
- The normative descriptions of processes in the main body of 12207.0 provide requirements for specific data that must be recorded in some manner.
- Clause 5 of 12207.1 lists seven "kinds" of generic information items (for example, plan, procedure, specification) and summarizes in a few hundred words the purpose and contents of each one. Clause 4 lists specific information items appropriate to the clauses of part 0, shows which "kind" of document is appropriate, and references other standards that may be helpful detailing them.
- Clause 6 of 12207.1 selects 30 of the most significant specific information items from Clause 4 and provides further details regarding recommended content.

It should be noted that Part 1 can be used as a conformance document even though it is labeled as a guide. Acquirers should refrain from using it to mandate documentation requirements, however, because it specifies requirements for the recording of data rather than the production of documents. Means for the appropriate and economical production of data are to be regarded as inherent to the deployment of the organization-level processes.

4.4.3. IEEE/EIA 12207.2-1997, IEEE/EIA Guide—Software Life Cycle Processes—Implementation Considerations   Part 2 of IEEE/EIA 12207 is a 101-page guide providing advice on the implementation of the processes prescribed by Part 0 in the context of US industrial and professional practices. The normative text of Part 0 is quoted and typographically enclosed in boxes. At appropriate intervals, guidance notes provide explanatory material and recommendations. In addition, several annexes have been added:

- A brief annex on the use of reusable software products.
- A list of 11 candidates for joint management reviews along with the purposes to which each might be applied.
- A brief discussion of software measurement categories.
- Guidance on development strategies.
- Guidance on categorization and prioritization of problem reports, along with a reference to IEEE Std 1044.
- A discussion of software product evaluation with references to ISO/IEC 9126, ISO/IEC 12119, and ISO/IEC 9127.
- A discussion of risk management.
- A summary matrix of IEEE and ISO/IEC standards that may usefully be applied in the implementation of the processes of 12207.

4.4.4. Conformance to IEEE/EIA 12207.0   ISO/IEC 12207 provides two types of conformance. The most typical type of conformance is appropriate to a project. In this case, conformance is achieved by executing the processes, activities and tasks selected by the tailoring process. The tailoring process permits the deletion of any process, activity, or task. The other form of conformance permits any organization (ranging from individual companies to national standards bodies) "imposing [the] standard as a condition of trade" to conform by "making public the minimum set of required processes, activities and tasks." IEEE/EIA 12207 is a public statement corresponding to this form of conformance. So the IEEE/EIA standard is a conforming adoption of ISO/IEC 12207.

The drafters of the IEEE/EIA adoption had several objectives concerning its provisions for conformance:

- They wanted to encourage organizational-level implementation of processes (as opposed to project-level implementation), hence they wanted to permit (nay, encourage) organizational-level conformance with the standard.
- They wanted to constrain the apparently free scope for tailoring provided by the international standard—in short, they wanted to standard to provide a meaningful minimum set of requirements.
- They wanted the standard to be usable in regulatory situations.

In tightening the provisions for conformance, one must deal with two difficult characteristics of the international standard: its dependence on tailoring to delimit the scope of work for a contract; and its inclusion of clauses containing phrases such as "in accordance with the requirements of the contract." The first characteristic implies that tailoring is "built into" the standard, that is, the standard cannot be applied without allowing some tailoring. The second characteristic implies that the full text of the standard cannot be applied in the absence of a contract, for example, at the organizational level. Both of these problems had to be solved to meet the objectives of the joint IEEE/EIA working group.

An annex of IEEE/EIA 12207 provides the definition of conformance with the IEEE/EIA standard. It describes two levels of conformance: *tailored*, similar to the conformance provisions of the international 12207 standard; and *absolute*, whereby adherence to all of the mandatory clauses of the standard is required. The annex permits absolute conformance to be separately claimed for specific processes. For example, absolute conformance could be claimed individually for the verification process. It is hoped that the absolute level of conformance will be commonly used. Throughout the IEEE/EIA adaptation, guidance is provided indicating that the proper use of tailoring is to delimit the scope of work (for example, development but not maintenance) rather than the elimination of inconvenient provisions.

The provisions of the annex describe four conformance situations:

- *Organization level*: The organization claiming conformance asserts that it has implemented procedures and methods to meet all of the requirements of the standard. The organization is required to prepare a public document describing any tailoring of the standard and describing how it deals with the clauses of the standard that reference the "contract." The annex invites the organization to state that such clauses are to be detailed in the plans of specific projects.
- *Project level*: The project claiming conformance documents its tailoring of the standard and the clauses that reference the contract. The most highly desired situation for project conformance is within a conforming organization. In this case, the project simply cites the organizational documents describing conformance, explains any tailoring necessary for the specific project, and explains the interpretation to be place on clauses of the standard that reference the "contract."
- *Multiple supplier programs*: In this case, responsibility for the execution of some of the processes have been subdivided among one or more suppliers in a manner that does not allow any of them to sensibly claim conformance for their individual scope of work. However, the acquirer may claim conformance for the program as a whole by explaining how each of the provisions of the standard are accomplished.
- *Regulatory*: This provision permits the regulator, in effect, to give the desired tailoring to the developer. It permits tailoring to be constrained by regulatory requirements, supplemental standards, legal regulations, or sector-specific requirements.

One final provision is intended to deal with unusual situations. Sometimes, because of very special requirements of the job, the usual requirements of 12207 (or any standard for that matter) just do not make sense. Rather than encouraging free tailoring in such a case, the annex permits conformance by an alternative method. Two other annexes of the IEEE/EIA adaptation specify objectives for each of the processes of 12207 as well as data objectives. (These are the same objectives cited by the IEEE S2ESC process reference model.) One is allowed to claim conformance with a process by implementing procedures that directly achieve those objectives rather than the specific requirements stated in the main body of 12207.

4.4.5. Differences between ISO/IEC 12207 and IEEE/EIA 12207   IEEE/EIA 12207[38] is packaged into three parts designated 12207.0, 12207.1 and 12207.2. Part 0 is a "sandwich" that wraps US material around the full text of ISO/IEC 12207. The US additions include:

- An informative annex describing basic concepts of 12207.
- An annex listing a few errors that have been discovered in the text of the international standard.
- A set of process objectives and data objectives that assist in determining the intent of the process requirements specified in the standard as well as the data (paper or electronic) produced by those processes.
- A replacement conformance clause that shifts emphasis toward conformance at the organizational level and that requires documentation of the means of conformance.

Part 1 of IEEE/EIA 12207 is a guidance document providing recommendations expanding on the data objectives of Part 0. For those desiring guidance on how specific documents or electronic data should be associated with specific processes, this part provides recommendations on the content of various possible documents. However, Part 1 also contains conformance provisions allowing it to be used as a standard rather than a guide when so desired.

Part 2 of IEEE/EIA 12207 is a guidance document providing recommendations on the implementation of the 12207 processes in the context of industry best practices. The normative text of Part 0 is quoted and typographically enclosed in boxes. At appropriate intervals, guidance notes provide explanatory material and recommendations regarding the implementation of the processes.

The US adaptation of the standard, IEEE/EIA 12207, has shifted its focus toward conformance at the organizational level rather than at the level of the individual project.[39] The preferred usage is that an enterprise would develop its own set of processes and procedures that conform to the requirements of IEEE/EIA 12207 and which would be applied across the enterprise. Any individual project conducted by the enterprise would select the appropriate enter-

---

[38] The material in this section is adapted from [Moore97a].

[39] Although the international standard has a provision for organizational conformance, that provision is intended for use by an organization to specify "conditions of trade," that is, requirements on the processes of its suppliers rather than on its own processes.

prise processes and procedures and parameterize them for application to the individual project.

The material provided in the US adaptation has the effect of constraining the use of *tailoring*. The writers of the original 12207 standard understood that not all of the requirements of the standard might be applicable to every project. Therefore, they adopted a concept of tailoring, which allows the deletion of specified processes, activities and tasks from the standard for application to a specific project.[40] With the shift toward organization-level conformance in the US version, a more precise approach is needed. Conforming enterprises should implement organization-level processes capable of executing any requirement of 12207 when so tasked by a particular contract. The organization's projects should use those processes, constraining them to the needs of the specific contract. Therefore, the concept of tailoring in the US version is better understood as a parameterization of the organization-level processes to the contracted scope of work for a particular project.

IEEE/EIA 12207 offers some important advantages over the international version of the standard:

- It provides a set of process and data objectives that guide adaptation of the requirements of the standard in unusual situations.
- It incorporates specific references to other US standards that may be helpful in the detailed implementation of life cycle processes.
- It incorporates guidance based on industry "best practices" in the development of complex computer-based systems.
- It incorporates a set of recommended contents of data items produced by the execution of 12207 processes.

It remains, however, fully conforming with the international version of the standard, permitting US companies to develop a single set of enterprise processes applicable to both global and domestic business.

4.4.6. The ISO/IEC Guides to 12207

ISO/IEC JTC 1/SC 7/WG7 has itself written two Technical Reports that may be used as guides for the application of ISO/IEC 12207. The general guide, ISO/IEC TR 15271, elaborates on the factors to be considered in application of the standard. Although it disclaims the intention to provide a rationale for the standard, it does provide useful insight into the criteria for identification and selection of the particular processes chosen for 12207. Information provided by the guide includes:

- Basic concepts of the standard
- Approaches to implementing the standard, including examples of tailoring
- Application at the project level
- Application at the organizational level
- Relationship to system life cycle

[40] The ISO/IEC 12207 concept of tailoring should not be confused with the traditional usage of the DoD software process standards, in which tailoring means "change anything." ISO/IEC 12207 limits tailoring to simple deletion. Any additions to process requirements desired by the acquirer would have to be specified in the contract or the statement of work.

- A summary of the quality processes and evaluation requirements that appear in various parts of the standard
- Guidance (less extensive than that of IEEE/EIA 12207.1) concerning the data output from the various processes
- Application to three different life cycle models—waterfall, spiral, and evolutionary

Although the material of TR 15271 overlaps with the IEEE/EIA additions, organizations interested in international trade in software may find knowledge of this document to be advisable.

The second WG 7 guide, TR 14759, is more limited in scope, applying 12207 to "mock-up and prototype" efforts. A key objective of the report is to discriminate between three pairs of terms:

- Mock-up (throw-away) versus prototype (usable)
- Illustrative (nonfunctional) versus functional
- Demonstrative versus operational

Those pairs of terms are applied in various sensible combinations to enumerate eight different types of products. The report is intended to explain the appropriate role of 12207 in an incremental life cycle utilizing various selections from the eight types of products.

4.4.7. The ISO/IEC Amendment to 12207 ISO/IEC JTC 1/SC 7 has developed an amendment to their version of the 12207 standard and are, as of 2004, developing a second amendment. The primary purpose of the amendments is harmonization between the standard defining software life cycle processes, 12207, and the standard for assessing them, 15504. The amendment breaks the 12207 processes into a finer level of detail, adds some additional ones, and provides a statement of purpose and outcomes for all of them. The result is a set of processes that can be assessed under the provisions of ISO/IEC 15504.

The IEEE has not adopted the amendments for several reasons:

- The amendments have not yet stabilized. Two have been required so far, and more may be necessary to achieve the goal.
- The revision of ISO/IEC 15504 to a standard has not yet been completed.
- Ongoing work in SC 7 to harmonize system and software life cycle processes may induce changes in the process model.

With this degree of uncertainty, IEEE S2ESC decided that it is not appropriate to disturb its set of reference processes until a stable alternative is available.

4.5. ISO/IEC TR 15504 (Nine Parts), Information Technology—Software Process Assessment

This nine-part Technical Report was the first result of an international effort to define a common approach to process assessment. A companion effort—commonly known as SPICE (Software Process Improvement and Capability dEtermination)—developed the initial document baseline, conducted field trials for the purpose of empirical validation, continues to promote awareness, understanding, and adoption of the ultimate standard.

The project was born in the 1991 ImproveIT study [DEF91] conducted by the British Ministry of Defence into methods for assessing the software development capability of suppliers. The study considered two dozen existing methods and concluded that there was a need to supplement the reliance of software procurers on ISO 9001 with a standardized, widely accepted, public domain software capability assessment scheme directed toward continuous process and quality improvement positioned within the context of business needs. Based on the study's conclusion, the British Standards Institution proposed the initiation of a three-part standardization effort within ISO/IEC JTC 1/SC 7: a study period; development of a Type 2 Technical Report; and, finally, development of a full international standard. The planned standard is broader in scope than the CMM, dealing with all of the processes of ISO/IEC 12207—acquisition, supply, maintenance, operation, and supporting processes, in addition to development. It is intended that the standard may be used for organizational process assessment and improvement as well as supplier capability determination [Kitson96].

The report defines a framework for assessment methods and models, not a single method or model for universal application. The architecture of the document is structured to encourage the development of methods specifically tailored to particular domains or markets. On the other hand, the standard does include an example assessment model which, some critics claim, might itself become a de facto standard. Aside from differences in the breadth of scope, the most noticeable difference between CMM and 15504 is the contrast between a staged and a continuous model. CMM constrains process ratings to discrete maturity levels, while 15504 rates processes along a continuous capability dimension on a process by process basis.

4.6. ISO/IEC (Draft) 15504 (Five Parts), Software Engineering—Process Assessment

In ISO parlance, a Type 2 Technical Report is an intermediate publication on the way toward gaining the consensus needed for a standard. The original ISO/IEC 15504 was such a Technical Report. Immediately following its publication, ISO/IEC JTC 1/SC 7/WG10 commenced a revision effort targeted on the development of a full standard. The plan is to reduce the part count from nine to five. A major contribution to the reduction was a change in scope. Technical Report 15504 contained its own set of software processes that was regarded by some as competing with the definitions in ISO/IEC 12207. Defenders of 15504 responded that the particular form of the process description (statement of purpose plus a set of outcomes) was necessary to the role of 15504 in process assessment. The incompatibility was resolved with the creation of Amendment 1 to ISO/IEC 12207. That document contains a set of process definitions (defined by purpose and outcome) that will be shared by the new ISO/IEC 15504 and future revisions of ISO/IEC 12207.

As a result of removing the process definitions, the 15504 standard will describe only process capability without defining processes. The developers of the 15504 standard say that this approach is so successful that they believe 15504 will be usable to assess any kind of processes—systems process, even business processes—if the process descriptions meet a few simple rules.

4.7. ISO/IEC 15939:2002, Software Engineering—Software Measurement Process

This 37-page standard was completed in 2002 by a committee of ISO/IEC JTC 1/SC 7 as a "plug-in" to ISO/IEC 12207. Although IEEE has not adopted the standard, they have included it in the set of reference processes that provide a framework for their other standards. In addition, IEEE has adopted the measurement model and terminology from Annex A of the standard as a set of terms that will be applied in their other standards related to measurement.

The standard defines a software measurement process applicable throughout the scope defined by the 12207 standard. The process is described in a manner similar to 12207—it is decomposed into activities and then tasks. The standard can be applied at the project level or at the organizational level. It does not provide a set of measures; instead it defines a process for defining measures appropriate to the information needs of a particular project or organization.

The relationships of the activities are depicted in a manner very similar to Figure 15. Activities for establishment, planning, performance, and evaluation are executed iteratively while contributing to and taking from a measurement experience base. Externally, the information products of the measurement process are provided to other processes while information needs come back to the measurement process.

Perhaps even more important than the process of 15939 is the framework of terminology that it provides. The framework unifies a wide range of measurement concepts. Figure 17 shows how some of the key terms relate. Software measurement concerns the assessment and prediction of well-defined *attributes* of well-defined *entities* (for example, processes, products and resources). The *measurement information model* is a structure linking *information needs* to the relevant entities and attributes of concern. The measurement information model describes how the relevant attributes are quantified and converted to indicators that provide a basis for decision-making.

The selection or definition of appropriate measures to address an information need begins with a *measurable concept*: an idea of which measurable attributes are related to an information need and how they are related. The measurement planner defines measurement constructs that link these attributes to a specified information need. Each construct may involve several types or levels of measures. The model defines three types of measures: *base measures*, *derived measures*, and *indicators*. The information content of measures increases as they become closer in the model to the information need. The *measurement model* helps to determine what the measurement planner needs to specify during measurement planning, performance, and evaluation.

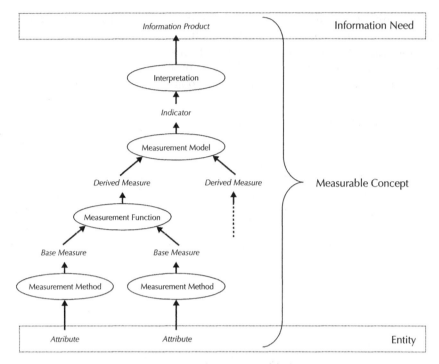

Figure 17. Measurement information model of ISO/IEC 15939

It is notable that this terminology framework has no use for the term "metric."

5. SUMMARY

This chapter has provided an overview of the Software Engineering Process knowledge area of the IEEE Computer Society's *Guide to the Software Engineering Body of Knowledge*. Sixteen IEEE and ISO/IEC standards have been offered as relevant to the knowledge area. The presentation has been divided into four subsections provided by the *SWEBOK Guide*:

- *Process Implementation and Change*: Organizations pursue process improvement because of the belief that better processes produce better products. An infrastructure is needed for process engineering.
- *Process Definition*: Of course, processes must be well-defined before they can be implemented. Four standards (IEEE/EIA 12207.0, ISO/IEC 15939, IEEE Std 1540 and IEEE Std 1517) can be combined to provide a set of reference processes for the software life cycle. Four other standards provide additional detail to some of the processes of 12207—IEEE/EIA 12207.2, IEEE Std 1008, IEEE Std 1219 and ISO/IEC 14764. Two standards—IEEE Std 1074 and IEEE/EIA 12207.1—assist in moving to the conceptual level of process abstraction, where the relationships among

processes must be considered. Finally, IEEE Std 1320.1 provides a notation, IDEF0, useful in describing processes.

- *Process Assessment*: Software process assessment is described in ISO/IEC 15504 and other de facto standards.

- *Process and Product Measurement*: To effectively improve processes, one must measure them or their outcomes. ISO/IEC 15939 describes a process for measurement. IEEE Std 1061 pays attention to the validity of measurement in predicting outcomes. IEEE Std 1044 can help in pursuing orthogonal defect classification. Process definition reviews and root cause analysis can be used to evaluate the success of processes. ISO/IEC 9126-1 provides a taxonomy of characteristics for product assessment and IEEE Std 14143-1 provides concepts for measurement of functional size.

Chapter 14

Knowledge Area: Software Engineering Tools and Methods

Tooling is almost as old as computing. It didn't take long for the pioneers to realize that the computer itself could relieve them of some of the drudgery in preparing machine code for the computer's execution. Assemblers were among the first tools; practical compilers followed in about a decade. The size, scope and difficulty of modern software-intensive systems requires tooling to assist the human programmers in maintaining consistency and thoroughness of treatment. Furthermore, it is difficult to attempt the adoption of organizational processes without some degree of automated support for their enactment and execution.

This chapter surveys the categories of software engineering tools and methods as well as the standards supporting them. The chapter is organized according to the subject's treatment in the *Guide to the Software Engineering Body of Knowledge* [SWEBOK04], and much of the text is paraphrased from that source. (The knowledge area editor for the chapter in the *SWEBOK Guide* was David Carrington.) The relevant IEEE software engineering standards are mentioned in the context of the knowledge described by the *SWEBOK Guide*. At the end of the chapter, the standards allocated to this knowledge area are described in greater detail. Cross-references to other chapters provide access to descriptions of the other relevant standards.

1. KNOWLEDGE AREA SCOPE

The scope of the Software Engineering Tools and Methods Knowledge Area is defined by [SWEBOK04] as being

The Road Map to Software Engineering: A Standards-Based Guide, by James W. Moore
Copyright © 2006 by IEEE Computer Society

Software development tools are the computer-based tools that are intended to assist the software life cycle processes. Tools allow repetitive, well-defined actions to be automated, reducing the cognitive load on the software engineer who is then free to concentrate on the creative aspects of the process. Tools are often designed to support particular software engineering methods, reducing any administrative load associated with applying the method manually. Like software engineering methods, they are intended to make software engineering more systematic, and they vary in scope from supporting individual tasks to encompassing the complete life cycle.

Software engineering methods impose structure on the software engineering activity with the goal of making the activity systematic and ultimately more likely to be successful. Methods usually provide a notation and vocabulary, procedures for performing identifiable tasks, and guidelines for checking both the process and the product. They vary widely in scope, from a single life cycle phase to the complete life cycle. The emphasis in this KA is on software engineering methods encompassing multiple life cycle phases, since phase-specific methods are covered by other KAs.

2. KNOWLEDGE AREA SUMMARY

The *SWEBOK Guide* divides the Software Engineering Tools and Methods Knowledge Area into two subareas—an organization followed by this chapter. The Introduction of the *SWEBOK Guide* summarizes this knowledge area as follows:

> *The Software Engineering Tools and Methods KA includes both software engineering tools and software engineering methods.*

> *The **Software Engineering Tools** subarea uses the same structure as the Guide itself, with one topic for each of the other nine software engineering KAs. An additional topic is provided: miscellaneous tools issues, such as tool integration techniques, which are potentially applicable to all classes of tools.*

> *The **Software Engineering Methods** subarea is divided into four subsections: heuristic methods dealing with informal approaches, formal methods dealing with mathematically based approaches, and prototyping methods dealing with software development approaches based on various forms of prototyping.*

The knowledge area breakdown is illustrated in Figure 18, which also shows the standards relevant to this knowledge area.

3. KNOWLEDGE AREA DESCRIPTION

In the original version of the *SWEBOK Guide*'s chapter on Tools and Methods, David Carrington reported [SWEBOK01] that,

> *there is a scarcity of recent technical writing on practical software engineering tools . . . Obviously, there are detailed manuals on specific tools and numerous research papers on innovative software tools, but there is a gap between the two.*

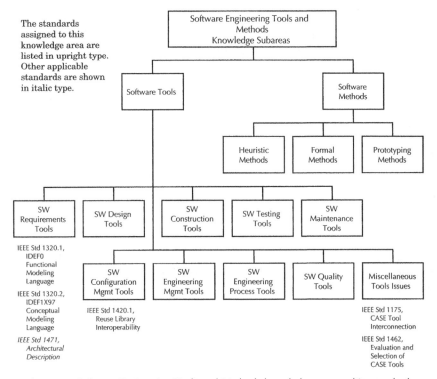

The standards assigned to this knowledge area are listed in upright type. Other applicable standards are shown in italic type.

Figure 18. *Software Engineering Tools and Methods knowledge area and its standards*

One difficulty is the high rate of change in software tools. There also seems to be an attitude that software engineering tools are prosaic and not worthy of study beyond the level required for use.

This chapter is among the briefest in the *SWEBOK Guide*. The paraphrase provided in this section is very close, often identical, to Carrington's text in [SWEBOK04].[41]

3.1. Software Tools

Software development induces a huge cognitive load on the developers. Tools that replace otherwise manual activity improve the work by reducing distraction from the intense intellectual activity, speeding operations, and enforcing consistency. Some tools provide all-purpose clerical support, while others are specific to particular development methods. Some are confined to individual tasks, while others support the complete life cycle.

3.1.1. Software Requirements Tools Tools for dealing with software requirements have been partitioned into two topics: modeling and traceability.

---

[41] I am grateful for his succinct writing.

Requirements Modeling Tools Tools used for eliciting, recording, analyzing, and validating software requirements belong in this category. Three IEEE standards are helpful. Two provide modeling languages and the third is useful in describing system and software architectures:

Tool

IEEE Std 1320.1-1998 (R2004)
IEEE Standard for
Functional Modeling Language—Syntax and Semantics for IDEF0
This standard defines the IDEF0 modeling language used to represent decisions, actions, and activities of an organization or system. IDEF0 may be used to define requirements in terms of functions to be performed by a desired system.
Allocated to: Software Engineering Tools and Methods Knowledge Area

Tool

IEEE Std 1320.2-1998 (R2004)
IEEE Standard for Conceptual Modeling Language—
Syntax and Semantics for IDEF1X 97 (IDEF object)
This standard defines two conceptual modeling languages, collectively called IDEF1X97 (IDEFObject). The language support the implementation of relational databases, object databases, and object models.
Allocated to: Software Engineering Tools and Methods Knowledge Area

Document

IEEE Std 1471-2000
IEEE Recommended Practice for
Architectural Description of Software Intensive Systems
This document recommends a conceptual framework and content for the architectural description of software-intensive systems.
Allocated to: Related Disciplines Chapter, Systems Engineering

Requirements Traceability Tools Requirements traceability tools are becoming increasingly important as the complexity of software systems grow, and since traceability tools are relevant also in other life cycle phases, they can be viewed separately from the other tools for requirements.

3.1.2. Software Design Tools This section covers tools for creating and checking software designs. There is a variety of such tools, with much of this variety being a consequence of the diversity of design notations and methods.

3.1.3. Software Construction Tools Software construction tools are concerned with the production and translation of the program representation (commonly known as source code) that is sufficiently detailed and explicit to enable machine execution.

- *Program editors:* Program editors are tools used for creation and modification of programs (and possibly associated documents). These tools can be general-purpose text or document editors, or they can be specialized for a target language.

- *Compilers and code generators:* Traditionally, compilers have been non-interactive translators of source code but there has been a trend to integrate compilers and program editors to provide integrated programming environments. This topic also covers preprocessors, linker/loaders, and code generators.
- *Interpreters:* Interpreters provide software execution through emulation. They can support software construction activities by providing a more controllable and observable environment for program execution.
- *Debuggers:* Debugging tools have been made a separate topic since they support the construction process but are different from program editors or compilers.

3.1.4. Software Testing Tools
Testing tools are categorized according to where in the testing process they are used.

- *Test generators:* Test generators assist the development of test cases.
- *Test execution frameworks:* Test execution frameworks enable the execution of test cases in a controlled environment where the behavior of the object under test is observed.
- *Test evaluation tools:* Test evaluation tools support the assessment of the results of test execution, helping to determine whether the observed behavior conforms to the expected behavior.
- *Test management tools:* Test management tools provide support for managing all aspects of the testing process.
- *Performance analysis tools:* This topic covers tools for measuring and analyzing software performance. It is a specialized form of testing where the goal is to assess the performance behavior rather than the functional behavior (correctness).

3.1.5. Software Maintenance Tools
Because software maintenance can be viewed as additional iteration of the development lifecycle, it makes use of tools for all other phases. This category encompasses tools that have particular importance in software maintenance where an existing system is being modified:

- *Comprehension tools:* This topic concerns tools to assist human comprehension of programs. Examples include visualization tools such as animators and program slicers.
- *Re-engineering tools:* Re-engineering tools allow translation of a program to a new programming language, or a database to a new format. Reverse engineering tools assist the process by working backwards from an existing product to create abstract artifacts such as design and specification descriptions that can then be transformed to generate a new product from an old one.

3.1.6. Software Configuration Management Tools
Tools for configuration management have been placed into three categories:

- *Defect, enhancement, issue and problem tracking tools:* Tools to track issues until they are resolved.
- *Version management tools:* Tools to manage multiple version (possibly for different computer configurations) of a software product.
- *Release and build tools:* Tools for configuring a version of software for a particular installation or managing the installation for the same result.

One IEEE standard is a force-fit in this category. IEEE Std 1420.1 supports the interconnection of software reuse libraries. These libraries would contain versions of software assets intended for reuse in other systems:

Tool

IEEE Std 1420.1-1995 (R2002)
IEEE Standard for Information Technology—
Software Reuse—Data Model for Reuse Library Interoperability:
Basic Interoperability Data Model (BIDM)
This standard describes information that software reuse libraries should be able to exchange in order to interchange assets.
Allocated to: Software Engineering Tools and Methods Knowledge Area

Tool

IEEE Std 1420.1a-1996 (R2002)
Supplement to IEEE Standard for Information Technology—
Software Reuse—Data Model for Reuse Library Interoperability:
Asset Certification Framework
This supplement to 1420.1 extends the standard model to asset certification information.
Allocated to: Software Engineering Tools and Methods Knowledge Area

Tool

IEEE Std 1420.1b-1999 (R2002)
IEEE Trial-Use Supplement to IEEE Standard for Information Technology—Software Reuse—Data Model for Reuse Library Interoperability: Intellectual property Rights Framework
This supplement to 1420.1 extends the standard model to intellectual property information.
Allocated to: Software Engineering Tools and Methods Knowledge Area

3.1.7. Software Engineering Management Tools

Management tools are subdivided into three categories:

- *Project planning and tracking tools*
- *Risk management tools*
- *Measurement tools*

3.1.8. Software Engineering Process Tools

This category of tools provides automated support in following the sometimes complex processes and procedures involved in modern software engineering:

- *Process modeling tools:* This topic covers tools to model and investigate software processes.

- *Process management tools:* These tools generally provide an integration of or a linkage to other tools.
- *Integrated CASE environments:* Computer-aided software engineering tools or environments that cover multiple phases of the software development life cycle belong in this section. Such tools perform multiple functions and hence potentially interact with the software process that is being enacted.
- *Process-centered software engineering environments:* This topic covers those environments that explicitly incorporate software process information and that guide and monitor the user according to a defined process.

3.1.9. Software Quality Tools This category of tools provides assistance in analysis and consistency:

- *Inspection tools:* This topic covers tools to support reviews and inspections.
- *Static analysis tools:* This topic deals with tools that analyze software artifacts, such as syntactic and semantic analyzers, and data, control flow and dependency analyzers. Such tools are intended for checking software artifacts for conformance or for verifying desired properties.

3.1.10. Miscellaneous Tools Issue This section covers issues that are applicable to all classes of tools. Three categories are identified: tool integration techniques, meta-tools, and tool evaluation.

Tool Integration Techniques Tool integration is important for making individual tools cooperate. This category potentially overlaps with integrated software engineering environments where integration techniques are applied, but it was felt that this topic is sufficiently distinct to merit its own category. The typical kinds of tool integration are platform, presentation, process, data, and control.

IEEE Std 1175.1 is the first of a family of standards providing mechanisms for integrating CASE tools:

Tool

IEEE Std 1175.1-2002
IEEE Guide for
CASE Tool Interconnections—Classification and Description
This document is the first of a planned series of standards on the integration of CASE tools into a productive software engineering environment. This part describes fundamental concepts and introduces the remaining (planned) parts.
Allocated to: Software Engineering Tools and Methods Knowledge Area

Meta-tools Meta-tools generate other tools; compiler-compilers are the classic example.

Tool Evaluation Because of the continuous evolution of software engineering tools, tool evaluation is an essential topic. IEEE offers an appropriate standard:

Tool

IEEE Std 1462-1998 (R2004)
IEEE Standard: Adoption of International Standard
ISO/IEC 14102: 1995, Information Technology—
Guideline for the Evaluation and Selection of CASE tools
This standard provides guidelines for the evaluation and selection of CASE tools.
Allocated to: Software Engineering Tools and Methods Knowledge Area

3.2. Software Engineering Methods

The software engineering methods section is divided into three subsections: heuristic methods dealing with informal approaches; formal methods dealing with mathematically based approaches; and prototyping methods. The three subsections are not disjoint; rather they represent distinct concerns. For example, an object-oriented method may incorporate formal techniques and rely on prototyping for verification and validation. Like software engineering tools, methodologies evolve continuously. Consequently, the Knowledge Area description avoids naming particular methodologies as far as possible.

3.2.1. Heuristic Methods This subsection contains four categories:

- *Structured methods*
- *Data-oriented methods*
- *Object-oriented methods*
- *Domain-specific methods:* including specialized methods for developing systems that involve real-time, safety or security aspects.

3.2.2. Formal Methods This subsection deals with mathematically based development methods and is subdivided by different aspects of formal methods:

- *Specification languages and notations:* Specification languages are commonly classified as model-oriented, property-oriented, or behavior-oriented.
- *Refinement:* How a method refines (or transforms) the specification into a form that is closer to the desired final form of an executable program.
- *Verification/proving properties:* The verification properties that are specific to the formal approach, covering both theorem proving and model checking.

3.2.3. Prototyping Methods This subsection covers methods involving software prototyping and is subdivided into three topics:

- *Styles:* The topic of prototyping styles identifies the different approaches: throwaway, evolutionary, and the executable specification.
- *Prototyping target:* Example targets of a prototyping method may be requirements, architectural design or the user interface.
- *Evaluation techniques:* This topic covers how the results of a prototype exercise are used.

4. STANDARDS IN THE SOFTWARE ENGINEERING TOOLS AND METHODS KNOWLEDGE AREA

4.1. IEEE Std 1175.1-2002, IEEE Guide for CASE Tool Interconnections— Classification and Description

Originally, this was a single-part standard published for trial use by the IEEE in 1992, and approved for full use two years later. In its recent revision, it has expanded to a five-part standard, but only the 14-page Part 1 has been completed as of late 2004. The 1992 version continues to be available.

The motivation of the standard is to help users of CASE tools interconnect those tools and integrate them into environments. The documents consider four things with which a computer *tool* might interconnect: *organizations, users, platforms*, and *other tools*. The word "interconnection" is used quite generally to encompass all of the associations between a tool and something in its environment. The two fundamental forms of interconnection are a passive interconnection (an interoperability agreement) and an active interconnection (a dynamic interaction).

The discussion of interconnections in this family actually has wider applicability to computing system tools in general, beyond only CASE tools. Most computing system tools have interconnections with organizations, users, platforms, and other tools, so consideration of these interconnections is important to them. Also, while most computing system tools do not need to communicate behavior descriptions of subject systems, their creators need to develop such descriptions for them.

The newly available IEEE Std 1175.1 is a guide to the remainder of the family. It provides overall concepts and an explanation of how the remaining parts of the family will apply the concepts to support effective integration of tools into environments. It describes the scope of each standard, the issues addressed in that standard, and the interrelationships between the family members. The additional planned parts will fill the roles indicated below:

Part	Type of Standard	Subject
1175-2	Recommended practice	Characterization of the four types of interconnections
1175-3	Standard	A reference model for specifying software behavior
1175-4	Standard	A reference model for specifying system behavior
1175-5	Standard	An explicit syntax for transferring behavior specification

4.2. IEEE Std 1320.1-1998, IEEE Standard for Functional Modeling Language— Syntax and Semantics for IDEF0

IDEF is a modeling language, combining graphics and text, used to analyze and define functions and requirements of a system. A model consists of a hierarchical series of diagrams, with accompanying explanation, depicting functions as well as the data and objects that relate the functions.

The IDEF notation was born in the 1970s Air Force program for Integrated Computer Aided Manufacturing (ICAM). (In fact, the "I" in "IDEF" originally stood for ICAM. Now, the acronym is usually decoded as "Integrated DEFinition.") Three notations were originally developed:

- IDEF0 for function models
- IDEF1 for information models
- IDEF2 for dynamics models

In 1991, a collaboration between the National Institute of Standards and Technology (NIST) and the DoD Office of Corporate Information Management produced Federal Information Processing Standard Publication 183 (FIPS Pub. 183), as a specification for IDEF0. Two years later, S2ESC initiated commercial standardization of IDEF0 using FIPS Publication 183 as the base document. IEEE Std 1320.1 describes the syntax and semantics of the IDEF0 language that are required to draw physical diagrams. It includes a mathematically based formulation of the language and separates that formulation from the physical representation.

IDEF0 is generally viewed as encompassing both a modeling language and a methodology for developing models. This standard does not address the methodology—only the syntax and semantics of the modeling language. Methodology is treated in several available textbooks. The 105-page standard includes an extensive set of example diagrams.

4.3. IEEE Std 1320.2-1998, IEEE Standard for Conceptual Modeling Language Syntax and Semantics for IDEF1X 97 (IDEFObject)

A 1983 Air Force project extended IDEF1 to perform semantic modeling, calling the resulting notation IDEF1X. Recently, object-oriented extensions to IDEF1X have been formulated; they go under the name IDEF1X97 or sometimes IDEFObject, and are the subject of IEEE Std 1320.2.

IDEF1X97 deals with a resource known as a conceptual schema. The primary objective in developing a conceptual schema is to define characteristics and relationships of concepts relevant to an enterprise. An IDEF1X97 model use boxes to depict things, lines to represent the relationships between the things, and annotations to describe the responsibilities of the things. Two styles of models are possible:

- A key style, representing structure and semantics, that is backward compatible with earlier versions of IDEF1X; and
- An identity style, representing objects and their collaboration, that can be used to develop executable prototypes.

The 303-page standard describes the syntax and semantics of IDEF1X97 along with a graphic form of representation. An appendix provides an extensive set of examples, including design patterns.

4.4. IEEE Std 1420.1-1995, IEEE Standard for Information Technology—Software Reuse—Data Model for Reuse Library Interoperability: Basic Interoperability Data Model (BIDM)

S2ESC's standards for reuse library interoperability grew out of a situation in the late 1980s and early 1990s when it became clear that various organizations within the federal government were each interested in establishing themselves as the sole software reuse library for all government users. Taking a contrary approach, the Reuse Library Interoperability Group (RIG) asserted that no single library could meet the needs of all communities of users and that libraries should instead promote interoperability [Moore91, Moore94]. This would permit each library to focus on the needs of its own community while still being able to access other components by obtaining them from other libraries.

To promote interoperability among libraries, the RIG specified an abstract data model for the description of assets. Following an approach of specifying in small, incremental pieces, the RIG produced a series of standards, parts and supplements gradually elaborating the model. The various specifications were adopted by the S2ESC. IEEE Std 1420.1 is the basic data model. A supplement, 1420.1a, elaborates the model by adding descriptions of certifications of quality and fitness. Another supplement, 1420.1b, further elaborates the model by adding intellectual property rights information.

4.5. IEEE Std 1462-1998, IEEE Standard—Adoption of International Standard ISO/IEC 14102:1995—Information Technology—Guideline for the Evaluation and Selection of CASE Tools

This 55-page standard is an example of the cooperation between IEEE S2ESC and ISO/IEC JTC 1/SC 7. IEEE once had its own standard, 1209, for evaluating CASE tools. Three years later, a working group of SC 7, involving many of the same individuals, developed a similar, but improved, standard, ISO/IEC 14102. Ultimately, as a step toward consistency between the two collections, S2ESC chose to drop their standard and adopt the international version. IEEE added a two-page "Implementation Note" providing some guidance for use of the standard. Unfortunately, IEEE assigned a different number to the result. IEEE reaffirmed the standard in 2004.

The standard describes the evaluation of tools for Computer-Aided Software Engineering (CASE) and their selection for deployment. The document describes processes for selection and evaluation, processes that include the determination of relevant selection criteria. All criteria are based on the viewpoint of a CASE tool user; hence they deal with externally visible characteristics. The criteria are based on the model provided by the ISO/IEC 12119 standard (IEEE Std 1465) on quality requirements for software packages, which, in turn, is an elaboration of the quality model provided by ISO/IEC 9126-1. The standard recognizes that the evaluation and selection process is complex and has organizational implications; therefore it does not generalize the processes beyond tools specifically applicable to software engineering. Furthermore, the standard does not advocate any specific development standards, design methods, or life cycle models.

In academic settings, the evaluation process of 14102 has been successfully expanded to a generic process for dealing with new technologies [Abran96].

5. SUMMARY

This chapter has provided an overview of the Software Engineering Tools and Methods knowledge area of the IEEE Computer Society's *Guide to the Software Engineering Body of Knowledge*. Six IEEE standards have been offered as relevant to the knowledge area.

The knowledge area is subdivided into two parts: Software Methods and Software Tools. The Software Tools part is further subdivided into ten areas patterned on the overall organization of the *SWEBOK Guide*:

- *Software Requirements Tools*: Two standards, IEEE Std 1320.1 and 1320.2, provide languages useful in modeling requirements. A third standard, IEEE Std 1471, places requirements on architectural descriptions.
- *Software Design Tools*
- *Software Construction Tools*
- *Software Testing Tools*
- *Software Maintenance Tools*
- *Software Engineering Process Tools*
- *Software Quality Tools*
- *Software Configuration Management Tools*: IEEE Std 1420.1 describes data models useful in transferring assets among software reuse libraries.
- *Software Engineering Management Tools*
- *Miscellaneous Tools Issues*, including CASE tool selection and integration: IEEE Std 1175.1 is the first of a five-part set for the interoperation of CASE tools. IEEE Std 1462 describes the evaluation and selection of CASE tools.

Chapter *15*

Knowledge Area: Software Quality

There was a time when "software quality" was used in a broad sense to mean roughly, "everything that one does beyond code and fix in order to produce good software." IEEE's first software engineering standard, IEEE Std 730-1984, *Software Quality Assurance*, described a wide variety of plans and methods for producing good software. As the discipline has progressed, our vocabulary has become more precise and descriptive. Various techniques once described as "software quality assurance" or simply "software quality" are now considered as systematic software development and are treated as part of process improvement or project management. The software quality area has become specialized to cover the specification of quality characteristics, the trade-offs among them, and the pursuit of their achievement. Despite this goal, it must be recognized that software product quality is still an immature subject. In many cases, software engineers must be content to pursue process improvement in the conviction that product quality will be correspondingly improved.

This chapter surveys the concepts, processes, and activities related to software quality as well as the standards supporting them. The chapter is organized according to the subject's treatment in the *Guide to the Software Engineering Body of Knowledge* [SWEBOK04], and much of the text is paraphrased from that source. (The knowledge area editors for the chapter in the *SWEBOK Guide* were Alain April and Larry Reeker.) The relevant IEEE software engineering standards, as well as a few from other sources, are mentioned in the context of the knowledge described by the SWEBOK. At the end of the chapter, the standards allocated to this knowledge area are described in greater detail. Cross-references to other chapters provide access to descriptions of the other relevant standards.

The Road Map to Software Engineering: A Standards-Based Guide, by James W. Moore
Copyright © 2006 by IEEE Computer Society

1. KNOWLEDGE AREA SCOPE

The scope of the Software Quality Knowledge Area is defined by [SWEBOK04] as follows:

> What is software quality, and why is it so important that it be pervasive in the SWEBOK Guide? Over the years, authors and organizations have defined the term "quality" differently. To Phil Crosby, it was "conformance to user requirements." Watts Humphrey refers to it as "achieving excellent levels of fitness for use," while IBM coined the phrase "market-driven quality," which is based on achieving total customer satisfaction. The Baldrige criteria for organizational quality use a similar phrase, "customer-driven quality," and include customer satisfaction as a major consideration. More recently, quality has been defined in ISO 9001 as "the degree to which a set of inherent characteristics fulfills requirements."
>
> Software quality is a ubiquitous concern in software engineering, and so it is also considered in many of the KAs. . . . In particular, this KA will cover static techniques, those which do not require the execution of the software being evaluated, while dynamic techniques are covered in the Software Testing KA.

This definition of quality from ISO 9001 gives direction to the *SWEBOK Guide*'s treatment of quality. Pertinent characteristics of software should be defined; it should be possible for users to place requirements on those characteristics; and it should be possible to develop and maintain software in a manner that fulfills those requirements.

2. KNOWLEDGE AREA SUMMARY

The *SWEBOK Guide* divides the Software Quality Knowledge Area into three sub-areas—an organization followed by this chapter. The Introduction of the *SWEBOK Guide* summarizes this knowledge area as follows:

> The Software Quality KA deals with software quality considerations which transcend the software life cycle processes. Since software quality is a ubiquitous concern in software engineering, it is also considered in many of the other KAs, and the reader will notice pointers to those KAs throughout this KA. The description of this KA covers three subareas.
>
> The first subarea describes the **Software Quality Fundamentals** such as software engineering culture and ethics, the value and costs of quality, models and quality characteristics, and quality improvement.
>
> The second subarea covers **Software Quality Management Processes**. The topics here are software quality assurance, verification and validation, and reviews and audits.
>
> The third and final subarea describes **Practical Considerations** related to software quality. The topics are software quality requirements, defect characterization, software quality management techniques, and software quality measurement.

The knowledge area breakdown is illustrated in Figure 19, which also shows the standards relevant to this knowledge area.

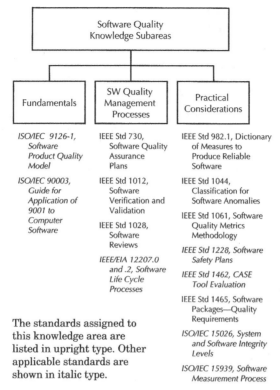

Figure 19. *Software Quality knowledge area and its standards*

3. KNOWLEDGE AREA DESCRIPTION

Because quality considerations are ubiquitous, they are mentioned in many areas of the SWEBOK. This knowledge area is intended to provide a unified treatment.

3.1. Software Quality Fundamentals

Achievement of quality characteristics is central to producing software that will satisfy the customer. Because they are often not described in functional terms, though, they are difficult to specify and measure. Nevertheless, the software requirements should specify the required quality characteristics with knowledge of how they will be measured. Acceptance criteria can be matched to the measurement approach. Although difficult, distinct treatment of quality facilitates communication between users, customers and developers.

3.1.1. Software Engineering Culture and Ethics Commitment to quality is an important facet of the software engineering discipline, sometimes rising to the level of an ethical issue. For example, the Software Engineering Code of Ethics[42]

---

[42] http://csciwww.etsu.edu/gotterbarn/SECEPP/default.asp

jointly developed by the IEEE Computer Society and the Association for Computing Machinery treats quality in several places, including the following:

Principle 3 PRODUCT Software engineers shall ensure that their products and related modifications meet the highest professional standards possible. In particular, software engineers shall, as appropriate:

3.01 Strive for high quality, acceptable cost, and a reasonable schedule, ensuring significant tradeoffs are clear to and accepted by the employer and the client, and are available for consideration by the user and the public. . . .

3.09 Ensure realistic quantitative estimates of cost, scheduling, personnel, quality and outcomes on any project on which they work or propose to work and provide an uncertainty assessment of these estimates. . . .

Principle 5 MANAGEMENT Software engineering managers and leaders shall subscribe to and promote an ethical approach to the management of software development and maintenance. In particular, those managing or leading software engineers shall, as appropriate:

5.01 Ensure good management for any project on which they work, including effective procedures for promotion of quality and reduction of risk. . . .

5.05 Ensure realistic quantitative estimates of cost, scheduling, personnel, quality and outcomes on any project on which they work or propose to work, and provide an uncertainty assessment of these estimates. . . .

Principle 8 SELF Software engineers shall participate in lifelong learning regarding the practice of their profession and shall promote an ethical approach to the practice of the profession. In particular, software engineers shall continually endeavor to: . . .

8.02 Improve their ability to create safe, reliable, and useful quality software at reasonable cost and within a reasonable time. . . .

3.1.2. Value and Costs of Quality   Quality is not a single-dimensional concept. There are many quality characteristics that must be traded against each other, if only in terms of attention and resources. Therefore, it is helpful to take a quantitative approach to quality and its cost. The costs related to quality can be modeled as prevention cost, appraisal cost, internal (project) failure cost, and external (customer) failure cost. Because the customer's perception of quality characteristics and their cost may be vague, it is important to achieve communication on this subject, typically during the requirements activity.

3.1.3. Models and Quality Characteristics   A number of different models have been proposed for software quality characteristics. Although similar in concept, they differ in terms of their hierarchy and terminology. Models of both process quality and product quality are described below.

Software Process Quality   Software process quality is important because it affects product quality. Because product quality characteristics are difficult to treat tangibly, it is important to address process quality. The most important standards for process quality are the famous ISO 9000 family of standards regarding the quality management system of an organization. The 2000 generation of these standards have been rewritten and the structure of the family has been simplified. ISO 9000, 9001, and 9004 contain concepts and vocabulary, requirements, and guidance, respectively. The ISO 9000 family is discussed in Chapter 16, Related Disciplines.

Of course, the ISO 9000 family treats quality management generically. Software organizations seeking certification to ISO 9001 sometimes complain that auditors who are not also software experts fail to understand how quality management concepts are treated in software development. For this reason, ISO/IEC JTC 1/SC 7 has developed a Guide:

Process

ISO/IEC 90003:2004
Software Engineering—Guidelines for the
Application of ISO 9001:2000 to Computer Software
This standard provides guidance for organizations in the application of ISO 9001:2000 to the acquisition, supply, development, operation and maintenance of computer software.
Allocated to: Related Disciplines Chapter, Quality Management

A treatment of process quality that is specific to software is provided by the Capability Maturity Model Integration (CMMI). Many organizations have decided that the two models are complementary and use both in evaluating and improving their organizational processes.

Software Product Quality   The software engineer has the responsibility to elicit the customers' requirements regarding quality characteristics. It is important to distinguish characteristics so that software can be designed with the specific requirements in mind, avoiding unnecessary cost. In distinguishing characteristics, it is helpful to have a taxonomical model of software product quality characteristics. Many have been proposed but one has been validated through consensus:

Terminology

ISO/IEC 9126-1:2001
Software Engineering—Product Quality—Part 1: Quality Model
This standard provides a model for software product quality covering internal quality, external quality, and quality in use. The model is in the form of a taxonomy of defined characteristics which software may exhibit.
Allocated to: Software Requirements Knowledge Area

ISO/IEC 9126-1 provides three views of quality:

- *Internal quality:* the totality of characteristics of the software product from an internal view during its development or maintenance.
- *External quality:* the totality of characteristics of the software product from an external view during its execution.
- *Quality in use:* the user's view of the quality of the software product when it is used in a specific environment and a specific context of use. It measures the extent to which users can achieve their goals in a particular environment, rather than measuring the properties of the software itself.

The first two views share a single hierarchical breakdown of six quality characteristics and a number of subcharacteristics. The final model is more simply decomposed into only four characteristics: effectiveness, productivity, safety, and satisfaction.

Software product quality evaluation is not limited to the final products of development. Intermediate products can also be treated. In fact, the relationship between the quality of the intermediate and final products is the reason that the internal and external quality models of 9126-1 share the same structure. It is posited that the measures used for the internal model are predictors of the external measures.

3.1.4. Quality Improvement   Quality improvement programs for software organizations often center on process improvement. It is generally agreed that the most effective approach is to try to build in quality at the outset rather than try to improve the quality of a partially completed product. Hence, defect prevention is valued more highly than defect removal and early defect removal is valued over late defect removal. These values lead directly to the quality management processes described in the next section.

3.2. Software Quality Management Processes

Several of the processes of the software life cycle are intended to address the quality of the resulting product—either by finding defects or by directing further examination. A definitive set of life cycle processes is available in a standard:

Process

IEEE/EIA 12207.0-1996
Industry Implementation of International Standard ISO/IEC
12207:1995, Standard for Information Technology—
Software Life Cycle Processes
This standard provides a framework of processes used across the entire
life cycle of software.
Allocated to: Software Engineering Process Knowledge Area

Five processes of that standard directly address software quality management:

- *Quality assurance:* assure that software products and processes conform to requirements and adhere to plans
- *Verification:* determine whether the software products of an activity fulfill the requirements imposed on them in the previous activities
- *Validation:* determine whether the requirements and the final product fulfills its intended use
- *Joint Review:* evaluate the status and the products of an activity
- *Audit:* determine compliance with the requirements, plans, and agreement

These processes are described in the sections that follow.

3.2.1. Software Quality Assurance The software quality assurance activity provides confidence that software products and processes conform to their requirements and are conducted according to plans. In effect, SQA is an overlay on the other plans and processes to ensure that quality goals are being appropriately treated. This relationship is clear in the 12207 standard; it defines activities of product assurance, process assurance, and assurance of quality systems.

The key feature of the 12207 quality assurance process is the development of a software quality assurance plan.

6.3.1.3 A plan for conducting the quality assurance process activities and tasks shall be developed, documented, implemented, and maintained for the life of the contract. The plan shall include the following:

a) Quality standards, methodologies, procedures, and tools for performing the quality assurance activities (or their references in organization's official documentation);

b) Procedures for contract review and coordination thereof;

c) Procedures for identification, collection, filing, maintenance, and disposition of quality records;

d) Resources, schedule, and responsibilities for conducting the quality assurance activities;

e) Selected activities and tasks from supporting processes, such as Verification, Validation, Joint Review, Audit, and Problem Resolution.

Some users may decide that the 12207 treatment of SQA planning is too terse for their needs. An IEEE standard provides additional detail:

Plan

IEEE Std 730-2002
IEEE Standard for Software Quality Assurance Plans
This standard specifies the format and content of Software Quality Assurance plans.
Allocated to: Software Quality Knowledge Area

The SQA plan prescribed by IEEE Std 730 defines a set of quality activities along with their costs and resource requirements, their objectives and their schedule, as related to the overall project schedule. In addition to management issues, the plan treats technical issues. It describes standards, practices, and conventions to be used in pursuing quality objectives, and identifies measures and procedures to be used for tracking progress toward the goals. Finally, it may provide acceptance criteria and reporting activities. Of course, the plan must be coordinated with others, like the Software Configuration Management Plan.

3.2.2. Verification and Validation The primary processes of the 12207 standard contain inherent provisions for evaluation. Some projects may desire additional evaluation effort. The 12207 standard provides the verification and validation processes for this purpose.[43] The purpose of verification is to determine whether the products of an activity fulfill the requirements imposed on them by previous activities. It is inherently incremental; it focuses on whether an activity accurately transformed its assigned inputs into the correct outputs. The purpose of validation is to determine whether the requirements correctly address the intended use of the product and whether the final software product actually fulfills its intended use. Rather than being incremental, validation takes an end-to-end look comparing three things: intended use, requirements, and completed product.

Despite this fundamental difference in goals, verification and validation are often treated as a single process—probably because they both employ the same techniques. The relevant IEEE standard treats the two together:

Process

IEEE Std 1012-2004
IEEE Standard for Software Verification and Validation
This standard describes software verification and validation processes that are used to determine if software products of an activity meets the requirements of the activity and to determine if software satisfies the user's needs for the intended usage. The scope includes analysis, evaluation, review, inspection, assessment, and testing of both products and processes.
Allocated to: Software Quality Knowledge Area

Perhaps the most important concept in IEEE Std 1012 is the use of an *integrity level* to economically focus V&V efforts. Simply stated, one should characterize every software component by an integrity level indicating its criticality to the quality goals of the product. Components with higher integrity levels should receive additional attention from V&V, in terms of both techniques and rigor.

3.2.3. Reviews and Audits   Throughout the literature of software engineering, there has been remarkable consensus on the value of reviews in improving the quality of software. Audits are also necessary in a two-party relationship to ensure that quality activities promised to the acquirer are, in fact, being performed by the supplier. The 12207 standard treats audits and reviews as two different processes. IEEE has one standard describing both:

Process

IEEE Std 1028-1997 (R2002)
IEEE Standard for Software Reviews
This standard defines five types of software reviews and procedures for their execution. Review types include management reviews, technical reviews, inspections, walk-throughs, and audits.
Allocated to: Software Quality Knowledge Area

---

[43] This is a slippery subject. The 12207 standard is clear that V&V represents additional evaluation beyond that provided by the primary processes. Some standards treat *all* evaluation, however, as if it were part of V&V.

IEEE Std 1028 describes five types of reviews:

- *Management review:* monitor progress and evaluate effectiveness of management approaches
- *Technical review:* evaluate products of the project to determine suitability and identify discrepancies
- *Inspection:* detect and identify anomalies in products
- *Walk-through:* a product evaluation less formal than an inspection, possibly for the purpose of educating an audience
- *Audit:* independent evaluation of compliance of products and processes to standards, regulations, plans, etc.

3.3. Practical Considerations

3.3.1. Application Quality Requirements
Various factors influence the planning and management of software quality including domain, external interfaces, methods, resources, etc. Perhaps none have an effect as profound as criticality. The need for the product to implement some critical property such as dependability, safety, security or privacy will have a far-reaching effect on the choice of quality assurance techniques and the intensity of their application. An international standard provides a gateway to the differential application of quality assurance:

Tool

ISO/IEC 15026:1998
Information Technology—System and Software Integrity Levels
This International Standard introduces the concepts of software integrity levels and software integrity requirements. It defines the concepts associated with integrity levels, defines the processes for determining integrity levels and software integrity requirements, and places requirements on each process.
Allocated to: Related Disciplines Chapter, Systems Engineering

ISO/IEC 15026 introduces the concept of an integrity level as an indicator of the contribution of a particular component in maintaining system risks within acceptable limits. Integrity level assignments result from a system-level evaluation of the design of the system in the context of the hazards that confront its use. Systems engineers and software engineers cooperate in adjusting design and re-evaluating risks, converging upon a design with assigned integrity levels. The integrity levels can be applied during development to allocate additional verification and validation efforts to high-integrity components, as described in IEEE Std 1012.

An IEEE standard describes additional quality techniques that are to be applied when safety is a concern:

Plan

IEEE Std 1228-1994 (R2002)
IEEE Standard for Software Safety Plans
This standard describes the minimum content of a plan for the software aspects of development, procurement, maintenance, and retirement of a safety-critical system.
Allocated to: Related Disciplines Chapter, Systems Engineering

IEEE Std 1228 is firmly grounded in a system view of software development. All of the measures provided by 1228 to pursue safety goals are premised upon a hazard analysis performed on the system containing the software.

3.3.2. Defect Characterization   By their nature, software quality assurance activities find defects. Simply fixing the defects might seem sufficient, but analysis of the discovered defects can be applied toward improving processes and reducing future defect rates. Defects are typically found in such numbers that effective analysis requires grouping them by categories. An IEEE standard includes provisions for the minimum classification of defect information and guidance for application of the information:

Tool

IEEE Std 1044-1993 (R2002)
IEEE Standard Classification for Software Anomalies
This standard provides a uniform approach to the classification of anomalies found in software and its documentation. It includes helpful lists of anomaly classifications and related data.
Allocated to: Software Quality Knowledge Area

Obviously, in analyzing defects, it is important to separate cause and effect. Consistent application of an appropriate terminology assists all participants. IEEE Std 610.12 describes the relationship among many of the key terms: "The fault tolerance discipline distinguishes between the human action (a *mistake*), its manifestation (a . . . *fault*), the result of the fault (a *failure*), and the amount by which the result is incorrect (the *error*). IEEE Std 1044 uses the neutral term, *anomaly*, to encompass all of these.

Collected anomaly data can be used to construct reliability data useful to predict reliability and determine when to stop testing. The data can also enable precisely directed process remediation and improvement. Of course, systematic defect collection and analysis requires appropriate tooling, procedures and management attention.

3.3.3. Software Quality Management Techniques   Software quality management techniques can be categorized as:

- *Static:* examination of artifacts without executing them. (Tools are available to support many important categories of static analysis.)
- *People-intensive:* review techniques of various degrees of formality and interaction
- *Analytical:* specific analyses aimed toward assessing formally defined characteristics
- *Dynamic:* exercising and observing the behavioral characteristics of the product

Examples of analysis include complexity analysis, control flow analysis and algorithmic analysis. Formal methods, including proofs of correct function, may also be grouped into this category. Formal methods can be used to ensure correct implementation of critical properties, such as security, without the effort inherent in providing a full proof of correctness.

Dynamic techniques include simulation, model checking and symbolic execution. Of course, testing is an important subcategory of dynamic techniques. Testing is treated elsewhere but two aspects of testing should be noted here because they relate to the quality of the materials to be used in the project:

- Evaluation (including testing) of tools to be employed in the project
- Conformance testing of components and COTS products to be incorporated into the product

These two forms of testing are covered by IEEE standards that are adoptions of ISO/IEC standards:

Tool

IEEE Std 1462-1998 (R2004)
IEEE Standard: Adoption of International Standard
ISO/IEC 14102: 1995, Information Technology—
Guideline for the Evaluation and Selection of CASE tools
This standard provides guidelines for the evaluation and selection of CASE tools.
Allocated to: Software Engineering Tools and Methods Knowledge Area

IEEE Std 1462 provides an overall approach to evaluating CASE tools for use in software projects.

Tool

IEEE Std 1465-1998 (R2004)
IEEE Standard: Adoption of International Standard
ISO/IEC 12119:1994(E), Information Technology—
Software Packages—Quality Requirements and Testing
This standard describes quality requirements specifically suitable for software packages and guidance on testing the package against those requirements.
Allocated to: Software Quality Knowledge Area

IEEE Std 1465 provides requirements for the quality and testing of software "packages." Although the requirements of the standard are mainly relevant to the supplier, clause 4 explains how the acquirer should test the supplier's claims.

Quality management activities are sometimes overlaid on testing activities. For example, a quality assurance organization might be asked to perform independent testing or to review the results of the developer's testing or even the adequacy of the developer's test plan.

3.3.4. Software Quality Measurement It would seem obvious that one cannot attain software quality without measuring the degree to which it is attained. Nevertheless, systematic measurement is often neglected in software project planning. Measurement can inform the management decision-making process (e.g., how much testing is enough?), find bottlenecks in development, and provide baselines for process improvement. Of course, a central purpose of measurement is to determine how well a product has achieved its quality goals.

Several standards are useful in quality measurement. The fundamental standard in this area is an international standard:

Process

ISO/IEC 15939:2002
Software Engineering—Software Measurement Process
This standard provides a life cycle process for software measurement
suitable for use with IEEE/EIA 12207.
Allocated to: Software Engineering Process Knowledge Area

ISO/IEC 15939 provides an overall process for performing measurement along with a framework of terminology fundamental to measurement. The standards listed below have not been fully reconciled with the terminology but are broadly consistent with the international standard.

This IEEE standard provides an overall approach to quality measurement:

Measure

IEEE Std 1061-1998 (R2004)
IEEE Standard for a Software Quality Metrics Methodology
This standard describes a methodology—spanning the entire life cycle—for
establishing quality requirements and identifying, implementing, and
validating the corresponding measures.
Allocated to: Software Quality Knowledge Area

IEEE Std 1061 provides for the selection of quality goals, their decomposition into specific attributes and the selection of measures for the attributes. The internal measures (those applied during development) are to be validated against external measures (those applied to the completed product) so that measurement during development can be used to predict the achievement of quality characteristics.

This IEEE standard provides specific treatment for the attribute of reliability:

Measure

IEEE Std 982.1-1988
IEEE Standard Dictionary of Measures to Produce Reliable Software
This standard provides a set of measures for evaluating the reliability of a
software product and for obtaining early forecasts of the reliability of a
product under development.
Allocated to: Software Quality Knowledge Area

The standard is a dictionary of various measures of software reliability.

4. STANDARDS IN THE SOFTWARE QUALITY KNOWLEDGE AREA

4.1. IEEE Std 730-2002, IEEE Standard for Software Quality Assurance Plans

IEEE Std 730 has a distinguished history, being the first standard to be approved (in 1979) by the predecessor organization of today's S2ESC. The current 10-page revision was approved in 2002. The first edition had the grand purpose of characterizing the difference between informal software development and disciplined software engineering. As the discipline has progressed, quality assurance is now viewed as the check on software engineering processes rather than being the totality of software engineering.

This standard provides minimum requirements for the content and preparation of a Software Quality Assurance Plan (SQAP) for the development and maintenance of critical software. Although the standard describes the SQAP itself, the requirements for the content of the various sections induce implicit requirements for various SQA activities. One would claim "content conformance" for quality assurance plans that contain—by inclusion or reference—the material required by the standard, or "format conformance" if the plan is also structured as provided by the standard. The format provides for the following sections:

- *Purpose:* the purpose and scope of the plan in terms of the software items covered, the intended use of the software and the extent of the life cycle treated
- *Reference documents:* cited documents including policies that motivate the plan as well as other documents providing additional details
- *Management:* the project's organization, along with the tasks, roles and responsibilities assigned to each element. Task descriptions include entry and exit criteria and the relationship to major checkpoints. Resource estimates are provided.
- *Documentation:* a list of the documentation for the development, verification, validation, use, and maintenance of the software along with the criteria for review or auditing the documents. A minimum set of documentation is required: software requirements description, software design description, verification and validation plans, V&V reports, user documentation, and software configuration management plan.
- *Standards, practices, conventions, and metrics:* identification of standards, practices, conventions, statistical techniques, quality requirements and measurements to be applied during the project and an explanation of how conformance to these items is to be assured
- *Software reviews:* a definition of the software reviews to be conducted and the schedule for performing them. A minimum set of reviews is required: software specifications review, architecture design review, detailed design review, verification and validation plan review, functional audit, physical audit, in-process audits, managerial review, software configuration management plan review, and post-implementation review.
- *Test:* identification of any testing other than that described in the V&V plan
- *Problem reporting and corrective action:* procedures for reporting, tracking and resolving problems or other issues
- *Tools, techniques, and methodologies:* the tools, techniques and methods used to support software quality assurance

- *Media control:* identification and plans for protecting the media used to store the work products
- *Supplier control:* assurance means for software to be provided by suppliers
- *Records collection, maintenance, and retention:* methods and facilities for assuring that records are available
- *Training:* training activities to support quality assurance
- *Risk management:* identification, assessment, monitoring and control of risks
- *Glossary*
- *SQAP change procedure and history*

The 730 standard is directly applicable to detailing the quality assurance process of 12207. It should be noted, though, that the efforts described in the SQAP could be appropriately applied to any of the other standards prescribing life cycle processes.

One might be tempted to complain that the SQAP required by 730 seems to be far larger in scope than the quality assurance process of 12207 and seems to address the entire scope of responsible software development. To some extent, this claim is justified because the 730 standard can be viewed as being, in some sense, an alternative to 12207. One could apply 730 to any software development project, regardless of whether 12207 is being used. It should be noted, though, that the recent revision of 730 was intended to make it thoroughly consistent with 12207. One can apply both standards to a project without fear of anything worse than redundant provisions.

IEEE Std 730 is also appropriate for providing the link between the quality management requirements of ISO 9001 and the software engineering standards of the S2ESC as a part of an overall program for conformance with the ISO 9000 series standards.

4.2. IEEE Std 982.1-1988, IEEE Standard Dictionary of Measures to Produce Reliable Software

The IEEE 982.1 standard is a dictionary, providing definitions and a taxonomy of measures that can be applied in the development of reliable software. This 40-page S2ESC document was approved in 1988 and is currently being revised. Emphasis is placed on measures that can be made early in the development process as indicators of the eventual reliability of the software product. Six categories of product measures and three categories of process measures are described along with the proper conditions for the use of a measure and its method of computation. Measures of errors, faults, and failures serve as primitives for many of the remaining measures.

4.3. IEEE Std 1012-2004, IEEE Standard for Software Verification and Validation

The current version of IEEE Std 1012 was approved in 2004—a minor revision following a major revision in 1998. The current version is a process standard describing the activities and tasks of the verification and validation processes as well as the content of an appropriate plan.

The 70-plus-page standard begins with the concept of a software integrity level—an indicator of the criticality of a software component. It provides minimum verification and validation tasks for each integrity level and provides a concept of differential intensity and rigor applied to V&V tasks depending on integrity level. Criteria for completion of the V&V tasks are provided. The standard reaches toward systems issues by defining system level V&V tasks such as hazard analysis, risk analysis, migration assessment, and retirement assessment. The standard is intended to be consistent with IEEE/EIA 12207.0 and the ISO/IEC version of that standard.

IEEE Std 1012 takes a broad view of the role of V&V, stating in Clause 1.4[44] that:

V&V processes provide an objective assessment of software products and processes throughout the software life cycle. This assessment demonstrates whether the software requirements and system requirements (i.e., those allocated to software) are correct, complete, accurate, consistent, and testable. The software V&V processes determine whether the development products of a given activity conform to the requirements of that activity, and whether the software satisfies its intended use and user needs. The determination includes assessment, analysis, evaluation, review, inspection, and testing of software products and processes. Software V&V should be performed in parallel with software development, not at the conclusion of the development effort.

The results of V&V create the following benefits to the program:

- Facilitate early detection and correction of software anomalies
- Enhance management insight into process and product risk
- Support the life cycle processes to ensure conformance to program performance, schedule and budget
- Provide an early assessment of software and system performance
- Provide objective evidence of software and system conformance to support a formal certification process
- Improve the software development and maintenance processes
- Support the process improvement for an integrated systems analysis model

---

Users are assisted by a number of tables, charts, and annexes that provide extensive cross-references between V&V provisions and other parts of the life cycle, e.g., the processes of 12207. In addition to requirements on the content of a Software V&V Plan, the standard recommends an outline for the organization of the plan as shown in Table 14:

---

[44] The source of this quotation is a pre-publication draft of IEEE P1012. Before final publication in IEEE Std 1012-2004, the text may be copy-edited or the containing clause may be renumbered.

TABLE 14. Outline of software V&V plan suggested by IEEE Std 1012

1. Purpose
2. Referenced Documents
3. Definitions
4. V&V Overview
   4.1 Organization
   4.2 Master Schedule
   4.3 Software Integrity Level Scheme
   4.4 Resources Summary
   4.5 Responsibilities
   4.6 Tools, Techniques, and Methods
5. V&V Processes
   5.1 Process: Management
      5.1.1 Activity: Management of V&V
   5.2 Process: Acquisition
      5.2.1 Activity: Acquisition Support V&V
   5.3 Process: Supply
      5.3.1 Activity: Planning V&V
   5.4 Process: Development
      5.4.1 Activity: Concept V&V
      5.4.2 Activity: Requirements V&V
      5.4.3 Activity: Design V&V
      5.4.4 Activity: Implementation V&V
      5.4.5 Activity: Test V&V
      5.4.6 Activity: Installation and Checkout V&V
   5.5 Process: Operation
      5.5.1 Activity: Operation V&V
   5.6 Process: Maintenance
      5.6.1 Activity: Maintenance V&V
6. V&V Reporting Requirements
7. V&V Administrative Requirements
   7.1 Anomaly Resolution and Reporting
   7.2 Task Iteration Policy
   7.3 Deviation Policy
   7.4 Control Procedures
   7.5 Standards, Practices, and Conventions
8. V&V Documentation Requirements

4.4. IEEE Std 1028-1997, IEEE Standard for Software Reviews

This 37-page standard was revised in 1997 and reaffirmed in 2002. It provides direction to the reviewer or auditor on the conduct of management and technical reviews and audits. Included are activities applicable to both critical and noncritical software and the procedures required for the execution of reviews and audits. The standard specifies the characteristics of five different types of reviews and audits (management review, technical review, inspection, walk-through, audit). It does not specify the reasons for conducting a review nor the requirements for using the results (other standards provide that); instead it focuses on the conduct of the review itself. For each review type, it specifies responsibilities, inputs, entry criteria, procedures, exit criteria, and outputs.

The standard is intended to support review and audit requirements of several other IEEE standards, including 730, 838, 1012, 1058, 1074, 1219, 1220, 1228, and 12207.

The life cycle process standard, IEEE/EIA 12207.0, specifies evaluations intrinsic to the primary processes and specifies Joint Review and Audit processes fundamental to a two-party relationship. IEEE 1028 could be applied to implement the intrinsic reviews and could satisfy some of the substantive requirements of the Joint Review and Audit processes.

Two useful annexes are included. Annex A looks at the reviews specified by other standards (IEEE 730, IEEE 1012, IEEE 1074, and IEEE/EIA 12207.0) and specifies which of the five review types is applicable. Annex B is a comparison of the characteristics of the review types.

4.5. IEEE Std 1044-1993, IEEE Standard Classification for Software Anomalies

IEEE Std 1044, approved in 1993 and reaffirmed in 2002, provides a uniform approach to the classification of anomalies found in software and its documentation. An *anomaly* is any condition that departs from the expected; the term is used as a generalization of terms such as error, fault, failure, incident, flaw, bug, etc. The standard describes the processing of anomalies from their initial discovery to their final disposition, as well as suggestions for categories into which anomalies may be classified. Conformance to the standard requires the use of a specified minimal set of classifications. The 26-page document may be employed to a number of ends, including software product measurements, quality records, and process improvement.

4.6. IEEE Std 1061-1998, IEEE Standard for a Software Quality Metrics Methodology

IEEE Std 1061 was developed by S2ESC in 1992, revised in 1998, and reaffirmed in 2004. The 20-page standard provides a methodology for establishing quality requirements and developing the supporting measurements. It may be applied by acquirers, developers, maintainers, users, or independent assessors. Some may believe that the word "quality" is misapplied in the title of this standard and is another example of the term being stretched to include anything that is good. Indeed, the introduction defines the purpose of the standard as follows:

> *Software quality is the degree to which software possesses a desired combination of attributes. This desired combination of attributes shall be clearly defined; otherwise, assessment of quality is left to intuition. For the purpose of this standard, defining software quality for a system is equivalent to defining a list of software quality attributes required for that system. In order to measure the software quality attributes, an appropriate set of software metrics shall be identified.*

Although the standard does not prescribe measures, the annexes provide exemplar measures along with two fully worked examples of application. The basic approach is to establish a measurement framework that is a three-level hierarchy. The framework begins with the establishment of quality requirements and an agreed set of attributes defining the requirements. Factors representing user and management views are associated with the attributes. "Direct metrics" are selected to quantitatively represent the factors. For example, mean time to failure might serve as the direct metric for a factor of reliability. At the second level of the hierarchy, the factors are decomposed into subfactors representing software oriented attributes that are more directly measurable and more meaningful to the developers. For example, a subfactor of reliability might be a measure of the system's ability to continue to operate in the presence of hardware failure. Finally, at the third level is found a decomposition of subfactors into metrics to be used to measure system products and processes during development. These third level metrics, that are to be validated against the direct metrics, are used to estimate factor values during the development process.

The word "metric" itself has become a bit suspect. The framework of measurement terminology provided by ISO/IEC 15939 provides no role for the term. Nevertheless, the 1061 standard is broadly compatible with 15939 despite the differences in terminology.

4.7. IEEE Std 1465-1998, IEEE Standard—Adoption of International Standard ISO/IEC 12119: 1994(E)—Information Technology—Software Packages—Quality Requirements and Testing

This 16-page standard, approved in 1994 and later adopted by IEEE, provides quality requirements for software packages, such as spreadsheets, word processors, utilities, etc. (The term "package" is intended to suggest a bundle of documentation, programs, and data.) Packages are required to include user documentation and a product description that enables prospective buyers to determine if the package is suitable for the intended use. General quality requirements are placed on the programs and data as well as specific requirements for the content of the user documentation and the product description. The standard also provides instructions for testing the product for compliance with quality requirements including the claims made in the product description. Additional material describing ISO/IEC 12119 can be found in [Wegner95].

ISO/IEC JTC 1/SC 7 is currently performing an extensive revision of this standard, including adjusting its scope to address commercial-off-the-shelf (COTS) software components. It is anticipated that IEEE will adopt the result, possibly using the number 12119 rather than 1465. Meanwhile, IEEE has reaffirmed its adoption of the standard, awaiting the results of the SC 7 revision project.

5. SUMMARY

This chapter has provided an overview of the Software Quality knowledge area of the IEEE Computer Society's *Guide to the Software Engineering Body of Knowledge.* Fifteen IEEE and ISO/IEC standards have been offered as relevant to the knowledge area. The presentation has been divided into four subsections provided by the *SWEBOK Guide*:

- *Fundamentals:* ISO/IEC 90003 provides the link between software quality assurance and the larger, more general disciplines of quality management. ISO/IEC 9126-1 provides a taxonomy of software quality characteristics.

- *Software Quality Management Processes:* Software quality management is provided by five software life cycle processes of IEEE/EIA 12207.0. Additional details for implementation of those processes can be found in IEEE Std 730 (quality assurance), IEEE Std 1012 (verification and validation), and IEEE Std 1028 (reviews and audits).

- *Practical Considerations:* Of the factors affecting software quality requirements, none is more profound than the need to implement a critical property. ISO/IEC 15026 describes the analysis leading to the assignment of integrity levels to software components. IEEE Std 1228 describes additional quality activities needed for software in systems where safety is a critical property. IEEE Std 1044 can assist in defect classification. IEEE standards 1462 and 1465 provide guidance in qualifying materials (tools and components) to be used in software projects. ISO/IEC 15939 provides a process for software measurement. IEEE Std 1061 provides an overall framework for pursuing quality measurement and IEEE Std 982.1 specifically addresses reliability measurement.

Chapter *16*

Related Disciplines

Although it is the purpose of the *SWEBOK Guide* to characterize the contents of software engineering, it is recognized that competent software engineers must have knowledge from other fields. The last chapter of the *Guide* is titled "Related Disciplines of Software Engineering." It defines the boundary of software engineering by describing eight strongly related disciplines from which software engineers will draw knowledge. The Guide selects one or more authoritative sources as providing an overview, including a knowledge breakdown, of each of the related disciplines.

The eight related disciplines are:

- Computer Engineering
- Computer Science
- Management
- Mathematics
- Project Management
- Quality Management
- Software Ergonomics
- Systems Engineering

Each related discipline is described in the sections that follow. Three of the disciplines—project management, quality management, and systems engineering—have important related standards. Those disciplines will be described in greater detail and the related standards will be discussed. The disciplines and the standards related to the disciplines are depicted in Figure 20.

The Road Map to Software Engineering: A Standards-Based Guide, by James W. Moore
Copyright © 2006 by IEEE Computer Society

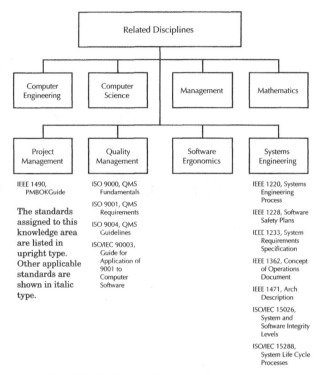

Figure 20. *Disciplines related to software engineering*

1. COMPUTER ENGINEERING

The Computing Curricula 2001[45] project is a joint project of the IEEE Computer Society and the Association for Computing Machinery to provide curricula relevant to the education of computing professionals. Four volumes are planned:

- Computer Science
- Computer Engineering
- Software Engineering
- Information Systems

The first volume is completed; the others are in various stages of preparation. This project is the source of several of the knowledge area breakdowns provided in this chapter.

The draft report of the volume on computer engineering states that "computer engineering embodies the science and technology of design, construction, implementation and maintenance of software and hardware components of modern computing systems and computer-controlled equipment." The report identifies the following knowledge areas:

---

[45] http://www.computer.org/education/cc2001/final/index.htm

- Algorithms and Complexity
- Computer Architecture and Organization
- Computer Systems Engineering
- Circuits and Systems
- Digital Logic
- Discrete Structures
- Digital Signal Processing
- Distributed Systems
- Electronics
- Embedded Systems
- Human-Computer Interaction
- Information Management
- Intelligent Systems
- Computer Networks
- Operating Systems
- Programming Fundamentals
- Probability and Statistics
- Social and Professional Issues
- Software Engineering
- Test and Verification
- VLSI/ASIC Design

2. COMPUTER SCIENCE

The final report of the volume on computer science of the Computing Curricula 2001 project identifies the following knowledge areas for computer science:

- Discrete Structures
- Programming Fundamentals
- Algorithms and Complexity
- Architecture and Organization
- Operating Systems
- Net-Centric Computing
- Programming Languages
- Human-Computer Interaction
- Graphics and Visual Computing
- Intelligent Systems
- Information Management
- Social and Professional Issues
- Software Engineering
- Computational Science and Numerical Methods

3. MANAGEMENT

The European MBA Guidelines defined by the European association of national accreditation bodies (EQUAL) covers the following area:

- Accounting
- Finance
- Marketing and sales
- Operations management
- Information systems management
- Law
- Human resource management
- Economics
- Quantitative analysis
- Business policy and strategy

4. MATHEMATICS

The *SWEBOK Guide* uses the guidelines of the Canadian Engineering Accreditation Board to identify the following knowledge areas for mathematics:

- Linear algebra
- Differential and integral calculus
- Differential equations
- Probability
- Statistics
- Numerical analysis
- Discrete mathematics

The *Guide* mentions that a more detailed list can be found in the draft software engineering volume of the Computing Curriculum 2001 project.

5. PROJECT MANAGEMENT

5.1. Scope

Project management is defined in the 2000 Edition of *A Guide to the Project Management Body of Knowledge (PMBOK® Guide)*, published by the Project Management Institute, as "the application of knowledge, skills, tools, and techniques to project activities to meet project requirements."

5.2. Knowledge Areas

The Knowledge Areas identified in the *PMBOK® Guide* for project management are:

- Project Integration Management
- Project Scope Management
- Project Time Management
- Project Cost Management
- Project Quality Management
- Project Human Resource Management
- Project Communications Management
- Project Risk Management
- Project Procurement Management

5.2. Related Standards

The IEEE's Computer Society's S2ESC recognized the close relationship between project management and software engineering several years ago when they decided to adopt the PMI PMBOK® Guide as their own standard for project management. The other S2ESC standard related to the subject— IEEE Std 1058, Software Project Management Plans—is to be regarded as a specialization of project management and is intended to be completely consistent with the PMBOK® Guide. In 2003, S2ESC updated their relationship with PMI by adopting the 2000 version of the PMBOK® Guide:

Terminology

IEEE Std 1490-2003
IEEE Guide: Adoption of PMI Standard, A Guide to the
Project Management Body of Knowledge (PMBOK® Guide)
This document is the IEEE adoption of the Project Management Body of Knowledge defined by the Project Management Institute. It identifies and describes generally accepted knowledge regarding project management.
Allocated to: Related Disciplines Chapter, Quality Management

6. QUALITY MANAGEMENT

6.1. Scope

Quality management is defined in ISO 9000:2000 as "coordinated activities to direct and control an organization with regard to quality." The year 2000 editions of three ISO standards—9000, 9001, and 9004—provide an authoritative reference to the discipline. Each will be considered below.

6.2. Knowledge Areas

The *SWEBOK Guide* selected knowledge areas from the material used by the American Society for Quality in certifying quality engineers:

- Management and leadership in quality engineering
- Quality systems development, implementation, and verification
- Planning, controlling, and assuring product and process quality
- Reliability and risk management

- Problem solving and quality improvement
- Quantitative methods

6.3. Related Standards

The ISO 9000 standards—developed and maintained by ISO TC 176—take a process-based view of the organization. The fundamental premise of the standards is that well-defined organizational processes are more likely to create high quality products than poorly defined ones. To implement a quality system an organization must define its processes and the interfaces among them. Of course, this premise corresponds exactly with accepted wisdom regarding the development of high-quality software. Many software engineers may be surprised to learn that practices they may have regarded as exclusive to software are described by ISO 9001 as general to all quality systems. Examples include configuration management, document control, product and process measurements, reviews, and audits. Even process improvement is described. In fact, the ISO 9000 approach has been criticized for aggregating all possible aspects of goodness under the label of "quality."

The three most important documents in the ISO 9000:2000 collection are listed below. ISO 9000 provides concepts and terminology that underlay all of the documents in the collection:

Terminology

ISO 9000:2000
Quality Management Systems—Fundamentals and Vocabulary
This standard describes fundamental concepts and vocabulary for the other quality management standards.
Allocated to: Related Disciplines Chapter, Quality Management

ISO 9001 provide the requirements for a quality management system:

Process

ISO 9001:2000
Quality Management Systems—Requirements
This standard specifies the requirements for an organizational quality management system aiming to provide products meeting requirements and enhance customer satisfaction.
Allocated to: Related Disciplines Chapter, Quality Management

ISO 9004 is a companion to 9001. It provides guidance in implementing the provisions of 9001. Because the two were written in a concurrent and carefully coordinated fashion, they are sometimes referred to as the "consistent pair":

Process

ISO 9004:2000
Quality Management Systems—
Guidelines for Performance Improvements
This is a guide to ISO 9004 focusing on the effectiveness and efficiency of the quality management system.
Allocated to: Related Disciplines Chapter, Quality Management

The application of the ISO 9000 standards to software development has always been a problem. Software developers follow many of the same principles, but have their own jargon. Furthermore, the complexity of software development can mislead auditors who are not themselves software experts. To help resolve this problem, the last two generations of ISO 9000 standards have been supplemented with a guide applying quality management principles to software. The companion to the 1994 generation was ISO 9000-3. ISO/IEC JTC 1/SC 7 took responsibility for preparing the guide for the 2000 generation; the result is ISO/IEC 90003, a number selected to be similar without suggesting that the document is maintained by the developers of ISO 9000:

Process

ISO/IEC 90003:2004
Software Engineering—Guidelines for the
Application of ISO 9001:2000 to Computer Software
This standard provides guidance for organizations in the application of ISO9001:2000 to the acquisition, supply, development, operation, and maintenance of computer software.
Allocated to: Related Disciplines Chapter, Quality Management

7. SOFTWARE ERGONOMICS

The *SWEBOK Guide* uses a definition of software ergonomics from ISO TC 159: "Ergonomics or (human factors) is the scientific discipline concerned with the understanding of the interactions among human and other elements of a system, and the profession that applies theory, principles, data and methods to design in order to optimize human well-being and overall system performance." The following knowledge areas were selected using a variety of sources:

- Cognition
- Cognitive AI I: Reasoning
- Machine Learning and Grammar Induction
- Formal Methods in Cognitive Science: Language
- Formal Methods in Cognitive Science: Reasoning
- Formal Methods in Cognitive Science: Cognitive Architecture
- Cognitive AI II: Learning
- Foundations of Cognitive Science
- Information Extraction from Speech and Text
- Lexical Processing
- Computational Language Acquisition
- The Nature of HCI: (Meta-)Models of HCI
- Use and Context of Computers: Human Social Organization and Work; Application Areas; Human-Machine Fit and Adaptation
- Human Characteristics: Human Information Processing; Language, Communication, Interaction; Ergonomics

- Computer System and Interface Architecture: Input and Output Devices; Dialogue Techniques; Dialogue Genre; Computer Graphics
- Dialogue Architecture
- Development Process: Design Approaches; Implementation Techniques; Evaluation Techniques; Example Systems and Case Studies

The *SWEBOK Guide* mentions that a list that is more narrowly focused on human-computer interface design can be found in the draft report of the volume on software engineering of the Computing Curricula 2001 project.

8. SYSTEMS ENGINEERING

8.1. Scope

The *SWEBOK Guide* uses a definition of systems engineering obtained from the International Council on Systems Engineering:

> *Systems Engineering is an interdisciplinary approach and means to enable the realization of successful systems. It focuses on defining customer needs and required functionality early in the development cycle, documenting requirements, then proceeding with design synthesis and system validation while considering the complete problem:*
>
> - *Operations*
> - *Performance*
> - *Test*
> - *Manufacturing*
> - *Cost and Schedule*
> - *Training and Support*
> - *Disposal*
>
> *Systems Engineering integrates all the disciplines and specialty groups into a team effort forming a structured development process that proceeds from concept to production to operation. Systems Engineering considers both the business and the technical needs of all customers with the goal of providing a quality product that meets the user needs.*

8.2. Knowledge Areas

The *SWEBOK Guide* takes its list of systems engineering knowledge areas from the process areas listed in INCOSE's "Systems Engineering Handbook— A 'How to' Guide for All Engineering" [INCOSE00]:

- Defining needs (acquisition and supply)
- Systems engineering technical management
- System design
- Product realization
- Technical analysis and evaluation

- Systems engineering product control
- Systems engineering process control
- Systems post-implementation support

8.3. Related Standards

The systems engineering standards are treated in a process-oriented manner in Chapter 20, System Life Cycle Processes. That treatment is organized around the system life cycle processes of ISO/IEC 15288. On the other hand, INCOSE's Systems Engineering Handbook is organized around a different set of process groups—a set derived from EIA-632:1999, *Processes for Engineering a System*. Instead of attempting to explain and reconcile the differing processes, this chapter will simply slot the standards into the process areas of EIA-632.

8.3.1. Defining Needs According to the SE Handbook, the output of this process area is as follows:

> *The output of mission level activities should be sufficient definition of the operational need or concept of operations to gain authorization and funding for program initiation and to generate a request for proposal if the system is to be acquired through a contract acquisition process, or to gain authorization to develop and market the system if market driven. These outputs can be documented in a mission needs statement, a system requirements document, a statement of work, and a request for proposal.*

IEEE has a standard for a Concept of Operations document, one suitable means for stating mission needs:

Document

IEEE Std 1362-1998
IEEE Guide for Information Technology—System Definition—
Concept of Operations (ConOps) Document
This document provides guidance on the format and content of a Concept of Operations (ConOps) document, describing characteristics of a proposed system from the users' viewpoint.
Allocated to: Related Disciplines Chapter, Systems Engineering

Alternatively, a Concept of Operations document could be produced as part of the requirements definition during system design, perhaps based on documents written during needs definition.

8.3.2. System Engineering Technical Management An important result of executing this process area is a Systems Engineering Management Plan. IEEE Std 1220—discussed later in this chapter—provides guidance on the content and format of such a plan.

8.3.3. System Design An important part of this process area is requirements definition. If a Concept of Operations document was not produced during needs definition, then it may be appropriate to produce one as part of requirements definition. In any case, it is necessary to produce a "System Requirements Document." IEEE Std 1233 makes recommendations regarding its content:

Document

IEEE Std 1233, 1998 Edition (R2002)
IEEE Guide for Developing System Requirements Specifications
This document provides guidance on the development of a System Requirements Specification, covering the identification, organization, presentation, and modification of requirements. It also provides guidance on the characteristics and qualities of requirements.
Allocated to: Related Disciplines Chapter, Systems Engineering

Requirements definition is followed by solution definition in this process area. The SE Handbook says that, "The overall objective . . . is to create a System Architecture." IEEE has a standard describing a multi-viewpoint approach to describing the architecture of a system:

Document

IEEE Std 1471-2000
IEEE Recommended Practice for
Architectural Description of Software Intensive Systems
This document recommends a conceptual framework and content for the architectural description of software-intensive systems.
Allocated to: Related Disciplines Chapter, Systems Engineering

8.3.4. Product Realization   Of course, the various software engineering standards are relevant to the realization of software components of the system.

8.3.5. Technical Analysis and Evaluation   The SE Handbook discusses many forms of technical analysis and evaluation. One important group consists of safety and health hazard analyses. The *SE Handbook* says that it is "useful to prepare a System Safety Program Plan, SSPP, which delineates hazard and risk analysis methodologies." The plan is used to drive various test and evaluation activities during component development and system integration. IEEE has a standard describing how software development is affected by a system safety plan:

Plan

IEEE Std 1228-1994 (R2002)
IEEE Standard for Software Safety Plans
This standard describes the minimum content of a plan for the software aspects of development, procurement, maintenance and retirement of a safety-critical system.
Allocated to: Related Disciplines Chapter, Systems Engineering

One aspect of designing a system with critical properties with critical properties, like safety or security, is to ensure that resources are directed toward assurance of the critical functions. ISO/IEC 15026 describes the collaboration between systems and software engineers to assign "integrity levels" to components so that their needs for special design and assurance measures can be noted:

Tool

ISO/IEC 15026:1998
Information Technology—System and Software Integrity Levels
This International Standard introduces the concepts of software integrity levels and software integrity requirements. It defines the concepts associated with integrity levels, defines the processes for determining integrity levels and software integrity requirements, and places requirements on each process.
Allocated to: Related Disciplines Chapter, Systems Engineering

8.3.6. Systems Engineering Product Control This area concerns configuration management and data management. Although IEEE has applicable standards for software components, it has no standards applicable to product control at the system level.

8.3.7. Systems Engineering Process Control This area concerns the adoption and evaluation of systems engineering processes to be applied upon a project. Two standards are relevant. IEEE Std 1220 describes how the "Systems Engineering Process" is applied and managed to develop a system:

Process

IEEE Std 1220-1998
IEEE Standard for the
Application and Management of the Systems Engineering Process
This standard describes the systems engineering activities and process required throughout a system's life cycle to develop systems meeting customer needs, requirements, and constraints.
Allocated to: Related Disciplines Chapter, Systems Engineering

ISO/IEC 15288 provides a broader set of processes that apply across the entire life cycle of a system:

Process

ISO/IEC 15288:2002
Systems Engineering—System Life Cycle Processes
This standard provides a framework of processes used across the entire life cycle of human-made systems.
Allocated to: Related Disciplines Chapter, Systems Engineering

8.3.8. System Post-Implementation Support This area concerns the support that systems engineers provide to manufacturing or sustaining operations following the development of a system. IEEE has no applicable standards.

9. DESCRIPTIONS OF RELEVANT STANDARDS

9.1. IEEE Std 1220-1998, IEEE Standard for the Application and Management of the Systems Engineering Process

This S2ESC standard was approved as a "trial use" standard in 1994 and revised, based in part on usage reports, for full-use status in 1998. The 76-page standard describes the interdisciplinary tasks that are required throughout a system's life cycle to transform customer needs, requirements, and constraints into a system solution. It applies to a performing activity within an enterprise that is responsible for developing a product design and establishing the life cycle infrastructure needed to provide for life cycle sustainment. It specifies the requirements for the systems engineering process and its application throughout the product life cycle. The requirements of this standard are applicable to new products as well as incremental enhancements to existing products.

The standard is useful in providing a view of systems engineering processes that is consistent with the software life cycle processes used in IEEE and other standards. This view provides a contextual anchor for software activities—like V & V, architecture, requirements engineering, integration, and qualification testing—that necessarily relate to systems-level engineering activity.

The standard makes no normative references but was prepared to be used with IEEE/EIA 12207.0 and ISO 9001:1994. Although ISO 9001 has been revised since the publication of IEEE 1220, there is no reason to believe that an inconsistency has been created.

The standard defines the Systems Engineering Process (SEP) shown in Figure 21. "The SEP is a generic problem-solving process, which provides the mechanisms for identifying and evolving the product and process definitions of a system. The SEP applies throughout the system life cycle to all activities associated with product development, verification/test, manufacturing, training, operation, support, distribution, disposal, and human systems engineering."

An important feature of IEEE Std 1220 is an informative annex describing the content of a Systems Engineering Management Plan. The suggested table of contents is shown in Table 15.

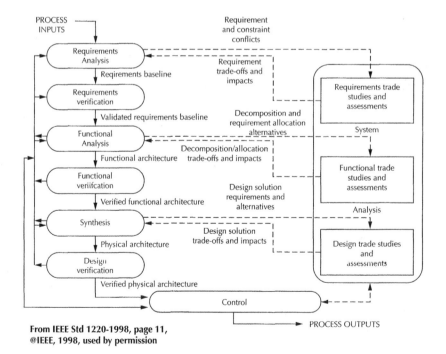

From IEEE Std 1220-1998, page 11,
@IEEE, 1998, used by permission

Figure 21. *Systems engineering process of IEEE Std 1220*

TABLE 15. Outline of systems engineering management plan suggested by IEEE Std 1220

1. Scope
2. Applicable Documents
3. Systems Engineering Process (SEP) Application
   3.1 Systems Engineering Process Planning
      3.1.1 Major Deliverables and Results
         3.1.1.1 Integrated Database
         3.1.1.2 Specifications and Baselines
      3.1.2 Process Inputs
      3.1.3 Technical Objectives
      3.1.4 System Breakdown Structure (SBS)
      3.1.5 Training
      3.1.6 Standards and Procedures
      3.1.7 Resource Allocation
      3.1.8 Constraints
      3.1.9 Work Authorization
   3.2 Requirements Analysis
   3.3 Requirements Baseline Validation
   3.4 Functional Analysis
   3.5 Functional Verification
   3.6 Synthesis
   3.7 Design Verification
   3.8 Systems Analysis
      3.8.1 Trade-Off Analyses
      3.8.2 System/Cost Effectiveness Analyses
      3.8.3 Risk Management
   3.9 Control
      3.9.1 Design Capture
      3.9.2 Interface Management
      3.9.3 Data Management
      3.9.4 Systems Engineering Master Schedule (SEMS)
      3.9.5 Technical Performance Measurement
      3.9.6 Technical Reviews
      3.9.7 Supplier Control
      3.9.8 Requirements Traceability
4. Transitioning Critical Technologies
5. Integration of the Systems Engineering Effort
   5.1 Organizational Structure
   5.2 Required Systems Engineering Integration Tasks
6. Additional Systems Engineering Activities
   6.1 Long-Lead Items
   6.2 Engineering Tools
   6.3 Design to Cost
   6.4 Value Engineering
   6.5 Systems Integration Plan
   6.6 Interface with Other Life Cycle Support Functions
   6.7 Safety Plan
   6.8 Other Plans and Controls
7. Notes
   7.1 General Background Information
   7.2 Acronyms and Abbreviations
   7.3 Glossary

IEEE Std 1220 is a central component in the ongoing activity to "harmo-nize" the systems and software engineering standards of ISO/IEC JTC 1/SC 7 and S2ESC. Currently, S2ESC is revising 1220 to be more consistent with the terminology and concepts of ISO/IEC 15288. This revision will probably be published in 2005. At that point, the IEEE standard will be "fast-tracked" to become a JTC 1 standard and will be further revised to take an appropriate place in the harmonized system and software engineering process standards.

9.2. IEEE Std 1228-1994, IEEE Standard for Software Safety Plans

This S2ESC standard, approved in 1994 and reaffirmed in 2002, applies to "the plan used for the development, procurement, maintenance and retirement of safety-critical software; for example, software products whose failure could cause loss of life, serious harm, or have widespread negative social impact." Probably due to liability considerations, the document does not state when such a plan is appropriate, nor does it claim that its provisions are sufficient to ensure software safety. An annex is devoted to five types of software safety analyses.

Although the 24-page document deals with only the safety aspects of soft-ware, its provisions cut across all of the subjects of interest to S2ESC, includ-ing management processes, product characteristics, and architectural aspects of the system enclosing the software.

IEEE Std 1228 establishes "minimum acceptable requirements for the content of a Software Safety Plan." It provides more than a format, though. Because the plan is required to address "processes and activities intended to improve the safety of safety-critical software," the standard levies implicit requirements on the activities applied to the development of the software. Other IEEE standards are cited as appropriate to achieving those require-ments. Table 16 shows the outline of the safety plan required by IEEE Std 1228 along with some of the standards cited as supporting execution of the plan.

It should be noted that IEEE 1228 requires that the software safety plan be prepared within the context of a more general system safety program; it recognizes that software safety must be considered in the context of its asso-ciated hardware, environment, and operators.

9.3. IEEE Std 1233, 1998 Edition, IEEE Guide for Developing System Requirements Specifications

S2ESC approved this 32-page guide document in 1996 as part of its efforts to describe the system-level context that necessarily encloses any software devel-opment effort. In 1998, it was supplemented with an annex reconciling it with IEEE/EIA 12207.1. This document is a guide to capturing system-level requirements including operational concepts, design constraints and design configuration requirements. The system requirements specification is impor-tant to the software development process because the requirements allocated to software components of the system are based on the system requirements. The 12207 standard specifically cites this connection, so 1233 is a key docu-ment in detailing the acquisition, supply, and development processes pre-scribed by 12207.

TABLE 16. Outline of software safety plan suggested by IEEE Std 1228

Section of Plan	IEEE Standards Referenced
1. Purpose	
2. Definitions, acronyms and abbreviations, and references	610.12
3. Software safety management	
3.1 Organization and responsibilities	
3.2 Resources	
3.3 Staff qualifications and training	
3.4 Software life cycle	1074
3.5 Documentation requirements	
(a) Software project management	1058
(b) Software configuration management	828
(c) Software quality assurance	730
(d) Software safety requirements	830
(e) Software safety design	1016
(f) Software development methodology, standards, practices, metrics and conventions	730, 982.1
(g) Test documentation	829, 1008
(h) Software V & V	1012
(i) Reporting safety V & V	1012
(j) Software user documentation	1063
(k)–(o) Safety analysis results	
3.6 Software safety program records	
3.7 Software configuration management activities	828
3.8 Software quality assurance activities	730
3.9 Software V & V activities	1012
3.10 Tool support and approval	
3.11 Previously developed or purchased software	
3.12 Subcontract management	
3.13 Process certification	
4. Software safety analyses	
4.1 Software safety analyses preparation	
4.2 Software safety requirements analysis	1028
4.3 Software safety design analysis	1028, 982.1
4.4 Software safety code analysis	1028
4.5 Software safety test analysis	1028
4.6 Software safety change analysis	
5. Post-development	
6. Approval	

**TABLE 17. Outline of system requirements specification suggested
by IEEE Std 1233**

Table of contents
1. Introduction
    1.1 System purpose
    1.2 System scope
    1.3 Definitions, acronyms, and abbreviations
    1.4 References
    1.5 System overview
2. General system description
    2.1 System context
    2.2 System modes and states
    2.3 Major system capabilities
    2.4 Major system conditions
    2.5 Major system constraints
    2.6 User characteristics
    2.7 Assumptions and dependencies
    2.8 Operational scenarios
3. System capabilities, conditions, and constraints
    3.1 Physical
        3.1.1 Construction
        3.1.2 Durability
        3.1.3 Adaptability
        3.1.4 Environmental conditions
    3.2 System performance characteristics
    3.3 System security
    3.4 Information management
    3.5 System operations
        3.5.1 System human factors
        3.5.2 System maintainability
        3.5.3 System reliability
    3.6 Policy and regulation
    3.7 System life cycle sustainment
4. System interfaces

The guide focuses more on the activities required to write the specification than the contents or format of the specification itself, although an example outline is provided. IEEE Std 1220 is cited as the source of process requirements for the development of the specification document.

The outline shown in Table 17 is offered as a possible organization for a System Requirements Specification.

9.4. IEEE Std 1362-1998, IEEE Guide for Information Technology—System Definition—Concept of Operations (ConOps) Document

The development of a Concept of Operations (ConOps) document has become an increasingly popular tool for the transmission of necessary information between systems and software engineers as well as other stakeholders. The 1998 IEEE document is a guide, but it also contains specific descriptions of desired content and format.

Preparation of a ConOps is a specification activity leading to a document bridging the gap between the users' understanding of their needs and technical specifications suitable for system development. The ConOps document has the following characteristics:

- It describes operational needs without performing detailed requirements analysis.
- It is intended to be verifiable by users with no special training beyond their normal duties.
- It provides a place for users to state their vision without the necessity for quantification or tradeoff.
- It is a mechanism for users to speculate on possible solutions.

A key feature of the IEEE ConOps document is the emphasis on describing the characteristics of both the current system and the proposed system. Furthermore, in long-lived systems, the document can point the way for anticipated evolution, all within the context of the operational environment. A major goal is avoiding the creation of a system that fails to fill a useful role despite the successful technical development of its constituent parts.

Table 18 shows an outline suggested for the ConOps document by IEEE Std 1362. An annex to the guide suggests small additions to the outline to ensure conformance to the requirements of IEEE/EIA 12207.1.

9.5. IEEE Std 1471-2000, IEEE Recommended Practice for Architectural Description of Software Intensive Systems

IEEE Std 1471 is intended to deal with one of software engineering's hot topics, the description of software architecture. In recent years, many practitioners have come to believe that successful development of modern distributed and client/server systems requires a description of the system that is more abstract than its design and which provides a focused and selective treatment of strategic issues crucial to the operation of the system while suppressing less important issues. Although there is much disagreement regarding the precise definition, most refer to the general concept as architecture.

The 23-page Recommended Practice was completed in 2000 following a lengthy development effort. As one might expect, a difficult issue was writing a definition for the word "architecture"; ultimately, the following was agreed:

> *Architecture is . . . the fundamental organization of a system, embodied in its components, their relationships to each other and the environment, and the principles governing its design and evolution.*

The emphasis upon relationships among components leads to the fundamental premise of the document. Architectures should be expressed by describing multiple viewpoints, each corresponding to a stakeholder concern. The document does not select or recommend viewpoints. Instead, each project should select viewpoints appropriate to the concerns of the system being developed.

Figure 22 is an Entity-Relationship diagram illustrating the concepts treated by 1471. A *system* exists within an *environment* for the purpose of per-

TABLE 18. Outline of concept of operations document suggested by IEEE Std 1362

Title page
Revision chart
Preface
Table of contents
1. Scope
    1.1 Identification
    1.2 Document overview
    1.3 System overview
2. Referenced documents
3. Current system or situation
    3.1 Background, objectives, and scope
    3.2 Operational policies and constraints
    3.3 Description of the current system or situation
    3.4 Modes of operation for the current system or situation
    3.5 User classes and other involved personnel
    3.6 Support environment
4. Justification for and nature of changes
    4.1 Justication of changes
    4.2 Description of desired changes
    4.3 Priorities among changes
    4.4 Changes considered but not included
5. Concepts for the proposed system
    5.1 Background, objectives, and scope
    5.2 Operational policies and constraints
    5.3 Description of the proposed system
    5.4 Modes of operation
    5.5 User classes and other involved personnel
    5.6 Support environment
6. Operational scenarios
7. Summary of impacts
    7.1 Operational impacts
    7.2 Organizational impacts
    7.3 Impacts during development
8. Analysis of the proposed system
    8.1 Summary of improvements
    8.2 Disadvantages and limitations
    8.3 Alternatives and trade-offs considered
9. Notes
Appendices
Glossary

forming a *mission*. Every system has an *architecture* regardless of whether it is actually described. When present, an *architectural description* identifies *concerns* that are important to *stakeholders*. *Viewpoints* are selected to address the concerns. *Views* are instances of what is seen from a viewpoint and may be treated with *models*.

The 1471 standard applies to any software-intensive system and is viewed as applicable for systems architecture activity as well as software architecture. It does not specify a particular form of architectural description; it simply recommends characteristics that an architectural description should have.

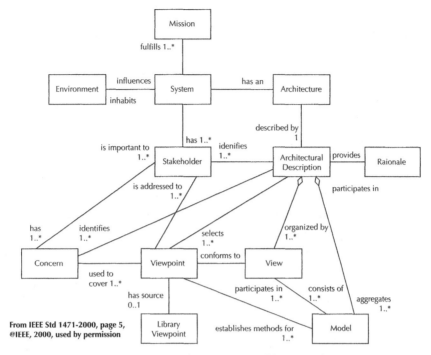

Figure 22. *Architecture concepts treated by IEEE Std 1471*

9.6. IEEE Std 1490-2003, IEEE Guide—Adoption of PMI Standard—A Guide to the Project Management Body of Knowledge

The most important tenet in the study of management is a principle called the *universality of management* [Fayol49, Koontz72] stating that:

- Management performs the same functions of planning, organizing, staffing, directing, and controlling regardless of the nature of the activity being managed.
- Management functions are characteristic duties of managers, but the specific practices, techniques and methods are particular to the nature of the activity being managed.

This concept permits us to apply general management principles to the particular needs of software project management [Thayer84].

The Program Management Institute (PMI) defines the Program Management Body of Knowledge as the sum of knowledge within the profession of project management. Their *Guide to the Project Management Body of Knowledge (PMBOK® Guide)* is intended to describe the subset of the PMBOK® that is generally accepted and to provide a common lexicon for discussion of project management. The *PMBOK® Guide* is used by the PMI in certification activities, including accreditation of degree-granting educational programs and professional certification programs.

IEEE S2ESC has chosen the *PMBOK® Guide* as its source of project management principles and has adopted it as an IEEE standard. The current standard adopts the PMI's 2000 edition of this document—216 pages.

The standard describes project management as an instance of *general management*—the planning, organizing, staffing, executing, and controlling the operations of an ongoing enterprise. Project management applies those techniques to the *project*—"a temporary endeavor undertaken to create a unique product or service." The temporary nature of the project implies, of course, that each one has a definite beginning and an end.

The standard describes five types of management processes:

- *Initiating:* Authorizing the project or phase
- *Planning:* Defining objectives and selecting from alternative courses of action to attain the project's objectives
- *Executing:* Coordinating people and other resources to carry out the plan
- *Controlling:* Ensuring that project objectives are met by monitoring and measuring progress and taking corrective action when necessary
- *Closing:* Formalizing acceptance of the project or phase and bringing it to an orderly end.

The standard then specializes those process types into 39 instances of processes that are applied to nine project management knowledge areas, as shown in Table 19.

9.7. ISO 9000:2000, Quality Management Systems—Fundamentals and Vocabulary

Since their first publication in 1987, the ISO 9000 series has become, arguably, the most successful set of standards ever written in any area that affects information technology and provide the baseline for quality management standards around the world. The ISO 9000 standards were originally developed to deal with the wide variety of national quality standards that were hindering the development of a single market in the European Union. The organization of the collection has evolved as its mission has broadened. The ISO web site claims implementation by 610,000 organizations in 160 countries, but this number will probably decline in the short term as organizations deal with the transition from the 1994 generation of the standard to the 2000 version.

The ISO 9000 series of standards are developed and maintained by ISO Technical Committee 176. (In the United States, the standards have been adopted by the American Society for Quality Control and are designated with similar numbers, for example, ASQC Q9001 corresponds to ISO 9001. Similar forms of adoption occur in several other countries.)

The premise underlying the standards is that an organization with well-defined processes is more likely to produce products meeting the needs of its customers than a poorly managed organization. The ISO 9000 series of standards and guidelines specifies an approach to quality management intended to achieve this goal.

TABLE 19. Processes and knowledge areas of IEEE Std 1490

Knowledge Area	Process	Process Type				
		I	P	E	Co	Cl
Project integration management	Project plan development		•			
	Project plan execution			•		
	Integrated change control				•	
Project scope management	Initiation	•				
	Scope planning		•			
	Scope definition		•			
	Scope verification				•	
	Scope change control				•	
Project time management	Activity definition		•			
	Activity sequencing		•			
	Activity duration estimating		•			
	Schedule development		•			
	Schedule control				•	
Project cost management	Resource planning		•			
	Cost estimating		•			
	Cost budgeting		•			
	Cost control				•	
Project quality management	Quality planning		•			
	Quality assurance			•		
	Quality control				•	
Project human resource management	Organizational planning		•			
	Staff acquisition		•			
	Team development			•		
Project communications management	Communications planning		•			
	Information distribution			•		
	Performance reporting				•	
	Administrative closure					•
Project risk management	Risk management planning		•			
	Risk identification		•			
	Qualitative risk analysis		•			
	Quantitative risk analysis		•			
	Risk response planning		•			
	Risk monitoring and control				•	
Project procurement management	Procurement planning		•			
	Solicitation planning		•			
	Solicitation			•		
	Source selection			•		
	Contract administration			•		
	Contract close-out					•

The standards were originally published in 1987 and revised circa 1994. A new 2000 generation of the standards makes substantial changes, notably moving to a process-oriented approach in place of the old documentation-driven approach.

ISO 9000:2000 describes the fundamental concepts of quality management systems and provides the terminology used by the remainder of the series. The 29-page document replaces two documents of the 1994 generation: ISO 8402 and ISO 9000-1.

The standard begins by providing eight quality management principles on which the ISO 9000 series is based:

- *Customer focus:* Organizations depend on their customers and therefore should understand current and future customer needs, should meet customer requirements and strive to exceed customer expectations.
- *Leadership:* Leaders establish unity of purpose and direction of the organization. They should create and maintain the internal environment in which people can become fully involved in achieving the organization's objectives.
- *Involvement of people:* People at all levels are the essence of an organization and their full involvement enables their abilities to be used for the organization's benefit.
- *Process approach:* A desired result is achieved more efficiently when activities and related resources are managed as a process.
- *System approach to management:* Identifying, understanding, and managing interrelated processes as a system contributes to the organization's effectiveness and efficiency in achieving its objectives.
- *Continual improvement:* Continual improvement of the organization's overall performance should be a permanent objective of the organization.
- *Factual approach to decision making:* Effective decisions are based on the analysis of data and information.
- *Mutually beneficial supplier relationships:* An organization and its suppliers are interdependent and a mutually beneficial relationship enhances the ability of both to create value.

These principles are further elaborated in a brochure published on the ISO web site.[46] The intent of the ISO 9000 series is to encourage "the adoption of the process approach to manage an organization." It defines a process as an "activity, or set of activities, that uses resources to transform inputs to outputs." Use of the process approach would enable the top management of an organization to establish quality objectives and utilize the processes to achieve those objectives throughout the organization. So the series of standards describe a quality management system used an organization to ensure that its products and service satisfy the customers' requirements and comply with applicable regulations.

---

[46] "ISO 9000 Quality Management Principles," http://www.iso.ch/iso/en/iso9000-14000/understand/qmp.html

IEEE Computer Society S2ESC has adopted a policy of consistency with the quality management standards of ISO TC 176.

9.8. ISO 9001:2000, Quality Management Systems—Requirements

This 23-page standard replaces three documents of the 1994 generation: 9001, 9002, and 9003. According to the ISO web site, the primary reasons for the revision were to

- Improve provisions for monitoring customer satisfaction
- Make the standard more user-friendly
- Improve the consistency between requirements and guidelines
- Promote use of generic quality management principles
- Improve compatibility with ISO 14000

The previous version of the standards had raised issues in application to small businesses, software developers, and service providers. An important change is a shift from the manufacturing-oriented, record-driven approach of the 1994 version to a process-oriented approach intended to be applicable to all sectors. Furthermore, the process-oriented approach is expected to be more compatible with other organizational initiatives like Total Quality Management and Baldrige.

ISO 9001:2000 is used to establish a management system that provides confidence that an organization's products and services meet established or specified requirements as well as applicable laws and regulation. In addition, the standard requires continual improvements of the quality management system to increase customer satisfaction. Unlike ISO 9000 and 9004, this standard contains requirements for the quality management system. Some organizations will choose to simply conform to the requirements of the standard. Others, for competitive reasons, will desire an independent audit of conformance, leading to "certification" or "registration" as a conforming organization. The approach to auditing is described in ISO 19011:2002, *Guidelines for quality and/or environmental management systems auditing.*

Major provisions of ISO 9001 require:

- Establishment of a quality management system and continual improvement of its effectiveness
- A commitment by top management to customer satisfaction evidenced by an organizational quality policy, measurable quality objectives throughout the organization, with appropriate responsibilities and review
- Providing appropriate resources
- Product realization processes to satisfy customer needs and expectations
- Continual measurement, analysis, and improvement

Only the product realization processes are tailorable. The other requirements are regarded as generic and applicable in all situations. Because of the generic nature of the standard, it is expected that some sectors may desire versions specific to their industry. In fact, TC 176 developed such a specification—ISO TS 16949—as a pilot for the auto industry.

IEEE Computer Society S2ESC has adopted a policy of consistency with the quality management standards of ISO TC 176.

9.9. ISO 9004:2000, Quality Management Systems—Guidelines for Performance Improvements

The 56-page ISO 9004 was developed concurrently with ISO 9001 to create a "consistent pair." ISO 9004:2000 replaces ISO 9004-1:1994 and incorporates key provisions from many of the other guidance documents in the 1994 generation of ISO 9000 standards. It quotes the text of ISO 9001 in boxed paragraphs and provides additional guidance. According to 9004, "ISO 9004 gives guidance on a wider range of objectives of a quality management system than does ISO 9001, particularly for the continual improvement of an organization's overall performance and efficiency, as well as its effectiveness. ISO 9004 is recommended as a guide for organizations whose top management wishes to move beyond the requirements of ISO 9001, in pursuit of continual improvement of performance. However, it is not intended for certification or for contractual purposes." ISO 9004 does not contain requirements and is useful only for guidance and self-evaluation.

ISO TC 176 has prepared other guidance documents on specific subjects related to quality management:

- ISO 10006 for project management
- ISO 10007 for configuration management
- ISO 10012 for measurement systems
- ISO 10013 for quality documentation
- ISO TR 10014 for managing the economics of quality
- ISO 10015 for training
- ISO 19011 for auditing

IEEE Computer Society S2ESC has adopted a policy of consistency with the quality management standards of ISO TC 176.

9.10. ISO/IEC 15026:1998, Information Technology—System and Software Integrity Levels

This 12-page standard was completed in 1998 as the result of a collaboration between ISO/IEC JTC 1/SC 7, responsible for software engineering, and IEC TC 56, responsible for dependability engineering.

Integrity is the concept that serves as the link between the dependability of a software or system product and the practice of software engineering. "Dependability" is a term relevant to the user's perception of the external characteristics of the system while "integrity" is relevant to the developer's view of the internal design of the system and processes employed in its development. The determination of integrity level is based on risk analysis. As a result of determining integrity level, software integrity requirements are derived and levied on the software developers.

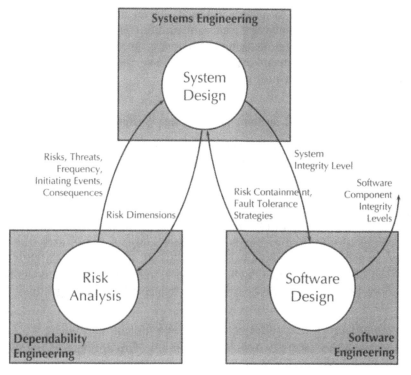

Figure 23. *Determination of software integrity levels*

The software aspects of dependability address the performance of the software as a part of a system functioning in its operational environment. The software, system, and operational aspects are inseparably related. The concept of integrity is intended to achieve the relationship.

ISO/IEC 15026 defines *integrity level* as a fundamental unifying concept. "A software integrity level denotes a range of values of a software property necessary to maintain system risks within tolerable limits. For software that performs a mitigating function, the property is the reliability with which the software must perform the mitigating function. For software whose failure can lead to a system threat, the property is the limit on the frequency or probability of that failure."

The integrity level is used to establish benchmarks intended to balance the consequences of the risk against the consequences of mitigating the risk. Due to the importance of this trade-off, determination of the desired integrity level is best considered as a negotiation between two parties, the developer and the buyer, user, or regulator [Tripp96]. "The concept of an independent integrity assurance authority is fundamental to the proper use of this International Standard. The integrity assurance authority is the person or organization responsible for certifying compliance with the integrity requirements."

As shown in Figure 23, determination of software integrity levels inherently involves iteration among the disciplines of dependability, systems engineering, and software engineering. The risk analysis techniques of dependability engineering are used to analyze threats, their frequency, and their consequences. This analysis is used to determine an integrity level for the system, and based on its design, to assign integrity levels for software components. Based on this analysis, software risk containment requirements can be postulated and provided to the systems engineering process for consideration in modifying the system concept and design. These results, in turn, lead to a revised risk analysis, continuing the iteration.

9.11. ISO/IEC 15288:2002, Systems Engineering—System Life Cycle Processes

The possibility of writing a systems engineering standard was conceived in ISO/IEC JTC 1/SC 7 during the early 1990s. Work began in roughly 1995, but extended discussions of the nature of the work slowed progress. The standard was finally completed and published in 2002. A companion guide, ISO/IEC TR 19760 was published the following year. Most of the 62-page 15288 standard is concerned with the definition of a set of life cycle processes for a system. The processes are defined in terms of purpose, outcomes and activities. Conformance is achieved by "demonstrating that all of the requirements of the declared set of processes have been satisfied using the outcomes as evidence."

The 25 system life cycle processes are categorized into four groups:

- Agreement processes: Relationships between organizations
- Enterprise processes: Strategic management of an enterprise, notably creation of projects
- Project processes: Managing the resources and assets allocated to a project
- Technical processes: Transform the system product from idea to completion.

Table 20 lists the life cycle processes in their process categories.

The processes of 15288 are described in more detail in Chapter 20, System Life Cycle Processes. The 15288 standard also requires that the user should assemble the selected processes into a life cycle model comprising a set of stages, along with a statement of purpose and outcomes for each of the stages. An example set of stages is provided in an informative annex.

Despite the obvious relationship between systems and software engineering, ISO/IEC 15288 has a less-than-perfect fit with its software life cycle counterpart, ISO/IEC 12207. That fact motivates a "harmonization" project that is underway to improve the fit.

IEEE Computer Society S2ESC is in the process of adopting ISO/IEC 15288. The plan is for the bodies of the two standards to be identical. IEEE plans only to add an annex providing a mapping to IEEE standards. The IEEE version is expected to be published in 2005.

9.12. ISO/IEC 90003:2004, Software Engineering—Guidelines for the Application of ISO 9001:2000 to Computer Software

It has always been difficult for ISO 9001 auditors to deal with software producers. Although software engineering implements many of the same quality management principles as ISO 9001, the jargon is so different that auditors often demanded excessive amounts of evidence or even denied certification. In

TABLE 20. System life cycle processes of ISO/IEC 15288

15288 Process Group	15288 Process
Agreement	Acquisition
	Supply
Enterprise	Enterprise Environment Management
	Investment Management
	System Life Cycle Processes Management
	Resource Management
	Quality Management
Project	Project Planning
	Project Assessment
	Project Control
	Decision-Making
	Risk Management
	Configuration Management
	Information Management
Technical	Stakeholder Requirements Definition
	Requirements Analysis
	Architectural Design
	Implementation
	Integration
	Verification
	Transition
	Validation
	Operation
	Maintenance
	Disposal

1997, ISO TC 176 produced ISO 9000-3 as a guide for how the quality management principles of ISO 9001:1994 could be applied to software. When ISO 9001 was revised in 2000, a replacement was needed. It was determined that the project should be transferred to ISO/IEC JTC 1/SC 7. Ultimately, the number of the resulting standard was changed so that it would not be regarded as a product of TC 176. The 54-page document reproduces the text of ISO 9001 in boxed paragraphs and provides guidance explaining how the material should be interpreted for software producers. In addition, the guidance cites various SC 7 standards that may be helpful in dealing with some of the provisions. An informative annex describes the relationship between the quality planning provisions of ISO/IEC 12207 and the body of 90003.

IEEE Computer Society S2ESC is in the process of adopting ISO/IEC 90003 as of March 2004. It plans to add an annex providing a mapping to IEEE standards.

10. SUMMARY

This chapter has provided an overview of eight disciplines listed as related to software engineering by the IEEE Computer Society's *Guide to the Software Engineering Body of Knowledge*. In some cases, there are important standards related to these disciplines:

- *Computer Engineering*
- *Computer Science*
- *Management*
- *Mathematics*
- *Project Management*: IEEE Std 1490 adopts the Project Management Institute's *Guide to the Project Management Body of Knowledge*
- *Quality Management*: Three ISO standards for quality management systems—9000, 9001, and 9004—are described. In addition, ISO/IEC 90003 maps the requirements of the 9001 standard to international software engineering standards.
- *Software Ergonomics*
- *Systems Engineering*: Two international standards and five IEEE standards are described. ISO/IEC 15288 provides a set of life cycle processes and IEEE Std 1220 describes a Systems Engineering Process. IEEE 1362 and 1233 assist in requirements specification by describing, respectively, a Concept of Operations document and a System Requirements Specification document. IEEE Std 1471 contains provisions for description of architectures. ISO/IEC 15026 and IEEE Std 1228 assist in planning for the production of software systems that must exhibit critical properties, such as safety.

Chapter *17*

Other IEEE Software Engineering Standards

The classification by knowledge areas of the preceding chapters does not capture two S2ESC standards—one because it is too general and the other because it is too specific.

Two indications of a mature engineering discipline are agreement on the terminology used in the discipline and the application of the discipline to solve specific classes of problems. "Real" engineering generally involves adapting a "cookbook" solution to meet the circumstances of a specific problem—all within the context of an agreed set of concepts and terms. The two standards described in this chapter can be viewed as addressing those needs. IEEE Std 610.12 underlays all of the other standards in the collection as the source of the terminology used in the standards. IEEE Std 2001 is the first of a new class of S2ESC standards applying software and systems engineering principles to create solutions to specific classes of problems. Those two standards are described in this chapter.

Terminology

IEEE Std 610.12-1990 (R2002)
IEEE Standard Glossary of Software Engineering Terminology
This standard is a glossary of software engineering terminology.
Allocated to: Other Software Engineering Standards Chapter

**World Wide
Web**

IEEE Std 2001-2002
IEEE Recommended Practice for the Internet—Web Site
Engineering, Web Site Management, and Web Site Life Cycle
This document recommends practices for engineering World Wide Web pages for use in Intranet and Extranet environments.
Allocated to: Other Software Engineering Standards Chapter

The Road Map to Software Engineering: A Standards-Based Guide, by James W. Moore
Copyright © 2006 by IEEE Computer Society

1. STANDARDS NOT IN A KNOWLEDGE AREA

1.1. IEEE Std 610.12-1990, IEEE Standard Glossary of Software Engineering Terminology

According to its abstract, IEEE Std 610.12 identifies terms currently in use in the field of Software Engineering and provides standard definitions for the terms. It contains about 1,300 entries. Although the vocabulary is intended to be comprehensive, terms are excluded if they are trademarked or otherwise specific to a group or organization. Multi-word terms following from the definition of their constituent words and words whose meaning in the computer field can be inferred from the usual English meaning are also excluded. The vocabulary also notes synonyms, contrasting terms, and related terms.

The 88-page standard was approved in 1990 and reaffirmed in 2002. Those involved with software engineering standardization for many years will recall that 729 was the number of the original 1983 IEEE vocabulary on the subject of software engineering. Circa 1990, the IEEE Computer Dictionary project gathered all of the glossaries of the computing field into a single document, IEEE Std 610. The successor of IEEE 729 was chapter 12 of the 610 standard. Although centralization of management improved the consistency of the various vocabularies, it became difficult to recruit volunteers to manage the huge collection. Technological obsolescence has caused IEEE to withdraw most of the other parts of the 610 standard. Because the rate of knowledge change in software engineering is slower than some other fields of information technology, IEEE has decided to retain this standard until a replacement can be developed. Nevertheless, the age of the standard remains a disadvantage. All considered, though, the document remains as a valuable resource.

To update the document, S2ESC has joined with ISO/IEC JTC 1/SC 7 to develop a shared vocabulary for software and systems engineering. The current version of IEEE Std 610.12 has been contributed to the project as a baseline. We can hope for a replacement within a few years.

1.2. IEEE Std 2001-2002, IEEE Recommended Practice for the Internet—Web Site Engineering, Web Site Management, and Web Site Life Cycle

According to its abstract, IEEE Std 2001 recommends practices for engineering web pages based on various industry guidelines, notably those of the World Wide Web Consortium (W3C®). The document does not address style or human factors considerations in web page design beyond those reflecting good engineering practice. The 72-page standard (including an index) was revised in 2002 following its initial release in 1999.

The document addresses the design and implementation of managed web sites—either Intranet (for use within an enterprise) or Extranet (for access by others). The goal is to facilitate ease of use (e.g., making it easy to find relevant information) while protecting the implementer from legal liabilities and increasing the effectiveness of development and maintenance. The recommended practice achieves these goals by providing guidance for the designers and developer of web pages and for the managers responsible for their development and maintenance.

From the viewpoint of software engineering, the standard is notable for describing a life cycle concept for web pages and relating that life cycle to various IEEE software engineering standards. A few examples are:

- IEEE/EIA 12207.0 for life cycle processes
- IEEE Std 1028 for reviews
- IEEE Std 1058 for project management

The standard goes well beyond software engineering practice, though, in recommending specific content and design goals for web sites.

One important feature of the standard is a large bibliography citing many other relevant standards and providing brief descriptions of their utility in web site design. Another annex provides a handy checklist of requirements. Another annex provides guidance on meeting the so-called "Section 508" requirements for access to web sites by users with disabilities.

2. SUMMARY

This chapter has described two standards that do not fit into any of the knowledge areas of the IEEE Computer Society's *Guide to the Software Engineering Body of Knowledge*.

- IEEE Std 610.12 is a glossary of software engineering terminology.
- IEEE Std 2001 applies software engineering principles to the engineering of web sites.

Part 3

A Process-Oriented View

Chapter *18*

History and Concepts

Of all of the topics in software engineering, process is the one receiving the most attention today. It is commonly believed that the implementation of a sound software development process is strongly correlated with the production of high-quality software products. Of course, this attitude is not unique to software development—the ISO 9000 standards apply the same premise to the manufacturing of systems.

Even in the early days of the software discipline, it was recognized that some crucial aspects of the software development, such as configuration management, had to be rigorously defined and enforced. Since Winston Royce's seminal presentation in 1970 [Royce70], emphasis has been broadened and placed on a disciplined approach to defining and improving the processes for software development and, more recently, maintenance and operation. More recently, systems engineering processes—at least, those related to software-intensive systems—have received similar attention. The body of available standards represents a range of viewpoints—spanning singular processes and life cycle frameworks. An important challenge for the standards organizations is to rationalize their collections, merging the viewpoints by harmonizing the standards that define processes. An additional dimension is the interest during the last decade in the systematic assessment and improvement of processes. Both IEEE S2ESC and SC 7 are pursuing the goals of integrating individual processes into life-cycle frameworks—frameworks that include approaches for self-improvement. S2ESC has led the way, assembling a set of reference software processes from available standards. ISO/IEC JTC 1/SC 7 is tackling the bigger job of "harmonizing" both software and system life cycle processes as well as the quality management processes of ISO 9001.

This chapter will provide a brief history of software life cycle process standards (including some "future history") and the "Basili model," intended to clarify the relationships among various kinds of process standards. The framework of software reference processes used by IEEE S2ESC will be introduced. In subsequent chapters, the Basili model will be applied to differentiate some of the available alternatives. The framework of software reference processes will be used to organize most of the important software engineering process standards. A chapter will discuss system life cycle process standards. Finally, a chapter will describe important alternative life cycle process standards.

1. HISTORY

One of the difficult questions in selecting a software life cycle process standard is to understand why so many of them are available at all. This section provides historical and technological background to help you select from the alternatives.

The Royce paper was presented at a time when even the concept of "software engineering" was in its infancy—the term itself had been coined only two years previously. Royce's paper introduced the concept that software development follows a "life cycle" with different activities appropriate at different points in the cycle. The paper suggested that it was possible to organize software development as a series of phases with staged objectives rather than following the simple-minded "code and fix" cycle typically practiced at the time, a process that today we would call "hacking." Largely because of the appearance of his diagrams, the Royce model was dubbed the "waterfall," a term that he did not use.[47]

The decades of the 1970s and 1980s saw a proliferation of life cycle definitions and standards, mostly adding details to the waterfall concept. Inspired by the Royce paper, numerous military, regulatory, commercial, and standards organizations wrote life cycle standards that, although boringly similar in concept, were maddeningly different in the details. Some of those standards are still in use and are pertinent to the current discussion.

1.1. Defense Life Cycle Standards

All of the current major life cycle (and development cycle) process standards have an ancestry that includes important Department of Defense (DoD) devel-

---

[47] This historical episode provides an important lesson—names *are* important. As managers put the waterfall model into practice, they were persuaded by the name that, just as water never goes up the waterfall, a particular piece of software should never move backward in the life cycle. In practice, the prototyping and cyclical activities that Royce built into his model were systematically ignored on the premise that each of the staged activities could and should "get it right the first time." Ironically, many of the reforms that modern models introduce were, in fact, present in Royce's original model. The persistence of unenlightened application of the waterfall model, despite repeated failure, is remarkable and is perhaps explained by its convenience to the manager. Applying the unenlightened waterfall model, a manager can summarize the status of even a large software development project on a single sheet of paper, an important advantage. Reformers will have to demonstrate that their proposed models are capable of similarly succinct summarization before they will make much headway in displacing the waterfall model.

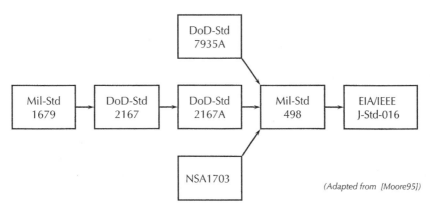

(Adapted from [Moore95])

Figure 24. Family tree of DoD software life cycle standards

opment standards (see Figure 24). In 1974, the US Navy initiated the project to write Mil-Std 1679, *Weapons System Software Development*, one of the first standards treating the usage, control and management of embedded computer resources [SESC93]. It was followed, in the early 1980s, by DoD-Std 2167, intended as applicable to all mission-critical defense computing systems. A subsequent revision, DoD-Std 2167A, corrected some technical characteristics that complicated use with modern programming languages and techniques and created a link between the software and its encompassing system. In the late 1980s, the DoD decided to consolidate DoD-Std 2167A and DoD-Std 7935 standard (for information systems) to produce a single standard, Mil-Std 498, that unified the requirements of its predecessors. After seeing the result, the National Security Agency also dropped its own standard, 1703, in favor of the new one.

Just as Mil-Std 498 was completed, the DoD announced its "acquisition reform" policy emphasizing the use of commercial standards; DoD canceled many of its own standards, including the predecessors of 498. Because no equivalent commercial standard was in place, 498 was approved for an interim period while a suitable commercial standard was developed. The IEEE and the EIA formed a joint committee to develop the replacement, largely similar to Mil-Std 498 with some of the defense-specific jargon removed. The result was issued under a number suggesting the collaborative nature of the project, EIA/IEEE J-Std-016, where the J stands for "Joint."[48] Despite the commercial designation, the result still very much represents three decades of DoD experience in the development of very large, complex software systems. Although new defense software development projects should prefer the IEEE/EIA 12207 standard, the J-Std-016 document may still be useful to legacy projects where it is desirable to retain the documentation structure of previous defense efforts or to organizations that have existing organization-level processes conforming to those military standards.[49]

---

[48] The "J" nomenclature is used by ANSI for standards developed jointly by two or more standards organizations.

[49] IEEE regarded J-Std-016 as a "trial use" standard and EIA regarded it as an "interim" standard. Accordingly, both organizations have withdrawn the standard.

1.2. Commercial Life Cycle Standards

Many of the early commercial standards on the software life cycle were either proprietary—regarded as trade secrets bestowing competitive advantage—or specific to an industry sector. Some industry sectors still employ their own standards; modern examples include RTCA DO-178B, used in the avionics industry, and IEC 880, used in the nuclear industry.

IEEE Std 1074 was developed with the goal of being independent of any particular industry sector and independent of any specific life cycle model. It specified life-cycle process fragments and how they could be connected to create life-cycle processes. Meanwhile, there was growing interest in the international community in developing a life-cycle framework, primarily as an aid to an anticipated international market for software development services. SC 7 initiated the ISO/IEC 12207 project to develop a high-level life cycle framework suitable primarily for use in two-party acquisition situations but also appropriate for internal use within an enterprise. Both Mil-Std 498 and IEEE 1074 were used as base documents for this development, even though the result, which was approved in 1995, is quite different from either (see Figure 25).

Completion of ISO/IEC 12207 put the IEEE S2ESC in an awkward position. It now had two national standards, IEEE 1074 and EIA/IEEE J-Std-016, already quite different in nature, and perceived that the ability of the United States to compete in the international software marketplace might depend on the adoption of a third, very different standard, ISO/IEC 12207. It responded in several ways:

- A joint IEEE/EIA committee adopted a US version of 12207, called IEEE/EIA 12207.0.

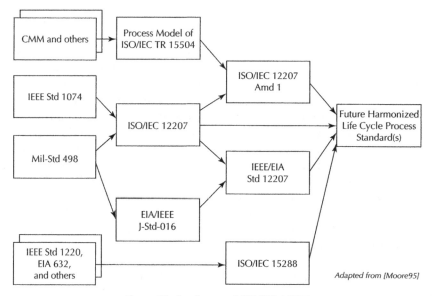

Figure 25. *Family tree of ISO/IEC 12207*

- The joint committee developed two guides, 12207.1 and 12207.2, providing guidance for process data and process implementation.
- S2ESC adopted policies explaining the relationships and intended use of IEEE/EIA 12207, EIA/IEEE J-Std-016, and IEEE Std 1074.

IEEE S2ESC was not alone in its problems integrating the standards. ISO/IEC JTC 1/SC 7 had problems too. Concurrent with the development of ISO/IEC 12207, another working group, WG10, was developing a process assessment guide, ultimately published as ISO/IEC Technical Report 15504.[50] The working group that developed TR 15504 believed that the processes of 12207, particularly the development process, were too large to be assessed. So the WG developed their own process framework that showed substantial differences from that of 12207.

Following the publication of ISO/IEC 12207, ISO/IEC JTC 1/SC 7/WG7 turned its attention to a system life cycle process standard that would make the same contribution to systems engineering that 12207 had made to software engineering. ISO/IEC 15288 was finally published in 2002, but had no clear interface with 12207.

SC 7 is dealing with these problems in two ways. First, an agreement was reached between WG7 and WG10 that the process assessment standard would not define a process model but would be rewritten to be applicable to any process model meeting certain characteristics. The new ISO/IEC 15504, currently under development, will have this characteristic. An appropriate process model was added to ISO/IEC 12207 by the adoption of Amendment 1 in 2002. Of course, this leaves the 12207 with two process models. Resolution of that problem awaits the completion of the effort mentioned next. Second, WG7 has initiated a harmonization project that will result in the revision of ISO/IEC 15288, ISO/IEC 12207, and possibly other standards to implement a single, uniform process model. After substantial preparatory work, this project began in 2003.

As of this writing, in the summer of 2003, these standards have the following status:

- Mil-Std-498 was effectively superseded by EIA/IEEE J-Std-016.
- EIA/IEEE J-Std-016 has never been updated beyond its original Interim (EIA) / Trial Use (IEEE) status. In accordance with its rules, IEEE no longer recommends use of the standard, and EIA has withdrawn it.
- IEEE 1074 was revised in 1997 to be more easily applied in conjunction with the 12207 standard. It is being revised again.
- ISO/IEC 12207 was completed in 1995.
- ISO/IEC 12207 Amendment 1 was completed in 2002. It provides an alternative process model for use with the forthcoming ISO/IEC 15504.

---

[50] ISO/IEC TR 15504 is a Type 2 Technical Report. A type 2 report is one on which work continues after publication. The principle is that the need for consensus is relaxed so that preliminary work can be exposed to a larger community. An ISO Technical Report is not a standard. ISO/IEC JTC 1/SC 7/WG 10 continues work on a multi-part standard that will replace the Technical Report.

- ISO/IEC TR 15504, a nine-part document, was completed during the late 1990s.
- ISO/IEC 15504 is a five-part standard to replace the Technical Report. It is expected to be completed in 2005 and will be used with externally specified process models, such as the one in ISO/IEC 12207 Amd 1.
- IEEE/EIA 12207.0 and its two guides, 12207.1 and 12207.2, were completed and approved by IEEE circa 1997. IEEE has written additional standards and revised other standards to be compatible with 12207.0. S2ESC's current set of reference processes is based strongly on 12207.0.
- ISO/IEC 15288 was completed in 2002.

The life cycle process harmonization project commenced in 2003 and can be expected to continue for three or more years.

Of course, this appears to represent a complicated situation—an appearance exploited by those who choose to term the situation as a "quagmire." In fact, the situation is similar to that of any marketplace where vendors seek to provide some stability for their current users while incorporating new technology. Newer, better products are sometimes not completely usable with older products; vendors sometimes introduce interim products to help bridge the gap between older technology and newer technology. Nevertheless, the fundamental direction is clear and simple—SC 7 plans to provide a unified and consistent treatment of both system engineering and software engineering processes, embracing both process definition and process assessment. The purpose of this part of the book is to assist the reader is dealing with the temporary superficial complexity to find the underlying simplicity.

2. MODEL OF PROCESS ABSTRACTION

Process standards provide a representation of ideal processes[51] intended to be implemented by the users of the standards. Part of the difficulty in applying the documents is that different standards present their views of the desired processes at different levels of abstraction. To relate the process standards, it is helpful to have an overall architecture for process abstraction. For this we use a framework developed by Basili for his *component factory* [Basili92] and applied by Heineman to general process modeling [Heineman94]. In this discussion, their terminology will be modified slightly to be closer to that used by 12207. The framework provides for three levels of abstraction in representing processes:

- The *reference* level, representing agents that carry out the processes. Decisions represented at this level are the selection of a coherent and cohesive set of activities that may be sensibly performed by a single agent. Such a set of activities is a process.

---

[51] Strictly speaking, process standards don't describe the processes. Rather, they specify required characteristics of the processes. In nearly all real-world situations, users will have to add to the set of requirements provided by the process standards, and then describe the processes in some way.

- The *conceptual* level, representing the flow of control and data among the agents. Decisions at this level include the logical relationships among the agents both for control and for the communication of data.
- The *implementation* level, representing the implementation, both technical and organizational, of the agents and their interfaces. Decisions at this level include mapping the agents to the management organization of the particular project or enterprise and the selection of policies, procedures, and tools to enable the agents to perform their tasks.

These levels are not to be regarded as successive functional decompositions. In fact, any one of them can be independently refined into greater details. The distinction between the former two levels permits discussion of the objectives of the processes independently of their fine-grained relationships. The distinction between the latter two levels permits discussion of specific processes independently of the structure of the organization that will implement them (see Figure 26).

The 12207 standard is an example of specifying software life cycle processes at the reference level. The writers of the standard identified processes, in part, by applying the criterion that it should be possible to assign the responsibility for a process to a single organization or party, the "agent" in the framework described above. The requirements of 12207 are, then, the specified responsibilities placed upon the agents executing the processes. From this viewpoint, one can view 12207 as a list of agents and their minimum responsibilities.

In applying the process standards, the next step would be to move to the conceptual level. The generic processes of ISO/IEC 12207 must be instantiated in terms of specific processes with specific flows of control and data. IEEE Std 1074 is useful at this level. It provides "activity groups," collections of related activities each with specified inputs and outputs. These activities can be assembled into processes. A process architect could apply IEEE Std 1074 to specify conceptual-level processes implementing the requirements of 12207, or other reference-level process standards.

The final step is at the implementation level, where the processes of the conceptual level are mapped to the specific characteristics of the organization that is implementing the processes. The agent roles must be assigned to organizational units and various policies and procedures implemented to ensure that the agents execute their assigned responsibilities.

Another distinction—the difference between *process* and *procedure*—is crucial to understanding the role of the 12207 and 1074 standards. The processes described in the standards are not to be understood as a series of steps (procedures) to be performed; instead the processes are assignments of continuing responsibilities to agents. Those assignments of responsibility persist for the duration of the life cycle. For example, when 12207 states that the developer should evaluate the software architecture, it does not necessarily mean that a single review should be conducted, or even that a sequence of reviews should be conducted. Instead, it means that for the duration of the development activity, the developer is assigned the responsibility for evaluating the architecture for the specified characteristics. To derive a time-phased sequence of activities to be

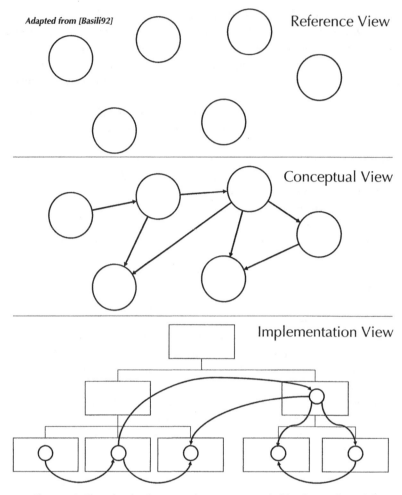

Figure 26. Three levels of process abstraction provided by the Basili model

performed, one must first select a life cycle model and then implement procedures describing the steps to be performed. Neither 12207 nor 1074 provides a
life cycle model and neither provides procedures for implementation.

Traditionally, process standards have been targeted for implementation at
the project level. In recent years, though, there has been increasing emphasis
on organizational process capability, and the Basili model supports this
emphasis. ISO/IEC 12207 viewed some project processes as instances of enterprise-level processes and encouraged enterprise-level adoption of processes but
still evaluated conformance at the project level. The US adaptation of 12207
shifted emphasis from project-level conformance to conformance by entire
enterprises via implementation of conforming organizational policies and
procedures.

To briefly recap this discussion, both the international and the US versions
of 12207 are examples of reference-level process descriptions. IEEE Std 1074

is a tool that can be applied by a process architect to create conceptual-level process descriptions implementing the requirements of the 12207 standard. Organizations—or, less desirably, projects—develop policies and procedures that provide the implementation-level descriptions of the processes complying with the standards.

Most of the other software process standards of IEEE S2ESC straddle the reference and conceptual level of abstraction. Written when process description tools were not in general usage, the authors of these standards generally resorted to the artifice of specifying a plan, the contents of which implicitly impose process requirements. Flows of data were generally unspecified except for the flows to and from the plan's manager.

3. FRAMEWORK OF REFERENCE PROCESSES

The complexity of choices provided by the number of existing process standards presented a problem to IEEE S2ESC. It wasn't reasonable to expect users of software engineering standards to make choices when the consequences of their choices were remote and unclear. Furthermore, the lack of a consistent set of reference processes made it difficult for S2ESC to refer to processes in its own standards. In short, S2ESC needed to adopt a set of processes to be shared across its standards, much as it was counseling its users to do with their projects.

S2ESC's framework of reference processes is based on IEEE/EIA 12207 with a small number of controlled additions. The current list of reference processes and their source is provided in Table 21.

For each process, the table references a set of process objectives that serve to summarize the goals of implementing and executing the process.[52] The processes contained in the list of the five primary processes, eight supporting processes, and four organizational processes of IEEE/EIA 12207.0. They are supplemented with a measurement process provided by ISO/IEC 15939, a risk management process provided by IEEE Std 1540, and a set of reuse processes provided by IEEE Std 1517. In each case, the additional processes were written from the outset to "plug into" the framework provided by the 12207 standard.

Using this framework provides a growing but controlled set of processes as the basis for adopting organizational processes and applying additional standards. However, the model makes a few sacrifices:

- The forthcoming ISO/IEC 15504 process assessment standard will not be applicable to this process framework. Of course, in many countries, there are other, de facto, standards for process assessment.
- There are no systems engineering processes, except for the minimal set of activities provided in the development process of the 12207 standard.

---

[52] ISO/IEC 12207 Amendment 1 describes each process by a statement of its purpose and its outcomes. This is an alternative way to the same end.

TABLE 21. Reference processes of S2ESC

Process Category	Process Name	Objectives Defined by
Primary-Business	Acquisition	IEEE/EIA 12207.0, G.1 and IEEE Std 1517, C.1
	Supply	IEEE/EIA 12207.0, G.14 and IEEE Std 1517, C.8
Primary-Technical	Development	IEEE/EIA 12207.0, G.4 and IEEE Std 1517, C.3
	Operation	IEEE/EIA 12207.0, G.11 and IEEE Std 1517, C.6
	Maintenance	IEEE/EIA 12207.0, G.9 and IEEE Std 1517, C.5
Supporting	Documentation	IEEE/EIA 12207.0, G.5
	Configuration Management	IEEE/EIA 12207.0, G.3
	Quality Assurance	IEEE/EIA 12207.0, G.13
	Verification	IEEE/EIA 12207.0, G.17
	Validation	IEEE/EIA 12207.0, G.16
	Joint Review	IEEE/EIA 12207.0, G.8
	Audit	IEEE/EIA 12207.0, G.2
	Problem Resolution	IEEE/EIA 12207.0, G.12
	Measurement	ISO/IEC 15939, 4.1
	Asset Management	IEEE Std 1517, C.2
Organizational	Management	IEEE/EIA 12207.0, G.10
	Infrastructure	IEEE/EIA 12207.0, G.7
	Improvement	IEEE/EIA 12207.0, G.6
	Training	IEEE/EIA 12207.0, G.15
	Risk Management	IEEE Std 1540, 5.0 (without sub-clauses)
	Reuse Program Administration	IEEE Std 1517, C.7
Cross-Project	Domain Engineering	IEEE Std 1517, C.4

It can be expected that this framework will remain stable, growing in a controlled fashion, at least through the completion of the harmonization activities by ISO/IEC JTC 1/SC 7. At that point, a harmonized set of SC 7 processes may offer sufficient advantage to consider changing to a new framework.

The next chapter will apply the S2ESC framework to provide a consistent view of software life cycle process standards. The other S2ESC standards will be organized according to that framework.

Chapter **19**

Software Life Cycle Processes

This chapter takes a process-oriented view of the software life cycle and describes how S2ESC and international standards can support definition, implementation, assessment, and improvement of software life cycle processes. The next chapter will look at system life cycle processes.

The chapter discusses the definition of software life cycle processes and how the various IEEE S2ESC standards can support the processes. The presentation is organized around the S2ESC framework of reference processes introduced in the previous chapter. That framework is based on IEEE/EIA 12207.0 with the addition of "plug-in" processes provided by IEEE Std 1540 and ISO/IEC 15939.

Process

IEEE/EIA 12207.0-1996
Industry Implementation of International Standard ISO/IEC
12207:1995, Standard for Information Technology—
Software Life Cycle Processes
This standard provides a framework of processes used across the entire
life cycle of software.
Allocated to: Software Engineering Process Knowledge Area

Process

ISO/IEC 15939:2002
Software Engineering—Software Measurement Process
This standard provides a life cycle process for software measurement
suitable for use with IEEE/EIA 12207.
Allocated to: Software Engineering Process Knowledge Area

The Road Map to Software Engineering: A Standards-Based Guide, by James W. Moore
Copyright © 2006 by IEEE Computer Society

Process

> **IEEE Std 1540-2001**
> **IEEE Standard for Software Life Cycle Processes—**
> **Risk Management**
> This standard provides a life cycle process for software risk management
> suitable for use with IEEE/EIA 12207.
> *Allocated to: Software Engineering Process Knowledge Area*

IEEE Std 1517 provides additional processes for systematic software reuse and adds provisions to the other processes of IEEE/EIA 12207.0.

Process

> **IEEE Std 1517-1999 (R2004)**
> **IEEE Standard for Information Technology—**
> **Software Life Cycle Processes—Reuse Processes**
> This standard provides life cycle processes for systematic software reuse
> suitable for use with IEEE/EIA 12207.
> *Allocated to: Software Engineering Process Knowledge Area*

In the following descriptions, the relationships of the various S2ESC standards to the reference processes will be depicted in a series of diagrams. Each diagram depicts a group of four-tiered stacks. At the top of each stack is listed the reference process to be described. The next tier down shows the standards that provide the requirements for that reference process. The next tier shows important context standards for the process. These are standards that may not be needed, but which provide a more general view of the process in question. The most obvious example is that ISO 9001 provides the context for the quality management process. Finally, the bottom tier shows the detailed standards that may be useful in defining and implementing the reference process. Standards listed in more than one place in the bottom tier are shown in italics. A similar chart will be used to describe the activities of the 12207 development process.

Like the 12207 standard, the S2ESC reference processes are grouped into categories: *primary*, *supporting*, and *organizational*. One additional category is added by IEEE Std 1517: *cross-project*. These categories may be characterized as follows:

- *Primary:* A primary process is executed by one of the project's principal parties to achieve the goals of the project. The five primary processes are sometimes subcategorized as business (*acquisition* and *supply*), and technical (*development, operation,* and *maintenance*).
- *Supporting:* A supporting process is executed by another process to achieve a distinct purpose contributing the overall success of the project. The 12207 standard provides eight supporting processes (*documentation, configuration management, quality assurance, verification, validation, joint review, audit,* and *problem resolution*). ISO/IEC 15939 adds one supporting process, *measurement,* and IEEE Std 1517 adds another, *[reuse] asset management.*
- *Organizational:* These four 12207 processes—*management, infrastructure, improvement,* and *training*—are inherent in any organization. For a given project, an instance of the process is created. IEEE Std 1540 adds

one organizational process, *risk management*, and IEEE Std 1517 adds another, *reuse program administration*.

- *Cross-project:* IEEE Std 1517 added this class to accommodate one special process, *[reuse] domain engineering*. This process inherently involves more than a single project within an organization.

The reference processes are deliberately broad and are intended to cover the entire life of software from conception through retirement—not just the development effort. Each of the reference processes is hierarchically decomposed into a set of *activities* and then *tasks*—although the tasks are better regarded as simply requirements on the activities. Each of the processes is described at the reference level of the Basili model described in the previous chapter.

It should be clear that not all of the reference processes are required for any given project. An important part of project planning is to select the appropriate processes for use on the job.

The writers of ISO/IEC 12207 chose to factor some activities into separate processes and chose to leave others distributed among the processes; these decisions are respected in the S2ESC reference processes. For example, the requirements for reviews are factored into separate processes: *joint review* and *audit*. On the other hand, every process contains the requirement to evaluate its own work. There are processes for verification, validation, and quality assurance, but these are all additions to the fundamental requirements for evaluation incorporated in each process. The integral nature of evaluation is a consequence of a more general principle of total quality management—each of the primary processes incorporates its own "plan-do-check-act" cycle inherited from its instantiation of the organizational management process.

1. PRIMARY PROCESSES

In the model provided by 12207, the acquirer and the supplier enter into a business agreement[53]; the supplier then executes one or more of the three primary technical processes to provide the agreed product or service. It is important to understand that, since 12207 is at the reference level of abstraction, the agents performing the processes are *roles* to be assumed rather than permanent organizational entities. For example, a developer choosing to purchase a component of the software system would additionally execute the acquirer role in order to make the purchase. Or, a maintainer electing to rewrite a portion of the system could execute the developer role to do that job or could execute the acquirer role to arrange for some other organization to perform the development. The primary processes are depicted in Figure 27.

In each case, requirements for the process are provided by a clause of IEEE/EIA 12207.0. If an organization desires to institute systematic software

---

[53] The agreement does not have to be a formal one. The standard is written in terms of a legal contract, but such a contract is not required. The standard is intended to apply to even the most informal forms of agreement within two parts of an organization. Contractual language was used so that the standard's application would be clearer in the more complex situation of agreements between companies.

Primary Process	Acquisition	Supply	Development	Operation	Maintenance
Basic Standard(s)	IEEE/EIA 12207.0, clause 5.1 IEEE Std 1517, clause 5.1	IEEE/EIA 12207.0, clause 5.2 IEEE Std 1517, clause 5.2	IEEE/EIA 12207.0, clause 5.3 IEEE Std 1517, clause 5.3	IEEE/EIA 12207.0, clause 5.4 IEEE Std 1517, clause 5.4	IEEE/EIA 12207.0, clause 5.5 IEEE Std 1517, clause 5.5
Context Standards					
Detailed Standards	IEEE Std 1062, SW Acquisition *IEEE Std 1362, Concept of Operations Document*		(See separate chart.)		IEEE Std 1219, SW Maintenance ISO/IEC 14764, SW Maintenance

Figure 27. *Primary processes of the S2ESC reference model*

reuse, the provisions for the primary processes of 12207.0 should be supplemented by those from the corresponding clauses of IEEE Std 1517.

1.1. Acquisition Process

The acquisition process begins with the "definition of the need to acquire a system, software product or software service." It specifies five activities:

- *Initiation:* description of concept or need, system requirements, and, optionally, software requirements analysis; make-buy-contract decision; acquisition planning; and acceptance strategy
- *Preparation of the Request for Proposal (RFP):* documenting requirements, scope of work, and contract terms; defining contract milestones
- *Contract preparation and update:* supplier selection; contract negotiation; contract change control
- *Supplier monitoring:* application of the supporting processes to monitor contract performance, including Joint Review, Audit, Verification and Validation as needed
- *Acceptance and completion:* acceptance review and testing

The contract-oriented language of 12207 may seem inapplicable to less formal procurement methods, but the standard is intended to be useful even for the least formal of agreements. The standard was written in contractual language from the conviction that it would be easier for users to interpret formal provisions for less formal purposes rather than the other way around.

Two IEEE standards are useful in implementing the provisions of the acquisition process:

Process

IEEE Std 1062, 1998 Edition (R2002)
IEEE Recommended Practice for Software Acquisition
This document recommends a set of useful practices that can be selected and applied during software acquisition. It is primarily suited to acquisitions that include development or modification rather than off-the-shelf purchase.
Allocated to: Software Engineering Management Knowledge Area

TABLE 22. Correspondence of IEEE Std 1062 with the 12207 acquisition process

"Step" from IEEE Std 1062	"Activity" from the Acquisition Process
Planning organizational strategy	Initiation
Implementing organization's process	(Not specifically covered[54])
Defining the software requirements	Initiation
Identifying potential suppliers	(Not specifically covered)
Preparing contract requirements	Preparation of the Request for Proposal
Evaluating proposals and selecting supplier	Contract preparation and update
Managing for supplier performance	Supplier monitoring
Accepting the software	Acceptance and completion
Using the software	(Not specifically covered)

Document

IEEE Std 1362-1998
IEEE Guide for Information Technology—System Definition—
Concept of Operations (ConOps) Document
This document provides guidance on the format and content of a
Concept of Operations (ConOps) document, describing characteristics of
a proposed system from the users' viewpoint.
Allocated to: Related Disciplines Chapter, Systems Engineering

IEEE Std 1062 recommends a set of practices that are useful across the entire scope of the acquisition process. It is organized into nine "steps" that fit reasonably well with the process activities listed previously, as shown in Table 22.

This sort of fit is to be expected when one considers that 12207 was intended to provide a minimum set of requirements and that 1062 provides additional recommended practices. IEEE Std 1062 provides a number of helpful checklists in Annex A and recommends format and content of an Acquisition Plan in Annex B. The suggested plan would satisfy the requirements of the 12207 standard for an acquisition plan.

IEEE Std 1362 recommends format and content for a Concept of Operations document. Such a document would be useful in accomplishing the first two tasks of the acquisition process:

---

[54] This is an example of a peculiar blind spot in the 12207 standard. The original writers were largely from communities where acquirers dominated the marketplace, e.g., defense, and could impose processes on suppliers but didn't necessarily apply processes to their own activities. Unlike most of the other processes of 12207, the acquisition process does not include a "process implementation" activity. Furthermore, the acquisition process is described using the verb "will" (defined as indicating an intention) rather than the verb "shall" (indicating a requirement). In short, the original writers of the 12207 standard did not seem to expect scrupulous conformance by acquirers.

From IEEE/EIA 12207.0, clause 5.1, Acquisition Process:

5.1.1.1 The acquirer begins the acquisition process by describing a concept or a need to acquire, develop, or enhance a system, software product, or software service.

5.1.1.2 The acquirer will define and analyze the system requirements. The system requirements should include business, organizational, and user as well as safety, security, and other criticality requirements along with related design, testing, and compliance standards and procedures.

If one uses IEEE Std 1517 to perform systematic software reuse, then seven tasks are added to the initiation, RFP preparation, and acceptance and completion activities of the acquisition process. These tasks involving incorporating reuse considerations into the acquisition plan and the RFP, and testing for reusability prior to acceptance.

1.2. Supply Process

Of course, the 12207 supply process is the complement of the acquisition process. It is important to note that the supply process does not directly incorporate the engineering activities of development, operation, and maintenance. The supply process would invoke one of those processes to perform the engineering. The supply process is intended to factor out those common activities characteristic of being a supplier regardless of whether the product is development, operation, or maintenance.

The supply process is initiated in either of two ways: (1) when the supplier decides to prepare a proposal; or (2) when the supplier enters into a contract through other mechanisms. The process has seven activities:

- *Initiation:* review of RFP requirements; bid-no-bid decision
- *Preparation of response:* writing the proposal
- *Contract:* negotiation and agreement on the contract; change request
- *Planning*: requirements review; management planning; assurance planning; life cycle model selection; resource planning; make-buy decisions; project plan development
- *Execution and control:* executing the project plan using the 12207 Development, Operation or Maintenance process; monitoring and controlling progress and quality; subcontractor management; independent verification and validation, if appropriate
- *Review and evaluation:* reviews with acquirer; verification and validation; reporting to acquirer; quality assurance
- *Delivery and completion:* delivery and assistance in support

Again, the fact that the provisions of 12207 are written in contractual language should not be considered as an obstacle to application in less formal situations.

There are no IEEE standards for the supplier process, but, since supply is the complement of acquisition, it may be helpful to consult IEEE Std 1062. In some cases, acquirers delegate responsibilities to suppliers; a common example is the preparation of a Concept of Operations document. In such cases, IEEE Std 1362, described above, would be helpful.

When one uses IEEE Std 1517 for systematic reuse, five tasks are added to the planning activity of the supply process. The tasks concern planning for reuse in both the software life cycle model and the project plan.

1.3. Development Process

The development process of 12207 is subdivided into 13 activities involving various types of analysis, design, coding, testing, integration, and acceptance, as depicted in Figure 28.

This diagram is slightly different than the others in this series. Rather than having a process at the top of each stack, an activity of the development process is shown. Otherwise, the figure uses the same conventions. The second tier lists the standards that provide the requirements for that activity. In all cases, the appropriate standard is IEEE/EIA 12207.0. If one desires processes supporting systematic software reuse, then the corresponding provisions of IEEE Std 1517 are also applicable.

Activities of Development Process	Process Implementation	System Requirements Analysis	System Architectural Design	Software Requirements Analysis	Software Architectural Design
Basic Standard(s)	IEEE/EIA 12207.0, clause 5.3.1 EEE Std 1517, I clause 5.3.1	IEEE/EIA 12207.0, clause 5.3.2 IEEE Std 1517, clause 5.3.2	IEEE/EIA 12207.0, clause 5.3.3 IEEE Std 1517, c lause 5.3.3	IEEE/EIA 12207.0, clause 5.3.4 IEEE Std 1517, clause 5.3.4	IEEE/EIA 12207.0, clause 5.3.5 IEEE Std 1517, clause 5.3.5
Context Standards					
Detailed Standards	IEEE Std 1074, Developing SW Life Cycle Processes	IEEE Std 1233, System Requirements Specification IEEE Std 1320.1, IDEF0 IEEE Std 1320.2, IDEF1X97	IEEE Std 1471, Architectural Description	IEEE Std 830, SW Requirements Specification ISO/IEC 9126-1, Quality Factors	IEEE Std 829, SW Test Documentation IEEE Std 1471, Architectural Description IEEE Std 1063, SW User Documentation
Activities of Development Process	**Software Detailed Design**	**Software Coding and Testing**	**Software Integration and Qualification Testing**	**System Integration and Qualification Testing**	**Software Installation and Acceptance Support**
Basic Standard(s)	IEEE/EIA 12207.0, clause 5.3.6 IEEE Std 1517, clause 5.3.6	IEEE/EIA 12207.0, clause 5.3.7 IEEE Std 1517, clause 5.3.7	IEEE/EIA 12207.0, clause 5.3.8, 9 IEEE Std 1517, clause 5.3.8, 9	IEEE/EIA 12207.0, clause 5.3.10, 11 IEEE Std 1517, clause 5.3.10, 11	IEEE/EIA 12207.0, clause 5.3.12, 13 IEEE Std 1517, clause 5.3.12, 13
Context Standards					
Detailed Standards	IEEE Std 829, SW Test Documentation IEEE Std 1016, SW Design Description IEEE Std 1063, SW User Documentation	IEEE Std 829, SW Test Documentation IEEE Std 1008, SW Unit Testing IEEE Std 1063, SW User Documentation	IEEE Std 829, SW Test Documentation IEEE Std 1063, SW User Documentation	IEEE Std 829, SW Test Documentation	

Figure 28. Activities of the development process

The third tier would show important context standards for the activity—but there aren't any. Finally, the bottom tier shows the detailed standards that may be useful in defining and implementing the activity. Standards that are allocated to more than one activity are shown in italics. Virtually all of the activities have evaluation and review requirements. Rather than being separately cited for each process, the appropriate S2ESC standard for review and audit, IEEE Std 1028, will be described when we get to the supporting process, joint review and audit.

1.3.1. Process Implementation Activity

The development process begins with the process implementation activity. A major requirement of this activity is to define or select a software life cycle process model appropriate to the project. The activities and tasks of the development process are then to be mapped onto the life cycle model. The activity also requires that detailed plans for conducting the activities of the development process be formulated and documented, including the selection of organizational procedures and methods. IEEE Std 1074 can be useful in performing this activity:

Process

IEEE Std 1074-1997
IEEE Standard for Developing Software Life Cycle Processes
This standard describes an approach for the definition of software life cycle processes.
Allocated to: Software Engineering Process Knowledge Area

IEEE Std 1074 provides a building-block set of "activities" organized into "activity groups." (It is a minor source of confusion that 12207 and 1074 use the word "activity" to mean different things. In this text, the two are distinguished by writing "12207 activity" or "1074 activity" when confusion seems to be possible.) Each 1074 activity lists a required set of input information; with each item of input is listed the 1074 activity that provides the information. Similarly, each 1074 activity lists output information along with its destination. Using these building blocks, networks of 1074 activities can be constructed through assembling single instances of 1074 activities, iterations of the activities, or invocations of them. One can build networks of 1074 activities that satisfy the requirements of the 12207 processes and activities. This effectively moves one from the reference level of process abstraction, provided by 12207 and 1517, to the conceptual level of abstraction through the specification of data flows internal to the processes and connecting the processes.

If IEEE Std 1517 is applied for systematic software reuse, then four tasks are added to the process implementation activity. The tasks provide for selecting appropriate reuse standards and incorporating reuse into the life cycle model and the project plans.

1.3.2. System Requirements Analysis Activity

Although 12207 does not prescribe systems engineering life cycle processes, it does prescribe the minimum systems engineering context necessary for the successful execution of the software processes. The systems engineering context is specified as a set of tasks intended to be shared with systems engineering activities. These tasks include system requirements, system architecture, system integration, and system qualification testing.

System requirements analysis is the first of the front-end interfaces to the systems engineering. The activity requires analyzing the intended use of the system, documenting the requirements, and evaluating the requirements for various aspects of traceability, consistency, testability, and feasibility.

Three IEEE standards would be useful in performing this activity:

Document

IEEE Std 1233, 1998 Edition (R2002)
IEEE Guide for Developing System Requirements Specifications
This document provides guidance on the development of a System Requirements Specification, covering the identification, organization, presentation, and modification of requirements. It also provides guidance on the characteristics and qualities of requirements.
Allocated to: Related Disciplines Chapter, Systems Engineering

IEEE Std 1233 provides explanation of the requirements analysis activity that would be useful in process implementation at the organizational or project level. It describes characteristics of well-formed requirements that go beyond the evaluation characteristics listed in 12207. In particular, it suggests an outline for a System Requirements Specification. The outline has not been completely reconciled with the data recommended by IEEE/EIA 12207.1. An annex of IEEE Std 1233 provides clarifications and suggestions for additional content to meet the recommendations of 12207.1.

The requirements of 12207 for requirements analysis are minimal and do not include requirements for conceptual modeling nor the use of specific notations. In cases where conceptual modeling is appropriate, IEEE has two applicable standards:

Tool

IEEE Std 1320.1-1998 (R2004)
IEEE Standard for
Functional Modeling Language—Syntax and Semantics for IDEF0
This standard defines the IDEF0 modeling language used to represent decisions, actions, and activities of an organization or system. IDEF0 may be used to define requirements in terms of functions to be performed by a desired system.
Allocated to: Software Engineering Tools and Methods Knowledge Area

Tool

IEEE Std 1320.2-1998 (R2004)
IEEE Standard for Conceptual Modeling Language—
Syntax and Semantics for IDEF1X 97 (IDEF object)
This standard defines two conceptual modeling languages, collectively called IDEF1X97 (IDEFObject). The language support the implementation of relational databases, object databases, and object models.
Allocated to: Software Engineering Tools and Methods Knowledge Area

The IDEF0 standard provides a notation for assembling building blocks like the one shown in Figure 29 into networks that are particularly useful for describing business processes and their results. An example of an IDEF0 drawing is shown in Figure 30.

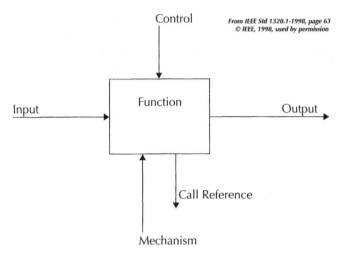

Figure 29. *Basic building block used for IDEF0 diagrams*

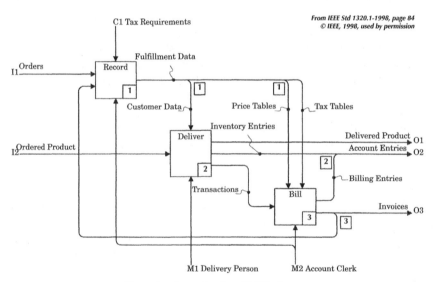

Figure 30. *Example of an IDEF0 diagram*

The IDEF1X97 standard provides a useful object-oriented notation for describing classes and instances of objects and their roles and responsibilities. The notation is rich and complex. Figure 31 provides a single example of a class of objects and a set of subclasses, some with additional capabilities.

An organization-level software reuse program requires some additional tasks during system requirements analysis. IEEE Std 1571 adds five tasks to this activity. Essentially, they require consultation and use of domain models in order to create opportunities for reuse.

1.3.3. System Architectural Design Activity According to the 12207 standard, the purpose of the system architectural design activity is to identify the

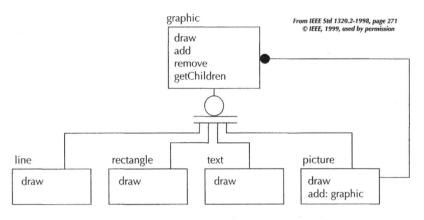

Figure 31. *Example of an IDEF1X97 diagram*

system's "items" of hardware, software and manual operation, and to allocate system requirements to those items. One would probably not need sophisticated tools to accomplish this minimal goal. However, for complex system development, the system architecture should describe how to meet the key requirements of the system at a "level of abstraction that allows designers to reason about system behavior" [Stevens98]. The architectural design exposes critical issues to examination and supports the pursuit of tradeoffs to deal with the issues. Typically, key issues are not all exposed by simple decomposition of the system into items. A richer form of expression is often needed. IEEE Std 1471 may be useful for this purpose.

Document

IEEE Std 1471-2000
IEEE Recommended Practice for
Architectural Description of Software Intensive Systems
This document recommends a conceptual framework and content for the architectural description of software-intensive systems.
Allocated to: Related Disciplines Chapter, Systems Engineering

The standard recommends provisions for architectural description that support multiple viewpoints to examine various issues of relevance and importance.

An organization-level software reuse program affects the system architectural design. IEEE Std 1517 adds four requirements concerning the incorporation of domain architecture material from applicable domain models.

1.3.4. Software Requirements Analysis Activity The software requirements analysis activity is performed by the developer on each of the software items identified by the system architecture. The purpose is to establish and document the requirements for each software item as a basis for its design, and to evaluate the requirements for various aspects of traceability, consistency, testability, and feasibility. IEEE/EIA 12207.0 specifically lists the following categories of requirements in clause 5.3.4.1:

- Functional and capability
- Interfaces
- Qualification
- Safety
- Security
- Human factors
- Data and database
- Installation and acceptance
- User documentation
- User operation and execution
- User maintenance

In addition, IEEE/EIA 12207.0 states that "guidance for specifying quality characteristics may be found in ISO/IEC 9126[55]:

Terminology

ISO/IEC 9126-1:2001
Software Engineering—Product Quality—Part 1: Quality Model
This standard provides a model for software product quality covering internal quality, external quality, and quality in use. The model is in the form of a taxonomy of defined characteristics which software may exhibit.
Allocated to: Software Requirements Knowledge Area

The 9126 standard provides a standard taxonomy of quality characteristics and subcharacteristics that can be applied by a requirements analysis as a useful framework or classification tool.

The product of the software requirements analysis activity is a document describing the requirements. IEEE Std 830 provides an outline and suggested contents of such a document, as well as describing the characteristics of well-formed software requirements:

Document

IEEE Std 830-1998
IEEE Recommended Practice for Software Requirements Specifications
This document recommends the content and characteristics of a Software Requirements Specification. Sample outlines are provided.
Allocated to: Software Requirements Knowledge Area

The 830 standard is not completely reconciled with the data requirements of IEEE/EIA 12207.1. An annex of 830 lists a few clarifications and additions that should be considered. There is also a minor issue of terminology. According to IEEE/EIA 12207.1, the software requirements document is a description because it is derived from another document, the system requirements specification. Nevertheless, IEEE Std 830 refers to the document as a speci-

---

[55] The cited version is ISO/IEC 9126:1991. It has been superseded by the version listed here.

fication. Of course, this is an issue of no practical importance; it merely complicates the life of process architects.

The software requirements analysis activity concludes with an important outcome—a joint review of the software requirements of the item.[56] When viewing a provision such as this, it is important to remember that the 12207 standard prescribes continuing responsibilities rather than discrete events. This provision does not necessarily call for a single "big-bang" event that will review all requirements once and for all. Instead, it provides that as each software item is analyzed, its requirements should be reviewed—and re-reviewed—as appropriate to the life cycle model being employed on the project.

The pursuit of systematic software reuse provides a benefit at this point. The domain model can provide some software requirements and may provide aids to characterizing others. When appropriate, the requirements analyst should write additional requirements related to reusability. In all, IEEE Std 1517 adds five tasks to this activity.

1.3.5. Software Architectural Design Activity   The software architectural design activity is the first of three activities that construct the software items of the system. IEEE/EIA 12207.0 assigns the following responsibilities to the activity:

- Decompose each software item into components and allocate the item requirements to the components.
- Design the external interfaces and the interfaces among components.
- Develop a preliminary version of the user documentation.
- Define preliminary test requirements and the software integration schedule.
- Document the results.
- Evaluate the results for various aspects of traceability, consistency, appropriateness, and feasibility.
- Conduct a joint review.

It is clear that the 12207 standard treats this as a high-level design activity rather than an architectural activity—at least in the sense that architecture deals with selected key issues. For those who take the latter approach, the architectural description standard described previously, IEEE Std 1471, would continue to be useful in this activity.

It should be noted that this activity kicks off work on two items that will be revisited in subsequent activities. The user documentation is initiated here and revisited in the next three activities; IEEE Std 1063 will be useful in all of these activities. Software test planning is also initiated here and revisited in the next six activities; IEEE Std 829 will be useful. The standard for user

---

[56] At this point, there is a difference between the requirements of ISO/IEC 12207 and IEEE/EIA 12207.0. The ISO/IEC standard requires the establishment of a baseline of software requirements at this point. The errata sheet (Annex J) of the IEEE/EIA standard deletes this requirement, as well as all other specific provisions for establishing baselines, and replaces them with a general requirement added to the process implementation activity: "Establish baselines for each configuration item at appropriate times, as determined by the acquirer and supplier."

documentation will be mentioned here, but the standard for test documentation will be deferred to the description of software coding and testing:

Document

IEEE Std 1063-2001
IEEE Standard for Software User Documentation
This standard provides minimum requirements for the structure, content and format of user documentation—both printed and electronic.
Allocated to: Software Construction Knowledge Area

The 12207 standard requires that the development of user documentation be started as a part of the software architectural design activity and updated as part of the software detailed design, software coding and test, software integration, and software qualification testing activities. IEEE Std 1063 contains provisions concerning the structure, content, and format of user documentation—whether paper or electronic.

In some cases, systematic software reuse provides benefits to this activity. The domain architecture may provide substantial portions of the architecture to be applied to the software under development, including interfaces, database designs, documentation, and test requirements. IEEE Std 1517 adds seven tasks to this activity.

1.3.6. Software Detailed Design Activity The software detailed design activity further refines the decomposition performed by the software architectural design. Software components are refined into software units and requirements are allocated downward. In effect, the activity is an analog of the software architectural activity, but operating one level lower in the hierarchy of refinement. However, some particular items should be noted:

- The refinement into smaller and smaller units continues until the units are appropriate for coding and testing.
- Requirements and a schedule for unit testing are defined. There is a recommendation to include stress testing.

During this activity, user documentation and software integration test requirements are updated. As you might expect, results are evaluated and a joint review is conducted.

Because the 12207 standard provides only minimum requirements, no particular design methodology is suggested and there are no specific requirements for the recording of the design. Those who would desire more guidance might turn to an IEEE standard on the subject:

Document

IEEE Std 1016-1998
IEEE Recommended Practice for Software Design Descriptions
This document recommends content and organization of a Software Design Description.
Allocated to: Software Design Knowledge Area

The document describes various ways of representing design characteristics and recommends an organization for a design description. Like IEEE Std 1471, it recognizes the value of multiple views, but goes on to recommend four specific views:

- *Decomposition:* To partition the software into design entities.
- *Dependency:* To describe the relationship between design entities and resources.
- *Interface:* To describe how entities are to be used.
- *Detail:* To describe the internal design of an entity.

The document is not yet well-integrated with the jargon of 12207 (for example, it uses the term "entity" rather than "unit"). An annex describes how to supplement a design description with additional data (mostly boilerplate) to meet the provisions of IEEE/EIA 12207.1.

This recommended practice is currently being revised and the result may be published before this book. It is likely that the revised standard will adopt some of the concepts of IEEE Std 1471 and will be better integrated with the 12207 standard.

The detailed design can also benefit from systematic reuse by inheriting designs, interfaces, database descriptions, documentation, and test requirements from the organization's asset library. This is provided in the six tasks that IEEE Std 1517 adds to this activity.

Because test planning and user documentation are revisited in this activity, IEEE standards 828 and 1063 continue to be relevant.

1.3.7. Software Coding and Testing Activity   The next activity, software coding and testing, also includes requirements for evaluating the results and providing appropriate documentation. User documentation is updated and the integration test requirements and schedule are revisited.

IEEE Std 1008 provides a standard approach to unit testing and is well integrated with the IEEE 829 standard for software test documentation:

Process

IEEE Std 1008-1987(R2003)
IEEE Standard for Software Unit Testing
This standard describes a sound approach to software unit testing, and the concepts and assumptions on which it is based.
Allocated to: Software Testing Knowledge Area

The standard provides substantial additional detail for the planning and conduct of unit testing. Of course, since it far predates the 12207 standard, terminology is slightly different, but the problem is of no practical significance. Interestingly, the standard includes an appendix describing the "fundamental software engineering concepts" and "testing assumptions" upon which the standard is premised.

Of course, during the coding of software, many other standards for programming languages and application program interfaces are applicable and usable. Those standards fall outside the scope of this book, however.

Systematic software reuse may provide huge benefits to this activity. For software that is well based in the domain models, software units, databases, test procedures and test data may be available from the organization's asset library. IEEE Std 1517 adds three tasks covering this possibility.

Because test planning and user documentation are revisited in this activity, IEEE standards 828 and 1063 continue to be relevant.

1.3.8. Software Integration Activity   The software integration activity marks "turning the corner" from the analysis and refinement activities of the front end of the development process to the synthesis and integration activities of the back end. The activity begins with the development of an integration plan. As the components and units of each software item are integrated, they must be tested against the requirements allocated to the item by the corresponding software requirement analysis. In addition, the developer must update the user documentation and begin planning for the next activity, Software Qualification Testing. Finally, the results are evaluated for various aspects of traceability, consistency, test coverage, appropriateness, conformance to expected results, and feasibility. A very useful standard for this activity is IEEE Std 829:

IEEE Std 829-1998
IEEE Standard for Software Test Documentation
This standard describes the form and content of a basic set of
documentation for planning, executing, and reporting software testing.
Allocated to: Software Testing Knowledge Area

Document

Actually, it understates the case to claim that the 829 standard is useful for this one activity. Application of the standard potentially spans seven activities of the development process and addresses four different levels of testing. Figure 32 depicts this relationship in two parts: the left side is reproduced from IEEE Std 829; and the right side has been added for explanation. The left side depicts the flow of planning and documentation:

- Test plans are created first.
- Continued work results in the specification of test design and test cases that are ultimately implemented in test procedures.
- The tests are executed resulting in test logs and incident reports that are finally summarized.

The right side shows how this generic testing approach maps to the four levels of testing provided in IEEE/EIA 12207.0. In unit testing, for example, the test planning and design are performed as a part of the software detailed design activity; while the development of test procedures, the execution of the tests, and the reporting of the results is performed in the software coding and testing activity.

From the diagram, we can see that the software integration activity completes the planning for software integration testing initiated by the three preceding activities and completes the test design, execution, and reporting. Furthermore, the activity performs the planning and design for the software qualification testing.

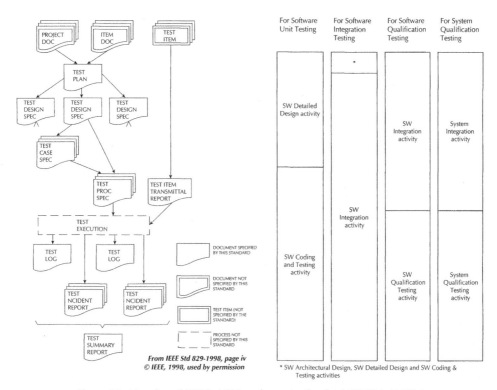

Figure 32. *Mapping of IEEE Std 829 to the testing levels of IEEE/EIA 12207.0*

A big advantage of IEEE Std 829 is its modular approach to test documentation, specifying a variety of small documents that can be produced at various times. Not only is the approach flexible, but it facilitates appropriate reuse of test cases and test procedures in later upgrades or related projects [Schmidt00]. The modular approach also permits a good mapping to the provisions of IEEE/EIA 12207.0 and supports the use of electronic records rather than paper documentation.

IEEE Std 1517 adds five tasks to the software integration activity covering the possibility that the organization's reuse library may provide assets helpful in performing the integration.

Because user documentation is updated in this activity, IEEE Std 1063 continues to be relevant.

1.3.9. Software Qualification Testing Activity The software qualification testing activity executes the qualification tests prepared by the previous activity and reports on the results. Qualification testing is performed against a set of *qualification requirements*. Qualification requirements are distinguished from other requirements in the provisions for software requirements analysis. The 12207 standard defines qualification testing as demonstrating that "the software product meets its specifications and is ready for use in its target environment." Therefore, the standard supports the concept of distinguishing a subset of requirements for focused treatment in determining the software's fitness for usage. Of course, IEEE Std 828 remains relevant for test documentation.

During this activity, user documentation is updated if necessary; so IEEE Std 1063 remains useful. An evaluation checks for test coverage, conformance to expected results, and feasibility to proceed in development. At this point, the developer may be required to support audits by the acquirer and must deliver software products for system integration.

When systematic reuse is being practiced, software qualification testing includes checking the completed items and other artifacts against the planned reusability criteria. For that purpose, IEEE Std 1517 adds three tasks to this activity.

1.3.10. System Integration Activity

At this point in the development process, the developer re-enters the set of activities that are part of the minimal required interface between software and system development. The developer may be required to perform this activity or may be required to support some other party in its performance. The main point of this activity is to integrate the various items of hardware, software and manual operation and test them against their allocated requirements and the system's overall requirements. The integrated system is evaluated for test coverage, appropriateness of test methods, conformance to expected results, and feasibility for continued development. IEEE Std 829 may be useful in documenting the testing results.

As shown in Figure 32, the system integration activity also performs the test planning and design for the following activity, system qualification testing.

An organization practicing systematic reuse will take advantage of reusable test cases and evaluate the results for reusability in the future. IEEE Std 1517 adds three tasks for this purpose.

1.3.11. System Qualification Testing Activity

The system qualification testing activity does just that. System qualification requirements are distinguished from other system requirements during the system requirements analysis activity. However, the wording of clause 5.3.11.1, "it shall be ensured that the implementation of each system requirement is tested for compliance and that the system is ready for delivery," suggests that all system requirements are to be tested during this activity. Apparently, successful testing of the qualification requirements—but not all the requirements—suggests that the system could be delivered with deficiencies noted for later correction. IEEE Std 829 may be useful in documenting the testing results.

The system is evaluated for test coverage, conformance to expected results, and feasibility of operation and maintenance. An audit is performed and the software developer delivers the software product.

IEEE Std 1517 adds two tasks for those practicing software reuse—evaluating the system for future reuse and reporting the results.

1.3.12. Software Installation Activity

This activity requires the developer to prepare a plan for installation of the software and assist the acquirer with set-up. In some cases, parallel operation will be required.

An organization's software reuse library may contain helpful materials. IEEE Std 1517 contains three tasks supporting this proposition.

1.3.13. Software Acceptance Support Activity   This activity provides for a closeout of the development process. The developer supports the acquirer's acceptance review and testing, considering the results of reviews, audits, and software and system qualification testing. The developer delivers the completed product and provides training and support as provided by the contract.

1.4. Operation Process

The operation process covers operating the software product and providing operational support to users. Because the software product cannot be operated without its containing system, this process actually refers to the system rather than its software items. The process contains four activities:

- *Process implementation:* develop a plan, set operational standards, establish procedures for dealing with problems and for testing and releasing software in the operational environment
- *Operational testing:* for each new version, perform operational testing and release the software for operational use
- *System operation:* operate the system in its intended environment
- *User support:* assist users, deal with user requests, provide temporary workarounds

Note that permanent corrections and improvements are performed with the maintenance process. IEEE does not have any standards specifically applicable to implementing the operation process.

IEEE Std 1517 anticipates the possibility that the process implementation activity may benefit from systematic reuse. Three tasks are added to the activity that call for reusing appropriate planning material, evaluating the result for future reuse, and reporting the results.

1.5. Maintenance Process

The maintenance process places requirements on the party responsible for maintaining the software after it has been completed and delivered. Of course, in some cases, the maintainer is the same organization that developed the software; nevertheless, the two roles are distinct. The objective of the process is to modify existing software products while preserving their "integrity." The process ends with the retirement of the product. It contains six activities:

- *Process implementation:* develop plans and procedures, deal with problem reports and modification requests using the problem resolution process, manage modifications using the configuration management process.
- *Problem and modification analysis:* analyze problems and requests for impact, replicate or verify problems, consider options for modification, obtain approval to modify
- *Modification implementation:* determine items to be modified, use the development process to implement the modification

- *Maintenance review/acceptance:* conduct reviews with the approving organization, obtain approval for completed modifications
- *Migration:* apply the 12207 standard to any products produced during migration, develop a migration plan, notify users, conduct parallel operation, document lessons-learned, archive old data
- *Software retirement:* develop a retirement plan, notify users, conduct parallel operation, archive data

When the development process is used to implement a modification, it is supplemented with provisions to develop test and evaluation criteria for both the modified and unmodified parts and test accordingly.

IEEE has a standard specifically dedicated to Software Maintenance:

Process

IEEE Std 1219-1998
IEEE Standard for Software Maintenance
This standard describes a process for software maintenance and its management.
Allocated to: Software Maintenance Knowledge Area

The IEEE standard provides much additional guidance but describes a process with different activities than those of the 12207 standard. For that reason, some users prefer to use an ISO/IEC standard for maintenance:

Process

ISO/IEC 14764:1999
Information Technology—Software Maintenance
This standard provides guidance on implementing the maintenance process provided in ISO/IEC 12207.
Allocated to: Software Maintenance Knowledge Area

The ISO/IEC 14764 standard has the advantage that it maps directly to 12207. In fact, it contains no requirements beyond those of 12207—merely guidance. IEEE S2ESC and ISO/IEC JTC 1/SC 7 have initiated a project to merge the two documents so that both organizations will share a single maintenance process standard that is fully compatible with 12207.

On the other hand, IEEE Std 1219 has the advantage of being very comprehensive and well integrated with the other standards in the S2ESC collection. In addition, the 1219 standard suggest categories of tools and useful measurements, and provides a suggested format for a maintenance plan which matches well with the data provisions of IEEE/EIA 12207.1. Furthermore, the mapping between 1219 and the maintenance process of 12207 is not difficult. Table 23 lists the "phases" of the 1219 maintenance process and suggests a rough match with the activities of the 12207 maintenance process:

The maintenance process is closely involved with practices for systematic software reuse. IEEE Std 1517 adds tasks to all but one of the activities of the maintenance process. The objectives of these tasks are summarized by subclause C.5 of the standard:

TABLE 23. Correspondence of IEEE Std 1219 with the 12207 maintenance process

Activities of the IEEE/EIA 12207.0 maintenance process	Specific clauses of the IEEE/EIA 12207.0 maintenance process	Phases of the IEEE Std 1219 maintenance process
Problem and modification analysis	5.5.2.1	Problem/modification identification, classification and prioritization
	5.5.2.1, 5.5.2.2, and 5.5.2.3	Analysis
Modification implementation	5.5.3.1	Design
	5.5.3.2	Implementation
	5.5.3.2	Regression/system testing
	5.5.3.2	Acceptance testing
Maintenance review and acceptance	5.5.4	Delivery

Analyze modification requests, problem reports, and implementation options in terms of their impact on any assets and opportunities to use assets to make the modifications.

Provide modification requests/problem reports, and maintenance analysis information to the asset manager.

Notify the asset manager of plans to migrate or retire software products that have been constructed from assets.

---

2. SUPPORTING PROCESSES

Any of the primary processes can invoke one or more of the supporting processes to accomplish appropriate objectives. The eight supporting processes are:

- Documentation
- Configuration Management
- Quality Assurance
- Verification
- Validation
- Joint Review
- Audit
- Problem Resolution

Two more supporting processes are added by ISO/IEC 15939 and IEEE Std 1517, respectively:

- Measurement
- [Reuse] Asset Management

Supporting Process	Documentation	Configuration Management	Quality Assurance	Verification	Validation
Basic Standard(s)	IEEE/EIA 12207.0, clause 6.1	IEEE/EIA 12207.0, clause 6.2	IEEE/EIA 12207.0, clause 6.3	IEEE/EIA 12207.0, clause 6.4	IEEE/EIA 12207.0, clause 6.5
Context Standards			ISO/IEC 9001, Quality Management Systems		
Detailed Standards	*IEEE Std 1063, SW User Documentation* IEEE/EIA 12207.1, SW Life Cycle Data	IEEE Std 828, SW Configuration Management	IEEE Std 730, SW QA Plans *IEEE Std 1061, SW Quality Metrics Methodology* IEEE Std 1465, SW Packages ISO/IEC 90003, SW Appl. of 9001	*IEEE Std 1012, SW Verification and Validation*	*IEEE Std 1012, SW Verification and Validation*

Supporting Process	Joint Review	Audit	Problem Resolution	Measurement	[Reuse] Asset Management
Basic Standard(s)	IEEE/EIA 12207.0, clause 6.6	IEEE/EIA 12207.0, clause 6.7	IEEE/EIA 12207.0, clause 6.8	ISO/IEC 15939	IEEE Std 1517, clause 6.1
Context Standards					
Detailed Standards	*IEEE Std 1028, SW Reviews*	*IEEE Std 1028, SW Reviews*	IEEE Std 1044, Classification for SW Anomalies	IEEE Std 982.1, Measures for Reliable SW IEEE Std 1045, SW Productivity Metrics *IEEE Std 1061, SW Quality Metrics Methodology* IEEE Std 14143.1, Functional Size Measurement	IEEE Std 1420.1, Reuse Library Interoperability

Figure 33. *Supporting processes of the S2ESC reference model*

Standards related to those processes are shown in Figure 33. The supporting processes of 12207, like subroutines, may be invoked by any of the other processes to execute the desired function. In one of the marvelous subtleties of 12207, ultimate responsibility for the requirements of any supporting process can be made to roll up to any party depending on who invoked the supporting process. For example, the development manager (more precisely, the party executing the development process) could choose to invoke the verification process to ensure traceability of requirements. On the other hand, if this responsibility is assigned to a separate department within the organization, then the verification process could be invoked by the supplier. Finally, if independent verification is desired, the acquirer could make an agreement with another supplier to execute the process.

In each case, requirements for the process are provided by a clause of IEEE/EIA 12207.0, ISO/IEC 15939 or IEEE Std 1517.

2.1. Documentation Process

The documentation process contains the activities needed to "plan, design, develop, produce, edit, distribute, and maintain" all of the documents needed by all of the parties to the project. It specifies four activities:

- *Process Implementation:* planning for all the documents to be produced during the software's life cycle
- *Design and Development*: designing, preparing, editing, and approving the planned documents
- *Production:* producing, distributing, and controlling the planned documents
- *Maintenance:* modifying documents in conjunction with the maintenance process

In general, the provisions of the 12207 for documentation are relaxed. Many provisions of the standard require that information should be documented or that documents should be updated. The standard is generally silent, though, on the form of the documentation. All of those considerations are factored into the documentation process for central treatment. We find that the documentation process permits the individual project to determine which documents are to be produced, how they are designed, and how they are produced and maintained. Furthermore, documents are permitted to be paper, electronic, or other material. No formats for documents are provided. Even content requirements are minimal.

Many users of 12207 are uncomfortable with the minimal nature of the guidance on content. Many of the users come from communities where it was customary to use "DIDs." These Document Item Descriptions placed detailed requirements on the content—and sometimes the format—of documents to be produced. They were particularly popular in the acquisition community of the US Department of Defense. In the mid-1990s, conventional wisdom shifted and the DIDs became viewed as over-prescriptive and a factor in high cost of Defense software. The writers of ISO/IEC 12207 decided that the minimal content requirements noted in the 12207 process descriptions were sufficient and that additional content requirements were inappropriate.

The minimalist approach of 12207 does cause some inconvenience, though. The documentation requirements of 12207 are scattered through the process descriptions. The minimal requirements on content are also scattered and there is no overall organizing guidance for documentation. When IEEE and EIA adopted the 12207 standard, they decided to address the problem by creating a supplementary standard, IEEE/EIA 12207.1.

Document

IEEE/EIA 12207.1-1996
Industry Implementation of International Standard ISO/IEC
12207:1995, Standard for Information Technology—
Software Life Cycle Processes—Life Cycle Data
This document provides guidance on recording data resulting from the
life cycle processes of IEEE/EIA 12207.0.
Allocated to: Software Engineering Process Knowledge Area

The heart of 12207.1 is a table listing all of the places where IEEE/EIA 12207.0 requires that data be documented or that documents be updated. The table consists of 84 rows, corresponding to 84 such requirements in 12207.0. Each row is an information item that could be produced. Table 24 provides some examples[57]:

---

[57] The rows have been modified slightly for the purpose of presentation.

TABLE 24. Example information items from IEEE/EIA 12207.1

Information item(s)	IEEE/EIA 12207.0 Clause	Kind of documentation	IEEE/EIA 12207.1 Clause	References (See Annex A)
Software life cycle model description	5.2.4.2, 5.3.1.1	Description	—	IEEE 1074
System requirements specification	5.1.1.2, 5.3.2.1, 5.3.2.2	Specification	6.26	IEEE 1220, IEEE 1233
User documentation description	5.3.4.1, 5.3.5.4, 5.3.6.4, 5.3.7.3, 5.3.8.3, 5.3.8.5, 5.3.9.2	Description	6.30	IEEE 1063

The first column provides a name for the information item. The second column lists each clause of IEEE/EIA 12207.0 that requires that the item be documented or updated. The third column classifies the item into one of seven categories: description, plan, procedure, record, report, request, or specification. Each of the seven categories provides some summary content requirements. The fourth column is used for 40 of the 84 rows. It references subclauses providing more specific content requirements for selected information items. The final column provides cross-references to other standards which may provide additional useful guidance.

None of the information provided by 12207.1 is intended to replace the documentation process of 12207.0. Instead, it is intended to provide assistance to the user in developing a documentation plan for the project. Basically, the user should select the appropriate rows from the table, determine how to combine the rows into physical documents (or databases), and design the documents keeping in mind both the generic and specific content recommendations derived from the entries of the third and fourth columns.

The user documentation for software is a matter of particular importance. As you can see from the table of 12207.1, the user document is referenced in seven clauses of 12207.0. Its importance is great enough that IEEE provides a separate standard on this subject. The standard contains provisions for the content of user documentation, not the process for creating it:

Document

IEEE Std 1063-2001
IEEE Standard for Software User Documentation
This standard provides minimum requirements for the structure, content and format of user documentation—both printed and electronic.
Allocated to: Software Construction Knowledge Area

2.2. Configuration Management Process

Responsibility for configuration management in 12207 is delegated to the configuration management process which has the purpose of establishing and maintaining the integrity of the software work products and making them available to concerned parties. The process includes six activities:

- *Process implementation:* Developing a configuration management plan for the project
- *Configuration identification:* Establishing a schema for identifying software configuration items and identifying their versions
- *Configuration control:* Recording change requests, evaluating their impact, approving the request, and releasing the results while maintaining an audit trail
- *Configuration status accounting:* Providing records and reports of the history and status of the controlled items
- *Configuration evaluation:* Ensuring the functional and physical completeness of software items
- *Release management and delivery:* Controlling the release and archiving of software products and documentation

In applying the configuration management process of 12207, it is important to note the things **not** covered by the process. Not all software items are controlled by CM; a software item only passes to CM control when it is identified as a software **configuration** item (emphasis added). This occurs sometime between the identification of items in the system architecture and the integration of those items into a system. A particular project uses the process implementation activity of the configuration management process to make an appropriate plan for this purpose. It should furthermore be noted that "baselines" are **not** established by the configuration management process despite phrasing in the standard that might make one think otherwise. Baselines are established by the developer and—in two-party situations—approved by the acquirer and the supplier. As its name suggests, the job of the configuration management process is merely to manage the baselines established by the developer, ensuring that appropriate approvals have been obtained.

The spare nature of the 12207 configuration management process is suitable for many projects. However, some will desire additional guidance. IEEE has a standard for this purpose:

Plan

IEEE Std 828-1998
IEEE Standard for Software Configuration Management Plans
This standard specifies the content of a Software Configuration Management plan along with requirements for specific activities.
Allocated to: Software Configuration Management Knowledge Area

The 12207 standard provides great freedom for the project managers, but the managers are expected to create a configuration management plan in the process implementation activity. IEEE Std 828 directly addresses this need with requirements and guidance in the preparation of a plan. The standard speaks of four "functions" of configuration management that directly map to four of the activities of the 12207 configuration management process.

2.3. Quality Assurance Process

In the 12207 standard, the objective of the quality assurance process is specified as "providing adequate assurance that the software products and processes in the project life cycle conform to their specified requirements and adhere to their established plans." The standard provides four activities:

- *Process Implementation:* Developing a process and a plan for quality assurance, ensuring that records are maintained and that organizational freedom is achieved
- *Product Assurance:* Assure that the software products comply with plans and the contract
- *Process Assurance:* Assure that processes comply with their plans, contract, applicable standards and procedures, and requirements that have been flowed-down from higher level contracts
- *Assurance of Quality Systems:* Conduct additional quality management activities in accordance with ISO 9001 if so required

It is important to note that the 12207 standard does **not** factor all quality provisions into the quality assurance process. Quality management is inherent to every process. The quality assurance process of 12207 provides an additional level of assurance that "products and processes . . . conform to their . . . requirements and adhere to their . . . plans." It can be interpreted as a checking process that is granted the power of organizational freedom to ensure that the quality-related tasks of other processes are, in fact, being appropriately executed.

Some managers will desire additional detail for the creation of the quality assurance plan required by the process implementation activity. A suitable standard for this purpose is:

Plan

IEEE Std 730-2002
IEEE Standard for Software Quality Assurance Plans
This standard specifies the format and content of Software Quality
Assurance plans.
Allocated to: Software Quality Knowledge Area

Frankly, this standard treats a much broader subject than the quality assurance process of 12207. It treats all of the quality assurance activities of the entire project, including those activities that are described in other processes of 12207. Some managers will prefer the centralized treatment of quality provided by IEEE 730 to the decentralized treatment provided by 12207.

Software packages intended for off-the-shelf purchase may have special needs for quality management. Those needs are treated by an ISO/IEC standard that has been adopted by the IEEE:

Tool

IEEE Std 1465-1998 (R2004)
IEEE Standard: Adoption of International Standard
ISO/IEC 12119:1994(E), Information Technology—
Software Packages—Quality Requirements and Testing
This standard describes quality requirements specifically suitable for software packages and guidance on testing the package against those requirements.
Allocated to: Software Quality Knowledge Area

Measurement of quality attributes may be important in assuring that the software product meets its requirements. An overall treatment of quality measurement is provided in this IEEE standard:

Measure

IEEE Std 1061-1998 (R2004)
IEEE Standard for a Software Quality Metrics Methodology
This standard describes a methodology—spanning the entire life cycle—for establishing quality requirements and identifying, implementing, and validating the corresponding measures.
Allocated to: Software Quality Knowledge Area

Finally, it has to be noted that 12207 contains a grand requirement for quality assurance in clause 6.3.4 of the quality assurance process.

6.3.4 Assurance of quality systems. This activity consists of the following task:

6.3.4.1 Additional quality management activities shall be assured in accordance with the clauses of ISO 9001 as specified in the contract.

In effect, this clause permits the acquirer to require the supplier's organization to become conformant to the provisions of ISO 9001:

Process

ISO 9001:2000
Quality Management Systems—Requirements
This standard specifies the requirements for an organizational quality management system aiming to provide products meeting requirements and enhance customer satisfaction.
Allocated to: Related Disciplines Chapter, Quality Management

This is a "grand" requirement because the requirements of ISO 9001 are aimed at an entire organization, not at a single project. For a project to conform, the entire organization that is conducting the project would have to change its practices. (Of course, in realistic situations, one would hope that acquirers who intend to apply this task would consider only suppliers who already conform to ISO 9001.) ISO 9001 conformance raises an additional problem—at least if audited conformance is desired. The ISO 9001 standard is not written in terms of software development, or even engineering activity. Auditors verifying conformance with the standard sometimes have difficulty interpreting and applying its provisions to software suppliers. For this reason, ISO/IEC JTC 1/SC 7 produced a derivative standard:

Process

ISO/IEC 90003:2004
Software Engineering—Guidelines for the
Application of ISO 9001:2000 to Computer Software
This standard provides guidance for organizations in the application of
ISO 9001:2000 to the acquisition, supply, development, operation, and
maintenance of computer software.
Allocated to: Related Disciplines Chapter, Quality Management

ISO/IEC 90003 quotes each provision of ISO 9001 and then interprets that provision in terms of practices and artifacts that an auditor might find in a software supplier. The standard also provides a cross-reference to SC 7 standards useful in conforming to ISO 9001.[58]

2.4. Verification Process

The 12207 standard separates verification and validation into two distinct processes. Of course, idiomatic usage so closely merges the two that some software engineers manage to pronounce the "V & V" acronym in not much more than a single syllable. The purpose of the verification process is to determine whether the products of a software activity fulfill the requirements or conditions imposed on them in the previous activities. For example, one might verify that a software design of an item meets the requirements for the item. It is important to note that the goal of evaluation is already an integral part of the primary processes of 12207. One uses a distinct verification process when one desires additional attention to verification. To this end, verification may be conducted with varying levels of independence. In cases where verification is conducted by a distinct organization, it is called "independent verification." The verification process only has two activities:

- *Process implementation:* Determine if verification is warranted and plan for it accordingly
- *Verification:* Perform the verification

A determination that verification is warranted is made by examining the requirements of the project for criticality. Criticality is judged by the potential for a software error to cause great losses—in terms of either human or financial costs, the risks associated with software technologies to be applied, and, of course, the availability of funds and resources to pay for additional verification activity. One must also decide the degree of independence that is to be granted to the verification process and accordingly select an organization to perform it, ensuring that is granted the appropriate independence and authority.

The verification activity contains tasks addressing the verification of:

- Contract
- Process

---

[58] It is anticipated that IEEE will adopt ISO/IEC 90003 and supplement it with an annex providing a cross-reference to IEEE standards.

- Requirements
- Design
- Code
- Integration
- Documentation

It is important to note that verification may not be equally applicable to all activities or to all software items. In fact, the cost-effective application of verification depends upon careful selection of appropriate activities and products and then further careful selection of verification techniques that are appropriate to the criticality. This understanding is central to the IEEE standard on this subject:

Process

IEEE Std 1012–2004
IEEE Standard for Software Verification and Validation
This standard describes software verification and validation processes that are used to determine if software products of an activity meets the requirements of the activity and to determine if software satisfies the user's needs for the intended usage. The scope includes analysis, evaluation, review, inspection, assessment, and testing of both products and processes.
Allocated to: Software Quality Knowledge Area

The IEEE standard posits four levels of software integrity to address criticality and defines verification tasks appropriate for each of the levels. Additionally, the standard suggests that varying levels of intensity and rigor are applied to the selected verification tasks based on the selected level of integrity. IEEE Std 1012 defines specific criteria for the performance of the verification tasks. The user of the standard would allocate an integrity level to each component or unit of each software item and use that integrity level to select appropriate verification tasks.

2.5. Validation Process

The purpose of validation is, "determining whether the requirements and the final as-built system or software product fulfills its specific intended use." The 12207 standard provides two activities for validation:

- *Process implementation:* Determine if verification is warranted and plan for it accordingly
- *Validation:* Perform the validation

As provided in 12207, validation is not as selectively targeted as verification—it is generally applied to the entire software or system product. The primary tool of validation is additional testing:

- Stress testing
- Boundary testing

- Testing inputs suspected of causing noncontinuous changes in behavior
- Testing for the ability to isolate and minimize the effects of faults
- Testing that users can actually complete their intended tasks
- Testing in the target environment

As mentioned above, the 12207 standard separates verification and validation into distinct processes. This makes sense because validation has a distinct purpose—"determining whether the requirements and the final as-built system or software product fulfills its specific intended use." From this viewpoint, validation is a natural adjunct of requirements analysis while verification is a natural adjunct of testing. The reason that the two processes are often combined is that they share many of the same techniques. Accordingly, the IEEE standard for validation is IEEE Std 1012, described in the previous section.

Process

IEEE Std 1012-2004
IEEE Standard for Software Verification and Validation
This standard describes software verification and validation processes that are used to determine if software products of an activity meets the requirements of the activity and to determine if software satisfies the user's needs for the intended usage. The scope includes analysis, evaluation, review, inspection, assessment, and testing of both products and processes.
Allocated to: Software Quality Knowledge Area

2.6. Joint Review Process

The joint review process provides for both technical and management reviews so that one party may evaluate the status of the products produced and the activities performed by another party. There are both technical and management reviews that occur throughout the life of the contract. The 12207 standard provides three activities:

- *Process Implementation:* The requirements for organizing a review and documenting its results.
- *Project Management Reviews:* Reviewing project status relative to plans, schedules, standards, and guidelines.
- *Technical Reviews:* Evaluating software products and services relative to technical requirements, development process, and plans.

The joint review process is used throughout the primary processes of 12207 to evaluate the outputs of technical activities and to establish baselines. The IEEE standard on this subject is:

Process

IEEE Std 1028-1997 (R2002)
IEEE Standard for Software Reviews
This standard defines five types of software reviews and procedures for their execution. Review types include management reviews, technical reviews, inspections, walk-throughs, and audits.
Allocated to: Software Quality Knowledge Area

For each of the five types of reviews, the standard provides:

- *Introduction*: The objectives of the review
- *Responsibilities*: The various roles played by reviewers and their respective duties
- *Input*: Information needed prior to the review
- *Entry criteria*: Criteria for initiating a review
- *Procedures*: Planning, preparing, recording results, and following up
- *Exit criteria*: Criteria for considering a review to be completed
- *Output*: Information to be produced by a review

2.7. Audit Process

The 12207 standard separates audit from joint review. In an audit, one party determines the other party's compliance with requirements, plans, and the contract. The 12207 standard provides two activities of the audit process:

- *Process Implementation:* The requirements for organizing an audit and documenting its results
- *Audit:* The kinds of things suitable for checking with an audit

The IEEE standard mentioned in the previous section, IEEE Std 1028, contains provisions suitable for conducting an audit.

Process

IEEE Std 1028-1997 (R2002)
IEEE Standard for Software Reviews
This standard defines five types of software reviews and procedures for their execution. Review types include management reviews, technical reviews, inspections, walk-throughs, and audits.
Allocated to: Software Quality Knowledge Area

2.8. Problem Resolution Process

The problem resolution process is used for "analyzing and resolving the problems (including nonconformances), whatever their nature or source, that are discovered during the execution of development, operation, maintenance, or other processes." The 12207 standard provides two activities:

- *Process Implementation:* The requirements for establishing a closed-loop process for entering, categorizing, prioritizing, evaluating and disposing of all problem reports.
- *Problem Resolution:* The role of a "problem report"

A specific requirement is that problems should be categorized. IEEE Std 1044 may be useful in implementing procedures for categorization of the problems:

Tool

IEEE Std 1044-1993 (R2002)
IEEE Standard Classification for Software Anomalies
This standard provides a uniform approach to the classification of
anomalies found in software and its documentation. It includes helpful
lists of anomaly classifications and related data.
Allocated to: Software Quality Knowledge Area

2.9. Measurement Process

ISO/IEC 12207 was originally published in 1995 after a development during the early 1990s. Although many researchers spoke of the need for quantitative measurement of software products and processes, measurement was not yet widely practiced except for critical properties such as reliability. (In fact, a large portion of the software measurement literature of the time was devoted solely to ways of estimating and measuring reliability.) So it's not particularly surprising that 12207 mentioned measurement but provided no process for treating measurement in a systematic manner. In the last ten years, it has become apparent that the need for measurement underlies many techniques for project management, quality assurance and other activities. Accordingly, ISO/IEC JTC 1/SC 7 developed a standard providing a process for software measurement:

Process

ISO/IEC 15939:2002
Software Engineering—Software Measurement Process
This standard provides a life cycle process for software measurement
suitable for use with IEEE/EIA 12207.
Allocated to: Software Engineering Process Knowledge Area

From the beginning, the measurement process of 15939 was designed to be a "plug-in" to 12207, as a supporting process. Four activities are provided for the measurement process:

- *Establish and sustain measurement commitment:* Accept requirement, commit to measurement, and assign resources
- *Plan the measurement process:* Identify the information needs, select appropriate measures, define collection procedures, define evaluation criteria, and provide resources
- *Perform the measurement process:* Integrate data collection into other technical and management processes, collect data, produce the desired information products, and communicate the results
- *Evaluate measurement:* Evaluate results and identify improvements

The 15939 measurement process owes much to the experience gained in the DoD's Practical Software Measurement Program [McGarry01] which, in turn, learned from Basili's Goal-Quality-Metric approach to measurement [Basili84].

A number of IEEE standards provide various measures useful for different purposes. IEEE Std 1045 provides an overview of measurements for productivity:

Measure

IEEE Std 1045-1992 (R2002)
IEEE Standard for Software Productivity Metrics
This standard provides a consistent terminology for software productivity measures and defines a consistent way to measure the elements that go into computing software productivity.
Allocated to: Software Engineering Management Knowledge Area

Of course, productivity measurements require some concept of the size of the work to be performed. Many of measures need a measurement of size in the denominator, e.g., the rate of problems reported may be expressed as the number of problem reports divided by the size of the job. A common measure for size is "source lines of code" but "function points" provide a popular alternative. This standard generalizes the concept of functions points to a concept of "functional size":

Measure

IEEE Std 14143.1-2000
IEEE Adoption of ISO/IEC 14143–1:1998, Information Technology—
Software Measurement—Functional Size Measurement—
Part 1: Definition of Concepts
This standard describes the fundamental concepts of a class of measures collectively known as functional size.
Allocated to: Software Requirements Knowledge Area

IEEE has a standard providing an overall methodology for measuring quality characteristics. It is not clear, though, that this standard is well integrated with either 12207 or 15939:

Measure

IEEE Std 1061-1998 (R2004)
IEEE Standard for a Software Quality Metrics Methodology
This standard describes a methodology—spanning the entire life cycle—for establishing quality requirements and identifying, implementing, and validating the corresponding measures.
Allocated to: Software Quality Knowledge Area

If reliability is a particular concern, there is an IEEE standard that addresses its evaluation during software construction:

Measure

IEEE Std 982.1-1988
IEEE Standard Dictionary of Measures to Produce Reliable Software
This standard provides a set of measures for evaluating the reliability of a software product and for obtaining early forecasts of the reliability of a product under development.
Allocated to: Software Quality Knowledge Area

2.10. [Reuse] Asset Management Process

The 12207 standard mentions software reuse in several places, but it is clear that the writers were considering reuse to be performed opportunistically—copying code from another source when the opportunity presents itself. The standard fails to deal with the situation where an organization practices reuse systematically. Systematic reuse involves making investments in understanding a problem domain and in creating software assets that will be reusable in several systems within the domain. Recognizing this shortcoming in 12207, IEEE wrote an appropriate standard.

The IEEE 1517 standard was designed to be used with 12207. It adds activities and tasks to the existing processes of 12207 and also adds complete processes to institutionalize the reuse activities of an organization. The asset management process—a supporting process—is one of the added ones. It addresses the need for developers to know of the existence of potentially reusable artifacts and to easily find and understand them. The process provides the following activities:

- *Process implementation:* Defining an asset management plan and process, including provisions for configuration management of assets
- *Asset storage and retrieval definition:* Providing a mechanism for storage, classification, and retrieval of assets
- *Asset management and control:* Operating the storage mechanism to accept, evaluate, and classify assets; perform configuration management, track usage, and notify users of problems

Additional information about IEEE Std 1517 and its use with the 12207 life cycle processes can be found in a book [McClure01] written by the chair of the working group that drafted the standard.

Of course, reusable software assets are not necessarily confined to a single organization. They might be shared among organizations within an enterprise, or between organizations connected by a contracting or purchasing relationship. One can even imagine an internet-enabled marketplace for trading the rights to reuse assets. Of course, the sharing of assets across organizational boundaries is hindered when each organization has its own unique reuse library. In the 1990s, a small consortium initiated by DoD—the Reuse Library Interoperability Group—developed specifications for sharing assets among reuse libraries. These specifications were adopted by the IEEE as a standard:

Tool

IEEE Std 1420.1-1995 (R2002)
IEEE Standard for Information Technology—
Software Reuse—Data Model for Reuse Library Interoperability:
Basic Interoperability Data Model (BIDM)
This standard describes information that software reuse libraries should
be able to exchange in order to interchange assets.
Allocated to: Software Engineering Tools and Methods Knowledge Area

Tool

IEEE Std 1420.1a-1996 (R2002)
Supplement to IEEE Standard for Information Technology—
Software Reuse—Data Model for Reuse Library Interoperability:
Asset Certification Framework
This supplement to 1420.1 extends the standard model to asset
certification information.
Allocated to: Software Engineering Tools and Methods Knowledge Area

Tool

IEEE Std 1420.1b-1999 (R2002)
IEEE Trial-Use Supplement to IEEE Standard for Information
Technology—Software Reuse—Data Model for Reuse Library
Interoperability: Intellectual property Rights Framework
This supplement to 1420.1 extends the standard model to intellectual
property information.
Allocated to: Software Engineering Tools and Methods Knowledge Area

3. ORGANIZATIONAL PROCESSES

The 12207 standard regards four processes as inherent to an organization at the enterprise level:

- Management
- Infrastructure
- Improvement
- Training

Two more organizational processes are added by IEEE Std 1540 and IEEE Std 1517, respectively:

- Risk Management
- Reuse Program Administration

Initiating any of the primary processes has the effect of instantiating the management process and the other appropriate organizational processes. The organizational processes of 12207 are expected to be inherent in the responsible organization; instances of those processes are instantiated for the execution of the specific project. Relevant standards for the organizational processes are shown in Figure 34.

3.1. Management Process

The management process is intended to provide management of all of the other processes of the project, including aspects of "product management, project management, and task management." The process provides four activities:

- *Initiation and Scope Definition:* Establish process requirements and ensure availability of resources
- *Planning:* Prepare plans for the execution of the process
- *Execution and Control:* Execute and monitor the process, resolve problems and report results
- *Review and Evaluation:* Evaluate products and plans to ensure satisfaction of requirements
- *Closure:* Ensure completeness of results

Upon initial reading, the provisions of the management process may seem vague. It is important to understand that the process is a generic one that is overlaid on all the other processes of the standard. For example, it is the instantiation of the management process that provides the "Plan-Do-Check-Act" (PDCA) cycle[59] inherited by the primary processes for the purpose of

---

[59] PDCA is a basic quality management concept on which ISO 9001 is based [Ling96].

Organizational Process	Management	Infrastructure	Improvement	Training	Risk Management
Basic Standard(s)	IEEE/EIA 12207.0, clause 7.1	IEEE/EIA 12207.0, clause 7.2	IEEE/EIA 12207.0, clause 7.3	IEEE/EIA 12207.0, clause 7.4	IEEE Std 1540
Context Standards	IEEE Std 1490, Project Management BOK				
Detailed Standards	IEEE Std 1058, SW Project Management Plans	IEEE Std 1175.1, CASE Tool Interconnection IEEE Std 1462, Evaluation and Selection of CASE Tools	ISO/IEC 15504, Process Assessment		

Organizational Process	Reuse Program Administration			Cross-Project Process	[Reuse] Domain Engineering
Basic Standard(s)	IEEE Std 1517, clause 7.1			Basic Standard(s)	IEEE Std 1517, clause 8.1
Context Standards				Context Standards	
Detailed Standards				Detailed Standards	

Figure 34. *Organizational and cross-project processes of the S2ESC reference model*

implementing general quality management principles. In short, all of the aspects of managing the processes of 12207 have been factored into the management process and expressed in a generic manner. So the plan described in the planning activity is not a distinct plan, instead it is a summary of characteristics applicable to all of the plans mentioned in other processes of the standard. These characteristics are listed in Clause 7.1.2 of the standard.

7.1.2 Planning. This activity consists of the following task:

7.1.2.1 The manager shall prepare the plans for execution of the process. The plans associated with the execution of the process shall contain descriptions of the associated activities and tasks and identification of the software products that will be provided. These plans shall include, but are not limited to, the following:

  a) Schedules for the timely completion of tasks;
  b) Estimation of effort;
  c) Adequate resources needed to execute the tasks;
  d) Allocation of tasks;
  e) Assignment of responsibilities;
  f) Quantification of risks associated with the tasks or the process itself;
  g) Quality control measures to be employed throughout the process;
  h) Costs associated with the process execution;
  i) Provision of environment and infrastructure.

A comparison with IEEE/EIA 12207.1 shows that these characteristics have been captured in the generic specifications for plans.

Because of the deserved emphasis on good project management, many users of 12207 will be uncomfortable with the brief 1–1/2 page treatment of management in 12207. IEEE has an additional standard that may be helpful:

Plan

IEEE Std 1058-1998
IEEE Standard for Software Project Management Plans
This standard describes the format and contents of a software project management plan.
Allocated to: Software Engineering Management Knowledge Area

The 1058 standard describes the content and format of a Software Project Management Plan similar to the one required by subclause 5.2.4.5 of the supply process of the 12207 standard. The description in the 1058 standard also references various subsidiary plans, including those required by other processes of 12207. For this reason, the 1058 standard can be applied as a unified treatment of planning across the entire software project.

It must be understood that project management is an important area of study in its own right. Many managers consider the Project Management Institute to be the leading professional group in this subject and consider their *Project Management Body of Knowledge (PMBOK® Guide)* to be the authoritative document. Recognizing the position of this important contextual standard, IEEE has chosen to adopt the *PMBOK® Guide* as one of its own standards:

Terminology

IEEE Std 1490-2003
IEEE Guide: Adoption of PMI Standard, A Guide to the
Project Management Body of Knowledge (PMBOK® Guide)
This document is the IEEE adoption of the Project Management Body of Knowledge defined by the Project Management Institute. It identifies and described generally accepted knowledge regarding project management.
Allocated to: Related Disciplines Chapter, Quality Management

The PMI updates the *PMBOK® Guide* from time to time; a new edition is expected in 2005. The IEEE adoption process tends to lag their updates by a few years. On the other hand, S2ESC makes an effort to revise their 1058 standard to achieve compatibility between it and the version of the *PMBOK® Guide* that they have adopted.

3.2. Infrastructure Process

The infrastructure process establishes and maintains the "hardware, software, tools, techniques, standards and facilities" required for the execution of the other processes. The process provides three activities:

- *Process Implementation:* Define and plan the infrastructure
- *Establishment of the Infrastructure:* Establish the infrastructure, considering cost, performance, safety, etc.

• *Maintenance of the Infrastructure:* Maintain the infrastructure so that it continues to meet its requirements

Trivially, of course, any standard utilized on a project or by an organization becomes part of the infrastructure. Perhaps the most important application of the infrastructure process considers the use of CASE tooling. An IEEE standard describes the consideration of CASE tools:

Tool

IEEE Std 1462-1998 (R2004)
IEEE Standard: Adoption of International Standard
ISO/IEC 14102: 1995, Information Technology—
Guideline for the Evaluation and Selection of CASE tools
This standard provides guidelines for the evaluation and selection
of CASE tools.
Allocated to: Software Engineering Tools and Methods Knowledge Area

Integration of CASE tools is a more challenging topic. IEEE provides a standard—the first in a planned family—for interconnecting these tools:

Tool

IEEE Std 1175.1-2002
IEEE Guide for
CASE Tool Interconnections—Classification and Description
This document is the first of a planned series of standards on the
integration of CASE tools into a productive software engineering
environment. This part describes fundamental concepts and introduces
the remaining (planned) parts.
Allocated to: Software Engineering Tools and Methods Knowledge Area

3.3. Improvement Process

The improvement process is intended for "establishing, assessing, measuring, controlling and improving" the software life cycle processes at the level of the enterprise. The process provides three activities:

• *Process establishment:* At the organizational level, establish and document a suite of software life cycle processes
• *Process assessment:* Develop, document, and apply a process assessment procedure
• *Process improvement:* Collect historical data and apply it to the improvement of the processes

The terminology of 12207 can confuse the unwary. Because only four processes are categorized as "organizational processes," it is easy to imagine that 12207 is intended for use at the project level. It is clear, though, that the improvement process requires definition, assessment, and improvement of processes at the organizational level for use throughout the organization.

The IEEE does not have any standards addressing process improvement. In the US, it is typical to use mechanisms that are not standards, such as one of the Capability Maturity Models (CMM®),[60] for this purpose. The international community does have an emerging standard in this area, though—a standard that may become very important outside the US. The original Technical Report can be regarded as a trial use standard while the final version is under development:

Process

ISO/IEC TR 15504 (nine parts)
Information Technology—Software Process Assessment
This technical report would provide requirements on methods for performing process assessment as a basis for process improvement or capability determination.
Allocated to: Software Engineering Process Knowledge Area

The version currently under development has been broadened to deal with the assessment of any business process—not just software. It provides a two-dimensional model of capability and processes. The process dimension is supplied by reference to an externally supplied process reference model that defines process based on a statement of purpose and a set of outcomes. The capability dimension is provided by the new 15504 and consists of six process capability levels and associated attributes. An assessment evaluates and records the process attribute ratings for each assessed process.

Process

ISO/IEC (Draft) 15504 (five parts)
Information Technology—Process Assessment
This draft standard would provide requirements on methods for performing process assessment as a basis for process improvement or capability determination.
Allocated to: Software Engineering Process Knowledge Area

The Technical Report and the draft standard both include an exemplar assessment model. If one takes the example model seriously, then one can perform process assessment based on 15504 itself. Some have done this and it is anticipated that others will. In general, though, it is assumed that one will use an assessment approach that conforms to the requirements of the 15504 standard. Because the standard is not yet completed, there are no conforming approaches, but it is possible that methods such as TickIT [DTI92], Trillium [April95], and Bootstrap [Bootstrap93] might make changes in order to conform to the standard.

Two methods popular in the US may not change—the Software CMM and the CMMI. The former because it is essentially frozen and the latter because it is maintained and extended by a DoD-centered community, which has other compatibility constraints. These two methods can be regarded as alternatives to 15504 and are briefly discussed below.

3.3.1. SEI CMM Probably the best known software process assessment approach in the US is the Software Engineering Institute's (SEI) Software

[60] Capability Maturity Model and CMM are registered service marks of Carnegie Mellon University.

Capability Maturity Model[61] (SW-CMM) [Paulk93]. The model characterizes five successive levels of maturity in the software process capability of the assessed organization. The model, along with an appropriate assessment method, may be applied to evaluate a developer's maturity either as an assessment (for purposes of self-improvement) or as an evaluation (for purposes of supplier qualification). The Department of Defense was particularly interested in the latter usage because its rules regarding open competition require objective evidence for vendor qualification (or, more pointedly, disqualification).

The SW-CMM has only a coincidental relationship with software engineering standards. The use of these standards does not guarantee a high CMM evaluation. Furthermore, a high CMM evaluation does not imply conformance to the standards. This is not completely bad. Using standards to define processes and CMM to assess them provides an independence of evaluation. Unfortunately, unenlightened organizations sometimes discard this advantage by "teaching to the test," i.e., they advise their process implementation team to directly implement the practices of the CMM.

The popularity of the SW-CMM triggered a wave of additional capability models treating different aspects of vendor capability. In recent years, several of these models were coalesced and revised, with DOD encouragement, to create the CMMI, discussed in the next section. However, the SW-CMM had achieved such wide popularity that replacing it is not easy. The Software Engineering Institute has announced plans to "sunset" the SW-CMM but it can be anticipated that usage will continue in the nondefense marketplace.

3.3.2. CMMI   The proliferation of capability models—even good models—created a problem for hopeful users. Each model required distinct training, deployment, and assessment. Additional complications were caused by overlap of scope. The Department of Defense created a combined government and industry team to develop a new CMM to integrate selected existing models. The result is the CMMI.

The initial CMMI unifies practices from a draft revision of the SW-CMM, EIA Interim Standard 731-Software Engineering Capability Model, and a CMM for Integrated Product and Process Development (IPPD). It is expected that additional disciplines will be added to the model. The CMMI product suite contains a number of components [Weszka00]:

- Integrated models for systems engineering, software engineering, and IPPD
- Assessment methods and instruments for the models
- Training products supporting the models and assessment method
- Common glossary and tailoring mechanism
- Framework for incorporating new disciplines

As with the SW-CMM, correspondence with the software and systems engineering standards discussed in this book is largely coincidental. The same

---

[61] Capability Maturity Model and CMM are service marks of Carnegie Mellon University.

advice applies—use standards as a source of requirements for process implementation and use maturity models for evaluating the success and effectiveness of the implementation.

3.4. Training Process

The final process of 12207 is training—activities for "providing and maintaining trained personnel." Three activities are provided:

- *Process Implementation:* Review project requirements to develop a training plan
- *Training Material Development:* Develop manuals and training presentations
- *Training Plan Implementation:* Provide training, maintain records, and ensure the availability of appropriate skill mixes.

There seem to be no software engineering standards—from any organization—specific to this subject.

3.5. Risk Management Process

Although the 12207 standard mentions "risk" in many provisions, it provides no unified treatment of the subject. IEEE decided to fill this need by developing an organizational process for risk management:

Process

IEEE Std 1540-2001
IEEE Standard for Software Life Cycle Processes—
Risk Management
This standard provides a life cycle process for software risk management
suitable for use with IEEE/EIA 12207.
Allocated to: Software Engineering Process Knowledge Area

This standard has been adopted by SC 7 and renumbered as ISO/IEC 16085. In order to reconcile comments received during the adoption process, IEEE and SC 7 are jointly revising the document. The revisions will be minor and both organizations will use the 16085 number for the result—expected in 2006.

The purpose of the process is to identify and mitigate risks continuously. The standard provides six activities:

- *Plan and implement risk management:* Establish a policy and a process for risk management, providing for resources, responsibility, and evaluation
- *Manage the project risk profile:* Maintain a complete and consistent view of the currently recognized risks and the status of their treatment
- *Perform risk analysis:* Identify risks, evaluate their probability and consequence, and recommend treatments
- *Perform risk monitoring:* Review the risks and assess the effectiveness of their treatment

- *Perform risk treatment:* Determine whether a risk is acceptable or initiate treatment to make it acceptable
- *Evaluate the risk management process:* Determine the success of risk management and improve policies and process when appropriate

When using this process in conjunction with 12207, risk treatment is performed by the other technical and management processes of 12207. In cases where the standard is used independently of 12207, it specifies requirements for risk treatment.

3.6. Reuse Program Administration

Reuse program administration is another of the processes supplied by IEEE Std 1517 (mentioned above) for the systematic practice of software reuse. Reuse program administration is the process capturing the organizational-level considerations in systematic reuse—how an organization should plan, establish, manage, control, and monitor its reuse program. The process provides the following activities:

- *Initiation:* Establish the organization's reuse program including strategies, resources, sponsors, responsibilities, and infrastructure
- *Domain identification:* Characterize a set of systems in terms of common properties that could be implemented with reusable software assets
- *Reuse assessment:* Evaluate the reuse maturity of the organization and the reuse potential of the domain(s) to motivate improvements
- *Planning:* Develop an appropriate plan for implementing reuse across the organization
- *Execution and control:* Execute the plan
- *Review and evaluation:* Review and evaluate the results

The standard recognizes that establishing a systematic reuse program in an organization requires substantial cultural adjustment. The three activities that precede planning address the cultural changes of the organization.

4. CROSS-PROJECT PROCESSES

This is a category of processes not found in the 12207 standard. The category was invented by IEEE Std 1517 to deal with aspects of software reuse that inherently span multiple projects but which might not demand management at the organizational level.

4.1. [Reuse] Domain Engineering

Domain engineering "covers the development and maintenance of the domain models, domain architecture, and other assets" for a domain. The domain engineering process of IEEE Std 1517 consists of the following activities:

- *Process implementation:* Create and document a domain engineering plan, selecting standards and tools to improve commonality and represent the domain models and architecture
- *Domain analysis:* Discover and describe the variations and commonalities among the systems within the domain
- *Domain design:* Define the domain architecture and characterize the reusable assets that could be used to build software products
- *Asset provision:* Develop or acquire the software assets
- *Asset maintenance:* Modify assets, including the domain model and architecture, to correct deficiencies or address new needs

Because a domain is, by definition, a collection of systems sharing common properties, the engineering of a domain must span multiple projects. The fundamental principle is that the domain has a life cycle of its own, independent of the life cycle of the systems within the domain. This leads to the concept that the domain should be managed distinctly, but in cooperation with, the systems that fall within the domain. This process provides that distinct life cycle management of the domain.

5. SUMMARY

This chapter has taken a process-based look at the standards of the IEEE Computer Society's Software Engineering Standards Committee along with a few standards selected from other organizations. The fundamental process framework is provided by IEEE/EIA 12207. In addition, IEEE Std 1540 and ISO/IEC 15939 provide processes for risk management and measurement, respectively, that plug-into the framework provided by 12207. IEEE Std 1517 provides additional processes, activities, and tasks for systematic software reuse. Taken together, these standards provide a single framework of reference processes used by all S2ESC standards. Most of the remaining S2ESC collection, as well as a few other standards, are allocated to the framework to demonstrate how they can support the software life cycle processes. The reference framework and supporting standards provide a basis for process definition and implementation.

Chapter *20*

System Life Cycle Processes

The relationship of software engineering to systems engineering has long been recognized, but its nature has long been a matter of disagreement. Both ISO/IEC JTC 1/SC 7 and the IEEE S2ESC began with a base of software engineering standards—and both found it necessary to describe a context of systems engineering within which software projects might fit. The writers of ISO/IEC 12207 assumed that all software products inherently require some sort of system—if only the computer on which the software is to be executed. Therefore, all software development would imply some minimal system development.

> "The standard provides the minimum system context for software. Software is treated as an integral part of the total system and performs certain functions in that system. This is implemented by extracting the software requirements from the system requirements and design, producing the software, and integrating it into the system."—IEEE/EIA 12207.0, E.7][62]

It was perhaps inevitable that both SC 7 and the IEEE would write systems engineering standards to complement their collections of software standards. A list is provided in Table 25.

This chapter takes a look at system life cycle processes. The key standard in this area, ISO/IEC 15288, considers the life cycle from two viewpoints—a set of processes that are performed during the life of a system and a set of stages through which the system passes during its life. Both views will be helpful to

---

[62] Annex E of IEEE/EIA 12207.0 was drafted by Raghu Singh, the editor of ISO/IEC 12207:1995.

TABLE 25. Standards supporting system life cycle processes

Standard	Title
IEEE Std 1220–1998	IEEE Standard for Application and Management of the Systems Engineering Process
IEEE Std 1228–1994	IEEE Standard for Software Safety Plans
IEEE Std 1233, 1998 Edition	IEEE Guide for Developing System Requirements Specifications
IEEE Std 1362–1998	IEEE Guide for Information Technology—System Definition—Concept of Operations (ConOps) Document
IEEE Std 1471–2000	IEEE Recommended Practice for Architectural Description for Software-Intensive Systems
ISO/IEC 15026:1998	Information Technology—System and Software Integrity Levels
ISO/IEC 15288:2002	Systems Engineering—System Life Cycle Processes
ISO/IEC TR 19760:2003	Systems Engineering—A Guide for the Application of ISO/IEC 15288 (System Life Cycle Processes)

us and will be considered separately in this chapter. Most of the IEEE standards will be considered from the life cycle process viewpoint; however, the key IEEE systems engineering standard, 1220, will be considered primarily from the viewpoint of life cycle stages.

1. ISO/IEC 15288—SYSTEMS ENGINEERING—SYSTEM LIFE CYCLE PROCESSES

Because ISO/IEC JTC 1/SC 7 developed a software life cycle process standard, ISO/IEC 12207, that explicitly places software into a context provided by a system life cycle, it is not surprising that they would turn their attention to system life cycle processes. The result—after seven years of work—is ISO/IEC 15288:2002 and its companion guide, ISO/IEC TR 19760:2003.

Unfortunately, 15288 uses a process architecture that is different than that of 12207. Each process is defined in terms of its purpose, a list of outcomes, and a list of activities. One achieves conformance to the standard by "demonstrating that all of the requirements of the declared set of processes have been satisfied using the outcomes as evidence." Because the activities are phrased using the verb "shall," the activities are required but the purpose and outcomes only count as evidence in demonstrating their achievement. One does not have to conform to all of the processes of the standard—only a "declared set" of them. The selected processes must be assembled into a life cycle model composed of a set of stages, which themselves have a statement of purpose and outcomes. An appendix of the standard describes an example set of stages.

The architectural differences between 12207 and 15288 have motivated a "harmonization" project that is underway as of 2005.

2. KEY CONCEPTS OF ISO/IEC 15288

Of course, ISO/IEC 15288 is concerned with man-made systems only.[63] It's necessary to make this obvious point because common language applies the same word to naturally occurring interacting collections, e.g., the "solar system." Man-made systems are created and operated to provide benefits for users and are composed of various kinds of elements: hardware, software, human participants, processes, procedures, facilities, and even naturally occurring entities, e.g., the water that powers a millwheel. Systems are provided in the form of *products* and/or *services*.

The definition of any particular system is relative to the observer. If one thinks of an airplane as a *system*, others might perceive it as a *system element* in an air traffic control system. Alternatively, the airplane can be viewed as the *operating environment* of the cabin pressure system. Since the system is defined by its perception, we can refer to the *system-of-interest* when we want to differentiate it from other related systems. To characterize a system, we must define its boundaries, boundaries that may include humans as elements of the system or exclude them as users of the system or both.

2.1. System Structure

Within the defined boundaries, a system is composed of a set of interacting system elements. Each element is to be implemented to fulfill specified requirements contributing to the functionality of the system. Because the element is distinguishable, its implementation may be delegated to another party through an *agreement*.

Of course, a complex system element may be considered as a system in its own right, leading to a viewpoint of the system-of-interest being at the apex of a hierarchical tree of systems, with system elements as leaves of the tree. Because the system life cycle is applied recursively to each subtree, each system could be the responsibility of a separate *project*, providing a hierarchy of projects mirroring that of the system-of-interest. Each project has the responsibility of *acquiring* from the level below it and *supplying* to the level above it.

2.2. Enabling Systems

As the system-of-interest progresses through its life cycle, services may be required from other systems. An obvious example is that to manufacture the widget system, we may need a widget factory, which itself is a system. With respect to the system-of-interest, these other systems are *enabling systems*. Typically various enabling systems are required throughout the life cycle of the system of interest. Note that the concept of the enabling system is distinct from the concept of interacting systems in the operational environment of the system-of-interest.

---

[63] This section is loosely based on Annex D of ISO/IEC 15288.

2.3. System Life Cycle Model

All systems go through a *life cycle*. Planned or not, man-made systems are originally conceived in some fashion and are ultimately discarded. The system progresses through the life cycle as the result of *processes* performed and managed by humans. It is possible to *model* the life cycle by characterizing processes and combining them and their results in a variety of ways. ISO/IEC 15288 provides a set of processes that can be used to model the life cycle of all systems.

2.4. System Life Cycle Stages

Despite wide variety in the details of various life cycles, commonality can be demonstrated by defining a series of *stages* through which the system passes. Each marks a major change in the state of the system and represents major progress and achievement. Each stage has a distinct purpose to be considered when planning the life cycle. Typically, life cycle stages are separated by *decision gates* that ensure that the prior stage was completed satisfactorily and has laid the basis for the following stage. In this way, stages provide a basis for management visibility and control of the project.

Stages can be arranged in a sequential, evolutionary, or iterative manner to satisfy a variety of management goals. ISO/IEC 15288 requires a project to define a set of stages in terms of their *purpose* and *outcomes* and to arrange the stages into a life cycle model for the system. A sample set of stages is provided in an informative annex.

An important reason for defining a system life cycle model is to appropriately synchronize the stages of the system-of-interest and its enabling systems. One can not manufacture the widget system until the widget manufacturing system is operational.

2.5. System Life Cycle Processes

As mentioned above, the system progresses through the life cycle because humans execute processes. The purpose of ISO/IEC 15288 is to define a set of processes that can be applied to any system. The processes are characterized by their essential goal, called *purpose*, and their results, called *outcomes*. Further detail for each process is provided by a set of *activities*, which, when executed together, produce the outcomes. The processes may be executed at any level in the system hierarchy, and—in principle—in any stage.

Obviously, any definition of a set of processes has some degree of arbitrariness. The writers of 15288 pursued two principles in defining processes—principles similar to those used in defining 12207. The two principles are:

- *Modularity:* The functions of a process should be cohesive and well decoupled from those of other processes.
- *Ownership:* A process is associated with a responsibility that is reasonable for a single party to fulfill.

The standard classifies the processes into three different organizational levels of responsibility—*enterprise processes*, *project processes*, and *technical processes.* Enterprise processes are typically used for the strategic management of an enterprise to ensure its continued capability to do business. In order to accomplish their goals, enterprises create projects that employ the project processes for managing the resources and assets allocated to the project by the enterprise. To achieve technical results, the project employs the technical processes to successively transform the system from idea to completion.

These three categories of processes are not yet complete, though. The reason for the existence of an enterprise is to engage in trade. For two enterprises to cooperate in this manner—one as an *acquirer* and one as a *supplier*—they must reach agreement on the product or service to be traded. A fourth category of processes—*agreement processes*—allows them to engage in a suitable relationship.

3. A PROCESS VIEW OF THE 15288 SYSTEM LIFE CYCLE

This section introduces the system life cycle processes of ISO/IEC 15288 and how the various S2ESC standards can support the processes. Of course, the processes of 15288 can be applied to systems of various types. In this treatment, though, we are assuming that important parts of the system's functionality are provided by software items. Given this viewpoint, we assume that software life cycle processes must fit into the overall system life cycle in order to implement the software items of the system. Table 26 illustrates the relationship between the life cycle processes of a system and the life cycle processes of its software elements.[64] The left-most column lists the four process groups defined by ISO/IEC 15288. The second column lists each system life cycle process of 15288 in its appropriate process group. The third column selects many of the processes and activities of 12207 and related standards and places them next to a roughly corresponding process of 15288. The final column lists S2ESC systems engineering standards (and one SC 7 standard) that are helpful in implementing the technical processes of 15288. One important S2ESC standard, IEEE 1220, *Application and Management of the Systems Engineering Process*, is omitted from this chart. It will be treated later in this chapter.

ISO/IEC 15288 groups its life cycle processes into four groups:

- *Agreement:* The activities necessary to establish an agreement between two organizations.
- *Enterprise:* Manage the organization's capability to acquire and supply products and services via the initiation, support, and control of projects.
- *Project:* Establish project plans, assess progress against plans, and control execution to completion.
- *Technical:* Define requirements for a system product and develop, produce, use, sustain, and dispose of the product.

---

[64] Please note that this mapping does not compare the processes of the two standards for similarity. Such a mapping is provided in Annex C of ISO/IEC 15288.

TABLE 26. Correspondence of the life cycle processes of a system and its software items

15288 Process Group	15288 Process	Corresponding 12207 Process: Activities	Helpful S2ESC Systems Engineering Standards
Agreement	Acquisition	Acquisition	
	Supply	Supply	
Enterprise	Enterprise Environment Management	Improvement	
	Investment Management	Infrastructure	
	System Life Cycle Processes Management	Improvement	
	Resource Management	Infrastructure Training	
	Quality Management		
Project	Project Planning	Management	
	Project Assessment		
	Project Control		
	Decision-Making		
	Risk Management		IEEE Std 1540, Risk Management
	Configuration Management		
	Information Management		
Technical	Stakeholder Requirements Definition	Development: System Requirements Analysis	IEEE 1362, Concept of Operations Document
	Requirements Analysis	Development: System Requirements Analysis	IEEE 1233 System Requirements Specification
	Architectural Design	Development: System Architectural Design	ISO/IEC 15026, System and SW Integrity Levels IEEE 1471 Architectural Description
	Implementation	Several development activities The supporting processes	IEEE Std 1228, SW Safety Plans
	Integration	Development: System Integration	
	Verification	Development: System Qualification Test	
	Transition	Development: SW Installation	
	Validation	Development: SW Acceptance Support	
	Operation	Operation	
	Maintenance	Maintenance	
	Disposal	Maintenance	

Each process of 15288 is defined in terms of a statement of purpose, a list of outcomes of successful performance, and a list of activities that are performed to produce the outcomes. The standard does not list specific tasks under each activity and is, therefore, less prescriptive than its software life cycle counterpart, 12207.

The key to understanding Table 26 is the realization that the process descriptions in 12207 extend beyond the implementation of a software item in a system to describe enterprise-level and system-level dependencies of the software processes. There are three major categories of dependencies:

- The organization processes of 12207 (management, improvement, infrastructure, and training) place dependencies upon the enterprise performing the software processes. The 12207 standard says that these four processes are project-level "instantiations" of processes that already exist at the enterprise level. If system development and the development of the software items are occurring within the same organization, then the enterprise processes of 15288 and the organizational processes of 12207 are necessarily addressing the same organization and must be reconciled.

- The description of the development process in 12207 contains the system-level activities that are necessary to enable the implementation and integration of the software items in the context of the enclosing system. So those activities must be reconciled with the corresponding processes of 15288.

- The other primary processes of 12207 (acquisition, supply, maintenance, and operation) contain software-specific provisions that should be incorporated in the execution of the corresponding system-level processes.

The alignment of the primary processes of 12207 with ISO/IEC 15288 is straightforward. The agreement-oriented primary processes of 12207 line up nicely with the like-named processes of 15288. Software operation and maintenance would align with the operation and maintenance activities of the system. From the viewpoint of the system life cycle, the 12207 standard is useful in **implementing** an identified software item of a system; so the 12207 development process would align with the implementation process of 15288. However, the 12207 development process also includes several activities that are regarded as providing the minimum system context for software development. So those activities have to be aligned with activities of 15288 that are outside the implementation activity. The alignment of the 15288 verification and validation processes shown in the table may strike some as odd. One must remember that the table describes the alignment of system-level processes with the processes of an item in the system. The system qualification test described in 12207 is one part of the overall system-level verification and the 12207 software acceptance test is one part of the overall system-level validation. There are verification and validation processes at the software level but they could be executed independently of the verification and validation processes at the system level. On the other hand, if a single organization is performing both system and software development using integrated processes, then it might be appropriate to align the two verification and validation processes.

The organizational processes provided by 12207, and IEEE Std 1540 also line up reasonably cleanly. The conclusion that both the training and infrastructure processes align with a single 15288 process, resource management, may suggest a shortcoming of 12207. Similarly, the alignment of 12207 infrastructure process with two processes of 15288 suggests a mixing of concerns in the 12207 process. The management process of 12207 aligns with four processes of 15288 because its writers chose to decompose management by providing four processes rather than one process with four activities. The risk management process of IEEE Std 1540 has been aligned with that of 15288; in fact, it seems likely that the IEEE standard would accomplish all of the outcomes and activities described for risk management in 15288.

One is tempted to align the 12207 documentation and configuration management processes with the information management and configuration management processes of 15288. However, these processes are so specialized to the needs of software that the alignment seems unenlightening. Of course, an organization using integrated processes might decide to make that alignment. The 12207 quality assurance process has not been aligned with 15288 quality management because the latter is more akin to enterprise-level treatment provided by ISO 9001. Alignments of the other supporting processes of 12207 seem even more unlikely, so all are assumed to be subsumed by the implementation process of 15288.

The following subsections will briefly describe the processes of 15288 in terms of their purpose as stated in ISO/IEC 15288. When appropriate, the text also describes helpful supporting standards as shown in the table.

3.1. Agreement Processes

The agreement processes allow two organizations to establish the means to conduct business with each other. The nature of the relationship is asymmetrical; one organization—the supplier—is providing a product or service to the other organization—the acquirer.

3.1.1. Acquisition   The purpose of the acquisition process is to obtain a product or service in accordance with the acquirer's requirements.

3.1.2. Supply   The purpose of the supply process is to provide an acquirer with a product or service that meets agreed requirements.

3.2. Enterprise Processes

Enterprise processes of 15288 are a selection—an incomplete selection—of the processes necessary for an organization to conduct business at an overall level. The processes manage the organization's capability to acquire and supply products and services. Organizations conduct projects to perform on this capability. The enterprise processes enable the organization to initiate, support, and control the projects.

3.2.1. Enterprise Environment Management   The purpose of the enterprise environment management process is to define and maintain the policies and procedures (within the scope of 15288) needed for the organization's business.

3.2.2. Investment Management   The purpose of the investment management process is to initiate and sustain sufficient and suitable projects in order to meet the objectives of the organization.

3.2.3. System Life Cycle Processes Management   The purpose of the system life cycle processes management process is to assure that effective system life cycle processes are available for use by the organization.

3.2.4. Resource Management   The purpose of the resource management process is to provide resources to projects.

3.2.5. Quality Management   The purpose of the quality management process is to assure that products, services, and implementations of life cycle processes meet enterprise quality goals and achieve customer satisfaction.

3.3. Project Processes

The enterprise accomplishes its objectives by conducting projects. The project processes are used to create and maintain project plans, to consider progress against the plans and to control the execution of the project until it is completed. Projects are sometimes viewed as a hierarchy of subprojects. So project processes may be invoked at any point to operate a new subproject.

3.3.1. Project Planning   The purpose of the project planning process is to produce and communicate effective and workable project plans.

3.3.2. Project Assessment   The purpose of the project assessment process is to determine the status of the project.

3.3.3. Project Control   The purpose of the project control process is to direct project plan execution and ensure that the project performs according to plans and schedules, within projected budgets and it satisfies technical objectives.

3.3.4. Decision-Making   The purpose of the decision-making process is to select the most beneficial course of project action where alternatives exist.

3.3.5. Risk Management   The purpose of the risk management process is to reduce the effects of uncertain events that may result in changes to quality, cost, schedule, or technical characteristics. An IEEE standard may be helpful:

Process

IEEE Std 1540-2001
IEEE Standard for Software Life Cycle Processes—
Risk Management
This standard provides a life cycle process for software risk management
suitable for use with IEEE/EIA 12207.
Allocated to: Software Engineering Process Knowledge Area

Although IEEE Std 1540 is written for software risk management, it seems completely satisfactory for system-level concerns. In fact, it is likely that SC

7 will ask IEEE to cooperate in revising the standard to provide a risk management process at both the system and software levels of technical projects.

3.3.6. Configuration Management   The purpose of the configuration management process is to establish and maintain the integrity of all identified outputs of a project or process and make them available to concerned parties.

3.3.7. Information Management   The purpose of the information management process is to provide relevant, timely, complete, valid, and, if required, confidential information to designated parties during and, as appropriate, after the system life cycle.

3.4. Technical Processes

Whereas the project processes are used to manage the project, the technical processes are used to actually create the results of the project. They are used to define the requirements for a system and design a product based on those requirements, to produce and use the product, and to dispose of the product when its life is completed.

3.4.1. Stakeholder Requirements Definition   The purpose of the stakeholder requirements definition process is to define the requirements for a system that can provide the services needed by users and other stakeholders in a defined environment. IEEE has a helpful standard:

Document

IEEE Std 1362-1998
IEEE Guide for Information Technology—System Definition—
Concept of Operations (ConOps) Document
This document provides guidance on the format and content of a
Concept of Operations (ConOps) document, describing characteristics of
a proposed system from the users' viewpoint.
Allocated to: Related Disciplines Chapter, Systems Engineering

During the 1970s, many experts emphasized the importance of rigor to improve software development. Generally, it was believed that the disciplined development of a requirements statement and its approval by the customer, followed by the disciplined development of the implementing software would result in the completion of a satisfactory software product. Despite success in these two objectives, though, software development projects often failed to satisfy the user of the software. More modern thinking has centered on communications rather than rigor. The premise is that all those with an interest in the productive deployment of the software, the stakeholders, should be able to suitably participate in the definition of the system. The list of stakeholders can be a long one and certainly includes the prospective users, operators, and maintainers of the intended software. In many cases, those responsible for other systems interfacing with the intended system would be included in the list. The Concept of Operations document was devised as a vehicle for communicating with stakeholders.

IEEE Std 1362 is a guide to the format and content of a ConOps document. It also provides some guidance on approaches to developing the ConOps document. The fundamental purpose of a ConOps is to describe the existing system, explain the changes, and describe the new system—all from the viewpoint of the users. It provides a place to:

- Describe the needs of the users, in their terms, without detailed consideration of technical issues.
- Document those needs in a manner that is accessible to user so that they can participate in verifying them
- Describe desires and expectations in a manner that is not quantified, e.g., a system that is "highly reliable"
- Express users' thoughts regarding possible solutions strategies

The standard suggests the top-level organization for the ConOps document as shown in Table 18 on page 266 IEEE Std 1362 works from the assumption that a new system is replacing an existing one of some sort. So it makes a systematic treatment of the old system, the changes desired, and the new system. To evaluate the utility of this standard in the stakeholder requirements definition process, Table 27 compares its suggestions with the activities provided in ISO/IEC 15288.

The comparison suggests that the format and content specified by IEEE Std 1362 for a ConOps document is a suitable product for recording and documenting stakeholder requirements, even though the standard does not provide guidance on the performance of the activities.

3.4.2. Requirements Analysis The purpose of the requirements analysis process is to transform the stakeholder, requirement-driven view of desired services into a technical view of a required product that could deliver those services. IEEE has a helpful standard:

Document

IEEE Std 1233, 1998 Edition (R2002)
IEEE Guide for Developing System Requirements Specifications
This document provides guidance on the development of a System Requirements Specification, covering the identification, organization, presentation, and modification of requirements. It also provides guidance on the characteristics and qualities of requirements.
Allocated to: Related Disciplines Chapter, Systems Engineering

One of the key ideas of this standard is that the system requirements specification is a document that must achieve communication between two audiences—the customer who is acquiring the system and the technical community that is creating the system. So the standard makes a distinction between the collected requirements and the means for presenting it to the various audiences. It emphasizes the specification of well-formed requirements and their collection into an aggregate. The top-level table of contents of IEEE Std 1233 is shown in Table 28.

TABLE 27. Correspondence of IEEE Std 1362 with the 15288 stakeholder requirements definition process

Activities of Stakeholder Requirements Definition process of ISO/IEC 15288	Correspondence of the ConOps document format and content as described in IEEE Std 1362
Identify the stakeholders	3.5 and 5.5 identify the user classes of the existing and proposed system
Elicit stakeholder requirements	Not specifically treated
Define constraints on solution	3.2 identifies constraints on existing system; 4.5 identifies constraints applicable to changes and new features; 5.2 identifies constraints that will apply to the new system
Represent anticipated operational and support scenarios	6 provides operational scenarios
Identify interaction between users and the system	Interactions are included in the scenarios of section 6; 3.5.2 describes interactions of users of existing system; 5.5.2 describes envisioned interactions with new system
Specify requirements for critical qualities	3.3 describes "provisions for safety, security, privacy, integrity, and continuity of operations in emergencies" in the current system; 5.3 describes them for the new system
Analyze the elicited requirements	4.8 provides "provides an analysis of the benefits, limitations, advantages, disadvantages, and alternatives and trade-offs considered for the proposed system"
Resolve requirements problems	Not specifically treated
Feedback requirements to ensure that needs and expectations have been expressed	Not specifically treated
Establish with stakeholders that requirements are expressed	Not specifically treated
Record stakeholder requirements in a form suitable for requirements management throughout life cycle	This is the reason for preparing a ConOps document
Maintain traceability of requirements to the stakeholder source, i.e. review periodically	Not specifically treated

TABLE 28. Top-level contents of IEEE Std 1233

1. Overview
2. Reference
3. Definitions
4. System requirements specification
5. SyRS development process overview
6. Well-formed requirements
7. SyRS development

Annex A (informative) System Requirements Specification outline
Annex B (informative) Bibliography
Annex C (informative) Guidelines for compliance with IEEE/EIA 12207.1-1997

TABLE 29. Correspondence of IEEE Std 1233 with the 15288 requirements analysis process

Activities of Requirements Analysis process of ISO/IEC 15288	Correspondence with IEEE Std 1233		
	Subprocesses	Other Guidance	Sections of recommended outline for SRS
Define the functional boundary of the system	7.1 Identify requirements	5.1 Raw requirements	2.1 System context 4 System interfaces
Define each function of the system	7.1 Identify requirements 7.2 Build a well-formed requirement	6.1 Definition of a well-formed requirement 6.2 Properties of a requirement	2.3 Major system capabilities 3 System capabilities, conditions and constraints
Define implementation constraints	7.1 Identify requirements	5.2 Environment	2.5 Major system constraints 3 System capabilities, conditions and constraints
Define measures to assess achievement	7.2 Build a well-formed requirement	6.1 Definition of a well-formed requirement	3 System capabilities, conditions and constraints
Specify system requirements and functions related to critical qualities	7.3 Organize requirements	5.2.3 Standards and technical policies influence 6.3 Categorization of requirements	3 System capabilities, conditions and constraints, notably 3.2, 3.3, 3.5 3.6 Policy and regulation
Analyze the integrity of the requirements	7.3 Organize requirements	4.2 Properties 4.3.1 Organizing requirements	
Demonstrate traceability to stakeholder requirements	7.4 Present requirements	4.1 Definition 5.1.1 Raw requirements 6.2c Traceable	
Maintain the requirements, along with rationale and assumptions, throughout the life cycle	Refers readers to IEEE Std 1220		3.7 System life cycle sustainment

The standard treats system requirements specification from three points of view: an outline of the resulting System Requirements Specification (shown in Table 17 on page 264); the process to create the document; and guidance in performing the process well. To evaluate the utility of IEEE Std 1233 in the requirements analysis process, we can compare its suggestions with the activities provided in ISO/IEC 15288. Table 29 lists the activities of the requirements analysis process of ISO/IEC 15288. For each activity, the table cites three types of corresponding information from IEEE Std 1233: the corresponding subprocess of 1233; other guidance provided by 1233; and the corresponding section(s) of the System Requirements Specification document recommended by 1233.

The comparison suggests that IEEE Std 1233 provides suitable guidance for the implementation of the requirements analysis process of ISO/IEC 15288.

3.4.3. Architectural Design

The purpose of the architectural design process is to synthesize a solution that satisfies system requirements. The process results in the description of a set of implementable system elements that would satisfy the requirements of the system. This process identifies among others, the elements of the system that will be implemented in software. IEEE does not have a standard that elaborates on the process of performing architecture, but it does have a Recommended Practice for the characteristics of an architectural description:

Document

IEEE Std 1471-2000
IEEE Recommended Practice for
Architectural Description of Software Intensive Systems
This document recommends a conceptual framework and content for the architectural description of software-intensive systems.
Allocated to: Related Disciplines Chapter, Systems Engineering

The IEEE standard is oriented primarily to software-intensive systems; however, there is nothing that precludes its use for any kind of system. The fundamental idea of the standard is that architectures should be expressed by describing multiple viewpoints, each corresponding to a stakeholder concern. The document does not select or recommend viewpoints. Instead, each project should select viewpoints appropriate to the concerns of the system being developed.

The 15288 standard seems to anticipate multiple architectural viewpoints:

"Prior to partitioning logical architecture to physical elements, conflicts among and between various logical descriptions are resolved and each logical architecture is shown to be complete and consistent by making mutual traceability checks with the defined system requirements." – 5.5.4.3 (a) Note

---

The phrase "each logical architecture" can be interpreted as an alternative way of referring to a single multi-view architecture.

For systems in which high confidence must be placed, special discipline is needed to ensure that appropriate development resources are allotted to the components with the most effect on failure probability or consequences. ISO/IEC 15026 describes how systems engineers and software engineers collaborate to assign integrity levels to components. The integrity levels may be used as a tool to allocate resource and trigger additional validation and verification activities.

Tool

ISO/IEC 15026:1998
Information Technology—System and Software Integrity Levels
This International Standard introduces the concepts of software integrity levels and software integrity requirements. It defines the concepts associated with integrity levels, defines the processes for determining integrity levels and software integrity requirements, and places requirements on each process.
Allocated to: Related Disciplines Chapter, Systems Engineering

This standard is grouped with the architectural design process because the determination of software integrity levels inherently involves iteration among the disciplines of dependability, systems engineering and software engineering. The risk analysis techniques of dependability engineering are used to analyze threats or hazards, their frequency and their consequences. This analysis is used to determine an integrity level for the system. Based on the system's architectural design, integrity levels are assigned to software elements. With this initial assignment, software engineers can postulate mechanisms for mitigating hazards, reacting to threats, tolerating faults, and confining the consequences of failure. These results are provided to the systems engineers for consideration in modifying the system architecture with the possible result of reallocated integrity levels. The iteration continues until a workable and beneficial architecture is completed.

3.4.4. Implementation The purpose of the implementation process is to produce a specified system element. (A system element is a distinct part of a system that fulfills an identified set of requirements.) For software elements, the 12207 standard provides appropriate processes to implement the element. IEEE standards supporting 12207 were already described in the previous chapter. One additional standard is discussed here, because it applies all of the processes of 12207 and may involve interaction with systems engineers:

Plan

IEEE Std 1228-1994 (R2002)
IEEE Standard for Software Safety Plans
This standard describes the minimum content of a plan for the software aspects of development, procurement, maintenance, and retirement of a safety-critical system.
Allocated to: Related Disciplines Chapter, Systems Engineering

IEEE Std 1228 establishes "minimum acceptable requirements for the content of a Software Safety Plan." It provides more than a format, though. Because the plan is required to address "processes activities intended to improve the safety of safety critical software," the standard levies implicit requirements on the activities applied to the development of the software. Other IEEE standards are cited as appropriate to achieving those requirements. Table 16 on page 263 shows the outline of the safety plan required by IEEE Std 1228 along with the standards cited as supporting execution of the plan.

It should be noted that IEEE 1228 requires that the software safety plan be prepared within the context of a more general system safety program; it recognizes that software safety must be considered in the context of its associated hardware, environment, and operators—a clear link to systems engineering. In particular, the Software Safety Plan required by the standard provides for "safety analyses preparation" when the system is designed:

4.4.1 Software safety analyses preparation (4.1 of the Plan)

This section of the Plan shall define the software-safety related activities for obtaining the following:

a) A Preliminary Hazard Analysis (PHA) and any additional hazard analyses performed on the entire system or any portion of the system that identifies
   1) Hazardous system states
   2) Sequences of actions that can cause the system to enter a hazardous state
   3) Sequences of actions intended to return the system from a hazardous state to a nonhazardous state
   4) Actions intended to mitigate the consequences of accidents
b) A high-level system design identifying those functions that will be performed by software and specifying the software safety-related actions that will be required of the software to prevent the system from entering a hazardous state, or to move the system from a hazardous state to a nonhazardous state, or to mitigate the consequences of an accident
c) The interfaces between the software and the rest of the system

---

This portion of the IEEE 1228 Software Safety Plan would seem to be a result of systems engineering activity.

3.4.5. Integration   The purpose of the integration process is to assemble a system that is consistent with the architectural design.

3.4.6. Verification   The purpose of the verification process is to confirm that the specified design requirements are fulfilled by the system. It should be noted that there is a mismatch of terminology (or emphasis, perhaps) between 12207 and 15288. In 15288, verification refers to examining the integrated system—apparently after the fact—to see that it performs its requirements. The 12207 standard performs this during system qualification testing. In 12207, "verification" refers to activities that go beyond normal evaluation of this sort.

3.4.7. Transition The purpose of the transition process is to establish a capability to provide services specified by stakeholder requirements in the operational environment.

3.4.8. Validation The purpose of the validation process is to provide objective evidence that the services provided by the system when in use comply with stakeholders' requirements.

3.4.9. Operation The purpose of the operation process is to use the system in order to deliver its services.

3.4.10. Maintenance The purpose of the maintenance process is to sustain the capability of the system to provide a service.

3.4.11. Disposal The purpose of the disposal process is to end the existence of a system or system element.

4. A STAGED VIEW OF THE 15288 SYSTEM LIFE CYCLE

Both 12207 and 15288 take the position that defining life cycle stages is the responsibility of the project rather than the standard. Unlike 12207, though, 15288 provides an exemplar set of life cycle stages that has been characterized by purpose and outcomes. Users of 15288 are required by clause 6 to define a life cycle model comprised of stages and to define a purpose and a set of outcomes for each stage. However, it seems likely that many users will elect to use the example model provided in informative annex B of the standard or use it as a starting point in defining their own stages. So the example model is briefly described here.

The example model contains six stages:

- *Concept:* Assess new business opportunities, develop preliminary requirements, and a feasible design solution
- *Development:* Develop a system of interest that meets acquirer requirements and can be produced, tested, evaluated, operated, supported, and retired
- *Production:* Produce or manufacture the product, test the product, and produce related and supporting and enabling systems
- *Utilization:* Operate the product, deliver services within the intended environments, and ensure continued operational effectiveness
- *Support:* Provide logistics, maintenance, and support services that enable continued operation and sustainable service
- *Retirement:* Remove the system-of-interest and related operational and support services, and operate and support the retirement system

One reason for describing the exemplar stages of the 15288 standard is that a reasonable explanation of the role of IEEE Std 1220 requires both the process view and the stage view. That will be done in the next section.

5. RELATIONSHIP OF IEEE STD 1220 WITH SYSTEM LIFE CYCLE PROCESSES

IEEE Std 1220, *Standard for the Application and Management of the Systems Engineering Process*, defines a Systems Engineering Process that can be roughly aligned with some of the life cycle processes of 15288. Performing that alignment, though, tends to disguise rather than expose the relationship between the two standards. In summary, the 15288 standard provides a broad and general view of the entire life cycle of a system beginning with the appreciation of its need and ending with its disposal. IEEE Std 1220 takes a viewpoint focused on the development of the system. Although it treats production, utilization, support, and retirement, its primary concern is the planning for these stages during development. The subsections below will provide an overall look at 1220, compare its Systems Engineering Process to the processes of 15288, and compare its life cycle treatment with the example stages of 15288.[65]

5.1. General Concepts of IEEE Std 1220

The IEEE standard for the systems engineering process is IEEE Std 1220. It was first issued for trial usage in 1994 and then revised to a full-use standard in 1998. As of early 2004, it is being revised again for improved consistency with ISO/IEC 15288:

Process

IEEE Std 1220-1998
IEEE Standard for the
Application and Management of the Systems Engineering Process
This standard describes the systems engineering activities and process required throughout a system's life cycle to develop systems meeting customer needs, requirements, and constraints.
Allocated to: Related Disciplines Chapter, Systems Engineering

IEEE Std 1220 has the objective of defining the requirements for an enterprise's total technical effort related to development of systems and consumer products (including computers and software) as well as the processes that will provide life cycle support for those products. The integrated technical approach prescribed by the standard requires the application and management of the systems engineering process throughout the product's life cycle. The process is applied recursively to the development of the system, its constituent components and its support processes. The approach is intended neither to provide a mission statement for a systems engineering organization nor a job description for a systems engineer. Instead, it prescribes what must be accomplished across the entire organization to produce the product. The standard is intended to be applicable for incremental enhancements to existing products as well as new products and to one at a time products, like a satellite, as well as mass produced

---

[65] Some of the material in these sections is based on an early draft of the planned 2004 revision of IEEE Std 1220, notably an informative annex intended to explain the relationship between 1220 and ISO/IEC 15288.

products. The scope of the standard treats all phases of the product's life from initial concept through development, operation and disposal.

An important concept of IEEE Std 1220 is the "building block." You will recall that 15288 recursively creates projects to create elements of a system, resulting in a hierarchy of systems and elements. IEEE 1220 also uses recursion, but each recursion produces a building block rather than an element. The building block includes a product, corresponding to the 15288 element, but also produces a set of processes. The processes are intended to be used downstream for development, test, manufacturing, distribution, support, operations, training, and disposal of the product. So 1220 does not use any concept of an enabling system. Instead, it packages all processes with the product in the system hierarchy, so that the processes can be executed later. For example, although the SEP is concerned with "manufacturability" and planning for it, the SEP does not encompass manufacturing. By packaging the processes with the product, 1220 is always looking downstream, but never actually goes downstream; its System Engineering Process is a development process.

5.2. The Systems Engineering Process (SEP)

Clause 6 of IEEE Std 1220 describes the system engineering process. The process consists of eight subprocesses:

- *Requirements Analysis:* Establish what the system should do by refining the requirements of the next system up in the hierarchy
- *Requirements Validation:* Validate the requirements against customer expectations, project constraints, and life cycle operation and support needs
- *Functional Analysis:* Decompose the system functions to lower level ones to be accomplished by parts of the system
- *Functional Verification:* Assess the functional architecture to verify that all requirements are met
- *Synthesis:* Develop a design architecture that provides an arrangement of system elements, their interfaces, and their relationships
- *Design Verification:* Verify that the requirements of the lowest level of the design architecture are traceable to the functional architecture and satisfy the requirements baseline
- *Systems Analysis:* Perform quantitative analysis in support of the other subprocesses
- *Control:* Manage and document the subprocesses of the SEP

The SEP of 1220 is so different from the processes of 15288 that it is difficult to make an insightful alignment between the processes of the two standards. Neglecting many complicating details, it would appear that the scope of the SEP essentially corresponds to the scope of two technical processes of 15288: requirements analysis and architectural design. Although consideration is paid to upstream and downstream activities, the execution of the SEP appears to essentially correspond to those two processes. The stakeholder requirements definition process of 15288 is omitted from the suggested alignment because it centers on identifying and eliciting requirements from stakeholders; 1220 seems to accept from a customer a set of requirements that are ready for analysis.

The SEP also touches upon aspects of many other processes of 15288, including verification, validation, and the project processes.

5.3. Applying the SEP to the Life Cycle

Clause 5 of IEEE Std 1220 applies the SEP across the life cycle of a system. This does not contradict the observation made in the preceding section that SEP maps to only two technical processes of 15288; in this section, we are considering the stages of the life cycle rather than its processes. The life cycle stages identified in 1220 are:

- *System Definition:* Establish the definition of the system with a focus on system products required to satisfy operational requirements
- *Subsystem Definition—Preliminary Design:* Initiate subsystem design and create subsystem-level specifications and design-to baselines to guide component development
- *Subsystem Definition—Detailed Design:* Complete subsystem design down to the lowest component level, and create a component specification and build-to component baseline for each component
- *Subsystem Definition—Fabrication, Assembly, Integration, and Test:* Resolve product deficiencies when specifications for the system, product, subsystem, assembly, or component are not met
- *Operation—Production:* Correct deficiencies discovered during production, assembly, integration, and acceptance testing of products and/or life cycle process products
- *Operation—Customer Support:* Evolve the product to implement an incremental change, resolve product or service deficiencies, or to implement planned evolutionary growth.

It is clear that the SEP is focused on development. Even in the later stages of the life cycle, the appropriate use of the SEP is to develop remedies for problems or improvements to the system. Nevertheless, one can conclude that IEEE Std 1220 clearly addresses four of the six example life cycle stages provided in ISO/IEC 15288—development, production, utilization, and support—lightly touches on the concept stage and largely omits the retirement stage.

5.4. Compatibility with ISO/IEC 15288

It is clear that IEEE Std 1220 and ISO/IEC 15288 have fundamental differences—terminology, life cycle concepts, coverage of life cycle stages, and description of processes. IEEE Std 1220 has a dedicated user community who desire to continue use of the standard but who also desire to apply the life cycle concepts of ISO/IEC 15288. The Software Engineering Standards Committee of the IEEE Computer Society is currently (circa 2004) revising the 1998 version of the standard to move it closer to compatibility with ISO/IEC 15288. It is anticipated that the revision will be "fast-tracked" to SC 7 for joint adoption by both SC 7 and S2ESC. Further maintenance, for improved compatibility, will be performed jointly by the two organizations.

6. SUMMARY

The proper engineering of a complex software product almost inevitably involves systems engineering. Of course, when the software is merely an element of a larger system, the relationship is inevitable. Both of the major organizations creating software engineering standards realize this relationship and have created standards treating the relationship.

The key standard in the collection of ISO/IEC JTC 1/SC 7 is ISO/IEC 15288, System Life Cycle Processes. This standard describes the life cycle of a system from two viewpoints—the processes that are executed in the life cycle and the stages through which the system passes from concept to retirement. As a result of applying 15288, the system-of-interest would be decomposed into a set of system elements. Although the fit between the two standards is a little uneasy, software elements of the system would be developed using ISO/IEC 12207, Software Life Cycle Processes or the IEEE/EIA version. Various IEEE standards would support the processes of 12207.

Aside from the use of 12207 in developing the software elements, some IEEE standards directly support the systems processes provided by 15288. They include:

- IEEE Std 1540 for risk management at the software level, and perhaps the system level.
- IEEE Std 1362 for developing a Concept of Operations document during the stakeholder requirements definition process.
- IEEE Std 1233 for developing a System Requirements Specification during the requirements analysis process.
- IEEE Std 1471 for characteristics of Architectural Descriptions created during the architectural design process.
- IEEE Std 1228 for creating a Software Safety Plan that provides a vital link between system and software design.

In addition, ISO/IEC 15026 provides a link between systems and software engineers in developing an architecture possessing desired critical properties.

The key standard in the collection of the IEEE S2ESC is IEEE Std 1220. It describes a Systems Engineering Process which anticipates life cycle considerations during the development of a system. The problematic fit of the 1998 version with the 15288 standard is the subject of a revision effort.

Appendix A

Standards Described in This Book

The standards are listed in order of their number regardless of their source.

Terminology	**IEEE Std 610.12-1990 (R2002)** **IEEE Standard Glossary of Software Engineering Terminology** This standard is a glossary of software engineering terminology. *Allocated to: Other Software Engineering Standards Chapter*
Project Plan **Plan**	**IEEE Std 730-2002** **IEEE Standard for Software Quality Assurance Plans** This standard specifies the format and content of Software Quality Assurance plans. *Allocated to: Software Quality Knowledge Area*
Project Plan **Plan**	**IEEE Std 828-1998** **IEEE Standard for Software Configuration Management Plans** This standard specifies the content of a Software Configuration Management plan along with requirements for specific activities. *Allocated to: Software Configuration Management Knowledge Area*

Document	**IEEE Std 829-1998** **IEEE Standard for Software Test Documentation** This standard describes the form and content of a basic set of documentation for planning, executing, and reporting software testing. *Allocated to: Software Testing Knowledge Area*
Document	**IEEE Std 830-1998** **IEEE Recommended Practice for Software Requirements Specifications** This document recommends the content and characteristics of a Software Requirements Specification. Sample outlines are provided. *Allocated to: Software Requirements Knowledge Area*
Measure	**IEEE Std 982.1-1988** **IEEE Standard Dictionary of Measures to Produce Reliable Software** This standard provides a set of measures for evaluating the reliability of a software product and for obtaining early forecasts of the reliability of a product under development. *Allocated to: Software Quality Knowledge Area*
Process	**IEEE Std 1008-1987 (R2003)** **IEEE Standard for Software Unit Testing** This standard describes a sound approach to software unit testing, and the concepts and assumptions on which it is based. *Allocated to: Software Testing Knowledge Area*
Process	**IEEE Std 1012-2004** **IEEE Standard for Software Verification and Validation** This standard describes software verification and validation processes that are used to determine if software products of an activity meets the requirements of the activity and to determine if software satisfies the user's needs for the intended usage. The scope includes analysis, evaluation, review, inspection, assessment and testing of both products and processes. *Allocated to: Software Quality Knowledge Area*
Document	**IEEE Std 1016-1998** **IEEE Recommended Practice for Software Design Descriptions** This document recommends content and organization of a Software Design Description. *Allocated to: Software Design Knowledge Area*
Process	**IEEE Std 1028-1997 (R2002)** **IEEE Standard for Software Reviews** This standard defines five types of software reviews and procedures for their execution. Review types include management reviews, technical reviews, inspections, walk-throughs, and audits. *Allocated to: Software Quality Knowledge Area*

Tool	**IEEE Std 1044-1993 (R2002)** **IEEE Standard Classification for Software Anomalies** This standard provides a uniform approach to the classification of anomalies found in software and its documentation. It includes helpful lists of anomaly classifications, and related data. *Allocated to: Software Quality Knowledge Area*
Measure	**IEEE Std 1045-1992 (R2002)** **IEEE Standard for Software Productivity Metrics** This standard provides a consistent terminology for software productivity measures and defines a consistent way to measure the elements that go into computing software productivity. *Allocated to: Software Engineering Management Knowledge Area*
Plan	**IEEE Std 1058-1998** **IEEE Standard for Software Project Management Plans** This standard describes the format and contents of a software project management plan. *Allocated to: Software Engineering Management Knowledge Area*
Measure	**IEEE Std 1061-1998 (R2004)** **IEEE Standard for a Software Quality Metrics Methodology** This standard describes a methodology—spanning the entire life cycle—for establishing quality requirements and identifying, implementing, and validating the corresponding measures. *Allocated to: Software Quality Knowledge Area*
Process	**IEEE Std 1062, 1998 Edition (R2002)** **IEEE Recommended Practice for Software Acquisition** This document recommends a set of useful practices that can be selected and applied during software acquisition. It is primarily suited to acquisitions that include development or modification rather than off-the-shelf purchase. *Allocated to: Software Engineering Management Knowledge Area*
Document	**IEEE Std 1063-2001** **IEEE Standard for Software User Documentation** This standard provides minimum requirements for the structure, content, and format of user documentation–both printed and electronic. *Allocated to: Software Construction Knowledge Area*
Process	**IEEE Std 1074-1997** **IEEE Standard for Developing Software Life Cycle Processes** This standard describes an approach for the definition of software life cycle processes. *Allocated to: Software Engineering Process Knowledge Area*

Tool

IEEE Std 1175.1-2002
IEEE Guide for
CASE Tool Interconnections—Classification and Description
This document is the first of a planned series of standards on the integration of CASE tools into a productive software engineering environment. This part describes fundamental concepts and introduces the remaining (planned) parts.
Allocated to: Software Engineering Tools and Methods Knowledge Area

Process

IEEE Std 1219-1998
IEEE Standard for Software Maintenance
This standard describes a process for software maintenance and its management.
Allocated to: Software Maintenance Knowledge Area

Process

IEEE Std 1220-1998
IEEE Standard for the
Application and Management of the Systems Engineering Process
This standard describes the systems engineering activities and process required throughout a system's life cycle to develop systems meeting customer needs, requirements, and constraints.
Allocated to: Related Disciplines Chapter, Systems Engineering

Plan

IEEE Std 1228-1994 (R2002)
IEEE Standard for Software Safety Plans
This standard describes the minimum content of a plan for the software aspects of development, procurement, maintenance, and retirement of a safety-critical system.
Allocated to: Related Disciplines Chapter, Systems Engineering

Document

IEEE Std 1233, 1998 Edition (R2002)
IEEE Guide for Developing System Requirements Specifications
This document provides guidance on the development of a System Requirements Specification, covering the identification, organization, presentation, and modification of requirements. It also provides guidance on the characteristics and qualities of requirements.
Allocated to: Related Disciplines Chapter, Systems Engineering

Tool

IEEE Std 1320.1-1998 (R2004)
IEEE Standard for
Functional Modeling Language—Syntax and Semantics for IDEF0
This standard defines the IDEF0 modeling language used to represent decisions, actions, and activities of an organization or system. IDEF0 may be used to define requirements in terms of functions to be performed by a desired system.
Allocated to: Software Engineering Tools and Methods Knowledge Area

Tool

IEEE Std 1320.2-1998 (R2004)
IEEE Standard for Conceptual Modeling Language—
Syntax and Semantics for IDEF1X 97 (IDEF object)
This standard defines two conceptual modeling languages, collectively called IDEF1X97 (IDEFObject). The language support the implementation of relational databases, object databases, and object models.
Allocated to: Software Engineering Tools and Methods Knowledge Area

Document	**IEEE Std 1362-1998** **IEEE Guide for Information Technology—System Definition—** **Concept of Operations (ConOps) Document** This document provides guidance on the format and content of a Concept of Operations (ConOps) document, describing characteristics of a proposed system from the users' viewpoint. *Allocated to: Related Disciplines Chapter, Systems Engineering*
Tool	**IEEE Std 1420.1-1995 (R2002)** **IEEE Standard for Information Technology—** **Software Reuse—Data Model for Reuse Library Interoperability:** **Basic Interoperability Data Model (BIDM)** This standard describes information that software reuse libraries should be able to exchange in order to interchange assets. *Allocated to: Software Engineering Tools and Methods Knowledge Area*
Tool	**IEEE Std 1420.1a-1996 (R2002)** **Supplement to IEEE Standard for Information Technology—** **Software Reuse—Data Model for Reuse Library Interoperability:** **Asset Certification Framework** This supplement to 1420.1 extends the standard model to asset certification information. *Allocated to: Software Engineering Tools and Methods Knowledge Area*
Tool	**IEEE Std 1420.1b-1999 (R2002)** **IEEE Trial-Use Supplement to IEEE Standard for Information Technology—Software Reuse—Data Model for Reuse Library Interoperability: Intellectual property Rights Framework** This supplement to 1420.1 extends the standard model to intellectual property information. *Allocated to: Software Engineering Tools and Methods Knowledge Area*
Tool	**IEEE Std 1462-1998 (R2004)** **IEEE Standard: Adoption of International Standard** **ISO/IEC 14102: 1995, Information Technology—** **Guideline for the Evaluation and Selection of CASE tools** This standard provides guidelines for the evaluation and selection of CASE tools. *Allocated to: Software Engineering Tools and Methods Knowledge Area*
Tool	**IEEE Std 1465-1998 (R2004)** **IEEE Standard: Adoption of International Standard** **ISO/IEC 12119:1994(E), Information Technology—** **Software Packages—Quality Requirements and Testing** This standard describes quality requirements specifically suitable for software packages and guidance on testing the package against those requirements. *Allocated to: Software Quality Knowledge Area*
Document	**IEEE Std 1471-2000** **IEEE Recommended Practice for** **Architectural Description of Software Intensive Systems** This document recommends a conceptual framework and content for the architectural description of software-intensive systems. *Allocated to: Related Disciplines Chapter, Systems Engineering*

Terminology	**IEEE Std 1490-2003** **IEEE Guide: Adoption of PMI Standard, A Guide to the** **Project Management Body of Knowledge (PMBOK® Guide)** This document is the IEEE adoption of the Project Management Body of Knowledge defined by the Project Management Institute. It identifies and describes generally accepted knowledge regarding project management. *Allocated to: Related Disciplines Chapter, Quality Management*
Process	**IEEE Std 1517-1999 (R2004)** **IEEE Standard for Information Technology—** **Software Life Cycle Processes—Reuse Processes** This standard provides life cycle processes for systematic software reuse suitable for use with IEEE/EIA 12207. *Allocated to: Software Engineering Process Knowledge Area*
Process	**IEEE Std 1540-2001** **IEEE Standard for Software Life Cycle Processes—** **Risk Management** This standard provides a life cycle process for software risk management suitable for use with IEEE/EIA 12207. *Allocated to: Software Engineering Process Knowledge Area*
World Wide Web	**IEEE Std 2001-2002** **IEEE Recommended Practice for the Internet—Web Site** **Engineering, Web Site Management, and Web Site Life Cycle** This document recommends practices for engineering World Wide Web pages for use in Intranet and Extranet environments. *Allocated to: Other Software Engineering Standards Chapter*
Terminology	**ISO 9000:2000** **Quality Management Systems—Fundamentals and Vocabulary** This standard describes fundamental concepts and vocabulary for the other quality management standards. *Allocated to: Related Disciplines Chapter, Quality Management*
Process	**ISO 9001:2000** **Quality Management Systems—Requirements** This standard specifies the requirements for an organizational quality management system aiming to provide products meeting requirements and enhance customer satisfaction. *Allocated to: Related Disciplines Chapter, Quality Management*
Process	**ISO 9004:2000** **Quality Management Systems—** **Guidelines for Performance Improvements** This is a guide to ISO 9004 focusing on the effectiveness and efficiency of the quality management system. *Allocated to: Related Disciplines Chapter, Quality Management*

Terminology	**ISO/IEC 9126-1:2001** **Software Engineering—Product Quality—Part 1: Quality Model** This standard provides a model for software product quality covering internal quality, external quality, and quality in use. The model is in the form of a taxonomy of defined characteristics which software may exhibit. *Allocated to: Software Requirements Knowledge Area*
Process	**IEEE/EIA 12207.0-1996** **Industry Implementation of International Standard ISO/IEC 12207:1995, Standard for Information Technology–Software Life Cycle Processes** This standard provides a framework of processes used across the entire life cycle of software. *Allocated to: Software Engineering Process Knowledge Area*
Document	**IEEE/EIA 12207.1-1996** **Industry Implementation of International Standard ISO/IEC 12207:1995, Standard for Information Technology—Software Life Cycle Processes—Life Cycle Data** This document provides guidance on recording data resulting from the life cycle processes of IEEE/EIA 12207.0. *Allocated to: Software Engineering Process Knowledge Area*
Process	**IEEE/EIA 12207.2-1997** **Industry Implementation of International Standard ISO/IEC 12207:1995, Standard for Information Technology—Software Life Cycle Processes—Implementation Considerations** This document provides guidance for the implementation of the life cycle processes of IEEE/EIA 12207.0. *Allocated to: Software Engineering Process Knowledge Area*
Measure	**IEEE Std 14143.1-2000** **IEEE Adoption of ISO/IEC 14143-1:1998, Information Technology—Software Measurement—Functional Size Measurement—Part 1: Definition of Concepts** This standard describes the fundamental concepts of a class of measures collectively known as functional size. *Allocated to: Software Requirements Knowledge Area*
Process	**ISO/IEC 14764:1999** **Information Technology—Software Maintenance** This standard provides guidance on implementing the maintenance process provided in ISO/IEC 12207. *Allocated to: Software Maintenance Knowledge Area*

 **Tool**	**ISO/IEC 15026:1998** **Information Technology—System and Software Integrity Levels** This International Standard introduces the concepts of software integrity levels and software integrity requirements. It defines the concepts associated with integrity levels, defines the processes for determining integrity levels and software integrity requirements, and places requirements on each process. *Allocated to: Related Disciplines Chapter, Systems Engineering*
Process	**ISO/IEC 15288:2002** **Systems Engineering—System Life Cycle Processes** This standard provides a framework of processes used across the entire life cycle of human-made systems. *Allocated to: Related Disciplines Chapter, Systems Engineering*
Process	**ISO/IEC (Draft) 15504 (five parts)** **Information Technology—Process Assessment** This draft standard would provide requirements on methods for performing process assessment as a basis for process improvement or capability determination. *Allocated to: Software Engineering Process Knowledge Area*
Process	**ISO/IEC TR 15504 (nine parts)** **Information Technology—Software Process Assessment** This technical report would provide requirements on methods for performing process assessment as a basis for process improvement or capability determination. *Allocated to: Software Engineering Process Knowledge Area*
Process	**ISO/IEC 15939:2002** **Software Engineering—Software Measurement Process** This standard provides a life cycle process for software measurement suitable for use with IEEE/EIA 12207. *Allocated to: Software Engineering Process Knowledge Area*
Process	**ISO/IEC 90003:2004** **Software Engineering—Guidelines for the Application of ISO 9001:2000 to Computer Software** This standard provides guidance for organizations in the application of ISO 9001:2000 to the acquisition, supply, development, operation, and maintenance of computer software. *Allocated to: Related Disciplines Chapter, Quality Management*

Abbreviations and Acronyms

ABET	Accreditation Board for Engineering and Technology
ACM	Association for Computing Machinery
AI	Artificial Intelligence
AIAA	American Institute of Aeronautics and Astronautics
Amd	Amendment
ASIC	Application-Specific Integrated Circuit
ASQC	American Society for Quality Control
ASTM	American Society for Testing and Materials
ANSI	American National Standards Institute
BOK	Body of Knowledge
BSR	ANSI Board of Standards Review
CASE	Computer-aided software engineering, sometimes extended to include systems engineering
CBA-IP	CMM-Based Appraisal for Internal Process Improvement
CD	(ISO and IEC) Committee Draft
CDV	(IEC) Committee Draft for Vote
CEN	European Committee for Standardization
CENELEC	European Committee for Electrotechnical Standardization
CI	Configuration item
CM	Configuration management
CMM®	Capability Maturity Model, a registered service mark of the SEI
CMMI®	Capability Maturity Model Integration, a registered service mark of the SEI
ConOps	Concept of Operations, also see OCD
Cor or **Corr**	Corrigendum

The Road Map to Software Engineering: A Standards-Based Guide, by James W. Moore
Copyright © 2006 by IEEE Computer Society

CoS	(AIAA) committees on standards
COTS	Commercial, off-the-shelf, as opposed to a product that is specially developed or modified for its intended usage
CS	(IEEE) Computer Society
CSDP	A certification program, Certified Software Development Professional, of the IEEE Computer Society
DID	Data Item Description
DIS	Draft International Standard
DoD	(US) Department of Defense
DoD-Std	A prefix for standards developed by the US Department of Defense
DTR	Draft Technical Report
EIA	Electronic Industries Alliance
ESA	European Space Agency
FAA	(US) Federal Aviation Agency
FCA	Functional configuration audit
FCD	(ISO) Final Committee Draft
FDIS	(ISO and IEC) Final Draft International Standard
FIPS	Federal Information Processing Standards
FSM	Functional size measurement
G	A prefix used by AIAA to denote a Guide
G-xx	Designation of EIA's standards committees
GEIA	(EIA) Government Electronics and Information Technology Association
HCI	Human-Computer Interface
ICAM	Integrated Computer-Aided Manufacturing
IDEAL	Initiating, Diagnosing, Establishing, Acting, and Learning, a process improvement model of the SEI
IDEF	Originally, ICAM Definition; now, Integrated Definition
IDEF0	IDEF Function Modeling
IDEF1X	IDEF Information Modeling Extended
IDEFObject	Alternative term for IDEF1X97, the most recent extension of IDEF1X
IEC	International Electrotechnical Commission
IEEE	Institute of Electrical and Electronics Engineers
IFPUG	International Function Point Users Group
INCITS	International Committee for Information Technology Standards, the committee formerly known as NCITS, and before that as X3
INCOSE	International Council on Systems Engineering
IPPD	Integrated Product and Process Development
IS	(EIA) Interim Standard
IS	(ISO or IEC) International Standard
ISO	International Organization for Standardization, sometimes (mistakenly) used to refer specifically to ISO 9000, 9001, and 9004
ISSB	Information Systems Standards Board of ANSI
IT	Information technology, the scope of ISO/IEC JTC 1

ITA	(ISO or IEC) Industry Technical Agreement
ITIC	Industry Technology Industry Council
ITU	International Telecommunications Union
J	An ANSI designation for a US standard jointly developed by two or more SDOs
JTC 1	ISO/IEC Joint Technical Committee 1 (information technology)
KA	(PMBOK® or SWEBOK) Knowledge area
Mil-Std	Prefix designating standards created by the US Department of Defense
NASA	(US) National Aeronautics and Space Administration
NIST	(US) National Institute of Standards and Technology
NP	New Work Item Proposal
NWI	New Work Item
OCD	Operational Concept Document, also see ConOps
PAR	IEEE's Project Authorization Request
PAS	(ISO or IEC) Publicly Available Specification
PCA	Physical Configuration Audit
PDCA	Plan-Do-Check-Act, a concept from quality management
pDTR	Preliminary Draft Technical Report
PINS	ANSI Project Initiation Notification System
PMBOK®	Project Management Body of Knowledge, a registered trademark of the Project Management Institute
P-member	Full, participating member of an ISO organ
PMI	Project Management Institute
PMP	Project Management Professional, a certification program of PMI
Pub	Publication
PWI	Preliminary Work Item
Pxxxx	An IEEE project. The "P" distinguishes the incomplete project from the eventual standard that is produced
QA	Quality Assurance
QIP	Quality Improvement Paradigm
R	A prefix used by AIAA to denote a Recommended Practice
R	A suffix used by some SDOs to note the date of reaffirmation of a standard
R	A suffix used by IEEE to indicate a project to revise a standard, for example, P1012 (R)
RFP	Request for Proposal
RIG	Reuse Library Interoperability Group
RP	(IEEE) Recommended Practice
RTCA	RTCA, Inc., formerly Radio Technical Commission for Aeronautics
S	A prefix used by AIAA to denote a Standard
S2ESC	The Software and Systems Engineering Standards Committee of the IEEE Computer Society
SA	(IEEE) Standards Association
SBS	System Breakdown Structure
SC	Subcommittee of an ISO or IEC Technical Committee

SC 7	ISO/IEC JTC 1 Subcommittee 7 (software and systems engineering)
SC 65A	IEC Subcommittee 65A (systems aspects of industrial process measurement and control)
SCE	Software Capability Evaluation
SCM	Software Configuration Management
SDD	Software Design Description
SDO	Standards Developing Organization
SE	Software Engineering or Systems Engineering, depending on context
SEC	(AIAA) Standards Executive Council
SEI	Software Engineering Institute, Carnegie Mellon University
SEMS	Systems Engineering Master Schedule
SEP	Systems Engineering Process
SEPG	Software Engineering Process Group
SESC	Software Engineering Standards Committee, the predecessor of S2ESC
SESS	Software Engineering Standards Subcommittee, the predecessor of SESC
SLCP	Software Life Cycle Process
SP	An AIAA Special Projects Report
SPICE	Software Process Improvement and Capability dEtermination
SPMP	Software Project Management Plan
SQA	Software Quality Assurance
SQAP	Software Quality Assurance Plan
SRS	Software Requirements Specification
SSPP	System Safety Program Plan
STC	(AIAA) Standards Technical Council
Std	IEEE designation for a standard
SW	Software
SW-CMM®	Software Capability Maturity Model, a registered service mark of the SEI
SWE	Software Engineering
SWEBOK	Software Engineering Body of Knowledge
SWG	(AIAA) Standards Working Group
SWLC	Software life cycle
SysRS	System Requirements Specification
TA	Technical Advisor
TAG	Technical Advisory Group
TC	Technical Committee, of ISO or IEC
TC 56	IEC Technical Committee 56 (dependability)
TC 62	IEC Technical Committee 62 (electrical equipment in medical practice)
TC 159	ISO Technical Committee 159 (ergonomics)
TC 176	ISO Technical Committee 176 (quality management and quality assurance)
TC 184	ISO Technical Committee 184 (industrial automation systems and integration

TC 210	ISO Technical Committee 210 (quality management and corresponding general aspects for medical devices)
TCSE	IEEE Technical Council on Software Engineering
TR	(ISO or IEC) Technical Report
TS	(ISO or IEC) Technical Specification
TS&S	(EIA) Technology Strategy and Standards department
TTA	(ISO or IEC) Technology Trend Assessment
UML™	Unified Modeling Language, a trademark of the Object Management Group
V & V	Verification and Validation
VLSI	Very Large Scale Integration
WD	Working Draft
WG	Working Group (in many SDOs); specifically the next level down from an ISO or IEC subcommittee

Bibliography

[Abran96] Alain Abran, "Teaching Software Engineering Using ISO Standards," StandardView, Vol. 4, No. 3, Sept. 1996, pp. 139–145.

[AIAA04] American Institute of Aeronautics and Astronautics, "Publication: Standards: Summary," 2004, http://www.aiaa.org/publications/index.hfm?pub=6 (viewed 27 July 2004).

[AIAA99] American Institute of Aeronautics and Astronautics, *Standards Program Procedures*, Revised Edition, 1999, http://www.aiaa.org/images/Publications/StdProc99F.pdf.

[Albrecht81] Alan Albrecht, "Measuring Application Development Productivity," *Programmer Productivity Issues for the Eighties*, C. Jones, ed., IEEE Computer Soc. Press, Los Alamitos, CA, 1981, pp. 34–43.

[ANSI04] American National Standards Institute, "About ANSI," http://www.ansi.org/about_ansi/overview/overview.aspx?menuid = 1, (viewed 27 July 2004).

[April95] Alain April and François Coallier, "Trillium: A model for the Assessment of Telecom Software System Development and Maintenance Capability," *Proc. IEEE Int'l Software Eng. Standards Symp.*, IEEE Computer Soc. Press, Los Alamitos, CA, 1995, pp. 175–183.

[Baron95] S. N. Baron, "The Standards Development Process and the NII: A View from the Trenches," in Brian Kahin and Janet Abbate, eds., *Standards Policy for Information Infrastructure*, MIT Press, Cambridge, MA, 1995.

[Basili84] V. Basili and D. M. Weiss, "A Methodology for Collecting Valid Software Engineering Data," *IEEE Transactions on Software Engineering*, pp. 728–738, November 1984.

[Basili92] Victor R. Basili et al., "A Reference Architecture for the Component Factory," *ACM Trans. Software Eng. and Methodology*, Vol. 1, No. 1, Jan. 1992, pp. 53–80.

[Batik92] Albert Batik, *The Engineering Standard: A Most Useful Tool*, BookMaster/El Rancho, Ashland, OH, 1992.

[BLS04] Bureau of Labor Statistics, *Occupational Career Handbook*, 2004–05 Edition, US Dept. of Labor, http://stats.bls.gov/oco/home.htm.

[Bollinger01] Terry Bollinger, "Software Construction," in [SWEBOK01].

[Bootstrap93] Members of the Bootstrap Project Team, "Bootstrap: Europe's Assessment Method," *IEEE Software*, Vol. 10, No. 3, May 1993, pp. 93–95.

[Bourque02] Pierre Bourque, Robert Dupuis, Alain Abran, James W. Moore, Leonard Tripp, and Sybille Wolff, "Fundamental principles of software engineering – a journey," *The Journal of Systems and Software* 62, 2002, pp. 59–70.

[Briand99] L. Briand, K. El Emam, and W. Melo, "An Inductive Method for Software Process Improvement: Concrete Steps and Guidelines," in *Elements of Software Process Assessment and Improvement*, K. El-Emam and N. Madhavji (eds.), IEEE CS Press, 1999.

[Brobeck96] Stephen Brobeck, "Consumer Participation in Standards Development," *ANSI Reporter*, Dec. 1996, pp. 5–6.

[Budgen94] David Budgen, *Software Design*, Addison-Wesley, 1994.

[Card91] David Card, "Understanding Process Improvement," *IEEE Software*, pp.102–103, July, 1991.

[Cargill97] Carl F. Cargill, *Open Systems Standardization: A Business Approach*, Prentice Hall PTR, Upper Saddle River, NJ, 1997.

[CMMI00] CMMI Development Team, *Capability Maturity Model-Integrated Systems/Software Engineering* (Version 1), Software Engineering Institute, Carnegie Mellon University, 2000.

[DEF91] DEF 5169/T1, *ImproveIT*, UK Ministry of Defense, London, 1991.

[DTI92] (UK) Department of Trade and Industry, *Guide to Software Quality Management System Construction and Certification*, 1992.

[EIA04] Electronic Industries Alliance, "How EIA Standards Activities are Organized," 2004, http://www.eia.org/new_policy/organization.phtml (viewed 27 July 2004).

[Fayol49] H. Fayol, *General and Industrial Administration*, Pitman & Sons, London, 1949.

[Fenton96] Norman Fenton, "Counterpoint: Do Standards Improve Quality?" *IEEE Software*, Vol. 13, No. 1, Jan. 1996, pp. 23–24.

[Gamma95] Erich Gamma et al, *Design Patterns: Elements of Reusable Software*, Addison-Wesley, Reading, MA, 1994.

[Gibson95] Richard B. Gibson, "The Global Standards Process: A Balance of the Old and the New," in Brian Kahin and Janet Abbate, eds., *Standards Policy for Information Infrastructure*, MIT Press, Cambridge, MA, 1995.

[Haase94] Volkmar Haase et al., "Bootstrap: Fine-Tuning Process Assessment," *IEEE Software*, Vol. 11, No. 4, July 1994, pp. 25–33.

[Heineman94] G. T. Heineman et al., "Emerging Technologies that Support a Software Process Life Cycle," *IBM Systems J.*, Vol. 33, No. 3, 1994, pp. 501–529.

[Humphrey95] Watts Humphrey, *A Discipline for Software Engineering*, Addison Wesley, 1995.

[IEC04] International Electrotechnical Commission, "About the IEC," 2004, http://www.iec.ch/about/ (viewed 26 July 2004).

[IEEE04] Institute of Electrical and Electronics Engineers, "About the IEEE," 2004, http://www.ieee.org/about/ (viewed 27 July 2004).

[IEEE04a] Institute of Electrical and Electronics Engineers, IEEE-SA Standards Board Operations Manual, January 2004, http://standards.ieee.org/guides/opman/index.html.

[IEEESA03] *IEEE Software Engineering Standards Collection*, 22 August 2003, (CD-ROM), IEEE Product SE113, Institute of Electrical and Electronics Engineers, 2003, New York.

[IEEESA97] *IEEE Software Engineering Standards Collection*, 1997 Edition, Institute of Electrical and Electronics Engineers, 1997, New York.

[IEEESA99] *IEEE Standards—Software Engineering*, 1999 Edition (Four volumes), Institute of Electrical and Electronics Engineers, 1999, New York.

[INCITS04] International Committee for Information Technology Standards, "Welcome . . . ," http://www.incits.org, (viewed 27 July 2004).

[INCOSE00] International Council on Systems Engineering, *Systems Engineering Handbook – A "How to" Guide for All Engineering*, Version 2.0, July 2000.

[INCOSE04] International Council on Systems Engineering, "Overview," 11 June 2004, http://www.incose.org/about/index.aspx.

[ISO03] International Organization for Standardization, "ISO 9000 and ISO 14000 – in brief," 2003, http://www.iso.org/iso/en/iso9000–14000/index.html (viewed 26 July 2004).

[ISO04] International Organization for Standardization, "About ISO," http://www.iso.org/iso/en/aboutiso/introduction/index.html (viewed 26 July 2004).

[ISO93] *International Vocabulary of Basic and General Terms in Metrology*, International Organization for Standardization, Geneva, 1993.

[Jabir98] Jabir (a collective name—James W. Moore was the point of contact), "A Search for Fundamental Principles of Software Engineering," *Computer Standards and Interfaces*, North-Holland, Elsevier, Amsterdam, 19(2), pp. 155–160.

[JTC1-04] ISO/IEC Joint Technical Committee 1, *ISO/IEC Directives, Procedures for the technical work of ISO/IEC JTC 1 on Information Technology*, (5th Edition), 2004 http://isotc.iso.ch/livelink/livelink/fetch/2000/2489/Ittf_Home/Directives/JTC 1_Directives.pdf.zip.

[Kitson96] David H. Kitson, "Relating the Spice Framework and the SEI Approach to Software Process Assessment," *Proc. 5th European Conf. Software Quality*, Dublin, Ireland, 1996.

[Knafl95] George J. Knafl, "Overview of SRE Standards Planning Activities," *Proc. Int'l Software Eng. Standards Symp.*, IEEE Computer Soc. Press, Los Alamitos, CA, 1995, p. 244–245.

[Koontz72] H. Koontz and C. O'Donnell, *Principles of Management: An Analysis of Managerial Functions*, 5th ed., McGraw-Hill, New York, 1972.

[Ling96] David Ling and Dale Misczynski, "ISO 9001 for the Supplier and the Purchaser," *ANSI Reporter*, Sept. 1996, pp. 8–9.

[Magee97] Stan Magee and Leonard L. Tripp, *Guide to Software Engineering Standards and Specifications*, Artech House, Boston, MA, 1997.

[McClure01] Carma McClure, *Software Reuse: A Standards-Based Guide*, IEEE Computer Society Press, Los Alamitos, CA, 2001.

[McGarry01] John McGarry et al, *Practical Software Measurement: Objective Information for Decision Makers*, Addison-Wesley, Boston, MA, 2001.

[Moore91] James W. Moore, "A National Infrastructure for Defense Reuse," *Proc. 4th Ann. Workshop Software Reuse*, Reston, VA, Nov. 18–22, 1991. Also available at: ftp://gandalf.umcs.maine.edu/pub/WISR/wisr4/proceedings/ps/moore.ps.

[Moore94] James W. Moore, "A Structure for a Defense Software Reuse Marketplace," *SIGAda AdaLetters*, Vol. 14, No. 3, May/June 1994.

[Moore95] James W. Moore and Roy Rada, "Organizational Badge Collecting," *Comm. ACM*, Aug. 1996, pp. 17–21.

[Moore97] James W. Moore, *Software Engineering Standards: A User's Road Map*, 1997, IEEE Computer Society Press, Los Alamitos, CA.

[Moore97a] James W. Moore, Perry R. DeWeese, and Dennis Rilling, "US Software Life Cycle Process Standards," *Crosstalk,* Vol. 10, No. 7, July 1997, pp. 6–8.

[Naur68] Peter Naur and Brian Randall, editors, "Software Engineering: Report on a Conference sponsored by the NATO Science Committee, Garmisch, Germany, 7–11 October 1968," NATO, Scientific Affairs Division, Brussels, 1969. (http://homepages. cs.ncl.ac.uk/brian.randell/NATO/).

[Parnas95] David Lorge Parnas, "Software Engineering: An Unconsummated Marriage," invited presentation at the *2nd IEEE Int'l Software Eng. Standards Symp.*, Montréal, Canada, 1995.

[Paulk93] Mark C. Paulk et al., *Capability Maturity Model for Software*, Version 1.1, Tech. Report CMU/SEI-93-TR-24, Software Engineering Institute, Carnegie-Mellon University, Pittsburgh, PA, 1993.

[Peach94] Robert W. Peach, ed., *The ISO 9000 Handbook*, 2nd ed., CEEM Information Services, Fairfax, VA, 1994.

[Pfleeger94] Shari Lawrence Pfleeger et al., "Evaluating Software Engineering Standards," *IEEE Software*, Vol. 11, No. 5, Sept. 1994, pp. 71–79.

[PMI00] Project Management Institute, *A Guide to the Project Management Body of Knowledge*, 2000 Edition, Newport Square, PA, http://www.pmi.org.

[PMI04] Project Management Institute, "Introduction to PMI," 2004, http://www. pmi.org/prod/groups/public/documents/info/AP_IntroOverview.asp?nav=0201 (viewed 27 July 2004).

[Pollak96] Bill Pollak, "The Role of Standards in Technology Transition," *Computer*, Vol. 29, No. 3, Mar. 1996, p. 102.

[Robillard02] Pierre N. Robillard, Philippe Kruchten, *Software Engineering Processes: with the UPEDU*, 2002, Pearson Addison Wesley.

[Royce70] Winston Royce, "Managing the Development of Large Software Systems: Concepts and Techniques," *Proc. WESCON*, IEEE Computer Soc. Press, Los Alamitos, CA, 1970.

[S2ESC-FP02] Software and Systems Engineering Standards Committee, "Mission," FP-02, June 2002, http://standards.computer.org/sesc/s2esc_pols/FP 02_Mission.htm.

[SC7-04] ISO/IEC JTC 1/SC 7, http://www.JTC 1-SC 7.org/.

[SC7-N3016] ISO/IEC JTC 1/SC 7/SWG5, "Framework for ISO/IEC system and software engineering standards," Draft 8.7, March 2004, SC 7 N3016. (Available at http://www.JTC 1-SC 7.org).

[SC7-N3069] ISO/IEC JTC 1/SC 7, "Vision of Liaison Outcomes: IEEE CS and ISO/IEC JTC 1/SC 7," June 2004, SC 7 N3069. (Available at http://www.JTC 1-SC 7.org).

[Schmidt00] Michael Schmidt, *Implementing the IEEE Software Engineering Standards*, SAMS, Indianapolis, 2000.

[Schneidewind96] Norman F. Schneidewind, "Point: Do standards improve quality?," *IEEE Software*, Vol. 13, No. 1, Jan. 1996, pp. 22–24.

[SEL96] Software Engineering Laboratory, "Software Process Improvement Guidebook. NASA/GSFC,", SEL-95–102, 1996. (available at http://sel.gsfc.nasa.gov/website/ documents/online-doc/95–102.pdf).

[SESC93] SESC Long Range Planning Group, *Master Plan for Software Engineering Standards*, Version 1.0, Dec. 1, 1993.

[Spring95] Michael B. Spring et al., "Improving the Standardization Process: Working with Bulldogs and Turtles," in Brian Kahin and Janet Abbate, eds., *Standards Policy for Information Infrastructure*, MIT Press, Cambridge, MA, 1995.

[Stevens98] Richard Stevens et al., *Systems Engineering: Coping with Complexity*, Prentice Hall Europe, London, 1998.

[SWEBOK01] Alain Abran and James W. Moore, Executive Editors, Pierre Bourque and Robert Dupuis, Editors, *Guide to the Software Engineering Body of Knowledge*, Trial Version, IEEE Computer Soc. Press, Los Alamitos, CA, 2001.

[SWEBOK04] Alain Abran and James W. Moore, exec. eds., Pierre Bourque and Robert Dupuis, eds., *Guide to the Software Engineering Body of Knowledge*, 2004 Version, IEEE Computer Society Press, Los Alamitos, CA. http://www.swebok.org/.

[TC159-01] ISO Technical Committee 159, "Draft Business Plan of ISO/TC 159 – Ergonomics," April 2001, http://isotc.iso.ch/livelink/livelink.exe/fetch/2000/2122/687806/ISO_TC_159__Ergonomics_.pdf?nodeid = 1162319&vernum=0.

[TC176-03] ISO Technical Committee 176, "ISO/TC 176 Business Plan," ISO/TC 176 N789, October 2003, http://isotc.iso.ch/livelink/livelink/fetch/2000/2122/687806/ISO_TC_176__Quality_management_and_quality_assurance_.pdf?nodeid = 852656&vernum=0.

[TC56-03] IEC Technical Committee 56, "Strategic Policy Statement," SMB/2736/R, December 2003, http://www.iec.ch/cgi-bin/getsps.pl/56.pdf?file=56.pdf.

[TC62-03] IEC Technical Committee 62, "Strategic Policy Statement," SMB/2711A/R, December 2003, http://www.iec.ch/cgi-bin/getsps.pl/62.pdf?file=62.pdf.

[TC65-03] IEC Technical Committee 65, "Strategic Policy Statement," SMB/2791/R, March 2004, http://www.iec.ch/cgi-bin/getsps.pl/65.pdf?file=65.pdf.

[Thayer84] R. H. Thayer and A. B. Pyster, "Guest Editorial: Software Engineering Project Management," *IEEE Trans. Software Eng.*, Vol. SE-10, No. 1, Jan. 1984.

[Thayer95] Richard H. Thayer, "Software Engineering Project Management," in Richard H. Thayer, ed., *Software Engineering*, IEEE Computer Soc. Press, Los Alamitos, CA, 1996, pp. 358–371.

[Tripp96] Leonard L. Tripp, "International Standards on System and Software Integrity," *StandardView*, Vol. 4, No. 3, Sept. 1996, pp. 146–150.

[Vincenti90] Walter G. Vincenti, *What Engineers Know and How They Know It*, Johns Hopkins University Press, Baltimore, MD, 1990.

[Wegner95] Eberhard Wegner, "Quality of Software Packages: The Forthcoming International Standard," *Computer Standards & Interfaces*, Vol. 17, 1995, pp. 115–120.

[Weszka00] Joan Weszka, Phil Babel and Jack Ferguson, "CMMI: Evolutionary Path to Enterprise Process Improvement," *Crosstalk*, July 2000.

Index

A

Absolute conformance, software engineering process standards, 208–209

Abstraction technology, software design, 102

Acceptance tests:
acquisition process, 296
software requirements, 93
software testing, 127

Accounting, software configuration management, 159–160

Acquisition process, life cycle framework, 296–298
systems agreement, 344

Activities planning:
software maintenance, 143–145
software testing, 132–133

Adaptation, software engineering process, 194

Adaptive software maintenance, 140

Adherence to process, for software engineering standards, 10

Agile methods, software construction, 116

Agreement process, systems life cycle framework, 344

AIAA. *See* American Institute of Aeronautics and Astronautics

AIAA G-010-1993 software standard, 31–32

AIAA R-013-1992 software standard, 31–32

Alpha/beta testing, software testing, 128

Alternative conformance, software engineering process standards, 209

American Institute of Aeronautics and Astronautics (AIAA):
ANSI and, 30
IEEE standards and, 35
structure and function, 30–32

American National Standards Institute (ANSI), structure and function, 29–30

American Society for Testing and Materials (ASTM), software engineering standards, 14

Analysis of software requirements, 84–88
architectural design, 85–87
classification, 84–85
conceptual modeling, 85
high-integrity systems, 88
life cycle processes framework, 303–305
negotiation, 87

The Road Map to Software Engineering: A Standards-Based Guide, by James W. Moore
Copyright © 2006 by IEEE Computer Society

Printed and bound by CPI Group (UK) Ltd, Croydon, CR0 4YY

09/06/2025

14685921-0003